# Contemporary Chinese America

A list of additional titles in this series appears at the back of this book.

# Contemporary Chinese America

*Immigration, Ethnicity, and Community Transformation*

Min Zhou

*Foreword by*
Alejandro Portes

TEMPLE UNIVERSITY PRESS
Philadelphia

TEMPLE UNIVERSITY PRESS
Philadelphia PA 19122
www.temple.edu/tempress

Copyright © 2009 by Temple University
All rights reserved
Published 2009
Printed in the United States of America

⊛ The paper used in this publication meets the requirements of the American National
Standard for Information Sciences—Permanence of Paper for Printed Library Materials,
ANSI Z39.48-1992

Library of Congress Cataloging-in-Publication Data

Zhou, Min, 1956–
    Contemporary Chinese America : immigration, ethnicity, and community transformation /
Min Zhou.
        p.   cm. — (Asian American history and culture)
    Includes bibliographical references and index.
    ISBN 978-1-59213-857-9 (hardcover : alk. paper)
    ISBN 978-1-59213-858-6 (paper : alk. paper)
        1. Chinese Americans—Social conditions.   2. Chinese—United States—Social
conditions.   3. Immigrants—United States—Social conditions.   4. Chinese American
families.   5. Chinese Americans—Ethnic identity.   6. Community life—United States.
7. Intergenerational relations—United States.   8. China—Emigration and immigration.
9. United States—Emigration and immigration.   I. Title.

E184.C5Z474  2009
305.895'1073—dc22                                                          2008049611

110611-P

*For Sam Guo, Philip Guo, Zhou Leiming, Yao Yaoping, Zhu Lin,
and my extended family in the United States and China*

# Contents

# List of Figures and Tables

# Foreword

It is commonly noted in the contemporary immigration literature in the United States that Asians are the fastest-growing segment of the foreign-born population. It is usually added that Asian immigrants, by virtue of their high levels of education and professional/entrepreneurial skills, do very well in the American labor market and usually reach middle- and even upper-class status in the course of one or two generations. Less emphasized are the great diversity of the Asian population and the fact that the positive characteristics associated with them are actually due to a few major groups, notably the Chinese. Even less often remarked are the vast differences in the immigration histories of individual Asian nationalities. Most of these immigrations are of recent vintage—the Chinese being an important exception. Chinese immigrants have been coming to America since the 1840s, although the circumstances of the earlier migrants' arrival and adaptation were a world away from those of the present.

The sociology and economics of immigration have made important strides during the last two decades through the formulation of novel concepts and hypotheses in sociology and the advent of an institutionalist perspective in economics. For the most part, however, studies of Asian minorities in the United States, including the Chinese, have paid more attention to chronicling the evolution and subjugation of a particular group or community than to linking them to more general theoretical concerns. This is where the work of Min Zhou comes in. For nearly twenty years now, she has painstakingly researched aspects of the experience of Chinese immigrants and, more broadly, Asian immigrants, in America, placing her results within a theoretical framework that gives them broader scope and relevance. She has made insightful use of the latest theoretical literature in the fields of immigration and ethnicity to formulate original hypotheses that, when tested against empirical data, produce lessons of general import. In this manner, Zhou has advanced both our factual knowledge of Asian-origin groups in America and general scientific knowledge about the process of immigrant adaptation and incorporation into the developed world.

An early example of this happy mix of theoretical acumen and attention to empirical evidence was her first book, *Chinatown: The Socioeconomic Potential of an Urban Enclave* (Temple University Press, 1992). In this book, Zhou made use of the then-novel concept of ethnic enclaves to show that areas of ethnic Chinese concentration were actually quite unlike what scholars and the public at large believed. Earlier journalistic and scholarly accounts of America's Chinatowns had depicted them as dangerous and alien places where a variety of strange and often unlawful activities were rampant: opium use, gambling, prostitution, and coethnic exploitation. Even the most sympathetic accounts portrayed ethnic enclaves as sites of refuge where an impoverished and highly discriminated-against minority sought protection from nativist xenophobia.

Zhou's work showed that although some of these descriptions may have applied in the past, they are quite inaccurate at present. Instead of impoverished ghettos where crime, health hazards, and labor exploitation flourish, Chinatowns are actually enclaves based on longstanding social structures whose ethnic organizations and enterprises not only help meet the survival needs of coethnic members but also offer them economic opportunities, including entrepreneurship, and paths to upward social mobility. Old-fashioned patriarchal nepotism exists, along with the exploitation of unskilled workers, women workers, and undocumented immigrants, and a wide variety of informal economic activities take place in these areas. But Zhou's work contended that characterizations of Chinese enclaves and Chinese-owned businesses in these terms were deeply flawed. Chinatowns are, above all, entrepreneurial engines creating an effective path of economic adaptation for many immigrants. The overall economic success and the rapid social mobility of the Chinese in America provide ample proof that this entrepreneurial strategy has paid off.

Zhou's work on the socioeconomic potential of Chinatown has profound implications for her study of another topic of great importance in the dynamics of contemporary immigration—namely, the adaptation of the new second generation. In this instance, she frames the study of the second generation within the novel theory of segmented assimilation that she herself has helped develop. In contrast to the conventional assimilation story, the concept of segmented assimilation highlights three key facts. First, assimilation into American culture and society does not necessarily lead to upward social mobility, since the direction of mobility depends on *what segment* of the society immigrants and their offspring assimilate to. Second, the economic advancement of immigrants and the successful adaptation of their children do not depend solely on human capital and economic resources; the level of internal cohesion and mutual support in immigrant communities—the *social capital*—is also important. Third, promptly shedding the cultural traditions and language brought from the home country is not the most effective path for economic and social progress among children of immigrants, since that loss can easily lead to *dissonant acculturation* in relation to the parental generation. In *selective acculturation,* parents and children learn the English language and American ways while preserving their own language and key elements of their culture. The theory hypothesizes that this strategy offers the best hope for educational success and economic advancement in the second generation because it preserves communication between parents and children and gives the latter a sense of their origins and history, reinforcing their self-esteem. Zhou has made use of her field research on the children of Chinese, Korean, and Vietnamese immigrants to test and refine these ideas, as shown in her influential *Growing Up American* (with Carl Bankston, 1998) and some of the chapters in this volume.

In her more recent work, Zhou has fruitfully contributed to the theories of ethnic enclaves, segmented assimilation, and transnationalism, advancing novel ideas and empirical results. For example, she links the theories of ethnic enclaves and immigrant transnationalism by showing that the viability and success of ethnic businesses depends largely on ties to the home country that provide access to capital, goods, labor, and markets, and that the strength of an ethnic community depends largely on the vitality and growth of the ethnic enclave economy. Zhou also notes the unexpected efficacy of entrepreneurial enclaves in promoting the adaptation of the second generation. Vibrant ethnic enterprises give children access to afterschool activities and programs and a wealth of information about educational opportunities that are not available to youths outside the coethnic community.

Throughout her career, Min Zhou has been a practitioner of the mid-range approach to social theory and research most prominently advocated by Robert K. Merton. A well-established and renowned sociologist in the United States and worldwide, she has made durable contributions to the study of immigration and ethnicity in general and of Asian minorities in particular. This book presents a comprehensive collection of major articles on the determinants and consequences of contemporary Chinese immigration to America. It is required reading for specialists in immigration and ethnicity—and of interest and value for the general public as well.

—Alejandro Portes
*Princeton University*
*November 2008*

# Acknowledgments

My work on contemporary Chinese America started in graduate school in the mid-1980s. Reflecting on my career as a scholar, researcher, and teacher, I realize that I am so deeply indebted to so many individuals and institutions that it is impossible to acknowledge every single name. First and foremost, I thank my graduate mentor, John R. Logan, for his trust, guidance, encouragement, and friendship. John also helped pull me out of a state of loss and hopelessness when I was stranded in Europe in 1989, unable to return to China in the wake of the Tiananmen Square events. He guided me onto a professional path in the U.S. academy. Nan Lin opened my eyes to a whole new world of sociology in 1982 when he visited Sun Yat-sen University. He showed me the way to graduate studies in the United States and provided the practical support that allowed me to settle comfortably in graduate school at SUNY–Albany. Alejandro Portes has always been an inspiration and a tremendous role model, as well as a mentor, collaborator, and friend.

I sincerely thank the numerous colleagues, friends, and students in the United States who have offered thoughtful critiques, innovative suggestions, instrumental assistance, and moral support: Richard D. Alba, Carl L. Bankston III, Frank D. Bean, Yanjie Bian, Wenhong Chen, Lucie Cheng, Elie Chrysostome, Angie Y. Chung, Paula England, C. Cindy Fan, M. Patricia Fernandez-Kelly, Nancy Foner, William H. Form, J. V. Gatewood, Margaret A. Gibson, Yoshinori Kamo, Philip Kasinitz, Rebecca Y. Kim, Susan S. Kim, Him Mark Lai, Jennifer Lee, Russell Leong, Minghuan Li, Wei Li, Zai Liang, Ivan Light, Howard X. Lin, Jan Lin, Huping Ling, Jinqi Ling, Haiming Liu, Harry H. Liu,

David Lopez, Ram Mahalingam, Douglas S. Massey, Pyong Gap Min, Don Naka-nishi, Victor Nee, Franklin Ng, Regina Nordquist, Paul Ong, Kyeyoung Park, Rubén G. Rumbaut, Myungduk Cho Sakong, Glenna Spitze, Carola Suárez-Orozco, Marcelo M. Suárez-Orozco, Wanning Sun, Betty Lee Sung, Todd Swanstrom, Roger Waldinger, Ling-chi Wang, Zuoyue Wang, Scott Waugh, Yu Xie, Yang Sao Xiong, Philip Q. Yang, Fenggang Yang, Xiaohuang Yin, Xiaojian Zhao, and Yu Zhou. I also thank my collaborators and colleagues outside the United States: Guoxuan Cai, Minghuan Li, Qirong Li, Xiyuan Li, Minggang Lin, Hong Liu, Liben Qiu, Yan-Fen Tseng, Ning Wang, Xiaohui Wang, Shaocong Zeng, Xiuming Zhang, and Guotu Zhuang. My students Amy Chai, Ly P. Lam, Angela Sung, Cindy Wang, and Jane Yu contributed tremendous technical and research assistance. I am especially grateful to members of my ethnic commu-nity, most of whom are post-1965 immigrants working or living in Chinatowns and Chinese ethnoburbs. They are unsung heroes whose values, ethos, opti-mism, actions, and activism inspire, orient, and motivate me and many others. They have assisted me in many different ways, offering their time and home space for interviews and observations and opening their hearts to share with me their personal stories of hardship and joy, and their determination and sense of identity.

I would like to acknowledge the institutional support from the University at Albany during my graduate career, Louisiana State University, and University of California, Los Angeles (UCLA). The California Policy Research Center, UCLA's Academic Senate, the Social Sciences Division of the College of Letters and Sci-ence, Asian American Studies Center, Center for International Business Educa-tion and Research, Institute for Research on Labor and Employment (formerly the Institute of Industrial Relations), Department of Sociology, and Department of Asian American Studies provided research grants. The Center for Advanced Studies in the Behavioral Sciences at Stanford (2005–2006), U.S. Department of Education (2000–2001), and Russell Sage Foundation (1994–1995) offered resi-dent fellowships.

This project could not have happened in the first place without Janet Fran-cendese, editor-in-chief of Temple University Press (TUP). Janet's vision of the possibilities of Chinese American Studies and her enthusiasm, encouragement, and editorial insight have made this project as intellectually challenging as it was fun. I am grateful to TUP's series advisor Linda Trinh Võ and TUP's anonymous reviewers, who offered critical and constructive comments and suggestions. Much appreciation also goes to TUP's editorial assistant Emily Taber and production editor Lynne Frost and to my copyeditor, Jane Barry, who read and edited the entire manuscript carefully, with her sharp eyes on substantive matters, intelligent input, excellent attention to detail, and meticulous treatment of words and style.

Last—but certainly not least—I thank my husband, Sam Nan Guo, my son, Philip Jia Guo, my parents, and members of my extended family in the United States and China, whose love, trust, and hope have never failed. I dedicate this book to them from the bottom of my heart.

# Introduction

*A Personal Reflection on the Study of*
*Chinatown and Beyond*

This book draws on and develops my previously published work on the multifaceted Chinese America of the late twentieth and early twenty-first centuries. My research on Chinese immigration and the Chinese American community began in the mid-1980s, when I was a graduate student at the University at Albany (formerly the State University of New York at Albany). Chinatown became my subject of study because of the circumstances of my own migration. I was intrigued by the Chinatown scene when I first arrived in New York City from China in the fall of 1984. Prior to that date I had never set foot in a foreign land. I knew nobody in the city except for a family friend who had immigrated just a year earlier and whose family put me up for a couple of days before I headed to Albany. My friend's family took me to *dim sum* in Chinatown the day after my arrival and showed me around Lower Manhattan. Juxtaposed against New York's magnificent skyline, the century-old ethnic colony immediately aroused my curiosity.

In my blurred childhood memory of the bedtime stories my grandmother told again and again, Chinatown was a faraway place—exotic, mysterious, and surreal. Until that day, they had been abstract tales of *gum san hak* ("guests of the Gold Mountain" in Cantonese). What shocked me outright was the seemingly irreconcilable paradox of Asian obsolete traditionalism and European avant-garde modernism: a movie set propped up against Lower Manhattan's skyscrapers. "How?" and "why?" I asked myself—questions that turned out to be relevant for sociological inquiry, much of it inspired by Herbert Gans's *Urban Villagers* and Gerald Suttle's *The Social Order of the Slum.*[1] When I considered a topic for my doctoral dissertation, Chinatown was a natural choice, even though I knew very little about Chinese Americans' decades of legal exclusion, social marginalization, and political struggle, and even though no one in the Sociology Department was then working on Asian American or Chinese American issues.

I chose Chinatown as my subject of sociological inquiry for practical reasons as well. I had originally intended to return to China as soon as possible after completing my graduate studies in the United States, both because of financial constraints and because of the urgent need to reunite with my family back in China.[2] Studying Chinatown and its residents, I felt, could help develop the field of overseas Chinese studies, which was fairly dormant in the Chinese academy in the early 1980s. I was a self-supporting foreign student with little knowledge of or access to private or public funding sources, but my ample family and kin connections to New York's Chinatown would provide instrumental support. My fluency in Cantonese and in a number of dialects from migrant-sending villages was another unique resource that proved to be crucial for my fieldwork. For strategic reasons—to circumvent my financial constraints and attain my graduate career goal—I conducted my Chinatown research on two fronts: quantitative data analysis based on the U.S. decennial censuses and fieldwork in Chinatown. Both efforts, I believed, were suited to my own resources and ability.[3]

## Original Study: New York City's Chinatown

My initial study of New York City's Chinatown became the foundation for much of my research on contemporary Chinese America. It addressed a single research question: how has a longstanding ethnic community assisted immigrants in their struggle to make it in America without losing their sense of identity? But I cast my analytic net more broadly to include a historical overview of New York's Chinatown, which evolved from a male-dominant bachelor society to a full-fledged family community; an analysis of the demographic and socioeconomic characteristics of Chinese immigrants, especially those who arrived after 1965; a detailed account of the enclave economy; a gendered analysis of the ethnic labor force, exploring the distinctive economic contributions of women and men; and an analysis of the gradual process of geographic decentralization that has become characteristic of the Chinese immigrant community since 1980.

My approach to Chinatown stood in contrast to the conventional view of immigrants as passive objects to be assimilated and of immigrant communities as isolated enclaves inhibiting assimilation. With a particular emphasis on the economic adjustment of post-1965 Chinese immigrants, I drew on, and empirically tested, the enclave economy theory—an emerging sociological theory developed by Alejandro Portes and his associates.[4] The gist of this theory asserts that ethnic enclaves can serve as mobility "platforms" or "engines" rather than "traps." In its original conceptualization, the enclave economy has both structural and cultural components. As a distinct type of the ethnic economy, it consists of a wide range of diverse economic activities that exceed the limits of small-scale trade and commerce and traditional mom-and-pop operations, and also contains ethnic institutions that mediate economic action. To some degree, the enclave economy resembles key characteristics of *both* the primary and the secondary labor markets of the mainstream economy.[5]

The enclave economy theory has an integral cultural component as well. From this perspective, economic activities are governed by bounded solidarity and enforceable trust—mechanisms of support and control necessary for economic life in the community and for reinforcement of norms and values and sanctioning of socially disapproved behavior.[6] Relationships between coethnic owners and workers, as well as customers, generally transcend a contractual monetary bond and are based on a commonly accepted norm of reciprocity.[7]

In reaffirming the ethnic community as a platform for social mobility rather than as a refuge for survival, I elaborated on a subject-centered ethnocultural approach to empirically test not only the economic dimension of the ethnic enclave, which was much studied and debated, but also the sociocultural dimension.[8] In my analysis, Chinatown is not an impoverished urban ghetto in the traditional sense of the word, despite the fact that its residents are predominantly poor, less skilled, and recent immigrants with little English-language proficiency. Instead, it possesses great potential, offering and generating tangible advantages and opportunities to immigrants that they would otherwise lack. In my view, ethnicity and ethnic attachments facilitate rather than impede social integration and mobility.

Three interrelated themes underlay my Chinatown study, which made a distinct contribution to the literature of the sociology of international migration. The first theme, drawn from the theoretical idea of the ethnic enclave, addressed a controversy over the character of ethnic labor markets. I conceptualized three ways to operationalize the enclave, using census data to measure the earnings returns on human capital in the enclave economy as opposed to the larger economy. I found that regardless of how the enclave was defined—by place of residence, place of work, or industrial concentration—male immigrant workers in New York's Chinatown were able to take advantage of human capital resources to increase their earnings.[9] However, similarly situated female immigrant workers, who made up almost half of the enclave labor force, were not able to reap similar advantages. This observation led to my second theme—gender and the ethnic enclave.[10]

Women had been absent or pushed to the sideline in the literature on the ethnic enclave. Bringing women to the center of my analysis, I took the position that immigrant women, despite many structural and cultural disadvantages, were agents of change capable of taking control over their destinies—not victims passively awaiting salvation. Using a subject-centered approach, I considered the labor force participation of immigrant women in Chinatown as an inseparable part of a family strategy for upward social mobility under extremely difficult circumstances. Employment in low-wage jobs was undesirable but generally accepted by these women as a means to raise their families out of poverty.[11]

For the third theme, residential resegregation, I questioned the best-developed model of residential mobility among immigrants, which predicted gradual and progressive assimilation. This theme was new in the ethnic enclave literature. I demonstrated that the formation of new middle-class ethnic enclaves and out-movement from Chinatown were not merely the result of increased economic status or interethnic contacts, as predicted by classical assimilation theories. Rather, residential mobility, and particularly the trend of resegregation, were jointly affected by the unique characteristics of contemporary Chinese immigration, the development of the enclave economy, the new immigrants' kinship ties to the ethnic community, and the ethnic segmentation of the housing market.[12]

I finished my doctoral dissertation in the spring of 1989, later publishing it as *Chinatown: The Socioeconomic Potential of an Urban Enclave* (Temple University Press, 1992).[13] *Chinatown* stimulated heated debate on the role of the ethnic enclave and the nature of ethnicity.[14] In 1995 a Chinese translation of the book was published in China.[15] But I myself was left with more questions than answers upon the completion of my dissertation, partly because of my limited disciplinary training and partly because of my "sojourning" orientation as a foreign student. If my *Chinatown* research was an accidental choice, my continued study of contemporary Chinese America is rooted in a greater sense of purpose and commitment. I have established myself in the subfields of international migration, race/ethnicity, and community studies in sociology. Since the transformation of contemporary Chinese America is one of my key research interests, I have gained immense inspiration and theoretical insights from the successful activism of Asian American movements of the 1960s and beyond and the groundbreaking work of both pioneers and young scholars in the fields of Chinese American and Asian American histories, Chinese American and Asian American historiographies, and Chinese American and Asian American studies.[16] I have also benefited tremendously from both constructive and judgmental critiques of *Chinatown* in particular and the enclave economy theory in general. Informed by my conclusions about ethnicity and the ethnic community in *Chinatown* and by the abundance of multidisciplinary research on Asian America, my work on contemporary Chinese America has expanded beyond the theoretical constraints of the classical assimilation perspective. I have developed a community perspective that takes into account the interaction of individual characteristics, group-specific cultural values and practices, and structural factors in explaining intergroup variations in immigrant mobility outcomes.

## Segmented Assimilation as an Alternative Way of Seeing and Thinking

My original Chinatown study may be interpreted as a deliberate challenge to the conventional wisdom about assimilation that has dominated sociological thinking since the 1920s. Central to the classical assimilation perspective are three assumptions: (1) that there is a natural process by which diverse ethnic groups come to share a common culture and gain equal access to the opportunity structure of the host society; (2) that this process entails the gradual abandonment of old-world cultural and behavioral patterns in favor of new ones; and (3) that this process, once set in motion, moves inevitably and irreversibly toward assimilation.

Classical assimilation scholars generally operate on the premise that the host society consists of a single mainstream dominated by a majority group (in the case of the United States, white Anglo-Saxon Protestants, or WASPs). Migration leads to the situation of the "marginal man": a member of an ethnic minority group pulled in the direction of the host culture but drawn back by his or her culture of origin.[17] As time goes by, diverse ethnic groups from underprivileged backgrounds will go through this painful bipolar process through a natural race relations cycle of contact, competition, and accommodation, as group members abandon their old way of life to "melt" into the host society's mainstream.[18] Classical assimilation scholars also acknowledge the potency of such institutional factors as family socioeconomic status (SES), phenotypical ranking, and racial/ethnic subsystems in determining the rate of assimilation. The assimilation of some ethnic minorities is especially problematic because their subordination is often based on ascribed characteristics such as skin color, language of origin, and religion. Readily identifiable minority groups, especially blacks, are likely to be confined within racial-caste boundaries, leading to intergroup differences in the pace of assimilation.[19]

From the classical perspective, distinctive ethnic traits such as old-world cultures, native languages, and ethnic enclaves, as well as ethnicity in the abstract, are disadvantages that hinder assimilation, but their negative effects diminish with each successive generation; native-born generations adopt English as their primary means of communication and become more and more similar to the mainstream American population in life skills, manner, and outlook. Although complete acculturation to the dominant American way of life may not ensure all ethnic groups' full social participation in the host society, immigrants are expected first to free themselves from their old cultures in order to begin rising up from marginal positions. Between the 1930s and the 1960s, America seemed to have absorbed the great waves of immigrants who arrived, primarily, from Europe.[20] Even Chinese Americans, who had been objects of legal exclusion, found themselves making significant inroads into mainstream America, albeit with limited social acceptance.[21]

Since the 1970s, the non-European immigrant groups have not converged into the middle-class mainstream in the ways predicted by assimilation theories. The first anomaly concerns persistent ethnic differences in socioeconomic outcomes across generations.[22] Another anomaly is what Herbert Gans describes as the "second generation decline."[23] Gans observed that immigrant children from less fortunate socioeconomic backgrounds struggled more than other middle-class children in school, and that a significant number of the children of poor, especially dark-skinned, immigrants risked being trapped in permanent poverty in an era of stagnant economic growth and too much of the kind of Americanization that glorifies pleasure and consumerism.[24] Still another anomaly is peculiarly counterintuitive. In America's fastest-growing knowledge-intensive industries, foreign-born engineers and other highly skilled professionals disproportionately occupy key technical or even ownership positions and bypass the conventional enclave-to-suburbia route. In immigrant enclaves, ethnic economies develop on the strength of ethnic human capital and transnational monetary capital, opening up new avenues to upward social mobility without the painful and lengthy process of climbing from the enclave into the mainstream economy.[25] In urban public schools, neither valedictorians nor delinquents are atypical among immigrant children, regardless of the timing of their arrival and their racial or socioeconomic backgrounds. These anomalies indicate a significant gap between theory and reality.

My work is associated with the idea of "segmented assimilation," a term coined by Alejandro Portes and introduced as a middle-range theory in our co-authored article, "The New Second Generation: Segmented Assimilation and Its Variants among Post-1965 Immigrant Youth" (published in *Annals of the American Academy of Political and Social Sciences* in 1993). The segmented assimilation theory responds to these anomalies, offering an alternative theoretical perspective on the process by which America's new second generation—the children of contemporary immigrants—are incorporated into the host society's system of stratification and the divergent outcomes of this process. Unlike classical assimilation theories, which posit an irreversible and unidirectional path leading *all* immigrants to their eventual incorporation into an undifferentiated, unified, and white middle-class mainstream, the segmented assimilation theory conceives of mainstream society as shaped by systems of class and racial stratification. The theory emphasizes the interaction between race and class and between ethnic communities and larger social structures that intentionally or unintentionally exclude nonwhites. It attempts to delineate the multiple patterns of adaptation that emerge among contemporary immigrants and their offspring, account for their different destinies of convergence (or divergence) in their new homeland, and address the ways in which particular contexts of exit and reception for national-origin groups affect outcomes.

Three main patterns are discernible. The first is the time-honored upward-mobility pattern: acculturation and economic integration into the normative structures of mainstream middle-class America. This is the old-fashioned pathway of severing ethnic ties, unlearning old-world values, norms, and behavioral patterns, and adapting to the WASP core culture associated with the middle class. The second is the downward-mobility pattern of acculturation and integration into the margins of American society. This is the pathway of adapting to native subcultures in direct opposition to the WASP core culture or creating hybrid oppositional subcultures associated with native racial minorities trapped on the bottom rungs of the host society's mobility ladder. The third pattern involves socioeconomic integration into mainstream America with lagged or selective acculturation *and* deliberate preservation of the ethnic community's values and norms, social ties, and institutions. This is the pathway of deliberately reaffirming ethnicity and rebuilding ethnic networks and ethnic social structures for socio-economic advancement into middle-class status.

According to the segmented assimilation theory, immigrant or ethnic groups assimilate into different segments of society, which are determined by group-specific contexts of exit and reception. The context of exit entails a number of factors, including pre-migration resources that immigrants bring with them (such as money, knowledge, and job skills), the social class status already attained by the immigrants in their homelands, motivations, and the means of migration. The context of reception includes the national-origin group's position in the system of racial stratification, government policies, labor market conditions, and public attitudes, as well as the strength and viability of the ethnic community in the host society. The segmented assimilation theory focuses on the interaction of these two sets of factors, predicting that particular contexts of exit and reception can create distinctive ethnocultural patterns and strategies of adaptation, social environments, and tangible resources for the group and give rise to opportunities or constraints for the individual, independent of individual socioeconomic and demographic characteristics.

Numerous qualitative and quantitative works have produced evidence supporting the prediction of segmented assimilation theory that members of the second generation are likely to assimilate upwardly, downwardly, or horizontally into an American society that is highly segmented by class and race—and to do so in different ways. This nuanced concept has attracted broad attention in the scholarly community since its inception. Some have joined forces to refine it and find innovative ways of measuring and operationalizing it for further empirical scrutiny and theoretical abstraction; others have raised critical issues and sought to stretch its intended meaning or develop alternative conceptions; still others have set up straw-man arguments against it, either out of confusion or because of a hidden ideological agenda. Despite the risks of being overused or misrepresented, segmented assimilation has become a powerful and increasingly influential theoretical perspective in the sociology of immigration and race/ethnicity and has been applied in the areas of education, psychology, criminology, and public health, as well as beyond the U.S. context.

It should be noted that downward assimilation is only *one* of several possible outcomes predicted by the segmented assimilation theory. Curiously, the theory is often misinterpreted as suggesting or predicting downward assimilation as the only outcome—and therefore criticized as overly pessimistic about the immigrant second generation. Nonetheless, to refute the segmented assimilation theory or to state that the second generation is doing just fine and is sooner or later moving into the mainstream middle class regardless of race/ethnicity or immigrant origin, one must demonstrate that *both* of the following cases are false: (1) that the proportions of those falling into the major indicators of downward assimilation—dropping out of high school, teenage pregnancy, and arrests for breaking the law—are insignificant for each national-origin or ethnic group; and (2) that the differences in outcome are randomly distributed across national-origin or ethnic groups, regardless of each group's modes of incorporation.

Although the segmented assimilation theory is informed by past research on immigrant communities such as Chinatown, I have applied it to my current study of contemporary Chinese America in two notable ways. One is to heighten the effect of ethnicity by documenting the ways in which it is constantly interacting with (adapting to while also resisting) larger structural circumstances in the homeland and in the host society, as well as in the processes of migration and globalization. The other is to foreground the role of the ethnic community in affecting socioeconomic incorporation.[26]

## Unpacking Ethnicity from a Community Perspective

Past and recent studies have consistently found that ethnicity significantly affects varied outcomes of social mobility among different immigrant groups and that such divergent outcomes in turn lead to further changes in the character and salience of ethnicity. Much of the intellectual debate on ethnic differences is between the cultural perspective, which emphasizes the role of internal agency and the extent to which ethnic cultures fit the requirements of the mainstream society, and the structural perspective, which emphasizes the role of social structure and the extent to which ethnic groups are constrained by the broader stratification system and networks of social relations within it.

Social scientists from both perspectives have attempted to develop statistical models to quantitatively measure the effects of "culture" and "structure" for the upward social mobility of immigrant groups. Under ideal circumstances, these models would include indicators illuminating pre-migration situations. But because of data limitations, many social scientists typically attempt to control for "structure" by documenting specific contexts of exit, identifying aspects of post-migration social structures, and operationalizing those components for which they have data. This is not only conventional but also reasonable, since many post-migration SES differences among adult migrants are likely to either reflect or be carryovers from pre-migration differences. However, even the most sophisticated statistical model accounts for only some of the variance, leaving a large residual unexplained. More intractable are questions of how to conceptualize and measure ethnicity. Given the constraints of the data, many social scientists have tried valiantly to make progress on this front and have come up with measures that are ingenious, though not fully convincing. In the end, many have had to place much weight on the effect of the ethnic dummy, whose exact meaning or contents remain unknown. I argue that ethnicity cannot be simply viewed as either a structural or a cultural measure; rather, it encompasses values and behavioral patterns that are constantly interacting with both internal and external structural exigencies. Unpacking ethnicity, however, requires the development of a community perspective, in which the concepts of ethnic enclaves, institutional completeness, ethnic capital, and multilevel social integration are helpful.

## Immigrant Neighborhoods versus Ethnic Enclaves

The idea that ethnic enclaves are significant contexts for immigrant adaptation stems from classical assimilation theories. However, the term "ethnic enclave" is often vaguely and loosely defined and used interchangeably with "immigrant neighborhood" to refer to a place where foreign-born and native-born racial/ethnic minorities predominate. As I have just discussed, the classical assimilation perspective suggests that ethnic enclaves are not permanent settlements but (at best) springboards assisting a gradual transition to the host society and (at worst) traps keeping immigrants apart from the mainstream middle class. In this view, ethnic enclaves and the institutions that emerge from them function in a non-linear fashion. They are beneficial only to the extent that they meet survival needs, reorganize migrants' economic and social lives, and alleviate resettlement problems in the new land. Classical assimilation theories predict that ethnic enclaves will eventually decline and even disappear as coethnic members become socioeconomically and residentially assimilated, or as fewer coethnic members arrive to replenish and support ethnic institutions.

Classical assimilation theories have abstracted from the experience of the European immigrants who arrived in large numbers at the turn of the twentieth century during a time of rapid industrial growth. Old Jewish, Polish, Italian, and Irish enclaves in America's major gateway cities have gradually been succeeded by African Americans and other native-born minorities or more recent immigrant groups. Some have experienced speedy declines into ghettos or "super-ghettos," while others have remained vibrant and resilient. But classical assimilation theories fail to explain why such ethnic succession transpires, much less why patterns of neighborhood change differ by race/ethnicity or national origin. Recent research, such as the work of William Julius Wilson and Douglas Massey, generally cites economic restructuring and white flight as principal causes of inner-city ghettoization.[27]

However, today's immigrant neighborhoods in urban America are quite different from past and present native-minority neighborhoods. Among the distinctive characteristics are a disproportionate share of noncitizen immigrants, both legal and illegal, and diversity in both national origins and social class backgrounds. A third factor is the significance of immigrant entrepreneurship, which transcends ethnic and national boundaries. Today's immigrant neighborhoods encompass multiple ethnic communities and thus may not be easily dichotomized as either a springboard or a trap. Rather, they may contain a wider spectrum of both resources and constraints than in the past, and they may constitute varied social environments, which are largely defined by ethnicity. Variations in these ethnic social environments, in turn, lead to significant differences in the socioeconomic outcomes of the first generation and the educational experiences of the second generation.

As the literature suggests, immigrant neighborhoods are constantly changing. Out-migration of upwardly mobile residents negatively affects social organization, social networking, and social life at the local level.[28] However, contemporary immigration and immigrant selectivity have shaped immigrant neighborhoods in diverse ways that both reinforce old constraints and create new opportunities. Thus, neighborhood and enclave may be viewed as two analytically distinct constructs. Such an analytic distinction is important in that local social structures—that is, all observable establishments including local businesses—tend to be ethnically bounded because of the cultural and language barriers that immigrants encounter.

## Institutional Completeness

In his study of immigrant adaptation in Canada in the early 1960s, Raymond Breton examined the conditions under which immigrants became interpersonally integrated into the host society.[29] Defining "institutional completeness" in terms of complex, neighborhood-based, *formal* institutions that satisfied members' needs, Breton measured the social organization of an ethnic community on a continuum. At one extreme, the community consisted of an informal network of interpersonal relations, such as kinship, friendship, or companionship groups and cliques without formal organization. Toward the other extreme, the community consisted of both informal and formal organizations ranging from welfare and mutual aid societies to commercial, religious, educational, political, professional, and recreational organizations and ethnic media (radio or television stations, newspapers). The higher the organizational density within a given ethnic community, the more likely was the formation of ethnic social networks, and the higher the level of institutional completeness.

Breton found that the presence of a wide range of formal and informal institutions in an ethnic community (i.e., a high degree of institutional completeness) had a powerful effect on keeping group members' social relations within ethnic boundaries and minimizing out-group contacts. The positive effect of institutional completeness on ethnic cohesiveness occurred *irrespective* of the group's orientation toward mainstream culture or ethnic culture. Ethnic institutions affected social relations not only for those who participated in them, but also those who did not, and the ethnic community did not prevent its members from establishing out-group contacts.[30] Like classical assimilation theorists, Breton concluded that the ethnic community would fade progressively, given low levels of international migration, because even a high degree of institutional completeness would not block members' eventual integration into the host society.

In the U.S. context, ethnic enclaves vary in the density and complexity of organizational structures, but few show full institutional completeness. In the current analysis, I propose a dual framework: at the institutional level (how institutions generate resources) and at the individual level (how patterned interpersonal relationships are structured by ethnic identity). I measure Breton's concept of "institutional completeness" in terms of the density and diversity of local institutions and add two additional dimensions.[31] The first is coethnicity—namely, the ethnic dominance of an institution's ownership, leadership, and/or membership—which I speculate strengthens within-group interpersonal interaction. The second dimension is the class composition of an institution's membership. Although the out-migration of middle-class coethnics from immigrant neighborhoods may exacerbate social isolation, their absence *as residents* in the inner city does not necessarily preclude their participation in local institutions in immigrant neighborhoods. In an ethnic enclave where there is a high degree of institutional completeness, those who have residentially out-migrated are likely to maintain communal ties through routine participation in its institutions, promoting interpersonal relationships across class lines. In my view, an ethnic enclave's institutional completeness, along with a significant presence of the coethnic middle class, positively influences immigrant adaptation through tangible resources provided by ethnic institutions and intangible resources, such as social capital, formed by institutional involvement.[32]

## The Embeddedness of Social Capital

Although the concept of "social capital" has come into wide use in recent years, there has been considerable debate over how to define and measure it and at what level of analysis to locate it. James Coleman defines social capital as consisting of closed systems of social networks inherent in the structure of relations between persons and among persons within a group—essentially a "dense set of associations" within a social group promoting cooperative behavior that is advantageous to group members.[33] Alejandro Portes and Julia Sensenbrenner define it as "expectations for action within a collectivity that affect the economic goals and goal-seeking behavior of its members," even if these expectations are not oriented toward the economic sphere.[34] Rob Sampson describes it as having variable utility values, arguing that not all social networks are created equal and that many lie dormant, contributing little to effective social action, social support, or social control.[35] Robert Putnam treats civic organizations as the main source of social capital because these organizations provide a dense network of secondary associations, trust, and norms, thereby creating and sustaining "civicness," or a sense of civic community that facilitates the workings of the society as a whole.[36] Demographic characteristics, such as SES or race and ethnicity, can also be part of the social capital process. For example, family educational background, family occupational status, and income are usually considered forms of human or financial capital. However, family SES can also connect individuals to advantageous networks and is thus related to social capital.[37] As Glenn Loury suggests, social connections associated with different class status and different levels of human capital give rise to differential access to opportunities.[38]

Despite variations in definition, scholars seem to agree that social capital is lodged not in the individual but in the structure of social organizations, patterns of social relations, or processes of interaction between individuals and organizations. That is, social capital does not consist of resources that are held by individuals or groups but of processes of goal-directed social relations embedded in particular social structures. Thus, social capital inheres immediately in social relations among individuals that are often determined and constrained by ethnicity; it is also embedded in the formal organizations and institutions within a definable ethnic community that structure and guide these social relations. Because of the variability, contextuality, and conditionality of the process, social relations that produce desirable outcomes for one ethnic group or in one situation may not translate to another ethnic group or situation. Although it is understood as a dense set of social relations with associated norms and values, social capital is embedded in and arises from institutions in a particular community—in this case not just any type of community but one in which the organizational structure and member identification are based on a shared ancestry and cultural heritage: the ethnic community.

Analyzing the formation of social capital in institutional and ethnic contexts is important in two respects. First, former social relations in families, friendship or kinship groups, and other social networks are often disrupted through the migration process. Many newcomers today experience difficulty in connecting to the larger host society and institutions because of their lack of English-language proficiency and cultural familiarity. Among coethnics in their own ethnic community, however, even as total strangers, they can reconnect and rebuild networks through involvement in ethnic institutions because of their shared cultural and language skills. Second, ethnic institutions differ from panethnic, multiethnic, and mainstream institutions at the local level in that they operate under similar cultural parameters, such as values and norms, codes of conduct, and, mostly importantly, language. In theory, immigrants can participate in and benefit from any local institutions in their new homeland. But many are excluded from participation in mainstream institutions, such as local government and "old boy" networks or schools and parent-teacher associations, because of language and cultural barriers. Ethnic institutions, in contrast, are not only more accessible but also more sensitive than other local institutions to group-specific needs and particularistic ways of coping. Further, they are more effective in resolving cultural problems. Thus, ethnicity interacts with local institutions to affect the formation of social capital.

## Conceptualizing Ethnic Capital

The interplay of financial capital, human capital, and social capital within an identifiable ethnic community can be broadly conceptualized as "ethnic capital" to explain causes and consequences of community development and transformation.[39] Thus, ethnic capital involves interrelated and interactive processes of financial, human, and social capital. Financial capital encompasses tangible economic resources, such as money and liquidatable assets. Human capital is generally measured by education, English-language proficiency, and job skills. Social capital, which I have discussed above, is more complex, entailing social relations, processes, and access to resources and opportunities.

How is ethnic capital related to community building? From the classical assimilation perspective, social capital in ethnic enclaves serves immigrants' survival needs well when they lack financial and human capital, but becomes "devalued" and eventually depleted as immigrants accumulate more and more financial and human capital. From a community perspective, in contrast, the interactive processes of financial, human, and social capital contribute to community development, which in turn perpetuates the accumulation of ethnic capital.

Old Chinatowns and new Chinese ethnoburbs are two ideal types illustrative of the dynamics of ethnic capital. Old Chinatowns had relatively weak human and financial capital but strong social capital. These communities had several distinctive features: (1) interpersonal relations were based primarily on blood, kin, and place of origin; (2) economic organizations were embedded in an interlocking ethnic social structure consisting of a range of ethnic organizations that guided and controlled interpersonal and interorganizational relations; and (3) the ethnic enclave as a whole operated on the basis of ethnic solidarity internally and interethnic exclusivity externally. Social capital, formed through a common origin, a common language, and a common fate, along with intimate face-to-face interaction and reciprocity within the enclave, provided the basis for economic and social organization, which in turn facilitated the accumulation of human capital in job training (and also, to a lesser extent, children's education) on the one hand, and the accumulation of financial capital through ethnic entrepreneurship and family savings on the other. The process of human and financial capital accumulation based on strong social capital resources in old Chinatowns heightened the significance of ethnic institutions, including ethnic business, which served as the basis for community development.

The processes of ethnic capital formation in new Chinese ethnoburbs are quite different. Compared with old Chinatowns, today's Chinese ethnoburb has several distinct features: (1) interpersonal relations are less likely to be based on strong ties defined by blood, kin, and place of origin, and more likely to be based on secondary, weak ties defined by common SES or other economic and professional characteristics; (2) economic organizations are less embedded in a locally based interlocking ethnic social structure and more diversified in type and more connected to the mainstream and global economies; and (3) the enclave economy as a whole operates on the basis of bounded solidarity and enforceable trust defined by a common ethnicity, but does not necessarily preclude interethnic cooperation and social integration. The interactive processes of ethnic capital in new Chinese ethnoburbs are not based on social capital because it is relatively weak. Instead, the community is built on strong financial and human capital. Social capital formation through ethnic interaction and organization comes *after* the formation of ethnoburbs. In ethnoburbs, the development of ethnic institutions, including ethnic businesses, creates opportunities and multiple sites for interpersonal relations.

## The Non-Economic Effects of Ethnic Entrepreneurship

From the community perspective, we can begin to see the complexity of group processes as opposed to individual processes, and the interplay between cultural and structural factors determining immigrant adaptation. My original study of Chinatown focuses on the economic potential of an immigrant enclave, highlighting the significant role of ethnic entrepreneurship in community building.[40] Research shows that contemporary entrepreneurial activities among ethnic and immigrant groups in the United States have grown exponentially and produced desirable outcomes for group members. However, this body of research has been more concerned with the effects of entrepreneurship on economic integration among immigrant and ethnic minorities than with its influence on the social contexts mediating ethnic economic life. It has largely overlooked such non-economic effects as serving as an alternative means to social status recognition, nurturing entrepreneurial spirit, providing role models, and strengthening social networks locally and internationally. Some of these effects are merely noted in the literature without further investigation into the mechanisms and conditions that produce them—a substantial conceptual gap.

Through *Chinatown* and my continued research on the development of ethnic enclaves and ethnoburbs in the Chinese immigrant community and other Asian immigrant and refugee communities, I have systematically examined these non-economic effects. Since ethnic entrepreneurs often embed their economic decisions and actions in specific social structures, variations in ethnic social structures may be conceptualized as both causes and outcomes of entrepreneurship. I propose that it is the social embeddedness of ethnic economic activities, rather than the enclave economy per se, that fosters a unique social environment conducive to upward social mobility. This ethnic social environment should not be defined by the neighborhood's characteristics, nor by residents' SES, nor by institutions that are located there; rather, a complicated set of interwoven social relationships between various institutions and residents, bounded by ethnicity, significantly facilitates or constrains educational and economic advancement.

My research on the ethnic system of supplementary education in the Los Angeles Chinese immigrant community provides a prime example.[41] It addresses how ethnic entrepreneurship shapes an ethnic environment conducive to education—an environment that benefits Chinese immigrant children to the exclusion of non-Chinese children sharing the same neighborhood. As part of the larger development of the Chinese enclave economy, a whole range of private afterschools have emerged in recent years, along with the growth of Chinese-language schools.[42] Like other ethnic businesses, private educational institutions and tutoring services are concentrated in Chinatown and Chinese ethnoburbs in

Los Angeles. They vary in scale, specialty, quality, and formality; some are transnational enterprises with headquarters or branches in Taiwan, Hong Kong, and mainland China, offering highly specialized curricula and formal structures; some are informal and relatively unstructured one-person or mom-and-pop operations. Some feature comprehensive academic programs; others tend to be highly specialized, with academic (as opposed to strictly linguistic) objectives. The latter may offer English, math, chemistry, or physics tutoring and intensive drilling solely to help children perform better in their regular K–12 schools, even if some of the instruction or tutoring is bilingual. Thus, these private institutions supplement, rather than compete with, public schools. Some of these for-profit services and programs are also embedded in nonprofit Chinese-language schools and other nonprofit ethnic organizations serving immigrants, such as family, kin, and district associations and churches.

This ethnic system of supplemental education not only generates tangible educational resources but also reinforces the overriding value placed on education by Chinese immigrants, and their extremely high educational expectations. Through participating in private afterschools, Chinese immigrant parents and children develop a more sophisticated understanding of the educational system and are better informed about college options than their peers of other national origins. They know which middle school is a feeder to a better high school, which high school offers adequate Advanced Placement (AP) classes and Scholastic Aptitude Test (SAT) preparation, how to prepare for standardized tests, and when to take them. The diversification of ethnic economic activities in the ethnic community also broadens the basis for social interaction between residents of Chinatown or the Chinese ethnoburbs and their geographically dispersed coethnics. Such relationships, though secondary and instrumental rather than primary and intimate, create channels for information exchange and thus ease the negative consequences of social isolation and ethnic segregation.

My analysis of the ethnic system of supplementary education contributes to the literature on ethnic entrepreneurship by shifting the focus from ultimate mobility outcomes (such as earnings or employment opportunities) to intermediate social processes: creating an ethnic social environment that mitigates immigrants' cultural and economic disadvantages. Social organization in immigrant neighborhoods varies by ethnicity, and the presence of an enclave economy, not just the concentration of a variety of local ethnic businesses, influences not only the economic life but also the social environment of coethnic group members.

Varied levels of enclave economic development among different immigrant groups affect community building, which in turn creates differences in the availability of and access to neighborhood-based resources, especially those pertaining to the socioeconomic integration of adult immigrants and the education of immigrant children. Social capital formed in different ethnic social environments appears to have different values, and what appears to be social capital for one ethnic group may not equally benefit another sharing the same neighborhood. In this respect, the enclave economy concept is superior for investigating specific ethnic social environments and processes of group mobility. It allows for a more focused and detailed examination of varied social contexts and their effects on mobility outcomes, thus unpacking the black box of ethnicity. A fuller account of the variations in ethnic social environments, in turn, can offer a better explanation of why ethnicity affects outcomes positively for some groups but negatively for others. It also allows for the development of an understanding of precisely how social resources are produced and reproduced in the ethnic community.

## Organization

My research on contemporary Chinese America follows the community perspective sketched above. The chapters that I have selected for this volume aim to shed light on the processes of community transformation in contemporary Chinese America from a sociological angle. Taken together, these chapters begin to unveil a reality. The resulting picture is imperfect and subject to diverse forms of interpretation and social construction, but, I hope, also informative and intellectually stimulating. As a sociologist by training and an Asian Americanist by acculturation, I have benefited from interdisciplinary scholarship in American studies, ethnic studies, and global studies. I am committed, in turn, to contributing to the subfields of international migration, race/ethnicity, and community studies. In conducting research, however, I cannot cover every angle and every subject under the sun. Thus, my research focuses on a limited range of topics, and my ethnographic research sites are primarily in Los Angeles and New York—two prominent immigrant gateway metropolises. And to state one modest goal simply: in the face of continual assertions that contemporary immigrants take jobs away from natives and "eat" social welfare, my work shows that they not only contribute tremendously to our economy (as immigrants have done historically), but are capable of creating new opportunities for themselves while making themselves new Americans.

I have organized this book on contemporary Chinese America into five parts. Part I consists of a single chapter that provides a historical overview of Chinese emigration and the formation of the Chinese Diaspora, of which Chinese America is a part.

Part II comprises three chapters documenting the patterns of contemporary Chinese immigration and demographic transformations. Chapter 2 offers a descriptive overview of the development of the ethnic Chinese community after World War II and the lifting of legal barriers to Chinese immigration. I provide a demographic profile of Chinese Americans, highlight significant trends and issues, and discuss the implications of drastic social change for identity formation and community development.

Chapter 3 examines the residential patterns of Chinese immigrants in New York City, historically a central gateway metropolis. I question whether the classic model of residential mobility adequately accounts for the differences in personal characteristics of the Chinese who live in different parts of the metropolis and for the segregation of the Chinese from other racial and ethnic groups. Factors such as SES, marriage, and fertility operate among the Chinese (as they do for other groups) to promote residential location outside the ethnic enclave. But I show that specifically ethnic factors, such as the enclave economy, immigrants' kinship ties, and the ethnic housing market, jointly structure residential patterns.

Chapter 4 (co-authored with Yan-Fen Tseng and Rebecca Kim) takes a close look at an emerging phenomenon: the Chinese ethnoburb. In the past three decades, the classical enclave-to-suburbia mobility model has been challenged. Urban neighborhoods that whites once dominated have evolved into either resegregated enclaves dominated by a single racial minority group or "global" neighborhoods where diverse native-born groups live side by side with new immigrants of different national origins. Some of the resegregated neighborhoods experience decline, a phenomenon that has been studied in great detail. Others, however, are thriving and growing, becoming home to immigrants possessing higher-than-average education and incomes who are capable of creating their own ethnic economies. The chapter focuses on the latter situation, illustrated by Chinese ethnoburbs in California's San Gabriel Valley.

Part III includes three chapters that reveal the organizational structure of the ethnic enclave. Chapter 5 examines Chinatown's enclave economy. I draw on the enclave economy theory—one of the most often cited yet most hotly debated theories in the field of international immigration—to empirically test whether there are significant earnings returns on human capital to immigrant entrepreneurs and workers participating in the ethnic enclave, based on the case of New York City's Chinatown. I offer three distinct operational definitions of the enclave as a place of residence, a place of work, and an industrial sector. Regardless of the definition employed, there is considerable evidence of positive returns for the earnings of male enclave workers from education, labor market experience, and English-language ability. By contrast, none of these human capital variables is positively related to income for female enclave workers. I use qualitative date to supplement and further explain these empirical findings.

Chapter 6 zooms in on a central ethnic institution. Chinese-language media have been on the American scene since the first Chinatown, but only recently have they achieved the status of an influential ethnic institution serving both social and economic functions. I show that since the late 1970s, Chinese-language media have taken on a dual role as both an ethnic social institution and an economic enterprise facilitating immigrant adaptation.

Chapter 7 unpacks ethnicity through a close examination of Chinese-language schools and the ethnic system of supplementary education in the immigrant Chinese community. I illustrate the specific ways in which ethnicity functions to create social capital and an environment conducive to immigrant children's educational achievement.

Part IV includes three chapters on the Chinese immigrant family. Chapter 8 deals with work and its place in the lives of Chinese immigrant women in the ethnic enclave. Working wives and mothers are traditionally considered secondary wage earners, and employment is not automatically accompanied by occupational attainment for individual workers. For immigrant women, the double burden of household work plus paid labor is compounded by their own lack of English-language proficiency, transferable education and job skills, and knowledge of the larger labor market—and, for many, by their husbands' labor market disadvantages, which make the women's labor force participation imperative for the family. This chapter illustrates the special meanings of immigrant women's work in the context of ethnic enclave employment and family responsibility.

Chapter 9 examines intergenerational relations in the Chinese immigrant family. Many Chinese parents have clearly articulated expectations that their children will attain the highest levels of educational and occupational achievement, help raise the family to middle-class status, and, most importantly, take care of parents when they are old and frail. However, the children often regard their immigrant parents as *lao-wan-gu* (meaning "old stick in the mud"), with feudal, outdated, and old-fashioned habits. Their rebellion against tradition is constant, inevitable, and intrinsic to their experience of growing up. This chapter explores the paradoxical family process through which parents and children cope with intricate relationships and negotiate priorities that benefit both individual family members and the family as a whole.

Although the bulk of Chapter 9 focuses on conflict, coping, and conciliation when parents and children live together, Chapter 10 considers intergenerational relations in the context of an altogether new type of living arrangement that has arisen in the Chinese immigrant community. "Parachute kids" come to the United States on their own, usually in their early teens, for a better education. Separated from their parents in those key years and in search of self-identities, the parachute kids and similarly situated immigrant children are subject to demands and pressures from their families, their American peers, and the host society. I discuss these young people as a social group and provide an analysis of the risks inherent in transnational families.

Part V addresses the future through a chapter on the issue of race and ethnicity in contemporary Chinese America. Chapter 11 argues that although Chinese Americans as a group have attained career and financial success equal to those of whites, and although many live near or have even married whites, they remain culturally distinct and suspect in a white society. Within America's racial hierarchy, Chinese Americans and their Asian American peers have occupied an in-between position. They have been labeled a "model minority" or considered "honorary whites" because of their socioeconomic attainments. At the same time, they continue to be stereotyped as the "perpetual foreigner." Today, globalization and U.S.-China relations, combined with persistently high rates of immigration and returned migration, continue to affect how Chinese Americans are perceived and positioned in American society.

# Future Work

Chinese America continues to intrigue me. Upon completion of each research project, I am exposed to new questions, interesting ideas, and exciting possibilities. Among the many unanswered questions on my Chinese American research agenda, several stand out. First, I would like to continue my work in ethnic enclaves. My research on economic adaptation speaks to the question of how visibly identifiable, low-skilled, and often stigmatized immigrants nonetheless make modest progress as they enter American society. My answer is that immigrants get ahead because they are able to take advantage of the resources generated through the ethnic community itself; the community provides a set of mechanisms that help newcomers get jobs, learn skills, and generate human, financial, and social capital. Thus, the enclave is not just a site for survival, but also a base for mobility. However, external circumstances, such as the power of local social organization or culture/acculturation, do not simply dictate socio-economic outcomes. Many factors interact at different levels. How to build empirically testable models and how to abstract empirical findings into theory remain challenging tasks for future research.

Second, I would like to dispel the "model minority" myth by examining in greater depth two interrelated issues: Chinese American educational hyper-attainment and the racialized glass ceiling in the workplace. Little empirical research has been done on the national level to get the facts straight. Hyper-attainment among Chinese Americans and other Asian Americans has now become so obvious in official statistics and in the public eye that the United States (and not just California) must address it in the next decade. Why do children of Chinese immigrants, including those from disadvantaged socioeconomic back-grounds, outperform native-born Americans in the educational arena? Conventional theories of social stratification are no longer sufficient; alternative theories must be developed to integrate theories of international migration, segmented assimilation, and the enclave economy. As for the glass ceiling, Chinese Americans and other Asian Americans have made tremendous inroads into mainstream America, but they have done so largely by educational hyper-attainment and excessive effort. Many hit a glass ceiling at some point in their careers and become stuck before the age factor chips in to negatively affect their career advancement. The conventional explanation is that they experience racial discrimination or that they voluntarily withdraw from the struggle to advance because they are content with their mediocre positions. To counter the model minority stereotype, we must not only show that it harms Asian Americans by holding them up as "the other," but also develop more sophisticated models to identify key determinants of immigrant and ethnic success and explain how they affect outcomes. In so doing, however, we must expand our data collection beyond ethnographic field sites and regional boundaries.[43]

Third, I would like to explore in greater depth global linkages between Chinese America, China, and the greater Chinese Diaspora. The rising economic power of

China and the Chinese diasporic communities around the world have facilitated the movements of people of Chinese ancestry across borders in unprecedented ways. Research has begun to address this trilateral relationship. Studies on transnationalism strongly suggest the emergence of alternative forms of economic incorporation into receiving societies that are quite different from what immigrants experienced in the past. However, the emerging literature on transnationalism falls short in explaining the phenomenon of return migration among highly skilled and productive immigrants. While small in scale, the sum total of all these return movements and the subsequent contributions of immigrants to families and communities left behind acquire "structural" importance for both sending and receiving countries. They affect both the pace and the forms of immigrants' incorporation into the host country and the prospects for economic development of those whom they have left behind.

Another gap in the literature involves immigrant adaptation. Little is known about whether highly assimilated Asian immigrants are satisfied with their current status and achievement in American society. The general assumption is that they are. But empirical evidence has increasingly found that successful economic incorporation into American society does not guarantee societal acceptance. The following questions are of particular interest to me. What prompts some highly skilled immigrants who are established in American society to return to China? Do such transnational movements imply permanent resettlement? How does the presence of Chinese transnationals affect local community developments in China and the United States? And how does the transnational flow of capital and labor shape economic and social developments at the local level—in *qiaoxiang* (migrant-sending communities) in China and ethnic enclaves in the United States?

Continuing to blend quantitative and qualitative methodologies, I intend to focus on these and other issues of a comparative nature—from a range of intra- and interethnic trajectories and a range of social contexts. The field of Chinese American studies involves many prospects and possibilities, and it is not up to a few individuals or a few disciplines to define its research directions and agenda. I am simply one among many social scientists who are passionate about research and determined to make a meaningful contribution.

# I

# Historical and
# Global Contexts

# 1

# The Chinese Diaspora and
# International Migration

Chinese America is a part of the Greater Chinese Diaspora. International migration among Chinese people is centuries old: long before European colonists set foot on the Asian continent, the Chinese moved across sea and land, seasonally or permanently, to other parts of Asia and the rest of the world to earn a living and support their families. In this chapter I offer a historical overview of Chinese emigration as a basis for understanding contemporary Chinese immigration to the United States.

History has witnessed distinct patterns of emigration from China to the outside world and from Chinese diasporic communities to other countries.[1] About 35 million overseas Chinese (*huaqiao* 华侨) and people of Chinese ancestry (*huayi* 华裔) live outside mainland China (including Hong Kong and Macao) and Taiwan.[2] People of Chinese ancestry have spread across the globe to more than 150 countries: over 80 percent in Asia (approximately 75 percent of the total in Southeast Asia) and about 13 percent in the Americas.[3] In the mid-1990s, countries with the largest number of people with Chinese ancestry included Indonesia (7.3 million), Thailand (6.4 million), Malaysia (5.5 million), Singapore (2.3 million), and the United States (2.7 million).[4] The extent of the Chinese Diaspora is captured in an old saying: "There are Chinese people wherever the ocean waves touch."[5]

How do the centuries-old Diaspora and its longstanding migrant networks interact with broader structural factors: colonization, decolonization, nation-state building, and changes in political regimes? In order to map the courses and patterns of international migration, I first provide a historical analysis of Chinese emigration and then discuss the implications of contemporary Chinese migration for both countries of origin and countries of destination. I identify distinct streams of emigration from China and remigration from the Chinese Disapora after World War II and demonstrate that each is contingent upon historical factors. As we will see, local and global economies, diasporic communities, and migration networks interact with the states at the origin as well as the destination to shape the direction and nature of international migration.

## The Chinese Trade Diaspora and
## *Huashang*-Dominated Intra-Asian Migration

Emigration patterns change over time and space. The Chinese people and the Chinese state have responded to, and influenced, migration differently depending on the circumstances. It is thus important to place migration in historical context, tracing the centuries-old Chinese trade diaspora and the migration networks that have emerged from it. Large-scale international migration across the Asian continent and the globe did not occur until the mid-nineteenth century. Chinese people had always moved from their places of birth in search of means and opportunities for survival and betterment, of course, but in the past they did so selectively and seasonally, usually traveling to neighboring towns and cities. Between the twelfth and the sixteenth centuries, few people, regardless of ethnicity, ventured off shore or traveled long distances from home. One of the significant groups that went overseas in large numbers was the Chinese.[6] *Huashang* (华商) is a Chinese term referring to traders, merchants, and artisans. This group dominated Chinese emigration, particularly to Southeast Asia, prior to the mid-1850s.[7] In this section, I examine how Chinese maritime commerce gave rise to the *huashang* class, and how the emerging *huashang* class and the resulting Chinese trade diaspora in Southeast Asia affected patterns of international migration in general and intra-Asian migration in particular.

### Pre-Nineteenth-Century Maritime Commerce

Prior to the nineteenth century, international migration largely consisted of tribute missions to the Chinese empire and the trading of indigenous tropical products and Chinese-manufactured commodities. As early as the Tang dynasty (618–907), when China was the largest, richest, most sophisticated state in the world, maritime trade was already well developed and thriving. The Chinese who ventured overseas were referred to as *Tangren*, "Tang people."[8] During the 1100s, they strengthened and extended their trade routes through the South China Sea to Southeast Asia, a region that the Chinese historically referred to as *Nanyang* ("southern ocean").[9] During that period, the Chinese empire had formal trade relations with neighboring Korea, Burma, Siam, Vietnam, and the kingdom of Ryukyu (Okinawa), while local officials and private traders conducted informal trade with foreign merchants through key Southeast Asian port-states, such as

Ayudhya, Malacca, and Brunei.[10] The Philippines and Borneo were then ruled by chieftains struggling to turn their territories into states.[11]

During the heyday of overseas trade, the Southern Song dynasty (1127–1279), porcelain, textiles, and lacquer production flourished, and printing and publishing technologies were well developed. Depictions of Southeast Asia and the Indian Ocean drawn from the perspective of Chinese trading ports appeared in books and other printed materials.[12] Trade continued to flourish and expanded into Russia and Persia under the rule of the Mongols, who conquered China and launched the Yuan dynasty (1279–1368). The Yuan imperial court promoted trade with the Arabs, allowed Islam to take root in China, and sponsored numerous expeditions to Japan, Java, Vietnam, Cambodia, and Burma. The court succeeded in pressing Vietnam, Cambodia, and Burma to recognize its suzerainty but failed to persuade Japan and Java.[13] After the fall of the Yuan dynasty, however, the succeeding Ming rulers (1368–1644) banned all private overseas trade in an attempt to exert tighter control on maritime commerce and curb foreign influences. Meanwhile, the Ming emperor aggressively sought to incorporate Southeast Asian states into the empire's tribute system, which defined the hierarchical relationship of imperial China with neighboring states and kingdoms.

Long before the arrival of the Europeans in the 1600s, the Chinese dominated trade in most of the *Nanyang* region, turning many Southeast Asian port-cities into entrepôts for Chinese silk, porcelains, and other manufactured goods. Unlike present-day trade, early trade often required that merchants physically travel from one place to another or even settle temporarily outside the home country.[14] As Chinese traders, merchants, and artisans proceeded from site to site, their circular movements from China to *Nanyang* and back became increasingly frequent and regular, giving rise to the *huashang* class and more stable overseas Chinese communities. *Huashang* would also take their workers abroad with them for a short period and then return home to prepare for the next journey. When the Dutch and English arrived in the *Nanyang* region in 1600, they found large and distinct Chinese resident communities already established in key port-cities such as Brunei, Malacca, Western Java, Batavia, Manila, southern Siam, and Phnom Penh. Thus, pre-colonial Chinese emigration was intertwined with trade and dominated by *huashang* and their seasonal workers, who were mostly their own relatives or village folk.[15] Those who were resettled in the foreign land acted as "middleman minorities," turning their areas of settlement into bustling marketplaces and dominating internal and international trade with their economic activities.[16] In the process, they planted the seeds for increased Chinese trade and subsequent emigration.

## The Role of the Imperial Chinese State

The imperial Chinese state had long been ambivalent about emigration. Sometimes it allowed Chinese to go overseas but discouraged their return; sometimes it favored out-migration, taking a keen interest in migrant remittances. At other times it closed off its borders and prohibited international migration altogether.[17] In times of prosperity or depression alike, the Chinese state played a paramount role in shaping patterns of international migration and the development of the Chinese Diaspora. In the early Ming dynasty, private trade and any trade outside the tribute system (e.g., trade with Japan) was banned, making it difficult for merchants and traders to move to and from China freely. Later on, the imperial state relaxed restrictions on private and localized maritime commerce but banned overseas residence.[18] The succeeding Qing imperial court (1644–1911) inherited this hostile attitude toward emigration and made overseas travel and residence a capital crime punishable by beheading.[19] Almost all trade with foreigners during that time was restricted to the port of Guangzhou (Canton).

By the time restrictive trade policies were implemented in the late fourteenth century, however, the *huashang* class had already developed innovative strategies to bypass state regulations. These were later institutionalized to facilitate migration and the formation of diasporic communities overseas. For example, the Ming court's restriction of overseas trade with Japan drove the Chinese seasonal merchants and traders, mostly Fujianese, to seek permanent refuge in Japan's port-cities, notably Nagasaki. This Chinese settlement, in turn, established new routes linking Fujian, Taiwan, and Manila.[20] Despite the ban, overseas and overland private trade in South and Southeast China boomed and showed little sign of slowing down. An ancient Chinese saying—"the mountain is high and the emperor is far away"—accurately described the attitude of local officials and traders in Guangdong and Fujian provinces. By the early fifteenth century, diasporic trade communities flourished in *Nanyang*. In 1567 the Ming court relaxed its ban on informal trade overseas, and new Southeast Asian port-cities flourished: Manila in the Philippines, Hoi An in the southern Vietnamese state, Phnom Penh in Cambodia, Patani in Malaya, the pepper port in West Java, and the Dutch port of Batavia.[21] Relaxation of the emigration policy led to a boom in the overseas junk trade, which was already rapidly developing, and a tremendous outflow of traders, miners, planters, shipbuilders, mariners, and adventurers of all kinds.[22] Most of the bans on private trade abroad were revoked in 1727. In 1754, the Qing imperial court declared for the first time that law-abiding emigrants could safely return home and that their property would be protected.[23]

At the peak of stability and prosperity, the Chinese empire acted aggressively toward its neighboring states, incorporating Korea into the tribute system during the 1630s (the late Ming dynasty) and invading Burma in 1766 and Vietnam in 1788 (Qing dynasty). In the last decade of the eighteenth century, tribute missions from Korea and Southeast Asian tribute states visited the Chinese emperor two to four times a year.[24] Intra-Asian trade and tribute missions to China reached a peak in 1790, despite Western colonization in Southeast Asia, and remained high until the decline of the Chinese empire in the mid-1840s. Trade and tribute missions, in turn, stimulated further emigration from, rather than immigration into, China.

During what the historian Anthony Reid calls the "Chinese century" (1740–1840), nearly one million Chinese were resettled in Southeast Asia, representing 3 percent of the region's population.[25] The ethnic Chinese population was estimated at around 30,000 in Bangka in the mid-1700s.[26] In Batavia, ethnic Chinese accounted for 10 percent of the total population in the early 1810s.[27] Siam, Java, and Borneo each had about 100,000 Chinese, representing 46 to 65 percent of the total population in the early 1820s.[28] Diasporic communities took root overseas, dominated by merchants and traders, who were both sojourners and settlers.[29] For example, almost all of the 11,500 seamen who were engaged in Bangkok's maritime trade were of Chinese descent.[30] But not all early Chinese emigrants were *huashang*. As the settling *huashang* started to invest in agriculture, mining, and other land-based ventures, they brought in workers from their ancestral villages to work on these new enterprises. During this period, most of the emigrants were Chaozhounese (Teochiu) from southeast Guangdong province or Fujianese from coastal regions of Fujian province. These pioneer emigrants were primarily involved in cash-crop farming, developing such goods as sugar, pepper, gambier, and rubber, as well as in tin and gold mining. Many of the products were developed by the Chinese merchant class and produced mainly for the Chinese and international markets.[31] The diasporic communities served to strengthen both formal and informal trade connections and facilitate subsequent emigration from China.

## Semi-Colonialism and *Huagong*-Dominated International Migration

European colonists arrived in Southeast Asian continental and island states in the early sixteenth century.[32] The Spanish occupied the central Philippine archipelago in 1521, captured Manila in 1571, and extended their control to Cebu and other islands in the Philippines.[33] The Dutch East Indies Company turned the scattered forts and trading posts in the archipelago into a colonial empire.[34] In the nineteenth century, Western colonization and expansion peaked. The Dutch took over Indonesia in 1799. The British occupied and ruled territories on the Malay Peninsula, including Singapore in 1819. In the mid-nineteenth century, the British defeated China in two Opium Wars, forcing it to open its ports and turn over Hong Kong to British control, and making China a semi-colonial state.[35] The French annexed Cochin China (three provinces in the southernmost part of Vietnam) in 1864 and the whole of Vietnam in 1885. By 1887 they had formed the Union Indochinoise, which included Cambodia and later Laos.[36] Japan, during the same period, rose from a long national seclusion and aggressively pursued industrialization and modernization. In 1894 it defeated China in the Sino-Japanese War, and the Qing dynasty ceded Taiwan and the Liaodong Peninsula in South Manchuria.[37]

Colonial expansion allowed Western private enterprises to develop plantation agriculture and mining and extract petroleum and other natural resources in the newly occupied colonies, while expanding their markets in the region. European colonists began to import Chinese contract laborers—often referred to as "coolies" (literally meaning "bitter strength" in Chinese)—to build infrastructure and work in plantations and mines.[38] The changing regional geopolitics significantly altered the nature and course of international migration.

## The Century of Defeat and Humiliation and the Fall of the Chinese Empire

What succeeded the "Chinese century" of stability and prosperity was a century of defeat and humiliation. Two Opium Wars (1840–1842 with Britain; 1856–1860 with Britain and France), combined with internal turmoil, shook the foundation of the Chinese empire. The first Opium War was ignited in 1839 when the imperial Qing government confiscated opium warehouses in Guangzhou. Britain sent warships to the city in February 1840 and won a quick victory. Consequently, China was forced to sign the Treaty of Nanjing (Nanking) on August 29, 1842, and a supplementary treaty the following year. Under these unequal treaties, China had to pay a large indemnity, open five ports to British trade and residence (Guangzhou to the south, Fuzhou and Xiamen to the southeast, Ningbo and Shanghai to the east), and cede Hong Kong. These same treaties gave British citizens in China the right to be tried in British courts and imposed on China the requirement that any rights granted to one foreign power must also be given to others.

The second Opium War further undermined the power of the Chinese empire. In October 1856 Guangzhou police boarded the British ship *Arrow* and charged its crew with smuggling. Eager to gain more trading rights in China, the British used this incident to launch another offensive. British forces, aided by the French, won another quick military battle in 1857 and presented China with the Treaty of Tianjin (Tientsin), demanding that China open additional trading ports, allow foreign emissaries to reside in the capital, admit Christian missionaries, and open travel to the interior. When China refused to ratify the treaty, fighting resumed. In 1860 British and French troops occupied Beijing and burned the imperial Summer Palace. The Qing government was forced to ratify the treaty. Later negotiations compelled it to legalize the importation of opium.[39]

During this period of attacks and defeats by foreign powers, the Taiping Rebellion in the south and a series of peasant uprisings elsewhere in the country weakened the power of the state and accelerated the empire's decline. The Taiping Rebellion (1851–1864), led by the Kejia (Hakka) "God worshipper" Hong Xiuquan (Hung Hsiu-ch'uan), was a popular uprising aimed at overthrowing the Qing regime and building an egalitarian society. Starting from Guangxi province, Hong proclaimed himself king of the Heavenly Kingdom, led his forces through Hunan and Hebei provinces and along the Yangtze River, and finally captured Nanjing in 1853. He declared it the capital of the Heavenly Kingdom and instituted an authoritarian government based on Christian beliefs and an ancient Chinese egalitarian ideal of dividing land equally among the peasants. In 1864 a new imperial Qing army, aided by foreign powers, put down the rebellion.[40] Hong committed suicide upon the fall of Nanjing. The 11-year revolt, which cost the lives of approximately 20 million people, had almost toppled the Qing dynasty.[41]

The declining Chinese empire was soon challenged and defeated by a rising Asian power. When Japan launched a war with the empire in 1894, China had little strength to resist and had to recognize Japan's control over Korea and give it the island of Taiwan. Britain, France, Germany, and Russia soon forced the crumbling Chinese empire to grant more trading rights and territories. It appeared likely that China would eventually be divided into colonies by Japan and the Western powers. However, a growing nationalism among the Chinese and rivalry among foreign powers prevented full colonization.[42] Grassroots rebels, nationalist intellectuals, and members of the government-backed secret societies rose up against foreign, particularly Christian, influence and subjugation. The best-known of these were the Boxers, whose 1900 rebellion attacked Western missionaries, "east ocean devils" (Japanese), "west ocean devils" (other westerners), and Chinese Christians. The Boxer Rebellion was soon suppressed by an allied force drawn from eight foreign nations. Afterward, a segment of the Qing government promoted Japanese Meiji-type reform to rebuild the regime, the economy, and a Western-style army, but the reform came too late. The last dynasty fell in 1911.

The decline of the Chinese empire into a semi-colonial state after the two Opium Wars coincided with rapid Western colonization and Japan's rise in the region. These trends had a profound impact on Chinese emigration. In particular, Western expansion into China and Southeast Asia broke the Chinese dominance of intra-Asian trade by transforming Asia's export economy and making East-West trade an arm of the world market for manufactured goods, food products, and industrial raw materials. On the one hand, the new East-West trade opportunities beyond Asia turned the *huashang* class, who had dominated intra-Asian trade for centuries, into agents for, or partners of, the European traders and colonists. The *huashang* class later played an important role in contract labor recruitment.[43] On the other hand, agricultural and industrial developments in new colonies opened new opportunities for Chinese diasporic communities to expand beyond trade into the plantation economy and mining, creating a tremendous demand for labor.[44] China's vast population became a limitless source of labor, and its centuries-old migration networks were in place to facilitate Chinese labor, or *huagong* (华工), migration.

## Huagong-*Dominated Emigration*

In the century between the mid-1840s and World War II, there were two distinct types of Chinese emigration. The *huashang*-dominated migration stream was more or less a continuation of pre-colonial emigration; the higher-volume *huagong*-dominated stream largely involved contract-labor.[45] Most of the latter headed for Southeast Asia, while much smaller numbers went to Hawaii, the South Pacific, and the Americas. Most Chinese contract laborers in Southeast Asia worked for Western colonists, but some worked for other overseas Chinese who owned plantations and mines in Western colonies.[46] Those heading elsewhere worked entirely for Western colonialists. *Huagong*-dominated emigration during the second half of the nineteenth century and the first four decades of the twentieth shared some remarkable similarities to earlier streams in terms of origins and destinations.

First, *huagong*-dominated emigration was based on dialect groups and originated in the same regions as the migration in the heyday of the maritime trade. These similarities indicate an intrinsic linkage between emigration and earlier trade diasporas. As I have noted, most of the earlier Chinese migrants were from Guangdong and Fujian provinces.[47] A small proportion was from areas bordering Vietnam in Guangxi province and from areas bordering Burma and Laos in Yunan province. Laborers who went to Korea and Japan during the 1920s and 1930s were mostly recruited by the Japanese colonial government from Shandong province on the east coast.[48] According to surveys conducted in the mid-1950s, there were approximately 20 million overseas Chinese spread around the world, 60 percent of them (12 million) in Southeast Asia. Among the Southeast Asian Chinese, 68 percent (8.2 million) were of Chaozhounese or Cantonese origin, and 31 percent (3.7 million) of Fujianese origin. These emigrants were not evenly distributed across destinations, however.[49] In the Philippines, the Chinese population was almost entirely Fujianese in 1800; a hundred years later, between 85 and 90 percent of the people of Chinese descent there were Fujianese, and the rest were Cantonese.[50] In Cambodia, the people of Chinese descent were dominated by two dialect groups from Guangdong—the Cantonese and Chaozhounese.[51] In Malaysia, Kejia (Hakka) was the dominant dialect group among the Chinese from Fujian and Guangdong. In contrast, almost all (99 percent) of the Chinese immigrants in North and South America and the West Indies in that period were from Guangdong.[52] Within a particular province, emigrants tended to come from just a few places. For example, most of the emigrants who went to Southeast Asia were from eastern Guangdong—particularly the Chaozhou-Shantou (Swatow) region—while the emigrants who went to the Philippines and the Americas were mostly from southwest Guangdong, and particularly the Si Yi (Sze Yap) and San Yi (Sam Yap) regions.[53] In Thailand (Siam before 1939), 95 percent of the Chinese immigrants or Sino-Thais could trace their origin to the Chaozhou-Shantou region.[54] In the Philippines, almost all the Cantonese emigrants were from the Si Yi region. As for the United States, close to 75 percent of the Chinese immigrants in San Francisco in the Chinese Exclusion era were from Taishan (Toishan—a part of Si Yi).

Second, *huagong*-dominated emigration disproportionately flowed toward established diasporic communities in Southeast Asia. Relatively small but fluctuating numbers went to Hawaii, North America, the West Indies, and South

America. It was estimated that 320,000 Chinese emigrated between 1801 and 1850: 63 percent of them went to Southeast Asian destinations, 6 percent to Hawaii and the United States, 5 percent to the West Indies, and 8 percent to Cuba and Peru. The next 25 years (1851–1875) saw record-high Chinese immigration to Hawaii, the United States, and Canada (17 percent), Cuba (11 percent), and Peru (9 percent).[55] But the volume pouring into Southeast Asia was still quite substantial: about 27 percent of the Chinese emigrants went to the Malay Peninsula, 20 percent to the East Indies, and 4 percent to the Philippines. Between 1876 and 1900, the period of Chinese exclusion in America, the figure for the Malay Peninsula rose to 48 percent and for the East Indies to 43 percent, while the total heading for Hawaii, the United States, and Canada dropped below 3 percent.[56]

Third, *huagong*-dominated emigration was circular, accompanied by high rates of return migration. Emigrant Chinese, merchants, traders, and laborers alike, were predominantly sojourning males. The patriarchal family system facilitated the formation of the bachelor society abroad, since sons, regardless of birth order, could claim an equal share of the patrimony upon their return, but daughters were forbidden to leave home. The male sojourner typically left his family behind; often he returned home to get married and then left his bride behind to take care of his parents and raise his children. He routinely sent remittances home and hoped to return in the not-so-distant future. Merchants and traders, who usually spent a considerable amount of time in an overseas location that served as a temporary home, traveled frequently between their homes in China and their places of business overseas. Laborers, especially those who worked on plantations and in mines and lived in camps near their work sites, were more constrained; many could not afford frequent home visits. Nonetheless, the overall return rates were high. The return rate in Thailand, for example, was 57 percent between 1882 and 1905, 78 percent between 1906 and 1917, and 68 percent between 1918 and 1945; it dropped to 40 percent between 1946 and 1955.[57]

## Pre-colonial and Colonial Migrations Compared

*Huagong*-dominated emigration during the colonial period highlighted the significance of the historical relationship between the centuries-old Chinese trade diaspora and emigration. It was distinct from pre-colonial *huashang*-dominated migration in several remarkable respects. First, even though *huagong* migrants came from roughly the same regions (i.e., Guangdong and Fujian provinces), they were mostly contract laborers working for Western colonists rather than for the Chinese. In the pre-colonial era, a typical worker was a relative or a fellow villager working for a coethnic merchant or trader who ran a shop, a farm, or a mine. In the colonial era, a typical worker was a contract laborer.

Moreover, even though most *huagong* migrants headed for the same destinations as laborers in the pre-colonial era, they were more responsive to labor demand. In the pre-colonial era, trade and local investment by the Chinese created labor demands that were easily met by a single extended family or by a clan from the home village, and labor migration routes followed the old diasporic trade routes. In the colonial era, large-scale developments in the plantation economy, mining, and infrastructure building demanded a disproportionately large amount of labor. Contract laborers were mostly recruited through diasporic Chinese family or clan networks, but were not evenly distributed to all Western colonies, or to places where Chinese diasporic communities were well established. For example, the Philippines, East Indies, and Malay Peninsula attracted over 95 percent of all contract labor to Southeast Asia. At the peak years (1851–1875), 350,000 laborers arrived in British colonies in the Malay Peninsula, 250,000 in the Dutch East Indies, and 45,000 in the Spanish-ruled Philippines.[58] Vietnam also attracted a considerable number; between 1923 and 1951, 1.2 million Chinese arrived in Vietnam to work as contract laborers (of whom 850,000 returned to China).[59] In contrast, few contract laborers went to French-ruled Cambodia and Laos.

Third, the financing of *huagong* emigration was distinct.[60] In the past, the *huashang* class themselves established home-village-based networks to sponsor migration. Colonial-era *huagong* migration was facilitated by two main means: the credit ticket system and labor contracts. Merchants and traders acted as labor brokers and agents to recruit prospective workers, not only from their own villages but also from similar dialect groups in the sending regions. Most of the laborers were poor and uneducated peasants who could not afford the journey. Either money was advanced by their labor brokers (their village kin or other overseas Chinese) or they signed labor contracts to pay the cost of the journey from wages earned at their destinations. Only those with direct connections to centuries-old diasporic communities or to labor migrant networks were likely to leave.

Fourth, *huagong* migration was highly organized and controlled, and emigrants were shipped off in large numbers from selected ports. For example, Chinese labor migrants to Malaysia were assembled in Macao and then shipped overseas. Once in the Malay Peninsula, they were often referred to as "Macaos" by the locals, even though they were Cantonese, Chaoshanese, Fujianese, Kejias (Hakkas), or Hainanese.[61] The British labor recruitment agencies also ran operations in Hong Kong, Guangzhou, and Shantou in consultation with Chinese authorities.[62] Those headed for Hawaii and the Americas during the same period primarily assembled in Macao and Hong Kong before sailing across the Pacific.[63]

Fifth, even when *huagong* migrants arrived in places with longstanding Chinese diasporic communities, many had to stay on plantations or in work camps, isolated in sojourning quarters away from the established Chinese communities. Those who were unable to send money home or could not afford to go home to find someone to marry often ended up marrying indigenous women and resettling permanently. Intermarriage thus became increasingly common in certain destinations. Many descendents of these marriages (e.g., *mestizos* in the Philippines, *jeks* in Thailand, *peranakan* in Indonesia, *babas* or *nyonya* in the Malay Peninsula, and *sino-Viets* in Vietnam) were assimilated into the local cultures; others were accepted as Chinese, becoming members of the overseas Chinese communities.[64]

In sum, during the colonial period, China was the largest labor-export country in Asia. Nearly two-thirds of Chinese emigrants went to Asian destinations, and most were contract laborers. Most of those who went to Southeast Asia returned home after their contracts ended, but some stayed and were integrated into the local Chinese communities. The countries in Southeast Asia that simultaneously received and sent out migrants were those ruled by Western colonists. For example, the Dutch East Indies received over 300,000 Chinese labor migrants, while the colonial government sponsored the resettlement of 30,000 natives of Java to the sparsely populated outer islands during the same period.[65] The Philippines under Spanish rule received over 65,000 Chinese laborers between 1850 and 1900 and continued to receive Chinese immigrants even after the country changed its colonial masters in 1898 and implemented restrictive and anti-Chinese immigration legislation. Meanwhile, thousands of Filipino laborers were shipped to Hawaii and the U.S. west coast to replace Chinese and Japanese labor: 45,000 in the 1920s.[66] During World War II, emigration from China ebbed; thereafter, intra-Asian migration took a crucial turn.

Large-scale emigration from China to Southeast Asia testified to the weakness of the Chinese state as well as the resilience of the Chinese Diaspora. Even though China was not colonized by any single nation, it had only limited control over the contract labor demands of Western colonists in Southeast Asia and the Americas, and little power to protect its nationals from harsh exploitation and mistreatment.[67] The apathy and incompetence of the Chinese government indirectly strengthened the cohesion and organization of diasporic Chinese communities overseas. These communities were initially established to provide aid to the sojourning workers, protect them from external competition and threats such as anti-Chinese violence and legislation, and enhance profits and economic opportunities for ethnic elite groups. The overseas *huashang* elite in diasporic communities played a more active role in labor migration than the state.

## Chinese Emigration in the Post–World War II Era

### Decolonization, Nation-State Building, and Restrictive Migration

From the late Ming dynasty to the end of World War II, more than 10 million Chinese emigrated to various parts of the world, with about two-thirds settling in Southeast Asia.[68] World War II shattered colonial dominance over Asia, causing Western colonists to struggle to regain colonial mastery. The Japanese lost the war along with their Greater East Asia Co-Prosperity Sphere and all their colonies. The British gave up the Indian subcontinent but resumed control over Malaya and Hong Kong; the French regained control over Indochina; and the Dutch attempted to take back the East Indies with British support.[69] However, inspired by Marxist ideologies, grassroots nationalist movements for independence sprang up everywhere in former colonies in Asia. Within one decade after the war, nearly all the Western colonies in Southeast Asia—the Philippines, Indonesia, Malaya, Vietnam, Cambodia, and Laos—collapsed.[70] With colonists gone, indigenous nationalist and socialist fractions in many newly independent nations competed for power and struggled to rebuild their countries while exercising stricter control over their borders, which had a profoundly negative effect on postwar Chinese emigration.

The slowdown of Chinese emigration can also be attributed to geopolitical developments in East Asia during the three decades following World War II. The surrender and departure of the Japanese in 1945 left China deeply divided between the ruling Kuomintang Nationalist Party (KMT) and the Chinese Communist Party (CCP). After the United State failed to mediate and build a two-party coalition, civil war broke out. The CCP forces fought well, with firm discipline and broad-based support from the peasants and the urban working class. The crumbling economy, record-high inflation, and rampant corruption in the KMT government and army alienated every social class, even the capitalists of Shanghai.[71] In 1949 the Communists won, despite massive U.S. arms supplies to the KMT and the latter's vastly superior numbers and full control of the air. The KMT retreated to Taiwan with about two million soldiers, officers, and their families, starting a bitter standoff and controversy summed up in two competing slogans: "one China, two systems" (the People's Republic of China [PRC] and Chinese Taiwan) versus "one Chinese ethnicity, two nation-states" (the PRC and the Republic of China [ROC]). Soon after the founding of the PRC came the Korean War and the lengthy Cold War, which isolated it from the West and from the Chinese diasporic communities until the late 1970s. Migration to and from China was strictly prohibited by the state. Border crossing became a crime, and overseas connections were viewed as evidence of espionage and treason, subject to punishment in a labor camp or jail.

While Hong Kong remained a British colony, Taiwan had been returned to the KMT-ruled ROC after the Japanese defeat in World War II. Driven by the CCP to Taiwan, the ruling KMT, with massive U.S. aid and military protection, successfully implemented a series of critical programs, including land reform, industrialization, and an educational system offering nine years of state-sponsored schooling. Yet the fear of a Communist takeover loomed large in Taiwan.

During the 1950s, a large group who had fled to Taiwan with the KMT from mainland China migrated again, this time to the United States. In the 1960s, children of ex-mainlanders, along with a smaller number of the children of islanders, having grown up in Taiwan and benefited from the reformed secondary educational system, began to arrive by the thousands in U.S. colleges and universities. For almost three decades Taiwanese students constituted one of the largest groups of international students in the United States. Most students of the 1960s and 1970s remained upon completion of their studies. The removal of the ROC from the United Nations in 1972 and the normalization of Sino-U.S. diplomatic relations in 1978 accelerated the brain and capital drain from the island to the United States, Canada, and Australia. In some sense Taiwan has been a skilled labor-export nation (with the United State as primary destination) since the mid-1960s.[72]

## Economic Developments and Contemporary Trends in International Migration

Nation-state building in Southeast and East Asia since the end of World War II has significantly realigned the region's political economy. Nation-states attempted to protect their sovereignty by erecting entry and exit barriers and instituting control over internal and international population flows.[73] At the same time, they pursued agricultural reforms and industrial development.[74] After two decades of wartime recuperation, many Asian nations rapidly rose to integrate themselves not merely into the world economy centered in Western developed economies, but also into a newly formed Asian core. The Association of Southeast Asian Nations (ASEAN) was founded in 1967, allying Indonesia, Singapore, Malaysia, Thailand, and the Philippines into an integral system for economic development. Brunei joined in 1984, Vietnam in 1995, and Myanmar (Burma until 1989) and Laos in 1997.[75] Japan emerged as Asia's industrial and financial superpower in the 1970s, and South Korea, Taiwan, Hong Kong, and Singapore won a reputation as Asia's "four little dragons" for their impressive economic growth and prosperity a decade later. Meanwhile, Malaysia and Thailand rapidly rose to Newly Industrialized Countries (NIC) status. The new Asian alliance, led by Japan and composed of Taiwan, Hong Kong, South Korea, and the ASEAN countries, challenged the single-core world system and brought about unprecedented economic growth in the region.

The development of regional interdependence through trade and investment set off massive state-sponsored intra-Asian labor migration in the 1980s. Japan, Singapore, Hong Kong, Taiwan, and Brunei became typical labor-import nation-states, while the Philippines, Indonesia, and China became major labor exporters.[76] South Korea, Malaysia, and Thailand witnessed equally significant labor inflows and outflows because of domestic labor market segmentation.[77] Japan had the largest pool of foreign workers in absolute numbers, but they amounted to only 2 percent of the total labor force. This was slightly lower than their proportion in South Korea, but Japan's economy was 5 times larger.[78] In contrast, foreign workers made up 5 percent of the employed labor force in Taiwan, 13 percent in Hong Kong, and 18 percent in Singapore.[79]

The prospect of high wages made Hong Kong and Taiwan attractive to workers from other Asian countries. But Hong Kong and Taiwan differed from each other (and from labor-short Japan, South Korea, and Singapore) in the type, number, and origin of the workers they allowed to enter. In the 1980s the rapid growth in construction and in labor-intensive manufacturing (apparel, toys, and home electronics), coupled with low fertility, created a severe labor shortage in Hong Kong.[80] Not long afterward, the exodus of the middle class to Australia and North America accelerated because of uncertainties surrounding the 1997 return of the colony to Chinese sovereignty.

Two streams of Hong Kong–bound migrant workers were highly noticeable. One stream responded to demands for labor-intensive domestic services, manufacturing, and construction. Filipinos formed the largest group of foreign workers (37 percent of the total), and most were educated (even professional) females, who worked uniformly as maids.[81] Recently, Indonesian women have begun to replace Filipinas in domestic service. The other stream consisted of skilled workers filling the technical and managerial jobs left vacant because of the middle-class exodus. Almost a third of the foreign workers in Hong Kong were educated professionals from Japan, the United Kingdom, the United States, Canada, and Australia.[82] More recently, two groups from the PRC—highly skilled professionals trained in the mainland and students with advanced training and degrees abroad—have become increasingly visible.

Taiwan, with laws strictly controlling immigration, received low-skilled workers from Vietnam, Thailand, Malaysia, the Philippines, and Indonesia. Filipinas and Indonesian women typically worked as maids, while their male counterparts worked in construction.[83] In the 1970s and early 1980s, Taiwan also experienced a middle-class exodus and a capital outflow to the United States, Australia, and Canada, due to political uncertainty surrounding Taiwan's removal from the United Nations and the normalization of China-U.S. diplomatic relations. But the trend of U.S.-bound migration reversed during the mid-1980s and 1990s. Many migrants returned to the island, and a new transnational migration eased the brain drain.[84]

Several concurrent demographic and economic trends affected migration patterns in Taiwan despite strict immigration controls: decreasing fertility, economic restructuring from labor-intensive manufacturing to capital-intensive high-tech and financial services, and public investment in highway construction.[85] These trends prompted a huge demand for domestic workers and construction workers. In the late 1980s and the 1990s, Taiwan imported workers mainly from Malaysia and the Philippines to work in manufacturing and construction (more than 70 percent of the foreign labor force).[86] No permits were issued for services, except for nurses' aides and private household maids (there were 13,007 maids in Taiwan as of the mid-1990s). Once China implemented the open-door reform policy in 1979, Taiwan also invested heavily in the mainland, and trans-Strait commerce flourished. Offshore fishing employed many mainland Chinese workers, but they were not allowed to come on shore.[87]

Singapore is a city-state. Its small land area (641 square kilometers) and population necessitated carefully managed strategies for development and globalization.[88] As the city-state rapidly rose to NIC status in the 1970s, it began to suffer from a severe labor shortage, rising labor costs, and declining population growth, like most Asian NICs. Importation of foreign labor, both high- and low-skilled, thus became a government priority. The government created two guest-labor categories, defined respectively by work permits and professional passes. Those holding work permits were barred from bringing in dependents (or, in the case of female migrants, from giving birth in Singapore), and their contract terms were strictly enforced. Holders of professional passes were more favorably received. Between 1985 and 1994, the number of foreign workers admitted into the country increased from 100,000 to 300,000 (or from 8 percent of the work force to 18 percent). Most were recruited from Malaysia and Thailand, with a smaller number from the Philippines.[89] In the 1990s, highly skilled workers from mainland China and Taiwan became increasing visible.[90]

Compared with the Philippines and Indonesia, the two major labor-export countries, China appeared to have no large-scale international labor migration. As long as the country was cut off from the rest of the world by the Cold War, migration to and from China was insignificant relative to the vast size of the domestic work force, but the potential for labor export was huge.[91] Beginning in the late 1970s and continuing through the Asian boom of the 1980s, China launched nationwide economic development programs: first agricultural reform, then market reform, and then industrial restructuring aiming at export manufacturing and the privatization of state enterprises. China's drive for modernization and industrialization, coupled with its population and the centuries-old "bamboo network," has tipped the balance in the regional politico-economic alignment.[92] These developments and trends have heralded a new "Pacific century,"[93] bringing tremendous changes in the pace, extent, direction, and nature of human movements.

Much of the labor migration from China to other parts of Asia in the late 1970s and the 1980s was more or less clandestine, following centuries-old diasporic networks and, to a lesser extent, guided by government sponsored and privately funded exchange-student programs. The Chinese government continued, encouraged by the West and neighboring countries, to exert tight control over emigration. Chinese workers in Korea and Japan were largely irregulars who entered as students or visitors and overstayed their visas. Relatively few Chinese workers were present in other Asian NICs. International migration from China to North America, however, has become massive since the United States and Canada relaxed their respective immigration policies. Because of accelerated immigration, the ethnic Chinese population in the United States increased from 237,292 in 1960 to 1,645,472 in 1990, and to nearly 3.6 million (including some 450,000 mixed-race persons) in 2006, making up more than one percent of the total U.S. population.[94] In Canada, the ethnic Chinese population surged from 58,197 in 1961 to 633,933 in 1991 to more than one million in 2001, forming the largest non-European ethnic group in the country, 3 percent of the total.[95] In fact, Chinese has become the third most commonly used language in Canada, next to English and French.[96] New patterns of intra-Asian and trans-Atlantic migration have in turn prompted a new challenge for Asian nations: managing migration.[97]

## Undocumented and Clandestine Chinese Immigration

Postwar intra-Asian migration was typically short-term and circular labor migration, with few possibilities for long-term settlement and integration. Both sending and receiving nation-states played a paramount role in negotiating and managing international labor flows.[98] However, globalization and integration of national economies into the world system over the past four decades have profoundly undermined any state's capacity to control emigrant and immigrant flows. In the process of regulating labor migration, both sending and receiving states have inadvertently created loopholes for undocumented or clandestine migration. China is a case in point. Emigration from China was strictly controlled between 1949 (the founding of the PRC) and 1976 (the end of the Cultural Revolution).[99] Since China opened its doors to the outside world and implemented economic reform in the late 1970s, it has experienced unprecedented economic growth. In its drive to build a market economy, China has unintentionally set off massive internal migration and facilitated international migration without the kind of sophisticated system to manage or sponsor migrations that many Asian sending countries had developed.[100] Starting in the late 1980s, accelerating in the 1990s, and continuing into the twenty-first century, Chinese immigrants have become highly visible in Asian NICs as well as in Australia, Canada, the United States, and many European countries. As many as 10 percent are undocumented, having either overstayed their visas or been smuggled into the destination countries.[101]

Total emigration from China was roughly 180,000 annually in the 1990s. Undocumented emigration is estimated to have grown by a factor of six in the early 1990s, and by a factor of 10 between 1995 and 2005, which would translate into a net of 200,000 to 300,000 annually.[102] Even a quarter of this outflow would have put tremendous pressure on the Asian NICs. For many Chinese emigrants, the preferred destinations are developed countries in the West: the United States, Canada, Australia, and Great Britain. Japan is also a desirable destination. However, the less developed countries have been affected by undocumented Chinese immigration because of the multiple smuggling routes employed by international crime organizations and tactics including "high seas transfer."[103] Hong Kong and Macao have traditionally served as entrepôts for Chinese immigration, and Thailand and Cambodia have recently emerged as both destinations and staging posts for Australia, Canada, the United States, and Europe.[104] Latin America, particularly Mexico, has also served as a staging post for illegal entry into the United States.

This rapidly rising and highly publicized undocumented emigration is linked to economic reform and structural changes in China's reconstructed political economy, especially since the early 1990s. First, rapid and uneven economic development increases the demand for labor in areas of growth, pulling surplus and idle labor from areas of stagnation. Second, the erosion of the welfare state, including the dissolution of food rationing and state-provided housing and healthcare, diminishes the incentive to stay in one place. When this powerful link is broken, urban workers feel free to consider migration, both internal and international, as a way to achieve a better life.[105] Third, market-style development greatly weakens the political and economic power of the central government while strengthening the powers of provincial and local officials. Corruption at the local level then makes it easier for well-connected and resourceful individuals and smuggling syndicates to function effectively. Fourth, centuries-old diasporic communities all over the world, now reconnected to the ancestral homeland, facilitate chain migrations initiated and sponsored by families, kin, and friends by serving as key sites of reception and meeting the survival and employment needs of undocumented immigrants, many of whom overstay tourist, student, or business visas. Fifth, Chinese syndicates and organized crime gangs use long-standing ethnic or kinship networks to ship their human cargo from China or from Chinese diasporic communities to various destination points via other countries with loose border controls, such as Russia's eastern region and various Eastern European countries.[106]

Governments in destination countries all have strict regulations to control or manage international migration, but attitudes and ways of dealing with undocumented immigration vary. Malaysia and Taiwan believe that undocumented emigration from China is part of that country's long-term plan for "nonviolent absorption" of the region, making it a national security concern.[107] Other countries, such as Singapore, fear that the continued pressure from human rights groups and democratization may break down order and control, flooding the city-state with refugees and work-seekers.[108] In reality, however, the capacity for repatriation and control hinges on the state's capacity for enforcement, on labor market conditions and access to migrant networks in sending countries, and on the state's labor-export policies at both origin and destination.[109] Curbing undocumented migration may not be in the best interests of receiving countries either, especially when the demand for migrant labor is high. Thus, while receiving countries are constrained in curbing undocumented immigration, given the demands of the local economy, labor market segmentation, and informal migrant networks, sending countries are also constrained, since repatriation would worsen domestic unemployment and reduce remittances and foreign exchange income.[110]

## Conclusion

Intra-Asian and international migration from China has been deeply affected by the centuries-old Chinese Diaspora and a wide range of geopolitical, economic, and social factors: colonization and decolonization, nation-state building, changing political regimes, and state-sponsored economic development programs. During the pre-colonial era, thanks to the dominance of the Chinese empire and the proliferation of Chinese trade to Southeast Asia, migrant flows within Asia were primarily defined by tribute missions and maritime trade centered on China. Other peoples might move beyond the boundaries of their native homelands to search for new land, fishing waters, or a better living, but they rarely ventured far off shore in large numbers. It was the Chinese, *huashang* in particular, who first developed and dominated trade entrepôts in port cities all over Southeast Asia, leading to the establishment of overseas Chinese communities and ethnic institutions. State control of trade and emigration gave rise to sophisticated migration networks and linkages between home villages and the Chinese

Diaspora, resulting in a unique pattern of emigration from China and permanent settlement at various destinations in Southeast Asia.

Western colonization overturned the dominance of Chinese trade and capsized the geopolitical centrality of the Chinese empire in the region. With the intricate networks of the trade diasporas already in place, Chinese merchants and traders turned brokers and agents of labor migration, bypassing the state to facilitate mass *huagong*-dominated emigration to Western colonies in and beyond Asia. Post–World War II nation-state building and economic development realigned the geopolitical order in East and Southeast Asia, and the Cold War severed China's ties to most parts of the world. During this time, newly founded nation-states aggressively pursued development and modernization strategies while also establishing entry and exit barriers, tight border controls, and strict emigration/immigration policies. As international migration became institutionalized bilaterally at the government level, diasporic communities, informal networks, and migrant syndicates also emerged or were revived in origin and destination states. These informal networks and institutions sometimes worked in tandem with the state to facilitate migration in response to economic changes, but sometimes functioned quite independently to facilitate migration without much state sponsorship or intervention. When pre-existing coethnic communities were well established in destination countries, individual emigrants could easily reactivate longstanding ethnic or kinship connections to evade state regulations and migrate on their own. Once this process was set in motion, migrants, networks, and diasporic communities undercut the power of the state to structure and manage international migration.[111]

Since China opened its door to the outside world and implemented economic reforms, tremendous pressures for international migration have built up. As the patterns of contemporary intra-Asian and international migration from China have shown, a direct, but unintended, consequence of China's economic reform is network-driven migration, along with undocumented or clandestine migrations. Migrant flows driven by social networks have a tendency to grow out of state control and the adjustment mechanisms of the free market. In the next 10 or 20 years, contemporary patterns of intra-Asian and international migration are likely to persist, with one exception: China, with the largest population and the most expansive (and best-developed) diasporic communities in the world, is potentially a huge labor-export country. As it has become increasingly integrated into the world system, as its marketization has continued to undermine the power of the state, and as the Chinese people have reconnected with their overseas diasporic communities, emigration, both legal and undocumented, may define a new "Chinese century" on a much greater scale than that of 1740–1840.[112] The potential for Chinese emigration has already been likened to a "Tsunami on the horizon."[113] This is a mixed blessing for China, Asia, and the world. The challenge for China and immigrant-receiving countries may be how to negotiate and manage it, given that the power of the state is severely constrained not only by the economy, but also by migration networks and ethnic institutions.

# II

# Immigration, Demographic Trends, and Community Dynamics

# 2

# Demographic Trends and Characteristics of Contemporary Chinese America

The United States has the largest ethnic Chinese population outside Asia. Chinese Americans are also the oldest and largest Asian-origin group in the United States. Their long history of migration and settlement dates back to the late 1840s and includes more than 60 years of legal exclusion. With the lifting of legal barriers to Chinese immigration after World War II and the enactment of liberal immigration legislation beginning with the passage of the Immigration and Nationality Act Amendments of 1965 (the Hart-Celler Act), the Chinese American community has increased 13-fold: from 237,000 in 1960 to 1.6 million in 1990 and to 3.6 million in 2006 (including half a million mixed-race persons), according to the official census.[1] Post-1965 immigration accounts for much of this growth. According to the U.S. Citizenship and Immigration Services, nearly 1.8 million immigrants were admitted to the United States from China, Hong Kong, and Taiwan as permanent residents between 1960 and 2006, more than four times the total admitted from 1850 to 1959.[2] China has been on USCIS's list of the top 10 immigrant-origin countries since 1980. The U.S. Census also attests to the important role of immigration. As of 2006, foreign-born Chinese accounted for nearly two-thirds of the Chinese American population, and more than half (56 percent) of the foreign-born arrived after 1990 (59 percent of the foreign-born were naturalized U.S. citizens).[3]

What is the current state of Chinese America? This chapter offers a demographic profile of Chinese Americans and discusses some of the implications of drastic demographic change for community development in the United States.

## A Historical Look at Demographic Trends

The Chinese American community remains an immigrant-dominant community, even though this ethnic group arrived in the United States earlier than many groups of southern or eastern European origin and earlier than any other Asian-origin group. While the majority of Italian, Jewish, and Japanese Americans are maturing into third and fourth-plus generations, Chinese Americans at the dawn of the twenty-first century are primarily of the first generation (i.e., foreign-born: 63 percent) or the second (the U.S.-born children of foreign-born parents: 27 percent). The third generation accounts for only 10 percent.

Legal exclusion largely explains the stifled growth prior to World War II, while post-1965 immigration policies explain the later surge of Chinese immigration. In the mid-nineteenth century, most Chinese immigrants came to Hawaii and the U.S. mainland as contract labor, working at first in the plantation economy in Hawaii and in the mining industry on the west coast and later on the transcontinental railroads west of the Rocky Mountains. These earlier immigrants were almost entirely from the Guangzhou (Canton) region of South China, and most intended to "sojourn" for only a short time and return home with gold and glory.[4] But few had much luck in the Gold Mountain, as they called America; many found little gold but plenty of unjust treatment and exclusion. In the 1870s, white workers' frustration with economic distress, labor market uncertainty, and capitalist exploitation turned into anti-Chinese sentiment and racist attacks. Whites accused the Chinese of building "a filthy nest of iniquity and rottenness" in the midst of American society and driving away white labor by "stealthy" competition. They also stigmatized the Chinese as the "yellow peril," the "Chinese menace," and the "indispensable enemy."[5] In 1882 Congress passed the Chinese Exclusion Act, which was renewed in 1892 and later extended to exclude all Asian immigrants. The act was in force until World War II.

Legal exclusion, augmented by extralegal persecution and anti-Chinese violence, effectively drove the Chinese out of the mines, farms, woolen mills, and factories and forced them to cluster in urban enclaves on the west coast that would evolve into Chinatowns.[6] Many laborers lost hope and returned permanently to China. Those who could not afford the return journey or were ashamed to return home penniless gravitated toward San Francisco's Chinatown for self-protection.[7] Still others traveled east to look for alternative means of earning a living. The number of new immigrants from China dwindled from 123,000 in the 1870s to 14,800 in the 1890s, and fell to a historical low of 5,000 in the 1930s. This trend did not change significantly until the 1960s—two decades after Congress repealed the Chinese Exclusion Act in 1943 (Fig. 2.1).

Chinatowns in the Northeast, particularly New York, and the Midwest, particularly Chicago, grew as they absorbed those fleeing the extreme persecution in California.[8] Consequently, the proportion of Chinese living in California decreased in the first half of the twentieth century, and the ethnic Chinese population in the United States grew slowly, with a gradual relaxation of the severely

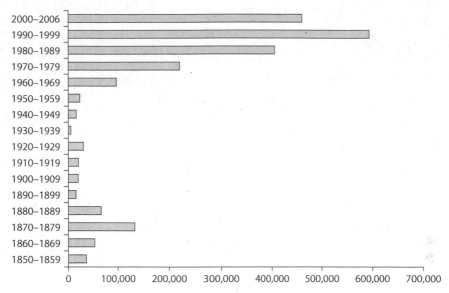

**FIGURE 2.1** Chinese Immigrants Admitted to the United States, 1850–2006.
(*Source:* U.S. Department of Homeland Security, 2007 Yearbook of Immigration Statistics, table 2.)

skewed sex ratio. As Table 2.1 illustrates, the population fluctuated by decade but basically remained stagnant in the half-century from 1890 to 1940. The 1890 sex ratio of 2,679 males per 100 females dropped steadily over time, but males still outnumbered females by more than two to one in the 1940s.

The shortage of women, combined with the "paper son" phenomenon and the illegal entry of male laborers during the Exclusion era, distorted the natural development of the Chinese American family.[9] In 1900, less than 10 percent of the Chinese American population was U.S.-born. Since then, the proportion of U.S.-born has increased significantly in each succeeding decade until 1960. Likewise, the proportion of children under 14 years of age increased substantially from a low of 3 percent in 1900 to a high of 33 percent in 1960. After the repeal of the Chinese Exclusion Act in 1943, more women than men were admitted to . the United States, mostly as war brides, but the annual quota of immigrant visas for the Chinese remained 105 for the next two decades.[10] At the founding of the People's Republic of China (PRC) in 1949, hundreds of refugees fled the Communist regime and arrived in the United States either directly or via Hong Kong, Taiwan, and other countries.

These demographic trends led to the appearance of visible second and third generations between the 1940s and 1960s, when the U.S.-born began to outnumber the foreign-born (see Table 2.1). In 1960, more than 60 percent of the Chinese American population was U.S.-born. However, the absolute number of U.S.-born was relatively small, and they were much younger (a third were under age 14) than the U.S. population as a whole.[11] In 2006, the proportion of U.S.-born

TABLE 2.1   CHINESE AMERICAN POPULATION: NUMBER, SEX RATIO,
NATIVITY, AND STATE OF RESIDENCE, 1890–2000

| Year | Number | Sex Ratio (Males per 100 females) | % U.S.-Born | % In California |
|------|--------|-----------------------------------|-------------|-----------------|
| 1890 | 107,475 | 2,679 | 0.7 | 67.4 |
| 1900 | 118,746 | 1,385 | 9.3 | 38.5 |
| 1910 | 94,414 | 926 | 20.7 | 38.4 |
| 1920 | 85,202 | 466 | 30.1 | 33.8 |
| 1930 | 102,159 | 296 | 41.2 | 36.6 |
| 1940 | 106,334 | 224 | 51.9 | 37.2 |
| 1950 | 150,005 | 168 | 53.0 | 38.9 |
| 1960 | 237,292 | 133 | 60.5 | 40.3 |
| 1970 | 435,062 | 110 | 53.1 | 39.1 |
| 1980 | 812,178 | 102 | 36.7 | 40.1 |
| 1990 | 1,645,472 | 99 | 30.7 | 42.9 |
| 2000 | 2,879,636 | 94 | 31.0 | 40.0 |
| 2006 | 3,565,458 | 93 | 37.0 | 33.3 |

Source: U.S. Census of the Population 1890–2000; 2006 figures from 2006 American Community Survey.

dropped to 37 percent. Even today, members of the second and third generations are young and have not yet come of age in significant numbers. The 2000 U.S. Current Population Survey indicates that 44 percent of second-generation Chinese Americans are 17 or younger, and 10 percent are between 18 and 24, compared with 8 percent in each of these younger age groups among the first generation.

## Intragroup Diversity

For much of the pre–World War II era, the Chinese American community was essentially an isolated bachelor society consisting of a small merchant class and a vast working class of sojourners whose lives were oriented toward an eventual return to their homeland. Most were from villages of the Si Yi (Sze Yap) region and spoke Taishanese (a local dialect incomprehensible even to the Cantonese); others came from the Pearl River Delta area in the greater Canton region, including Si Yi and San Yi.[12] Most left their families behind in China and came to America with the aim of making a "golden" fortune and returning home. And most were poor and uneducated and had to work at jobs that few Americans wanted: laundrymen, cooks or waiters, and household servants. They spoke very little English and seemed unassimilable in the eyes of Americans. In fact, the Chinese were not allowed to naturalize: they were "aliens ineligible for citizenship."

Since World War II, and particularly since the Hart-Celler Act of 1965, this bachelor society has experienced unprecedented demographic and social transformation into a family community. The 13-fold growth of the Chinese American population from 1960 to 2006 is not merely a matter of quantitative change; it marks a turning point. This new ethnic community is characterized by tremendous intragroup diversity in terms of place of origin, socioeconomic background, patterns of geographic settlement, and trajectories of social mobility.

In contrast to their earlier counterparts, contemporary Chinese immigrants have arrived not only from mainland China but also from the greater Chinese Diaspora—Hong Kong, Macao, Taiwan, Vietnam, Cambodia, Malaysia, the Americas, and other parts of the world. In Los Angeles as of 1990, for example, 23 percent of the Chinese American population was born in the United States, 27 percent in mainland China, 20 percent in Taiwan, 8 percent in Hong Kong, and 22 percent in other countries. Linguistically, Chinese immigrants come from a much wider variety of dialect groups than in the past: Mandarin, Cantonese, Fujianese, Kejia (Hakka), Chaozhounese, and Shanghainese; these are not always mutually intelligible. About 83 percent of Chinese Americans speak Chinese or a regional Chinese dialect at home. In the United States today, Chinese is second only to Spanish as the foreign language most commonly spoken at home.[13]

Contemporary Chinese immigrants also come from diverse socioeconomic backgrounds. Some arrive with little money, minimal education, and few job skills, forcing them to take low-wage jobs and settle in deteriorating urban neighborhoods. Others come with family savings, education, and skills far above the level of average Americans. Nationwide, levels of educational achievement among Chinese Americans have since 1980 been significantly higher than those of the general population. The 2004 American Community Survey reports that half of adult Chinese Americans (25 years or older) have attained four or more years of college education, compared with 30 percent of non-Hispanic whites. Immigrants from Taiwan display the highest educational levels, with nearly two-thirds having completed at least four years of college, followed by those from Hong Kong (just shy of 50 percent) and from the mainland (about a third). Professional occupations were also more common among Chinese American workers (16 years or older) than among non-Hispanic white workers (52 percent versus 38 percent). The annual median household income for Chinese Americans was $57,000 in 2003 dollars, compared with $49,000 for non-Hispanic whites. Yet the poverty rate for Chinese Americans was also higher (13 percent versus 9 percent for non-Hispanic whites); and their homeownership rate was lower (63 percent versus 74 percent).[14]

The settlement patterns of Chinese Americans at the dawn of the twenty-first century are characterized by concentration as well as dispersion. To some extent they follow a historical pattern: Chinese Americans continue to concentrate in the West and in urban areas. For example, over half of the ethnic Chinese population lives in just three metropolitan regions: New York, Los Angeles, and San Francisco.[15] Table 2.2 provides descriptive statistics for the Chinese American population by state. As of 2000, California by itself accounted for 40 percent of all Chinese Americans (1.1 million); New York for 16 percent, second only to California; and Hawaii for 6 percent. However, other states that historically received fewer Chinese immigrants have witnessed phenomenal growth: Texas, New Jersey, Massachusetts, Illinois, Washington, Pennsylvania, Florida, and

TABLE 2.2    CHINESE AMERICAN POPULATION BY STATE,* 2000

| State | Number of Chinese | % Of Total Population | State | Number of Chinese | % Of Total Population |
|---|---|---|---|---|---|
| Alabama | 7,358 | 0.17 | Montana | 1,204 | 0.13 |
| Alaska | 2,459 | 0.39 | Nebraska | 3,774 | 0.22 |
| Arizona | 26,419 | 0.51 | Nevada | 18,950 | 0.95 |
| Arkansas | 3,816 | 0.14 | New Hampshire | 4,774 | 0.39 |
| **California** | **1,114,047** | **3.29** | **New Jersey** | **109,640** | **1.30** |
| Colorado | 20,204 | 0.47 | New Mexico | 5,327 | 0.29 |
| Connecticut | 21,893 | 0.64 | **New York** | **450,910** | **2.38** |
| Delaware | 4,520 | 0.58 | North Carolina | 22,077 | 0.27 |
| District of Columbia | 4,291 | 0.75 | North Dakota | 756 | 0.12 |
| **Florida** | **59,031** | **0.37** | Ohio | 34,848 | 0.31 |
| Georgia | 31,797 | 0.39 | Oklahoma | 8,693 | 0.25 |
| **Hawaii** | **170,684** | **14.09** | Oregon | 27,021 | 0.79 |
| Idaho | 3,016 | 0.23 | **Pennsylvania** | **56,665** | **0.46** |
| **Illinois** | **85,840** | **0.69** | Rhode Island | 5,730 | 0.55 |
| Indiana | 14,618 | 0.24 | South Carolina | 7,094 | 0.18 |
| Iowa | 7,256 | 0.25 | South Dakota | 1,034 | 0.14 |
| Kansas | 8,977 | 0.33 | Tennessee | 10,951 | 0.19 |
| Kentucky | 6,259 | 0.15 | **Texas** | **120,776** | **0.58** |
| Louisiana | 8,895 | 0.20 | Utah | 10,691 | 0.48 |
| Maine | 2,452 | 0.19 | Vermont | 1,631 | 0.27 |
| **Maryland** | **54,889** | **1.04** | Virginia | 43,320 | 0.61 |
| **Massachusetts** | **92,123** | **1.45** | **Washington** | **75,464** | **1.28** |
| Michigan | 37,966 | 0.38 | West Virginia | 2,138 | 0.12 |
| Minnesota | 19,309 | 0.39 | Wisconsin | 13,322 | 0.25 |
| Mississippi | 3,713 | 0.13 | Wyoming | 802 | 0.16 |
| Missouri | 15,808 | 0.28 | | | |

*States with the largest Chinese populations are shown in boldface type.

Source: U.S. Census Bureau website: http://factfinder.census.gov/home/saff/main.html?_lang=en/, accessed September 7, 2007.

Maryland. Among cities with populations over 100,000, New York City (with 365,000), San Francisco (161,000), Los Angeles (74,000), Honolulu (69,000), and San Jose (58,000) have the largest numbers of Chinese Americans.

Within each of these metropolitan regions, however, the settlement pattern tends to be bimodal, with ethnic concentration and dispersion equally significant. Traditional urban enclaves, such as the Chinatowns in San Francisco, New York, Los Angeles, Chicago, and Boston, continue to receive immigrants, but they no longer serve as primary centers of initial settlement for many newcomers, especially members of the educated and professional middle class, who are bypassing inner cities to settle into suburbs immediately after arrival.[16] Currently, only 14 percent of the Chinese in New York, 8 percent of the Chinese in San Francisco, and less than 3 percent of the Chinese in Los Angeles live in old Chinatowns. The majority of the Chinese American population is spreading into outlying metropolitan areas or suburbs of traditional gateway cities as well as new urban centers of Asian settlement across the country. Half of all Chinese Americans live in suburbs. Mandarin-speaking coethnics from mainland China

TABLE 2.3    CITIES WITH THE HIGHEST PROPORTIONS OF
CHINESE AMERICANS, 2000

| City* | Number of Chinese Americans | % Of Total City Population |
|---|---|---|
| Monterey Park | 26,582 | 44.3 |
| San Marino | 5,616 | 43.4 |
| San Gabriel | 14,581 | 37.3 |
| Arcadia | 19,676 | 37.1 |
| Alhambra | 31,099 | 36.2 |
| Rosemead | 17,441 | 32.6 |
| Rowland Heights | 15,740 | 32.4 |
| Walnut City | 9,309 | 31.0 |
| Temple City | 10,269 | 30.8 |
| Hacienda Heights | 13,551 | 25.5 |
| Cupertino | 12,777 | 25.3 |
| San Francisco | 160,947 | 20.7 |
| Diamond Bar | 11,396 | 20.2 |

*All cities are in California and have populations over 10,000.

Source: U.S. Census Bureau website: http://factfinder.census.gov/home/saff/main.html?_lang=en/, accessed September 7, 2007.

or Taiwan and those of higher socioeconomic status tend to stay away from Cantonese-dominant old Chinatowns. Once settled, they tend to establish new ethnic communities, often in more affluent urban neighborhoods and suburbs, such as the "second Chinatown" in Flushing, New York, and "Little Taipei" in Monterey Park, California.[17] Meanwhile, the influx of contemporary Chinese immigrants is transforming the old Chinatowns in the United States in previously unimaginable ways. The transplanted village of shared origins and culture has evolved into a full-fledged family-based community with a new cosmopolitan vibrancy transcending territorial and national boundaries.

There are 13 U.S. cities with 10,000 people or more in which Chinese Americans make up over 20 percent of the population (Table 2.3). All but two are in the sprawling suburbs of Los Angeles. Except for San Francisco, all are suburban cities that emerged as identifiable middle-class immigrant ethnoburbs only after 1980.[18] Recent residential movements of affluent Chinese Americans into white middle-class suburban communities have tipped the balance of power, raising nativist anxiety about an ethnic "invasion" along with some anti-immigrant sentiment.[19]

Trajectories of social mobility among Chinese Americans also differ from those of the past because of the tremendous diversity in migrants' socioeconomic backgrounds. Three predominant trajectories are noteworthy. The first one is the familiar, time-honored path of starting at the bottom and moving up through hard work. This route is particularly relevant to those with limited education and English-language ability, few marketable job skills, and little familiarity with the mainstream labor market. However, in a post-industrial era and a globalized economy restructured in a way that has removed most of the middle rungs of the mobility ladder, low-skilled workers starting at the bottom often find themselves trapped there with little chance of upward mobility however hard they work. A majority of such low-skilled immigrants nevertheless consider their initial downward mobility or lack of mobility a necessary first step in their quest for the American dream or a means of paving the way for their children to do better.[20]

The second trajectory involves incorporation into professional occupations in the mainstream economy through extraordinary educational achievement. As noted above, more than a third of contemporary immigrants have attained college educations and advanced professional training either in their homeland or in the United States. Those who are equipped with U.S. degrees or professional credentials generally face fewer labor market barriers, especially in science and engineering fields, than those who have completed their education and training abroad.[21] It is worth noting that the influx of highly educated and highly skilled immigrants from mainland China into the United States in early 1990s was in part a direct result of the Tiananmen Square incident of June 4, 1989. The U.S. government passed legislation to grant permanent residency status to Chinese students, visiting scholars, and others who were in the country during that time. More than 60,000 Chinese on nonimmigrant visas (mostly J-1, for official exchange visitors, or F-1, for students) were granted permanent residency via the so-called June Fourth green cards.[22] This has led to a more diverse immigration from the mainland in terms of places of origin and a new trend of transnational movement as immigrants return to the homeland to seek better economic opportunities. It has also had profound implications for the development of ethnoburbs and suburban ethnic economies. The effects are evident, as well, in the enrollment of Chinese American youths in colleges and universities, from which they graduate with bachelor's and advanced degrees in disproportionate numbers. Such graduates may find labor market entry easier, but they often encounter a glass ceiling as they move up into managerial and executive positions.

The third trajectory is ethnic entrepreneurship. Since the 1970s, unprecedented Chinese immigration, accompanied by drastic economic marketization in China and rapid economic growth in Asia, has set off a tremendous influx of human capital and financial capital. This is a new stage of economic development in the Chinese American community as well as in the mainstream American economy. From 1977 to 1987, the U.S. Census reported that the number of Chinese-owned firms grew by 286 percent, compared with 238 percent for Asian-owned firms, 93 percent for black-owned firms, and 93 percent for Hispanic-owned firms.[23] From 1987 to 2002, the number of Chinese-owned businesses continued to grow by another 218 percent (from fewer than 90,000 to 286,000). As of 2002, there was approximately one ethnic firm for every 9 Chinese and for every 10 Asians, but only one ethnic firm for every 28 blacks and one for every 22 Hispanics. Chinese American–owned business enterprises made up 7 percent of the total minority-owned nonfarm business enterprises nationwide (and more than a quarter of all Asian-owned businesses), but accounted for 17 percent of the total gross receipts.[24] Ethnic entrepreneurship creates numerous employment opportunities for both entrepreneurs and coethnic workers.[25] However, problems also arise that leave some workers behind, such as abusive labor practices and overconcentration of jobs offering low wages, poor working conditions, few fringe benefits, and lack of prospects for mobility.[26]

## The Salience of Ethnicity and the Paradox of Assimilation

Contemporary Chinese immigration has heightened the salience of ethnicity, as the community continues to be dominated by first-generation immigrants. It has also created new challenges for assimilation. In the past, Chinese immigrants were concentrated in ethnic enclaves and had to rely on ethnic organizations and ethnic social networks for their daily survival because of pervasive racism, discrimination, and exclusion in the larger society and ethnic members' own lack of English-language proficiency, marketable or transferable skills, and information about their new homeland. But these immigrants, like their European counterparts, were expected to assimilate into mainstream American society as they achieved socioeconomic mobility.

Classical assimilation theories posit that the ethnic community and its ethnic institutions are initially instrumental in reorganizing immigrants' economic and social lives and alleviating social problems arising from migration and ghetto living. In the long run, however, ethnic communities either dissolve or fade into merely symbolic significance, since there are no newcomers to support them and no institutional roadblocks to inhibit assimilation. Institutional completeness—a situation in which an ethnic community's formal institutions satisfy all its members' needs—is said to create disincentives for learning the English language and American ways, decrease contacts with outsiders and mainstream institutions, and ultimately trap ethnic group members in permanent isolation.[27]

In the case of Chinese Americans, we have witnessed trends of upward social mobility that are predictable under classical assimilation theories. Members of the second or later generations are unlikely to live in ethnic enclaves or get involved in immigrant organizations.[28] Even many of today's first-generation immigrants, especially the educated, highly skilled, and middle class, are bypassing ethnic enclaves to assimilate residentially in suburban middle-class white communities. And yet we have also witnessed trends of ethnic revival. On the one hand, the growing presence and power of the first generation reinforce the sense of ethnicity. Many immigrants from mainland China, Hong Kong, or Taiwan never thought of themselves in ethnic terms until they arrived in the United States, because they were members of the majority group in their homelands. They have become Chinese as they strive to become American.

On the other hand, many new immigrants who have acculturated into American ways and residentially assimilated into white middle-class suburbs—as well as members of the second or later generations—are now returning to their own ethnic community to organize among their coethnics, culturally, socially, and politically. Some of the emerging ethnic organizations include suburban Chinese schools, alumni and professional associations, and ethnically based civil rights organizations, such as the Organization for Chinese Americans and the Committee of 100. New religious organizations, mostly nondenominational Christian groups, also tend to be coethnic. Some of these new organizations are located in Chinatowns or ethnoburbs; others are geographically dispersed, and some have members from the highly skilled, highly assimilated segment of the Chinese American population. While most have clearly stated religious missions, they often serve important social functions similar to those of professional and alumni associations. Some specify secular goals, mainly networking and information exchange to enhance the mobility prospects of Chinese immigrants.[29]

These trends point to a paradoxical outcome of immigrant adaptation. They imply that becoming American while maintaining Chinese ethnicity is not just a possibility but an increasingly preferred choice among Chinese Americans.[30]

In the past, immigration, Chinese exclusion, and structural constraints created opportunities for ethnic organizing, prompted the revalorization of the symbols of a common ethnicity, and consolidated a unified, though internally conflictual and fractional, ethnic community. Today's Chinese American community has become more diverse but less geographically bounded and less cohesive. Ethnic solidarity no longer necessarily inheres in the moral convictions of individuals or the traditional value orientations of the group. In my view, the very fact that Chinese immigrants are allowed to assimilate and that they then return to their own ethnic community indicates that a fixed notion of the ethnic community as an isolated entity no longer applies. Community transformation has been prompted by two internal forces: one from the immigrants, especially those lacking English-language proficiency, job skills, and employment networks linking them to the mainstream economy; the other from the highly assimilated coethnics. New immigrants are primarily concerned with three urgent issues of settlement: employment, homeownership, and children's education. In many cases, an immigrant would consider himself (or herself) successful if he runs his own business or becomes a *laoban* (boss), if he lives his own home (even if he has to cram his family into the basement and rent out the rest of the building), and if he sends his child to an Ivy League or equally prestigious college. The ethnic community and ethnic organizations must respond to and address these issues of immediate concern. In contrast, the more established and assimilated immigrants, and members of the second and later generations, tend to be morally committed to community work and are primarily concerned with addressing social justice issues through involvement in new ethnic or panethnic organizations or electoral politics. Progressive and assimilated coethnics run new social service agencies and other ethnic organizations in Chinatowns and put pressure on old ethnic organizations to adapt to changes.

The injection of new blood not only replenishes the ethnic community's organizational basis but also changes its mission from survival assistance to socioeconomic incorporation.

We should therefore start to look at the Chinese American community of the twenty-first century as integral to, rather than separate from, the mainstream society, and view Chinese cultural heritage, despite its distinct internal dynamics, as essentially contributing to, rather than competing with, the mainstream culture. Developments in the Chinese American community provide some useful insights into the paradox of ethnicization and assimilation. Is the ethnic community inhibiting, or contributing to, the assimilation of Chinese immigrants into American life? To the extent that they feel comfortable leading their own ethnic lives in America, the immigrants may be well adjusted. However, to the extent that their ethnic lives, intentionally or unintentionally, hinder opportunities for interethnic or interracial interactions at the personal and group level, the immigrants may be socially isolated. One of the main constraints on the ethnic community is its group exclusivity. We have seen signs that Chinese immigrants are not mixing well with U.S.-born non-coethnics in ethnic enclaves or ethnoburbs. This lack of primary-level or intimate interpersonal relationships may render Chinese immigrants and their children vulnerable to negative stereotyping and racial discrimination. For example, in communities like Monterey Park, California, and Flushing, New York, many non-Chinese residents feel that they are being pushed out of their own backyards and being un-Americanized by the influx of middle-class Chinese immigrants, with higher-than-average levels of education and household incomes, who move directly into the suburbs upon arrival.[31] While Chinese immigrants are perceived as foreign "invaders," U.S.-born Americans of Chinese or Asian ancestry are also stereotyped as foreigners—receiving praise for speaking "good" English when English is their first language or being told to go back to their own country when the United States is their native country. This perception of Chinese Americans, and other Asian Americans, as perpetual foreigners is deepseated in the American psyche.[32] Asian Americans perennially feel compelled to prove their loyalty and patriotism, despite having made impressive inroads into American society largely on the strength of their own ethnic communities. Therefore, ethnic communities need to find innovative ways to collectively counter societal stereotypes and foster greater interethnic and interracial understanding and inclusion.

## Conclusion

The Chinese American community in the United States has gone through enormous changes since Chinese immigration began in the late 1840s. Current demographic trends mirror the linguistic, cultural, and socioeconomic diversity of the Chinese American community and its multifaceted life in the United States.

These trends suggest a transformation in the twenty-first century from a predominantly immigrant community to a native ethnic community. While issues and challenges directly relevant to immigration and immigrant settlement continue to occupy a central place in community affairs, new issues and challenges concerning citizenship, civil rights, interethnic/interracial coalition, and political incorporation have acquired urgency. The future of Chinese Americans, foreign-born and U.S.-born alike, is intrinsically linked to the diversity of immigration and to the current social stratification system into which today's immigrants and their children are supposedly assimilating. Learning how to negotiate the culture of diversity and how to navigate through the new racial/ethnic stratification system is not only imperative but also inevitable.

# 3

# In and Out of Chinatown

*Residential Segregation and Mobility among
Chinese Immigrants in New York City*

Nㅔew York City has the second-largest concentration of Chinese
Americans in urban America. Its Chinatown has always been a distinctly contiguous geographic locality in which Chinese immigrants cluster. While other ethnic communities, such as Little Italy across
the street, have dwindled, Chinatown has survived for more than a century
and a half and has grown into a full-fledged immigrant community based
on a solid organizational structure and a thriving enclave economy. Yet even
though contemporary Chinese immigrants retain a strong desire to maintain their own language and culture, they are much less likely to live in ethnic enclaves than their predecessors. At the time of the 2000 census, about
451,000 Chinese Americans lived in New York City, making up more than
80 percent of New York State's Chinese American population. One fifth of
the city's Chinese (91,500) lived in Manhattan, 27 percent in Brooklyn
(125,000), and 33 percent in Queens (147,000). It was estimated that a
majority of Manhattan's Chinese lived on the Lower East Side, where Chinatown is located—"Old Chinatown," as we will call it here. Although the
absolute number of Chinese there or elsewhere in the city is much under-
estimated by official counts, current demographic trends suggest that New
York City's Chinese are rooted in the city but more dispersed than before in
relation to Old Chinatown. This chapter examines the residential patterns
of Chinese residents in and around New York City, based on 1980 census
data and analysis conducted in the late 1980s.

## Changes in Old Chinatown and Beyond

When Chinese laborers were shipped in large numbers across the Pacific to the west coast in the late 1850s and early 1860s, few Chinese resided in New York. The 1860 U.S. Census shows 120 Chinese in New York, one-fifth of one percent of the total Chinese population in the United States (63,199). New York's Old Chinatown emerged in a four-block neighborhood across Canal Street from Little Italy in Lower East Manhattan in the 1870s.[1] The first significant group of Chinese immigrants settled on Mott, Park, and Doyer Streets.[2] During the first decade of official Chinese exclusion, New York City gained a few thousand Chinese. The ethnic population increased by 147 percent in 1890, while in the rest of the country it dropped 16 percent. At the turn of the century, the proportion of Chinese living in California fell to 39 percent, while the proportion in New York increased to 6 percent. New York's Chinese population was relatively small but experienced steady growth (from 7,170 to 13,731) between 1900 and 1940, while California's Chinese population sank from 45,753 to 39,556. In the first half of the twentieth century, New York's Chinese community was fairly stable and experienced modest growth. Prior to the drastic changes of the 1960s, most Chinese immigrants in New York City clustered in Old Chinatown.

Although residential dispersal began in the late 1950s, substantial out-migration was not common until much later. Close to 60,000 Chinese were believed to live in Old Chinatown in 1980, compared with fewer than 25,000 two decades earlier. But in fact Chinatown has always sustained many more residents than the official counts reveal. The discrepancy is mainly due to the reluctance of Chinese immigrants to cooperate with census workers and also possibly to the presence of a considerable number of undocumented immigrants.[3]

Over the span of one and a half centuries, Old Chinatown has not experienced the neighborhood decline predicted by assimilation theories, unlike neighboring Little Italy and the Jewish Lower East Side. Instead of diminishing in significance, both the ethnic Chinese population and the territory of Chinatown are growing at accelerated speeds. As the tremendous influx of new immigrants and foreign capital brings life to the decaying area surrounding Chinatown, this enclave has necessarily spilled beyond its traditional boundaries, spreading over southeastern Manhattan into neighborhoods once solidly Jewish and Puerto Rican. Canal Street used to divide Chinatown from Little Italy. There was a time when Chinatown residents did not dare to venture into neighborhoods across the street, even for a stroll. This borderline no longer exists. The Chinese have not only crossed the street, all but smothering Little Italy, which is now a two-block relic amid buildings and businesses full of Chinese and Chinese-language signs; they have also bought up buildings and set up shops as far north as 14th Street. Figure 3.1 displays the residential concentration of Chinese in the extended Chinatown area on the Lower East Side as of 1980.

While high rates of Chinese immigration and foreign capital investment help sustain and develop the old core area of Old Chinatown, the Chinese population

FIGURE 3.1 Residential Concentration of Chinese in Extended Chinatown, New York City, Defined by 1980 Census Tracts. (*Source:* Adapted from Min Zhou, *Chinatown: The Socioeconomic Potential of an Urban Enclave* [Philadelphia: Temple University Press, 1992], p. 188, fig. 8-1.)

has grown rapidly and become much more spread out; more than two-thirds of New York City's Chinese now live in new Chinese neighborhoods, or "satellite Chinatowns," in Queens and Brooklyn. The two most visible Chinese enclaves are Flushing, known as the Chinatown of Queens, and Sunset Park, known as the Chinatown of Brooklyn.[4]

Flushing, located in north-central Queens, was mainly a white middle-income working-class area, whose residents were of Jewish, Irish, Italian, and German ancestry. In 1960, 97 percent of the population was non-Hispanic white. Prior to the 1970s, nonwhites were not welcome in the neighborhood. A long-time Chinese resident had arrived from China in 1946 to join her white husband in Jamaica, Queens. When they decided to move to Flushing, she had to send her husband to look for housing: "because they [whites] didn't want to see Chinese here. At that time, there were few Chinese around in the community. I was not the only one, but there weren't many." She recalled that the business district in Flushing had only one Chinese restaurant and one Chinese laundry in the early 1960s.[5] In more affluent parts of Flushing, there were neighborhood attempts in the 1950s to keep Chinese families from moving into the area.

Since the late 1980s, Flushing has changed its face. It is now referred to as the "second" Chinatown, or "Little Taipei." However, Flushing does not match Old Chinatown in ethnic density, because it is not dominated by a single ethnic group. In demographic terms, it is clearly a neighborhood that has experienced rapid transition and that contains a variety of ethnic and racial groups. Between 1970 and 1990, the non-Hispanic white population fell by 31 percent in the general Flushing area, while the total population increased by 5 percent, with a high proportion of foreign-born residents (more than 40 percent). Compared with those living on the Lower East Side, Flushing's residents had much higher levels of education and occupational status, lower poverty rates, and higher median household incomes. Overall, this is a relatively affluent urban area.

The core of Flushing, surrounding the downtown area, is especially Asian. At the core (defined by 11 census tracts), the proportion of whites in every tract has decreased drastically since the 1970s; only one tract still maintained a white majority. In 1990, whites constituted 24 percent of the population in the 11-tract area; Asians, 41 percent. Among the Asians, 41 percent were Chinese, 38 percent Koreans, and 15 percent Indians.[6] Representatives of all three Asian groups are clearly visible in the central business district. The concentrations, however, are rarely more than a few blocks wide. Indeed, only 2 of the 11 tracts had Asian majorities (no single ethnic group dominated); 9 tracts in the core area were 25 percent or more Asian.

Reflecting national trends, Flushing's Chinese immigrants come from three major regions: Taiwan, mainland China, and Hong Kong. Although most Taiwanese prefer Los Angeles—only 16 percent of the Taiwanese immigrants in the United States live in New York City—they are very visible in Flushing. Among Chinese immigrants, those from Taiwan are significantly better educated and are more concentrated in professional occupations. Many Taiwanese immigrants first came to Flushing because they did not identify with Manhattan's Old Chinatown, which is dominated by the Cantonese and by Cantonese culture. Moreover, Taiwanese had the educational backgrounds and economic resources to build their own enclave away from the existing center of Chinese settlement.[7] Once the Taiwanese movement to Flushing began, other Chinese followed, and after a while a new type of immigrant enclave has emerged that includes many from the mainland as well.

With the injection of massive amounts of capital and the influx of affluent, entrepreneurial, and highly skilled immigrants from Taiwan, Flushing's Chinese enclave economy began to develop in the 1980s. According to the Downtown Flushing Development Corporation, property values in Flushing increased 50 to 100 percent during the 1980s, and commercial vacancy rates plummeted from 7 percent in the late 1970s to less than one percent a decade later.[8] Since 1975 new retail and office development has rejuvenated the downtown area. Nowadays, the business center has expanded in all directions from the core. Commercial development is extraordinarily active, with new businesses literally springing up overnight. Modern office complexes house banks and service-oriented firms owned by Taiwanese immigrants and transnational Taiwanese, as well as subsidiary firms from the Asian Pacific region. In the heart of the downtown commercial and transportation hub, the multilingual signs of several mainstream bank branches and Asian-owned banks stand at the busiest intersection. Just a few blocks from the subway station, in what was until recently an aging neighborhood rapidly falling into decay, is a 14-story, pink granite and limestone tower—the Sheraton LaGuardia East Hotel. Such a sight in downtown Flushing would have been unimaginable in 1970. The hotel, Taiwanese-owned, is the only full-service hotel in Queens outside the airports.[9] In the immediate vicinity of the subway station, stretching up and down Main Street and onto the side streets, Chinese restaurants and shops, interspersed with green groceries, drug stores, and fast food restaurants, give the area an unmistakable look of Chinatown. The development of Flushing as a comprehensive business center means that suburban Chinese residents no longer have to go to Manhattan's Chinatown to visit a restaurant, to shop, or to satisfy their need for Chinese cultural activities. Yet Flushing's Chinese enclave economy also maintains strong ties to Old Chinatown, since the subway makes it relatively easy to commute there to work or shop.

Sunset Park, Brooklyn, is a working-class neighborhood of two-story houses and brownstones originally settled by European immigrants. It is conveniently located along the B, N, and R subway lines, about 30 minutes by subway from Old Chinatown. As in Flushing, the earlier European immigrants and their children have gradually moved to the suburbs since the late 1960s, leaving many absentee-owned houses and storefronts vacant. As white residents slowly abandoned the neighborhood, ethnic minorities and new immigrants—first Dominicans, then Puerto Ricans, then Asians, and Arabs—moved in.[10] Like Flushing, Sunset Park is a new multiethnic immigrant neighborhood, but it has a different racial and ethnic makeup. Of some 102,000 residents in the district in 1990, about 34 percent were non-Hispanic white, 4 percent black, 51 percent Latino, and 10 percent Asian, 78 percent of whom were Chinese. Between 1980 and 1990, the Chinese experienced a population growth of 319 percent, compared with a 26 percent loss among non-Hispanic whites.[11]

Sunset Park is more an outlet or extension of Old Chinatown than a newly founded Chinatown with its own unique character, as Flushing is. It houses recent arrivals as well as Chinatown's out-movers, who are mostly of working-class background. Among the out-movers, some families resettled in Sunset Park as they attained a measure of economic mobility, while others were pushed out of Chinatown because of overcrowding or the fear that their teenage children might be pressured into joining gangs. Sunset Park offers affordable housing and easy access to Old Chinatown. The more upwardly mobile immigrant Chinese are unlikely to move to Sunset Park because of the neighborhood's working-class characteristics, but they may purchase a home as a rental property. Hard-working though less upwardly mobile immigrants are often able to buy a house in Sunset Park, renting out part of it to coethnic immigrant families in order to meet the hefty mortgage payments. Mr. Fu of Brooklyn's Community Planning Board explained that with continued high immigration from China and Hong Kong, "more and more Chinese will be coming to New York. There is no more room in Manhattan, and Queens is too expensive for newcomers. Brooklyn, being affordable and easily accessible, is the logical place to be."[12] In fact, most immigrant Chinese in Sunset Park share similar socioeconomic characteristics with non-coethnic residents in the neighborhood. The arrival of immigrant Chinese families has helped revitalize the dying neighborhood by means of homeownership, and this in turn has attracted more immigrants from Old Chinatown and from abroad. Most of Sunset Park's Chinese immigrants are Cantonese-speakers from the mainland and Hong Kong. A sizable number of Fuzhounese have also moved into the neighborhood; most rent basement units from coethnic homeowners.[13]

As increasing numbers of Chinese immigrant families moved into Sunset Park, so did ethnic businesses. The ethnic economy that has developed along Eighth Avenue between 39th and 65th Streets can trace its origin to the opening of Fung Wong Supermarket, owned by a Hong Kong immigrant, Tsang Sun (Sunny) Mui, on Eighth Avenue in 1986.[14] In recent years the number of garment factories has grown along with ethnic service-oriented businesses, such as restaurants, grocery stores, beauty salons, herbal medicine stores, health clinics, and accounting and legal offices. By the early 1990s, there were an estimated 300 stores and 250 garment factories in the neighborhood.[15] Immigrant Chinese like to call Sunset Park "*Bat Dai Do*," a Cantonese translation of "Eighth Avenue" that also means "the road to good fortune and prosperity." Although it is not as well-developed as Flushing and the basis for ethnic social organization is not as solid as in Old Chinatown, Sunset Park has certainly served to accommodate the pressing needs of new immigrants for jobs, housing, and a place to rear children. Figure 3.2 maps out the distribution of New York City's Chinese residents in 2000.

## Segregation and Ethnic Residential Mobility

Examining whether the classical assimilation model applies easily to the Chinese immigrant experience is important for our understanding of race and ethnicity in North America, particularly as the Chinese are—primarily through immigration—a fast-growing segment of the U.S. population.[16] Prior research has often treated residential segregation as an indicator of general shifts in groups' relative social positions.[17] The assimilation theory, perhaps the most influential perspective on ethnic segregation, posits that all ethnic groups tend to be drawn into mainstream American society and gain social acceptance through their educational and occupational achievements. The initial establishment of an ethnic enclave—ethnic segregation—is regarded primarily as an adaptive strategy to

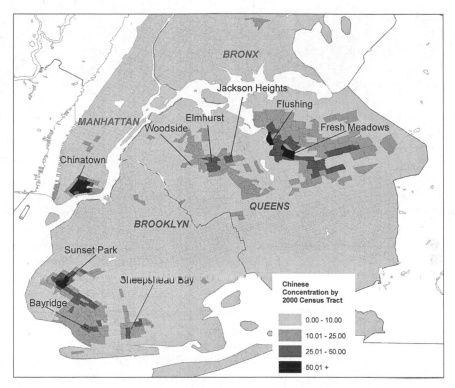

**FIGURE 3.2** Residential Concentration of Chinese in New York City, 2000. (*Source:* 2000 U.S. Census tract data; map created by and courtesy of Spatial Structures in the Social Sciences, Brown University.)

enable ethnic members to survive and overcome initial disadvantages and constraints in the early stages of assimilation. Residential segregation is temporary and will diminish as group members, having improved their labor market position and absorbed mainstream values, choose residences in new areas.

These hypotheses have gained credibility from sociological research on European ethnic minority groups, such as Italian Americans.[18] Their application to more recent non-European immigrant groups has not been fully tested. A classic study by Douglas Massey and Nancy Denton reports that suburbanization is strongly predictive of lower residential isolation and less segregation for both Asians and Hispanics, serving as a key factor in spatial assimilation, but it provides only weak evidence, based on the census data, that social mobility and acculturation underlie this process.[19]

Richard Alba and John Logan have also analyzed census data and estimated individual-level models of suburban residence for various racial and ethnic groups across the nation.[20] For the Chinese as well as some other groups, they report significant effects of marriage and the presence of children, English-language ability, and socioeconomic status (SES). They find a considerable amount of between-group variation in the process of spatial assimilation. The key predictors of location—SES and acculturation—do not operate the same way for members of all minority groups. Further, the effects of these predictors depend on the distinct social contexts in which group members live. Results at the national level may be modified by particular local situations.

The experience of adaptation for some immigrant groups suggests contrasting paths that do not agree with models derived from classical assimilation theories. Most relevant to my study is an enclave economy model put forward by Alejandro Portes, which emphasizes the crucial role of ethnic enclaves and ethnic social networks in mobility and status attainment processes.[21] Portes understands enclave participation as an alternative to assimilation for the labor market, specifically arguing that the enclave does not block the residential mobility of its members. Evidence from the Cuban enclave in Miami has shown that higher-ranking participants in the enclave tend to reside in more affluent neighborhoods or suburbs, leaving disadvantaged participants in or around the geographic enclave.[22]

Much recent research comparing racial minority groups describes persons of Asian ancestry as relatively privileged, experiencing relatively low levels of segregation and advancing toward spatial assimilation in proportion to their socioeconomic achievement. For example, Massey and Denton report that Asians in 1980 experienced a remarkably low level of spatial segregation, roughly equivalent to the 1970 levels for the "old" European ethnic groups.[23] Thus, Asians are depicted as part of a success story of ethnic incorporation into mainstream society. I wish to look more closely at this judgment, partly because the conclusions cited above depend on contrasts to the case of African Americans, who constitute an extreme reference point, and partly because the conclusions are based upon analyses that intermingle data from Asians of widely different national and cultural backgrounds. Are New York City's Chinese in fact being residentially assimilated? Does residence outside Old Chinatown coincide with socioeconomic mobility? Is participation in the enclave economy, and the ethnic social networks on which it is based, an obstacle to residential mobility? I approach these questions through three kinds of quantitative analysis.

The first analysis examined the degree of segregation of the Chinese from other groups, using the Index of Dissimilarity (D).[24] Results from my analysis showed that during the 1970s, the Chinese were fairly highly segregated from other racial and ethnic groups in New York City, with values of D ranging from .545 to .838. The Chinese in the New York metropolitan area were most segregated from non-Hispanic blacks (.838) and were also highly segregated from Hispanics (.654). Their level of segregation from non-Hispanic whites (.574) was high, but not as high as was often found for blacks.[25] When I compared Chinese segregation from non-Hispanic whites in Manhattan, the outer boroughs, and areas outside the city, some of my results were consistent with the assimilation hypothesis: Chinese segregation from non-Hispanic whites was much higher in

Manhattan (.740) than in the outer boroughs (.501) or outside the city (.376). Decentralization, particularly into the suburbs, was clearly associated with decreasing segregation.[26] These results undermine simple interpretations of the residential patterns. Chinese settlement in New York created a Chinatown located in Manhattan, the central core of the metropolis, which displays high levels of segregation, but residential segregation in Old Chinatown may not inhibit future residential mobility, a point that I discuss in the next section.

The second quantitative analysis addressed the determinants of place of residence for individual Chinese householders (defined as household heads). For comparing Chinese who resided in different subareas of the metropolitan area, I used logit regression models.[27] In its most common form, logit regression predicts a dependent variable with only two categories. My analysis therefore first predicted the odds of living outside New York City (coded 1) versus living within the city (coded 0), then the odds of living in the outer boroughs (coded 1) versus Manhattan (coded 0). In the first form, the dependent variable is whether or not the household head lived in New York City or outside it (coded 0 for New York City residence and 1 for outside the city). Both models examined how SES (education, household income, and occupational prestige),[28] sectoral (enclave) employment,[29] acculturation (English proficiency, citizenship status, and length of U.S. residence), age, and family situation (marital status and presence of children) affect the probability of place of residence. My analyses generated the following findings:

1. The coefficients of all three SES variables all significantly increased the likelihood of living outside New York City for the Chinese. For non-Hispanic whites, however, household income has a positive effect but education and occupational prestige have negative effects on living outside the city.[30]
2. Sectoral employment did not show any significant effect on the Chinese, but employment in these same industries, which of course did not constitute an "enclave" for whites, had a significantly negative effect on whites' residential mobility.
3. The acculturation variable—English proficiency, citizenship status, and years of immigration—showed significant effects for the Chinese and for whites. For the Chinese, only English made a difference in place of residence. For whites, only years of immigration had a significant effect; the U.S.-born and earlier immigrants were more likely to live outside the city than recent immigrants.
4. Age was not a significant factor for either group, but family situation variables were significant factors for both. For example, being married added about 6 percent to the likelihood of residence outside the city for the Chinese, and having children under 17 years of age also added approximately 6 percent. For the whites, the differences for these two variables were both around 8 percent.

The equation predicting residence in the outer boroughs, as opposed to Manhattan, was very similar to the one for suburban residence for the Chinese. The positive effects of most SES variables in both equations for the Chinese indicated a strong relationship between social mobility and residential decentralization. This finding was consistent with the assimilation theory. However, the absence of an enclave employment effect for the Chinese supported Portes' view that enclave participation did not restrict residential mobility.

The third quantitative analysis examined the type of neighborhoods into which the Chinese tend to move. The purpose was to estimate the independent effects of various neighborhood characteristics (e.g., the percentage of racial minorities, median household incomes, occupation, rental housing, and residential stability) on the percentage of Chinese living in a particular neighborhood. I employed multiple regression models to estimate the independent effects of various census-tract characteristics—percentages of non-Chinese Asians, percentages of non-Hispanic blacks, percentages of Hispanics, median household incomes, percentages of persons holding top-ranking occupations, percentages of rental housing, and level of residential stability—on the dependent variable, percentages of Chinese. I also included two additional analyses for comparison: one predicting the percentage of non-Hispanic whites and the other the percentage of non-Hispanic blacks. I suspected that segregation patterns for the Chinese might not be the same as those of whites and blacks.

Table 3.1 lists selected characteristics of census tracts in the New York metropolitan area. Overall, tracts located in New York City had fewer desirable characteristics than those outside it. The percentage of non-Hispanic white residents in the city was just over half (54 percent), much lower than that outside the city (81 percent). In contrast, the percentages of racial minorities and of foreign-born residents were much higher in the city than outside it. Moreover, the city had older housing stock and more residents living in rental and multifamily housing. A similar pattern held for Manhattan versus the outer boroughs, except that Manhattan had a higher percentage of foreign-born residents, as well as higher percentages of those with a college education and in top-ranking occupations.

Results from multivariate regression analyses for the Chinese showed that in New York City they were most likely to share a census tract with other Asians and least likely to do so with either blacks or Hispanics.[31] However, none of the census-tract characteristics seemed to significantly affect where the Chinese were concentrated at the tract level, except for the percentage of residents holding top-ranking occupations. Median household income, generally believed to be a strong predictor, did not have a significant effect. In suburban areas outside the city, the Chinese lived in much better neighborhoods. Most of the census-tract characteristics had significant effects in the expected direction, except the effects of percentage of blacks, percentage of rental housing, and level of residential mobility, which failed to reach statistical significance. The overall explanatory power ($R2$) of the multivariate regression models for the Chinese was very weak but confirmed my observation about different patterns of residential segregation.

TABLE 3.1   SELECTED CHARACTERISTICS OF CENSUS TRACTS IN THE NEW YORK
METROPOLITAN AREA, 1980

| Characteristics | New York City | Outside New York City | Manhattan | Outer Boroughs |
|---|---|---|---|---|
| Number of tracts with population >50 | 2,148 | 2,396 | 289 | 1,859 |
| % Chinese | 1.5 | 0.3 | 3.0 | 1.3 |
| % Non-Chinese Asian | 1.4 | 1.0 | 1.5 | 1.4 |
| % Non-Hispanic white | 53.6 | 81.1 | 50.3 | 54.1 |
| % Non-Hispanic black | 24.2 | 10.7 | 23.5 | 24.2 |
| % Hispanic | 18.8 | 6.5 | 21.0 | 18.4 |
| % Foreign-born | 22.7 | 11.3 | 22.4 | 22.7 |
| % With college education | 26.0 | 33.5 | 43.3 | 23.3 |
| % Managerial-executive | 23.9 | 29.8 | 38.2 | 21.7 |
| Median household income in 1979 | $14,845 | $22,794 | $14,012 | $14,973 |
| % Houses built before 1940 | 52.3 | 32.0 | 57.5 | 51.5 |
| % Rental housing | 68.6 | 34.4 | 92.8 | 64.9 |
| % Multifamily housing | 81.3 | 38.9 | 99.6 | 78.5 |
| % Same residence as in 1975 | 54.8 | 58.8 | 49.4 | 55.7 |

Source: U.S. Bureau of the Census, *Census of Population and Housing 1980* (STF3A)

On the one hand, residential movement of the city's Chinese was highly selective
and directed toward relatively disadvantaged tracts, which implied that their
residential movements might not necessarily be associated with socioeconomic
achievement. Unless the Chinese moved out of the city altogether, they would
still have a high probability of being segregated from whites and members of
other racial minority groups. On the other hand, the poor performance of
median household income in the models predicting the percentage of Chinese
indicated that ethnicity might trump class in determining their residential patterns: that is, higher- and lower-income households might be mixed in the neighborhoods where the Chinese were concentrated.

## Residential Mobility and Resegregation

It appeared that in the 1980s New York's Chinese had a much better chance to
achieve spatial assimilation if they moved farther away from the city. It also seemed
that they were less segregated from non-Hispanic whites than non-Hispanic
blacks were. Chinese immigrants have always wanted to convert their economic
gains to real estate properties by purchasing homes in nice neighborhoods away
from, but easily accessible to, Chinatown. They have pursued this strategy for
quite some time, so the patterns I present here were not entirely unexpected.

The quantitative analyses revealed a number of contradictions and pointed
to a more complex reality than one could derive from a simple reading of statistical data based on assimilation models. The interesting question here was why New
York's Chinese were so overwhelmingly concentrated in the city. There were certain mechanisms working to enforce or reinforce residential segregation within
the Chinese immigrant community that statistical models could not sufficiently

document. Findings from quantitative analyses might be understood better in light of the fieldwork that I conducted within the Chinese immigrant community. What actually happened to the Chinese in New York during the 1980s reflected three main factors: development pressures in Old Chinatown, reliance on family and kinship networks to obtain housing, and a resilient preference for proximity and access to the ethnic enclave. All of these factors were emphasized in my field interviews.[32]

## Developments in the Ethnic Enclave

One obvious reason for Chinese immigrants to concentrate in New York City is the existence of a Chinatown in Manhattan and growing satellite Chinatowns in Queens and Brooklyn. Here "Chinatown" does not simply refer to a residential enclave; rather, it indicates economic opportunities—jobs—created by the Chinese themselves. Jobs generated by coethnics are generally accessible to Chinese immigrants. Indeed, these jobs are perhaps the only ones available to many recent arrivals, especially those without a college education, English proficiency, and transferable job skills or work experiences. Many newcomers find work in restaurants, garment factories, and a wide range of Chinese-owned retail and service businesses.

During the 1980s, when I conducted my fieldwork, immigrants who worked in New York's Old Chinatown but lived elsewhere relied heavily on subway lines for daily transportation. Some restaurant workers (and others) who did not even work in Chinatown still went there by subway in order to meet the company vans that brought them to Chinese restaurants scattered over the city or in the suburbs. Every morning between 9 and 10, the vans, some with restaurant names on the side, lined up to pick up workers in places like Confucius Plaza in Old Chinatown or a street corner just outside a subway stop on Main Street in Flushing.

As might be expected, the relationship between job location and residence was reciprocal. To some extent the ability of ethnic businesses to expand outside the city was limited by the shortage of Chinese workers in suburban areas. Mr. Yung, who ran a restaurant in Port Washington, Long Island, turned to Old Chinatown to recruit workers:

> I run a Chinese restaurant and prefer Chinese employees, in part because I can easily communicate with the workers, and also my patrons would expect to see Chinese waiters serving the food. But it is hard to find Chinese workers in the local area. So I have to rely on one of about 20 Chinatown employment agencies to hire workers.
>
> The problem is that since these workers live with their families in the city, transportation to work by train is expensive and time-consuming. If we did not provide transportation, we simply could not get the workers. So I have to send a van every day to Chinatown to pick up workers for work.
>
> Nowadays, Chinese restaurants have sprung up in the suburbs, where it is hard to find ethnic workers. Some restaurants have set up dormitory-type

facilities in apartments and have not had to take the workers back and forth every morning from Chinatown or from Flushing. I also have a dormitory for my workers, but they do not want to stay there; they want to be with other Chinese. So this type of transporting workers to work has become a pattern.[33]

For Chinese workers who did not live in Old Chinatown, access to dispersed job opportunities required them to go to Chinatown by subway first. Mr. Lin, a waiter in Yung's restaurant, said in an interview:

I live in Corona [Queens]. Every morning I go to Flushing to wait for the company van to take me and other co-workers to work in Long Island. It usually takes about 45 minutes each way, the same amount of time as it would take one to go from Corona to [Old] Chinatown by subway train. If the restaurant provides transportation, I would prefer to work outside the city. Working in the suburbs, I get higher pay, because suburban restaurants usually have more affluent patrons, and we get more tips. But I definitely do not want to move out to live near that restaurant, because I am not sure when I would switch jobs again.[34]

The development of the enclave economy in the 1980s certainly affected the residential pattern of the city's Chinese, who found it important to live either in Chinatown or near the subway lines. In fact, outer neighborhoods that had a considerable number of Chinese were all in accessible and convenient places. For example, residents of Woodside, Elmhurst, Jackson Heights, Corona, and Flushing in Queens could take the subway to Manhattan, allowing ethnic enclave workers, and not just the more affluent, to live in the outer districts.

Chinatown's enclave economy in the 1980s provided jobs for Chinese immigrants, helped them adjust to the new country, and smoothed their path to economic incorporation. Meanwhile, however, the growth of the enclave economy had created a tremendous demand on the limited space in Chinatown, then experiencing an economic boom due to influxes of foreign capital and immigrants in the late 1970s and early 1980s. The capital influx stemmed in part from political uncertainty in Hong Kong, Taiwan, and Southeast Asia, and in part from the worldwide recession of the early 1970s, which had forced U.S. financial markets to offer higher interest rates.[35] Foreign investors were especially interested in low-risk, nonliquid assets—namely, real estate development in Chinatown.[36] Residential space gave way to commercial development, while the desire of Chinese retailers to locate in the heart of Chinatown further boosted land prices. According to a study by the Real Estate Board of New York in 1986, the annual rent per square foot for commercial space in the core of Chinatown ($275) was far higher than that on Wall Street ($175); it was also higher than the most desirable commercial location in Manhattan's central business district—for example, on Madison Avenue above 42nd Street ($255).[37] John Wang, former director of the Chinatown Planning Council in New York, was startled by the pace of change in the enclave:

I can't keep up with it! I mean, I work here and the next day I come to work, "Boom! What is that?" Stores and buildings seem to change faces every day. In the past 10 or 15 years, because of the tremendous influx of immigration and foreign capital, Chinatown has become a battlefield for developers and investors. . . . Poor immigrant families have been priced out and displaced in other areas; and more and more better-to-do Asians, and even some of the non-Chinese artists and Wall Street yuppies, have started to purchase converted condominiums in Chinatown at the average price of $150,000. The community has been gentrified; it has become a place for the wealthy, rather than just a poor immigrant ghetto.[38]

Real estate transactions in Chinatown yielded tremendous profits for investors and landowners. Residential rents increased by 200 to 300 percent within a short period during the first half of the 1980s. Illegal "key money" has brought additional profit to investors. Key money is a lump sum collected up front by the landlord upon renting an apartment. For residential units, the key money was usually 10 times as much as the rent; for commercial space, it could be as high as $20,000.[39] Mr. Lu, who had lived and worked in Chinatown for over 20 years, was shocked at the profitability of converting a building from residential to commercial use:

Some lucky owners could make a lot of money through conversion. For example, before conversion of a five-story building on Canal Street, the ground floor was an electronics store, the second and the third floor used to be garment shops, and the top two floors housed about eight families. From what I know, the first four floors have converted to commercial space. Instead of collecting rents from two garment shops and a store, the owner now has 12 commercial tenants, each paying at least $1,800 a month, plus the key money. Key money is illegal and everybody knows it. But no one can do anything about it. In the 1970s key money ranged from $500 to $2,000. Now it is usually 10 times the rent.[40]

The most serious threat to Chinatown residents originating from this property development and speculation was tenant harassment and eviction. Mr. Mui, an activist from Asian Americans for Equality, described what happened when Chinatown tenants filed legal complaints or sued their landlords over leaky ceilings, peeling plaster, poor security, or drastic rent increases:

The Chinese immigrants are usually very tolerant and they know little about their rights as tenants. They do not want any trouble; they do not want to have anything to do with a lawsuit. If they did, it would mean they were very serious. For example, in 1984, 22 tenants of two tenements on Henry Street in Chinatown filed a legal complaint against their landlords for excessive rent increases. Most of these tenants were longtime residents who had been working in Chinatown. They suspected that the increases were a prelude to getting them out and getting in those with more money to spend on rent. Among them, there was a Mrs. Wong, a 66-year-old garment worker who had lived there for almost 40 years. She said she would have no place else to go and that this had been her home. Mrs. Wong's landlord, Mr. Sung, won the endorsement of the Chinatown Planning Council for a plan to rehabilitate his Henry Street building in 1982. After making some improvements—new storm windows, light fixtures, an intercom system, and a coat of paint—the landlord received an approval for rent increases of up to 30 percent. But the actual rent increase was much higher than what was legally allowed. For example, the new rent for 88-year-old Mr. Yuen, another longtime resident, who lived alone in one room there, was $200.68, from $77.44. Mr. Yuen's Social Security check could barely cover the increased rent. The tenants decided to pay the old rents while they challenged the increases. However, the landlord, Mr. Sung, simply put the building up for sale. The tenants did not win the case.[41]

I found, in short, that the cost of property, particularly renovated space, in the core Chinatown area became so high that little affordable housing remained on the fringes. This was not simply caused by a gentrification trend that created greater demand for space throughout Manhattan; there had also been a specific change in Chinatown. Chinatown used to be a residential enclave based on a social structure of sojourning; now, it was increasingly a hotbed for investment and real estate speculation by more affluent coethnics from abroad. Whether they were priced or pushed out of Chinatown, recent immigrants were adapting to this transformation. This finding explained why neither citizenship status nor recency of immigration was significantly related to place of residence in the regression models for the Chinese.

## Family and Kinship Ties

In the quantitative analysis, I found that family situation variables—being married and having children—were significant predictors of living outside the ethnic enclave, but that none of the immigration variables had significant effects. These findings suggested that it might be unnecessary for recent Chinese immigrants to live in Chinatown first and then move on to better neighborhoods as time went by, as was predicted by the classical model of spatial assimilation. Immigrants today might be able to bypass Chinatown to find their first settlement elsewhere in the city. Apparently missing in the logistic analyses were the effects of family ties or kinship networks, which were closely associated with immigration in determining where one would live.

The convergence of Chinese immigrants in immigrant gateway cities such as San Francisco, Los Angeles, and New York is usually explained by the history of Chinese immigration. The first place of residence often depends upon the location of family or kin. More than 80 percent of Chinese immigrants to the United States in the 1970s and 1980s were sponsored by family members. Thus, family ties played a significant role in shaping the settlement patterns of new waves of Chinese immigrants.

"Why did you come to settle in New York?" The immediate response to my question would be: "Because my relatives are here." Mr. Lee recalled the first few months after his family of six came to New York:

> My wife and I and our four children, the oldest being 15 years old, immigrated in 1979 from Taishan. My sister-in-law Ah Ling, who is a naturalized U.S. citizen, helped us out.
>
> When we were about to leave China, my fellow villagers [in Taishan] asked me where in America I would go. I told them New York. They wondered why not San Francisco. All I could tell them was because my sister-in-law Ah Ling was there, and she was the only one who would receive us in the U.S. Actually, I, like my fellow villagers, knew nothing else other than San Francisco and New York, where most of our relatives lived.
>
> When we arrived at JFK International Airport in New York, Ah Ling and her husband came to pick us up. She said, "You have to live with us for the time being. I hope you don't mind." I was only grateful. How could I possibly resist such a generous offer?
>
> Ah Ling's family lived in a small two-bedroom apartment in Jackson Heights, Queens. They had three kids similar to the age of mine. They gave us a bedroom and the 11 of us all crammed into this small apartment, with three of the older kids sleeping on the living room floor at night.

Lee shared with almost all Chinese immigrants the idea that where they will live depends on the location of the relatives who sponsored their immigration. He continued:

> We did not have a choice but listened to what Ah Ling had to say. We did not have any money; we did not know anybody else; we did not speak a single word of English; and everything here was so foreign to us that we were basically scared.
>
> I knew that a lot of immigrant families had to go through this. I did the same thing for my own brother's family when I got them out a couple of years ago. I had to put them up in my apartment for half a year. This is a tradition that has been going on for a long time; it is a family obligation which you are not supposed to avoid.[42]

Lee never lived in Old Chinatown, simply because his relatives did not live there. Another family, which had lived in Old Chinatown since immigrating, told the other side of the story. Mrs. Chen, who came from Zhongshan to join her husband, has lived in Old Chinatown since 1980. Her husband immigrated in 1969 as a refugee from Hong Kong at the age of 18. With little education, no English-language ability, and few relatives here, Mr. Chen turned to Chinatown for support. He first worked in a restaurant as a dishwasher. He then became a self-trained cook for another Chinese restaurant in Chinatown. He shared a unit (one room with a small kitchen and a bathroom) with three co-workers in one of the bachelors quarters there. Like many Chinatown bachelors, he had to go to China to find a wife. When Mrs. Chen arrived, they managed to rent the whole unit. Chen's three roommates volunteered to move out, but Chen had to pay each $500 to cover their moving expenses, a common practice in Chinatown. The rent itself was only $75 because units in the building were rent-controlled, but the Chens had to pay $800 in key money every two years to renew the lease. Mrs. Chen had two children at the time of the interview, and the family of four lived in that same unit. When asked whether her family had considered moving, she replied:

> Not at the moment. Maybe when the kids grow older, we would move into a bigger apartment somewhere. Living in Chinatown is just so convenient. We don't have to spend time on the subway train; my husband and I only walk a few blocks to work. It is also safer. My husband gets off work at 11 p.m. with cash wages in his pocket. Riding on a subway train at night is not very safe; besides, it is time-consuming. Also, I can leave my kids next door at my neighbors'. If you lived elsewhere, even if there were other Chinese around, you could not possibly find a babysitter so close by, and you would have to hurry off every day in the morning to send you kids to the babysitter and then catch the train to work, or you couldn't work at all. Moreover, I don't have to pack my refrigerator; I can bring in fresh vegetables and food every day after work. I feel life is much easier when you are close to an environment similar to the one you grew up in.[43]

Mrs. Chen came right to Old Chinatown. She did not make her own residential choice; she lived in Chinatown because her husband was there. She had gotten so used to Chinatown's conveniences that she could tolerate cramped quarters and poor housing.

Her case had one thing in common with Lee's. Both came to join relatives and settled wherever their relatives were. In the Old Chinatown area, where the growth of the Chinese population far exceeds the scale of residential expansion, the level of segregation has increased along with the density. In other parts of the city, family and kinship networks have directed immigrants into neighborhoods where a considerable number of Chinese families have already concentrated, thus establishing new enclaves and leading to resegregation.

While developments in Old Chinatown's enclave economy push Chinese immigrants into other areas of the city, family and kinship networks also account for much of the decentralization. During the 1970s New York City's Chinese population grew from 69,000 to 124,000 by census count. Other areas, such as Queens and Brooklyn, have developed Chinese populations, partly from the outward movement from Old Chinatown and partly from new immigrants' family networking. During the same decade, Queens's Chinese population grew by 207 percent and Brooklyn's by 121 percent.[44] Census data for the following decades suggest an acceleration of Asian population growth, largely outside Manhattan.

## The Development of the Ethnic Housing Market

A growing ethnic housing market helps Chinese immigrants find affordable housing outside Old Chinatown, which in turn accounts, at least in part, for the unexpectedly high level of residential segregation among the Chinese in the city's outer boroughs.[45] Since many new immigrants speak little English and have limited knowledge about the larger housing market, they have to depend on the ethnic market to satisfy their housing needs, whether they intend to rent or buy. Real estate is one of the fastest-growing businesses in the enclave economy: not only the land development and speculation discussed above, but also buying, selling, and rental services. Many immigrants depend on Chinese-run real estate companies in renting or purchasing their homes. Even if they search for housing by themselves to save money, they are often confined to the ethnic housing market. "It is a pain and time-consuming to look for a suitable apartment all by yourself," said Mr. Lee when he talked about his house-hunting experience, and many new families would echo his statement. "After my wife and I both got a job," he continued:

> we decided to look for an apartment by ourselves. We picked up a Chinese newspaper in Chinatown, and started making phone calls at night. If the landlord was not a Chinese, I would hang up on him, because I could not speak English. Most of the available units rented out by Chinese owners seemed to be in convenient locations because the owners themselves lived in the same house. But when you actually went there to see the unit, it might not be the one you wanted. Those houses look pretty nice from outside, but from inside many units we could afford were not in very good shape. The owners did not seem to do much to maintain their rental units, let alone renovate them. Housing was in such great demand that those landlords did not have to worry about whether their units could be rented out or not. Most of the time, it was the landlord who chose his tenants rather than the other way around.
>
> We had looked at five or six houses before we decided on one in a neighborhood a few block away from my sister-in-law's in Jackson Heights. We did not dare to move far, since we barely knew anybody here. It took us three weekends just to look from one house to another. Some people would simply pay a hundred dollar fee and leave the whole thing to the real estate agent. I would have done so if I had anticipated the hectic experience.[46]

To a great extent Chinese-owned real estate companies shape the residential patterns of the Chinese while making good money off newcomers' desperate housing needs. Moreover, some real estate companies, with the support of foreign capital, manage to buy into working-class neighborhoods where homeowners are eager to sell off their properties for cash to invest in homes elsewhere. In such cases, real estate agencies can buy at relatively low prices and then turn around and immediately sell to Chinese immigrant families, usually without any repairs or improvements, at prices ranging from 25 to 50 percent above the takeover prices. The new owners commonly rent out a good part of the home, again without much repair work, to other Chinese immigrant families.

The ethnic housing market, combined with ethnic economic resources and foreign capital, effectively shapes the residential movement of the Chinese, promoting the development of satellite Chinese enclaves in new locations in Queens and Brooklyn. Ms. Liang, who is an immigrant herself and runs a real estate agency in Flushing, commented:

> Our customers are exclusively Chinese, most of whom are immigrants and speak very little English. They want to rent or buy a house, but they don't know how and where. They come to us, and we provide them with all the necessary information and help in every step to their satisfaction. We deal with our customers in Chinese and in ways that they are familiar with.[47]

Chinese immigrants have two basic concerns when it comes to housing. Practically speaking, they need a decent place to live. Culturally speaking, they measure success not so much by what they do for a living but by how much land or real estate they own. The golden dream of old sojourners was to save enough money to buy land in their homeland, because they saw it as something they could pass on to the next generation. The American dream of new immigrants, who have no intention of returning to their homeland, is to own a home like other Americans. Many of them must sacrifice to achieve this goal. Mr. Cheung, 67 years old and recently retired from his restaurant job, explained how he did so, in an interview at his home in Jackson Heights:

> I immigrated with my family in 1965 from Hong Kong. I worked in a restaurant for 23 years. The whole family—my wife and I and six kids—used to cram into a small two-room apartment in Chinatown. Both my wife and I worked right away, and three years later my two elder daughters worked to help bring in income. We worked hard and lived on a very tight budget with a goal of buying our own home. In 1984 we purchased this three-story house. Now my wife and I with our two youngest children live on the second floor; the first and the third floors are rented out to two immigrant families recently arrived from Canton. Only since then have I started to think of retiring, because I finally have something that can be left for my children.[48]

Those who cannot afford to buy now remain optimistic. Mrs. Lai said:

> My husband and I want to buy our own home somewhere in the city. We both feel that if we have a job, work hard, and live on a frugal budget, we can save money to invest in housing. For us, buying a home is a more secure and practical investment than starting up a small business. Not everybody is successful in business. My family of six, including my parents-in-law, who also work, now live in a three-bedroom apartment in Sunset Park, Brooklyn. We pay $630 rent a month. With four workers in the household, it is not difficult to pool money to purchase a house.[49]

The real estate agent Ms. Liang agreed that "because rents are so high, immigrants who have been here for a while would rather buy their own housing and rent part of it out to help pay off their mortgage." Almost all my informants, particularly those who worked in the enclave, shared the views of Mr. Cheung, Mrs. Lai, and Ms. Liang about housing. Even if their earnings may not transfer into higher occupational status, they can be converted into a residential gain, which implies a collective effort—a family strategy—distinct from the generally assumed path of socioeconomic mobility.

The settlement patterns for New York's Chinese also suggest a voluntary process. Old Chinatown was established as a defense against the hostile environment that immigrant Chinese confronted. Later it was part of a strategy of voluntary segregation in order to preserve group solidarity for mutual help and linguistic and cultural security.[50] Today, that voluntary aspect has become more resilient despite the decreasing amount of hostility actually faced by the group. Chinese immigrants' preference for proximity and access to the ethnic enclave largely determines their residential choices. Again, informants offered some interpretations. A Chinese realtor explained:

> Chinese immigrants have some essential preferences concerning where they would like to live. First, the location has to be convenient—near the subway lines, for many of the immigrants work in Chinatown and the subway is their only means of transportation. Second, the neighborhood has to be safe, with a good mix of ethnic groups. The Chinese prefer to live in a neighborhood with at least a Chinese family, some Asians, and maybe some Hispanics. People used to joke that the Chinese had a herd instinct; they were inclined to herd around their own folks. They don't want to be the first ones to move into a non-Chinese neighborhood, but as soon as one makes such a move, others will follow. There is rarely such a thing as just one Chinese family in a neighborhood.[51]

While New York City's Chinese continue to cluster on the Lower East Side of Manhattan, those who disperse mainly concentrate in Flushing, Elmhurst, Corona, Jackson Heights, Astoria, and Rego Park in Queens; and in Borough Park, Flatbush, Bay Ridge, Park Slope, Midwood, Sheepshead Bay, and Sunset Park in Brooklyn.[52] Many immigrant families in outer boroughs are more affluent than those in Old Chinatown. However, there are also a large number of poor immigrant families bypassing Old Chinatown to settle elsewhere. These families are resegregated in certain neighborhoods, some of which share characteristics with Old Chinatown. These findings suggest, on the one hand, that ethnicity is perhaps more important than class in their residential choice, and, on the other hand, that the formation of the ethnic housing market largely determines resegregation in satellite Chinatowns.

## Conclusion

My study of residential patterns in New York City during the 1970s and 1980s led me to several tentative conclusions. The Chinese were more highly segregated than one might have anticipated from the research literature. Decentralization was strongly associated with less segregation from non-Hispanic whites for both Chinese and other Asian subgroups. However, while segregation from non-Hispanic whites for the Chinese was higher in Manhattan than in other boroughs, segregation for other Asian subgroups was lower in Manhattan than in outer boroughs. These findings only partially support a key prediction of assimilation theory. The discrepancy serves as a reminder that there is no intrinsic link between such abstract categories as "centralization" and "segregation," or "suburbanization" and "assimilation." One needs more information. Where are the areas of initial settlement? How distinctive are these areas? Under what housing market conditions do immigrants resettle? What is the economic basis of the ethnic group? How do labor market factors affect residential location? Chinatown is an important point of orientation for Chinese immigrants; for many whose jobs are tied to the enclave economy, it serves as an anchor for their residential choices.

The residential patterns of the Chinese in New York City were related to SES—as the assimilation model predicted. That is, the Chinese were more likely to live outside Manhattan and outside the city if they have achieved higher SES and if their family situation (marital status and presence of children) promoted that residential choice. Field interviews confirmed that many Chinese perceived the purchase of a home in Queens or Brooklyn as a prime achievement and a symbol of success. In many cases, residential mobility was an expression of socio-economic mobility.

However, my study suggests that residential decentralization may not serve as a good indicator of assimilation into mainstream society. Recent immigrants were just as likely as the native-born to live in the outer boroughs or suburban areas, even though English-language ability made a difference. An important factor to take into account was the social organization of the Chinese community, which I examined in terms of developments in the enclave economy, family and kinship networks, and the ethnic housing market. For immigrants, the key questions were where their jobs were, where their relatives lived, and where they got assistance in finding housing. The influence of all these factors was clearly reflected in the lack of association of U.S. citizenship and year of immigration with place of residence. Beyond access to jobs and family networking, a formal real estate market organized through Chinese realtors reinforced tendencies toward clustering in certain neighborhoods. Moreover, Chinese immigrant families in New York expressed a strong inclination to live close to other Chinese and to build their own ethnic community in the new neighborhoods. For these reasons, immigrants simply did not participate widely in the open housing market. The set of market conditions that traditionally operated to restrict such persons to the deteriorated, old, and dense housing stock of the inner city did not apply to them; and at the same time, housing prices in the core area tended to force them out.

Another complication for the assimilation model is the existence of an enclave economy centered in the traditional core of Chinatown. My study showed that employment in an enclave industry had no direct effect on residential location, even though these industries were concentrated in Manhattan. Whether one lived in Manhattan (which was more convenient), one of the outer boroughs, or even in the suburbs (which were less expensive and accessible by subway or train), the tie to the enclave was persistent. Chinese families were able to maintain links to the enclave even while enjoying upward social mobility and even while living outside Chinatown.

These findings may have implications for the future evolution of settlement patterns. Given cultural preferences and the strength of an ethnic and kinship-based real estate market, it is not obvious that location outside Chinatown will long remain associated with markedly lower segregation. Based on the field interviews, a strong hypothesis would state that Chinese segregation is in large part voluntary, and their residential segregation may not be as disadvantageous as it is for other racial minority groups. In this interpretation, the enclave economy and the ethnic housing market provide the Chinese with a positive mode of incorporation distinct from assimilation into the larger society. This interpretation is consistent with what is known about the operation of the enclave labor market.[53] But the Chinese pay a price: wages in the enclave industries are low, housing prices in the Chinese market are high, and extended families live for long periods in crowded quarters. Further research is needed to evaluate to what extent the Chinese residential pattern avoids the disadvantages faced by other racial and ethnic minority groups.

# 4

# Suburbanization and New Trends in Community Development

*The Case of Chinese Ethnoburbs in the San Gabriel Valley, California*

With Yen-Fen Tseng and Rebecca Y. Kim

Classic assimilation theories have long stressed the transitory nature of ethnically distinct urban enclaves as springboards for immigrants' eventual integration into the mainstream. New York's Little Italy and Los Angeles' Little Tokyo are well-known examples of spatial assimilation, places where immigrants toiled to enable their children to "melt" into suburbia and become "indistinguishably" American. In the past three decades, however, this classic urban-to-suburban residential mobility model has been challenged.[1] America's largest metropolitan regions have witnessed trends of suburbanization not simply among native-born non-Hispanic whites but also among racial/ethnic minorities. The latter trend—the direct insertion of large numbers of new immigrants into white middle-class suburbs—does not follow the incorporation patterns predicted by classical assimilation theories. Some of the suburban communities that whites once dominated have evolved into "global" neighborhoods in which native-born groups live side by side with middle-class native minorities and immigrants of different national origins. Others have been rapidly transformed into "ethnoburbs" by new immigrants possessing higher-than-average levels of education, occupational status, and incomes, as well as social networks that branch out to tap financial resources and markets in Asia.[2]

In this chapter, we examine new patterns of spatial assimilation through the case of the sprawling Chinese ethnoburbs in California's San Gabriel Valley, focusing on several questions. How have Chinese immigrants of diverse origins and socioeconomic backgrounds negotiated their way into the suburbia of an immigrant gateway metropolis? What is a Chinese ethnoburb like, and how does it differ from traditional Chinatowns and from typical American suburban communities? What implications does the ethnoburb phenomenon have for our understanding of spatial assimilation? We base our analysis on census data, prior case studies in the existing literature, and our own field observations. Overall, we seek to understand the ways in which contemporary globalization and international migration challenge the notion of assimilation. We also speculate on how new patterns of immigrant settlement create new issues for the Chinese American community while contributing to our understanding of twenty-first-century urban dynamics.

## The Changing Contexts of International Migration: Exit versus Reception

Global economic restructuring has moved people and capital, leading to sweeping changes in local economies of both sending and receiving countries. In many of the sending countries, global economic restructuring has significantly altered the structures of local economies and opportunities for social mobility, causing people and capital to move within and across borders in ways that render neoclassical economic theories of international migration inadequate. Wage differentials and access to better employment opportunities are no longer the main forces that push people to move. Other compelling causes include access to formal and informal migration networks, access to well-established institutionalized credit and insurance markets, and the need for risk diversification, as well as extreme hardships arising from war, political and religious persecutions, (de)colonization, and military involvement.[3]

As a result, the contexts of exit for contemporary international migrations have been substantially reshaped. Since the 1960s, international migrants to the United States constitute not only the tired, the poor, and the huddled masses "yearning to breathe free," as is inscribed on the Statue of Liberty, but also the affluent, the highly skilled, and the entrepreneurial. Contemporary immigrants from Asia, for example, include low-skilled urban workers, uneducated peasants, and penniless refugees. But they also include professionals such as engineers, scientists, physicians, entrepreneurs, and wealthy investors.[4] The influx of large numbers of resource-rich immigrants creates new modes of immigrant settlement, the most remarkable of which is the detour from central-city ethnic enclaves to white middle-class suburbia.

Globalization has also changed the contexts of reception. In the United States, economic restructuring divides urban labor markets into two parts: a dominant core sector characterized by knowledge-intensive or capital-intensive jobs that offer high salaries with fringe benefits, good working conditions, and ample opportunities for upward social mobility—and a marginal but sizable sector characterized by low-skilled, labor-intensive jobs that offer minimum wages with no benefits, poor working conditions, and few opportunities for upward social mobility.[5] The urban employment base of unionized, blue-collar manufacturing jobs that used to facilitate intergenerational mobility for the working-class is shrinking. Consequently, the jobs available in local labor markets either require advanced education and skills or do not pay decent wages, and less skilled natives or immigrants living in the central city are trapped in the ranks of the unemployed or working poor.[6]

Parallel to this economic restructuring is the trend of accelerating suburbanization. Most of the country's large metropolises have witnessed "white flight"— middle-class Americans, mainly whites, leaving the city for the suburbs. Much like New York, Los Angeles has witnessed the decline of non-Hispanic whites as a proportion of the metropolitan population, from over 85 percent in 1960 to less than a third (31 percent) in 2000. In fact, by 2000 most of the country's major urban centers had become numerically minority-dominant.[7]

The changing contexts of reception have rendered the conventional notion of spatial assimilation outdated. On the one hand, central-city ethnic enclaves and larger urban contexts in which immigrants first settle may be composed disproportionately of minority natives or immigrants. Thanks to accelerating white flight, immigrants may have little contact with the native-born middle-class whites to whom they are expected to assimilate. They are now more likely to experience varied pathways of segmented assimilation than to follow a linear pathway of assimilation into a single mainstream. On the other hand, suburbs that used to be exclusively white and middle-class may now be settled by affluent immigrants perceived by natives as "unacculturated" because they are non-English-speaking and nonwhite.

Changing contexts of exit and reception thus lead to varied modes of immigrant incorporation, which defy conventional notions of straight-line assimilation into the white middle class. In the following section, we unfold the processes and consequences of contemporary Chinese immigration to highlight new forms and mechanisms for immigrant settlement and community development.[8]

## Contemporary Chinese Immigration to Los Angeles: Growth and Diversification

Chinese immigration to the United States began several decades before the mass migration from southern and eastern Europe. But unlike those early European immigrants, who were expected to assimilate into mainstream society as quickly as possible, and have done so in the course of two to three generations, early Chinese immigrants were legally barred from immigration, naturalization, and assimilation by the Chinese Exclusion Act (1882–1943). They were forced to take refuge in Chinatowns, creating their own means of survival via ethnic economies and organizations in order to avoid direct competition with native workers while keeping alive the sojourner's dream of one day returning to China with gold and glory.[9] Sixty years of legal exclusion confined Chinese immigrants to Chinatowns and prevented them from living elsewhere, reinforcing their ethnicity, bounded by the enclave, as well as the stereotypes of their clannishness and unassimilability.

In the wake of the new millennium, the Chinese American community remains largely an immigrant community despite its long history of immigrant settlement and its current phenomenal population growth. Between 1960 and 2006, the number of Chinese in the United States grew more than 13-fold: from 237,292 in 1960 to 2,879,636 in 2000 (including half a million mixed-race persons). As of 2006, the ethnic population reached 3.6 million. This rapid growth was largely attributed to international migration: first-generation migrants made up nearly 70 percent of the population, and more than three-quarters of the foreign-born arrived in the United States after 1980.[10]

Unlike the old-timers, who were mostly unskilled laborers from the southern region of Guangdong province, new Chinese immigrants come from diverse regions and socioeconomic backgrounds. The three main sources of Chinese immigration are mainland China, Taiwan, and Hong Kong. In recent years, Chinese immigrants from Southeast Asia and the Americas have also been visible. For example, as of 1990, 15 percent of the Chinese American population lived in the Los Angeles metropolitan area. Among L.A.'s Chinese Americans at that time, 23 percent were born in the United States, 27 percent in mainland China, 20 percent in Taiwan, 8 percent in Hong Kong, and 22 percent in other countries.[11] Immigrant Chinese from different regions do not necessarily share the same culture or lived experiences. Language is perhaps the most significant cultural barrier, creating a subtle social distance between coethnics who speak Cantonese or other regional dialects and those who speak Mandarin. The new Chinese immigrants are also disproportionately drawn from highly educated and professional segments of the sending societies. The 2000 census showed that young people (aged 25 to 34) with four or more years of college education were more than twice as prevalent among foreign-born Chinese as among U.S.-born non-Hispanic whites (65 versus 30 percent).[12]

The divergent origins and socioeconomic backgrounds of contemporary Chinese immigrants, combined with global developments in the Pacific Rim region, have drastically changed the Chinese American community. Shifting from homogeneous Chinatowns into global ethnoburbs, the residential patterns of the Chinese are now characterized by concentration as well as dispersion. Geographic concentration to some extent follows a historical pattern: Chinese Americans continue to concentrate in the West and in urban areas. California has accounted for a disproportionate share of the Chinese ever since they first set foot on the American shore. Prior to 1950, California accounted for more than half of all Chinese in the United States, and it still has close to 40 percent. California's Chinese today continue to concentrate in the Bay Area to the north and the Los Angeles metropolitan region to the south, but they tend to disperse into suburbs rather than cluster in central cities. As of 2000, less than 3 percent of the Chinese in Los Angeles, 8 percent of the Chinese in San Francisco, and 14 percent of the Chinese in New York lived in old inner-city Chinatowns. However, demographic changes influenced by international migration do not appear to be associated with the disappearance or significant decline of Chinatowns. Traditional Chinatowns show little sign of decline, but have actually grown and expanded.[13] In Los Angeles' Chinatown, for example, two tracts located at the core had a Chinese majority, and two adjacent census tracts contained 25 percent or more Chinese.[14]

While inner-city Chinatowns continue to receive newcomers as well as attract economic investment from coethnics, they no longer serve as primary centers of initial settlement. The majority of new immigrants, especially the affluent and highly skilled, are bypassing central cities to settle into suburbs immediately after arrival. The majority of Chinese are spreading out into the suburbs outside traditional immigrant gateway cities as well as into new urban centers of Asian settlement across the country. As of 2000, half of all Chinese in the United States lived outside central cities. There are few new urban Chinese enclaves in the country where more than half of the residents are coethnics. For example, in New York City's Flushing, known as the "second [urban] Chinatown," only 2 of the 11 census tracts contained 25 percent or more Chinese, and none had a Chinese majority.[15] In Los Angeles' Monterey Park, known as "the first suburban Chinatown," 10 of the 13 tracts contained 25 percent or more Chinese, but only one tract had a Chinese majority. Small suburban cities in Los Angeles and the San Francisco Bay Area have witnessed extraordinarily high proportions of Chinese Americans in the general population and the emergence of a new and distinct phenomenon—"ethnoburbs."

## Monterey Park and Beyond: Chinese Ethnoburbs in the San Gabriel Valley

The notion of ethnoburb was first proposed by the Chinese American geographer Wei Li to refer to the hybridity of inner-city ethnic enclaves and middle-class suburbs:[16] suburban ethnic clusters of people and businesses. According to the ethnoburb model, the suburbanization and residential re-concentration of an immigrant group may not necessarily be accompanied by complete assimilation, as predicted by classical assimilation theories. Instead, this drastic spatial transformation is affected by a combination of global and local forces, including the movements of people and capital and the dynamics of community and networks.

### The Demographic Transformation of an American Suburb

The San Gabriel Valley is a vast suburban region to the east of the city of Los Angeles, to the north of the Puente Hills, to the south of the San Gabriel Mountains, and to the west of the Inland Empire, encompassing 31 municipalities and 14 unincorporated communities of Los Angeles County.[17] The kind of Chinese ethnoburb that we explore in this chapter is defined rather loosely to refer to the emerging immigrant Chinese community in the metropolitan area. At the core of the development is Monterey Park, a Chinese ethnoburb.[18] Monterey Park is an incorporated municipality with its own elected city council in suburban Los Angeles. From the beginning of World War II until 1960, Monterey Park prospered as the wartime economy brought new people from across the country to southern California.[19] In the decade immediately after the war, it was one of the most affordable suburban bedroom communities—a cozy town with single-family homes, tree-lined streets, and spacious green lawns. In the 1960s, about 85 percent of the housing consisted of detached single-family homes, and 4 percent consisted of buildings with 10 or more units. About two-thirds of the housing was owner-occupied, and vacancy rates were about 5 percent.

Postwar Monterey Park was predominantly white. But because of its suburban atmosphere and proximity to downtown Los Angeles, it began to draw upwardly mobile Mexican Americans from neighboring East Los Angeles, Japanese Americans from the Westside, and Chinese Americans from Chinatown.[20] By 1960 its ethnic makeup was 85.0 percent non-Hispanic white (down from 99.9 percent in 1950), 12.0 percent Hispanic, 2.9 percent Asian, and 0.1 percent black; by 1970, it was 51.0 percent white, 34.0 percent Hispanic, and 15.0 percent Asian (two-thirds Japanese American, one-third Chinese American). Many of the Hispanic and Asian Americans arriving in Monterey Park during the 1950s and 1960s were educated, acculturated, and middle-class second- or third-generation immigrants driven by the American dream of upward mobility and suburban life. By 1970, it had become the first ethnically diverse middle-class suburb, with non-Hispanic whites holding a slight majority. The process of ethnic integration was fairly smooth, since it very much conformed to the conventional model of spatial assimilation. The new residents were not perceived as a threat to existing Anglo political and institutional dominance.[21]

The arrival of immigrants and investors from Taiwan and the Pacific Rim, and the influx of foreign capital that started in the 1970s and then accelerated, set off a dramatic demographic transformation in Monterey Park. By the mid-1980s, the city had been completely remade: from a native bedroom town into an immigrant suburb with an Asian majority and a visible presence of foreign-born Chinese. Non-Hispanic white residents declined from 51 percent in 1970 to 26 percent in 1980, 12 percent in 1990, and 7 percent in 2000. In contrast, the proportion of Asian residents increased from 15 percent in 1970 to 34 percent in 1980 and 56 percent in 1990, making it the first Asian-majority city in the United States. As of 2000, Monterey Park's racial composition was 7 percent white, 41 percent Chinese, 21 percent other Asian, 30 percent Hispanic, and 1 percent African American. Those in the "other Asian" category included Japanese Americans (mostly U.S.-born), Vietnamese, Filipinos, and other Southeast Asians. In 1980, less than a third of the Monterey Park population was foreign-born, but the proportion increased to 54 percent by 2000. Not surprisingly, more than three-quarters of those in Monterey Park spoke a language other than

English at home. Clearly, this suburban city has been transformed into a typical immigrant-dominant ethnoburb.

Unlike earlier Chinese immigrants, who were mainly from rural regions in South China, Monterey Park's Chinese immigrants of the early 1980s were mostly from Taiwan, either investors and entrepreneurs or professionals.[22] Once the Chinese community took shape, family migration and migration from mainland China, Hong Kong, and Southeast Asia followed. By the mid-1980s, the number of mainland Chinese immigrants surpassed the number of Taiwanese. According to the Immigration and Naturalization Service, among Chinese immigrants who selected Monterey Park as their preferred destination between 1983 and 1990, 44 percent were from the mainland and 42 percent from Taiwan.[23] Yet the visibility of Taiwanese money, Taiwanese-owned businesses, and Taiwanese involvement in local politics earned Monterey Park the nickname "Little Taipei."

What made Taiwanese immigrants in Monterey Park distinct was that they were disproportionately highly skilled and capital-rich, and many had obtained immigration visas through direct investment or employment by Chinese-owned or mainstream American businesses. As of 1990, the Chinese immigrants were more highly skilled than Los Angeles County's population: about a quarter of the adult Chinese population had completed four years of college, and another 17 percent had post-college education, compared with 14 percent and 8 percent respectively of residents countywide; close to 40 percent had professional occupations, compared with 27 percent countywide; and 16 percent of the work force was self-employed, compared with 10 percent countywide. A telephone survey of Chinese business owners in Los Angeles in the early 1990s also showed that Chinese immigrant entrepreneurs had much higher levels of educational attainment than other immigrant entrepreneurs: 88 percent of those surveyed reported having four years or more of college education, compared with 35 percent of white male business owners.[24] Moreover, Chinese immigrant business owners were nearly twice as likely as Korean business owners (who are known for their propensity for entrepreneurship) to have been members of the business-owner class prior to migration (43 percent versus 24 percent), and some of these entrepreneurs continue to run their businesses in the homeland after migration, or become transnational.[25] This selective group of entrepreneurs were not only highly educated with entrepreneurial expertise and skills; they also had extensive homeland and transnational business ties that had been established prior to their arrival in the United States, and that were further strengthened through frequent visits to the homeland.[26]

Another distinctive characteristic of Monterey Park was the visibility of transnational migrants. In contrast to the traditional male sojourner who left his family behind to find riches in America, a new group of Chinese transnationals—"spacemen" or "astronauts" as the media call them—settled their wives and children in Monterey Park while shuttling back and forth over the Pacific Ocean. In other cases, the children—known as "parachute kids"—were left alone to obtain an education in the United States while both parents

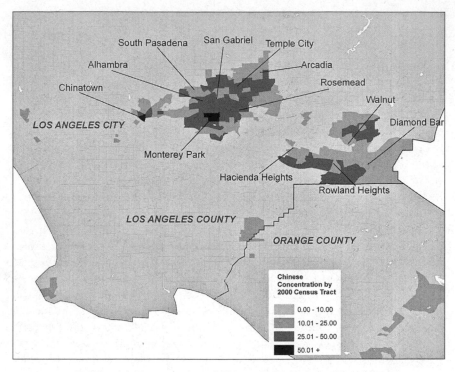

**FIGURE 4.1** Residential Concentration of Chinese in Los Angeles County, 2000. (*Source:* 2000 U.S. Census tract data; map created by and courtesy of Spatial Structures in the Social Sciences, Brown University.)

remained in Asia.[27] Transnational household arrangements became an alternative model of immigrant settlement. Indeed, Monterey Park's newcomers represented a brand new stream of immigrants and a new mode of incorporation. Instead of moving from immigrant enclaves like other native-born Latino or Asian Americans, the new Chinese immigrants inserted themselves directly into the middle-class suburb without a period of acculturation.

As more Chinese immigrants put down their roots in Monterey Park, newer arrivals started to settle in adjacent suburban communities, such as Alhambra, Rosemead, San Gabriel, and Temple City. They branched out north to Arcadia and San Marino, and southeast to Diamond Bar. This trend of residential movement out of, or bypassing, the ethnoburb's core area is less noticeable to non-coethnic outsiders than it is to coethnics. Part of the reason is the diversity of the newcomers' socioeconomic backgrounds. In recent years the undocumented immigrants of lower socioeconomic status (SES) who serve the growing Chinese enclave economy have become more visible. Figure 4.1 maps out the spatial distribution of Chinese Americans at the census-tract level for Los Angeles County. Patterns of Chinese American settlement generally reflect the duality of concentration and dispersal. These patterns are distinct insofar as the ethnic population has grown beyond the boundaries of the central city and has become increasingly concentrated in several locations that expand eastward into the San Gabriel Valley. As Figure 4.1 shows, Chinese settlement is most concentrated in Monterey Park, San Marino, Arcadia, San Gabriel, Alhambra, Rosemead, Temple City, and as far southeast as Hacienda Heights, Rowland Heights, Walnut, and Diamond Bar.

Making up only 3.5 percent of Los Angeles County's total population (and one percent of the total U.S. population), Chinese Americans are overrepresented in many suburban cities in the San Gabriel Valley even though none of these cities has a Chinese majority. As shown in Table 4.1, there are 13 U.S. cities with over 10,000 people in which the proportion of ethnic Chinese is at least 20 percent. All are in California, and all but two are in Los Angeles' San Gabriel Valley.[28] Except for San Francisco, all the cities listed in Table 4.1 can be considered typical ethnoburbs, which were barely visible before 1980. Table 4.1 reveals another marked characteristic of the ethnoburb: ethnic plurality; here, non-Hispanic whites are a numerical minority.[29]

Also shown in Table 4.1 is a trend of socioeconomic diversity. As time goes by, some Chinese ethnoburbs have begun to attract less resourceful Chinese immigrants from the mainland and other parts of Asia. Some have arrived in the ethnoburb to join their families; others, many of whom are low-skilled and undocumented, are drawn there because the expanding enclave economy has a demand for their cheap labor and because they can easily find housing through

TABLE 4.1   CALIFORNIA CITIES AND ETHNOBURBS, 2000: WHITE, ASIAN, AND ETHNIC CHINESE POPULATIONS

| City | Total Population | % Non-Hispanic White | % Asian | % Chinese | Median Household Income |
|------|------|------|------|------|------|
| Los Angeles County | 9,519,338 | 31 | 12 | 3.9 | $42,189 |
| Los Angeles City | 3,694,820 | 30 | 10 | 2.0 | $36,687 |
| Monterey Park | 60,051 | 7 | 62 | 44 | $40,724 |
| San Marino | 12,945 | 45 | 49 | 43 | $117,267 |
| Arcadia | 53,054 | 40 | 45 | 37 | $56,100 |
| San Gabriel | 39,084 | 18 | 50 | 37 | $41,791 |
| Alhambra | 85,804 | 14 | 47 | 36 | $39,213 |
| Rosemead | 53,505 | 8 | 49 | 33 | $36,181 |
| Temple City | 33,377 | 38 | 39 | 31 | $48,722 |
| Rowland Heights | 48,553 | 16 | 50 | 32 | $52,270 |
| Walnut | 30,004 | 18 | 56 | 31 | $81,015 |
| Hacienda Heights | 53,122 | 22 | 36 | 26 | $59,485 |
| Diamond Bar | 56,287 | 31 | 43 | 20 | $68,871 |
| Cupertino | 50,546 | 48 | 44 | 25 | $100,411 |
| San Francisco | 776,733 | 44 | 31 | 21 | $55,221 |

Source: U.S. Census of the Population, 2000 (http://factfinder.census.gov/).

relatives and friends. For example, the median household income in ethnoburbs such as Monterey Park, Alhambra, Rosemead, and San Gabriel was significantly lower than that in Los Angeles County. As a result of intertwined ethnic ties, the Chinese population has become increasingly diverse along class lines.

## The Development of the Enclave Economy in the San Gabriel Valley

Without doubt, contemporary Chinese immigration has driven much of the demographic transformation in the suburbs of Los Angeles. The development of the Chinese enclave economy in the San Gabriel Valley was initially set off in Monterey Park in the late 1970s, transforming the character of the American suburb and making the emerging ethnoburb distinctly Chinese. Prior to 1970, a handful of small specialty shops, supermarkets, and restaurants dominated commercial activities in Monterey Park. At night, streets were quiet as residents retired into their comfortable homes. A former police chief recalled, "You could shoot a cannon off at Atlantic and Garvey [one of the main intersections], and it could fly through the air and roll to a stop without hitting a soul."[30] Today, Chinese-owned office buildings and mini-malls have replaced this bedroom community's commercial core with a cosmopolitan Asian Pacific hub. Varied Chinese-owned businesses, with prominent Chinese-language signs, line the main streets. The vibrant commercial center expands block after block and is active from early in the morning until late at night, seven days a week. As a resident recalled, "At 3:30 in the morning . . . I counted 34 cars stopped at a red light at Atlantic and Garvey. It looked like rush hour."[31] While many Chinese-owned businesses still resemble those in Chinatowns—such as "mom and pop" or "husband-wife" family-run restaurants, gift shops, food stores, and small-scale services—newer establishments are bigger and more diverse and modern, much like those in mainstream economies in the United States and in Asia.

The development of the Chinese enclave economy in the ethnoburbs was initially fueled, and has continued to be affected, by foreign capital, which was combined with family assets and savings that immigrants brought to or accumulated in the new country. During the early period of economic transformation, real estate development was perhaps the most significant economic activity in Monterey Park. It should be noted that in the 1980s, rampant and speculative land development all over southern California turned many small bedroom towns into cities with high-density commercial and residential overdevelopment. Monterey Park was simply part of the trend. What made it unique, however, was that the economic boom had an Asian face and responded mainly to the demands of coethnic transnationals and immigrants.

The arrival of many Taiwanese investors, realtors, developers, and entrepreneurs, and later the mainland Chinese *nouveaux riches,* played a crucial role in reinvigorating a formerly inactive economy and boosting real estate values. In the 1970s, transnational investors and immigrant entrepreneurs from Taiwan invested in Monterey Park because of its growth potential and its convenient location, with access to Chinatown and the Pacific Rim. By the late 1970s, 30 percent of the city's business licenses were registered under Asian names.[32] Foreign capital flows accelerated in the following decade as Hong Kong, China, and Southeast Asia started to transfer capital to the United States. With sufficient capital, these investors bought up properties and converted or developed them into both commercial and residential housing. Lots that were vacant in the 1970s were now built up, and old bungalows were torn down to make room for commercial or mixed-use real estate developments. By the 1980s, the price of land skyrocketed. Many lots for commercial development were sold at $40 to $50 per square foot, much higher than the $8 to $10 a square foot that supermarkets or department stores could afford to pay during that time. With these inflated prices, developers had to recoup their costs through intensive development. Huge, luxurious single-family homes were built on joint lots alongside multiple-family apartments and condominiums and high-density office buildings and mini-malls. The total number of housing units in Monterey Park jumped from 12,833 in 1960 to 19,331 in 1980, and again to 20,209 in 2000, representing a 57 percent increase in 40 years. The proportion of apartments with 10 units or more jumped from 5 percent in 1960 to 14 percent in 2000. A leading business real estate company in the region reported that 60 percent of the shopping and retail property transactions it handled in the San Gabriel Valley in 1989 were for Chinese investors, and 50 percent of the warehouse purchases there in 1991 involved Chinese immigrant investors or Chinese-owned firms.[33]

Accompanying real estate development was transnational advertising and marketing to lure Chinese businesses and immigrants to settle in the region. The constant flow of foreign capital toward real estate and land development stimulated tremendous demand for residential and commercial space, not only from Chinese immigrants already in the United States, but also from potential immigrants abroad. As local real estate brokers and developers rushed to capitalize on the highly specialized immigrant market, they promoted Monterey Park in Asia as the "Chinese Beverly Hills" and "a Mecca for Chinese businesses."[34] A brochure distributed in Taiwan read: "In Monterey Park, you can enjoy the American life quality and Taipei's convenience at the same time."[35] Soon after the establishment of Little Taipei in Monterey Park, the Taiwanese dispersed to neighboring cities. This was referred to as the "Taiwan Syndrome": enterprising Taiwanese investors purchased commercial properties and homes in the San Gabriel Valley in order to sell them later to wealthy newcomers from Taiwan.[36] Consequently, much of the real estate development was absorbed by Chinese-owned businesses and immigrant families, and home and business purchases in Monterey Park and adjacent cities became a viable channel for further immigration and transnational economic development.

Foreign investments also had a not-for-profit flavor because investments in real estate and local businesses were viewed as tickets to immigration. Many investors and entrepreneurs were even willing to take losses to secure a place in the United States through immigrant visas or nonimmigrant visas that could later be adjusted for permanent residency.[37] Consequently, Monterey Park evolved into a commercial and banking hub for transnational businesses and an economic center for producer, retail, and professional services for local Chinese businesses, drawn from an even bigger Chinese community that has spilled over rapidly into San Marino, Arcadia, South Pasadena, and throughout the San Gabriel Valley.[38] Potential emigrants in Taiwan, Hong Kong, and mainland China were attracted to Monterey Park and neighboring areas because of the availability of new and affordable homes and a business environment favorable not only to local development, but to transnational ventures as well.

The proliferation of real estate and commercial developments in Monterey Park and other suburbs in the San Gabriel Valley mirrors a new trend of sprawling Chinese immigrant settlement in Los Angeles. In the early 1980s, about one-third of all Chinese businesses in the Los Angeles metropolitan area listed in the Chinese-language telephone books were located in Chinatown, and another third were in the San Gabriel Valley. As of 1992, more than 11,000 Chinese-owned firms in Los Angeles were listed in the Chinese-language telephone books; of these, only 6 percent were located in Chinatown, whereas about 12 percent were located in Monterey Park and another third in neighboring cities in the San Gabriel Valley.[39] Valley Boulevard, which runs parallel to Interstate 10 through at least 10 cities in the San Gabriel Valley, serves as a window on Chinese business development in the region. Along the boulevard are numerous mini-malls, commercial plazas, professional office complexes, restaurants, shops, hotels, and industrial plants with Chinese-language signs, creating the impression of a series of prosperous Asian marketplaces.

Like businesses in the various Chinatowns, many businesses in the Chinese ethnoburbs concentrate in niches characterized by low entry barriers, or those industries in the manufacturing and service sectors shunned by the larger economy. Unlike Chinatowns, however, Chinese ethnoburbs also concentrate a wider and more diverse range of businesses of much larger size and scale, and they create new economic niches that are not commonly found in Chinatown. Typical Chinatown businesses—restaurants, eateries, grocery stores, gift shops, herbal stores, and garment factories—have been replaced by a large spectrum of upscale restaurants, trendy cafes and coffee houses, huge supermarkets, multifunction shopping centers, and professional service parks. These require either much larger startup capital or much higher human capital: printing and publishing, high-tech manufacturing of computer hardware and software, biotechnology, wholesale commercial equipment, real estate, banking, security and commodity brokerage, hotels and motels, data processing, and financial, accounting, advertising, medical, and engineering services.

The Chinese enclave economy in the San Gabriel Valley embodies key characteristics of *both* primary and secondary sectors of the mainstream economy, serving the diverse social mobility and settlement needs of new immigrants and transnationals. However, such development has also produced a hidden suburban inequality. For example, the labor force that supports the Chinese enclave economy includes a significant number of low-skilled Chinese, Latino, and other Asian workers. A segment of suburban residents, coethnic and non-coethnic immigrants alike, lives in ghettoized housing. Moreover, the proliferation of Chinese businesses in ethnoburbs produces some conditions very similar to those in old Chinatowns, such as high informality of work and proletarianization of labor, but also social dynamics much unlike those in old Chinatowns, such as the lack of bounded solidarity and enforceable trust.[40] These changes raise new questions about spatial assimilation. For example: may socioeconomic mobility—a measure of assimilation or immigrant success—entail the possibility of downward mobility or immigrant failure in American suburbia?

## Social Development in Chinese Ethnoburbs

Demographic transformation and the development of the Chinese enclave economy in the San Gabriel Valley go hand in hand. Ethnic population and business growth have not only become increasingly interdependent, but have also promoted unprecedented social and political developments. One key conceptual distinction between the ethnic economy and the enclave economy is that the latter requires not only a sizable coethnic entrepreneurial class but also a geographic core.[41] San Gabriel's Chinese ethnoburbs, though sprawling, serve to anchor communities where a wide variety of ethnic organizations have emerged side by side with ethnic businesses.

Ethnic organizations are pillars of the ethnic community.[42] In the old Chinatown under Chinese exclusion, three types of ethnic organizations were dominant: family associations (based on common surname, ancestral descent, and village of origin), district associations or *hui guan* (based on a common dialect and/or common region of origin), and merchant associations and *tongs* ("brotherhoods" based on professions).[43] In new Chinese ethnoburbs, these traditional associations are less visible and play a smaller role in members' social and economic lives. The most visible of the new ethnic organizations there are the nonprofit social service organizations, run by educated immigrants or the children of immigrants, which support community cultural centers, cultural programs in public libraries, history projects, English classes, job training centers, employment referral services, health clinics, youth programs, daycare centers, and welfare, housing, legal, and family counseling services. Although many similar ethnic social organizations have long existed in old Chinatowns, the new ones in the suburbs tend to be horizontal and democratic, serving specialized functions.[44] Unlike members of the old ethnic elite, who, as "cultural managers," supported traditional Chinese culture, ethnic identity, self-determination, and the status quo in Chinatown,[45] the organizers and leaders of the new social service organizations are more concerned with interethnic relations, citizen and immigrant rights, civic duties, equality, and the general well-being of the large, ethnically diverse community as a whole.

Also visible in Chinese ethnoburbs are Chinese-language schools and ethnic institutions serving young children and youth.[46] Chinese schools have histori-cally been another pillar of the organizational structure of U.S. Chinatowns as well as in the worldwide Chinese Diaspora.[47] For much of the pre–World War II era, Chinese schools aimed to preserve language and cultural heritage in the sec-ond and succeeding generations. Since the 1980s, these ethnic language schools have evolved to fulfill a much broader range of functions. In addition to language and cultural classes, contemporary Chinese schools offer K–12 children a variety of academic and enrichment courses and extracurricular activities, ranging from Chinese music, folk dance, calligraphy, calculation with an abacus, and ping-pong to SAT and SAT-II (Chinese) prep courses and academic tutoring.[48] Most schools are registered as nonprofit organizations and rely on parental volunteer-ism and fundraising from the ethnic community. Parental involvement is much more intense than in public schools; many parents volunteer to serve as princi-pals or administrative officials and teaching assistants.[49]

The development of Chinese schools has also paralleled the development of private supplementary educational institutions since the late 1980s: *buxiban* (academic tutoring), early childhood educational programs, and college prep centers. These children- and youth-oriented institutions have joined the existing Chinese-language schools to constitute a comprehensive system of supplemen-tary education whose core curricula supplement, rather than compete with, pub-lic school education.[50]

Other spatially rooted new ethnic organizations include religious institutions of all sorts, from Protestant and Catholic churches to Buddhist, Taoist, and other folk religious temples and worship houses. For example, Hsi Lai Temple, a gran-diose structure in classical Chinese architectural style, was built in 1988 by a Taiwanese Buddhist organization. Situated on the foothills of Hacienda Heights, it is the largest Buddhist temple in North America, offering Dharma services and performing Dharma functions and rituals regularly. But the temple is much more than a religious center. It houses a university offering academic degrees: bachelor and master of arts programs in Buddhist studies and comparative religious stud-ies, and a master of business administration program. It also offers workshops and seminars on Buddhism as well as secular programs on a wide range of topics, including education, immigration, marriage and family, taxation, and legal issues. It serves as a popular site for school field trips, business trips, meetings, and interreligious dialogue. The temple attracts worshipers, visitors, and tourists from near and far.

Other ethnic organizations emerging in the Chinese ethnoburb include pro-fessional and alumni groups and homeland district associations, which seek to aid Chinese immigrants' social mobility. They encourage professional and social networks and promote information exchange on opportunities in the United States, China, and other Chinese diasporic communities. Other goals include building U.S.-China economic relations, fostering economic exchanges within the Chinese Diaspora, raising funds for relief of natural disasters in China, Hong

Kong, and Taiwan, and protecting the interests of Chinese immigrants in the United States. These ethnic organizations depend on sponsorships and funds raised from Chinese immigrants and Chinese-owned businesses and from mainstream businesses and private foundations.

Last but not least, ethnic political and civil rights organizations can be found. Most are run by second-generation Chinese Americans who came of age in the late 1960s and formed the core of the Asian American Movement on college campuses on the west coast. Inspired by the civil rights movement, these political organizations are concerned primarily with minority and immigrant rights, representation in the mainstream economy and politics, and inter-group relations. In effect, these ethnic political organizations have brought ethnic group members together in line with the norms and standards of the civil society rather than those of the narrowly defined ethnic community. In doing so, they have strengthened Chinese Americans' political power base.

One common characteristic of the various ethnic organizations in the Chinese ethnoburb is that leadership and staff are composed mainly of U.S.-born Chinese Americans or Chinese immigrants who are upwardly mobile, as measured by levels of English proficiency, education, occupation, income, and place of residence. The fact that ethnic organizations and networks are actually built and maintained by the socioeconomically mobile indicates that assimilation is not a clear-cut, zero-sum process. The formation of the Chinese ethnoburbs in the San Gabriel Valley demonstrates that high ethnic concentration and organization and linguistic isolation are not incompatible with immigrants' successful adaptation to American society. Moreover, resources mobilized by coethnic businesses and institutions tend to benefit coethnic members to the exclusion of non-coethnic members, which creates potential for intergroup conflicts as well as possibilities of multiethnic coalition.

## Political Participation

Because many suburban communities are independent municipalities, the concentration of ethnic populations makes it possible for powerful voting blocs to form and for coethnic members or those who are sensitive to immigrant and ethnic minority issues to get elected. These possibilities, in turn, promote meaningful political participation even among first-generation immigrants.

Monterey Park is a case in point. It is an independent municipality. From the 1940s to the mid-1970s, politics were dominated by an "old-boy network" of white Republican professionals and businessmen. This power structure was challenged by the arrival of Japanese Americans and Mexican Americans in the 1950s and 1960s and the unprecedented arrival of Asian immigrants, mainly Chinese, in the mid-1970s and 1980s.[51] While some Democrats were willing to adapt previously all-white institutions to accommodate new immigrants and minorities, others sided with conservatives against the Chinese newcomers and their ethnic community development. When immigrants with strong economic resources form a numerical majority, however, politicians cannot ignore them. The large-scale arrival of Chinese immigrants and the dominance of Chinese businesses tipped the power balance and transformed local politics into a politics of diversity.[52]

The shrinking non-Hispanic white population, along with the decreasing influence of the old white conservative elite, has created an opportunity for young multiethnic businesspeople, minorities, immigrants, women, and multiculturalists as well as nativists to engage in politics, opening up a new political order in Monterey Park.[53] In 1983, the year Lily Lee Chen was inaugurated as the first Chinese American mayor, Monterey Park's five-member city council became truly multiethnic, seating one white, two Mexican Americans, one Filipino American, and one Chinese American.[54] *Time* magazine featured this "majority minority" city council as representative of multiculturalism and as a "successful suburban melting pot."[55] Growing resentment against demographic, cultural, and economic changes related to the Chinese newcomers, however, soon swept the minority incumbents out of office. In 1986, three city council members were replaced by long-established white residents, returning the council to white control. It promptly launched an anti-immigrant campaign under the banner of the defense of Americanism: "English, the family, God, the nation, and the neighborhood."[56]

The backlash was short-lived. More immigrant Chinese became naturalized citizens and mobilized politically. Since 1988 Monterey Park's city council has had a Chinese American presence. Judy Chu, a second-generation Chinese American, served on the council from 1988 to 2001. Samuel Kiang, David Lau, Betty Tom Chu, and Mike Eng have served or are currently serving. Betty Tom Chu served as mayor in 2006, and David Lau was mayor in 2007–2008. These local elections indicate the political maturity of Monterey Park's Chinese immigrants, who have used their increasing demographic presence and economic power to challenge traditional Anglo domination.

The electoral success of the Chinese immigrant community reaffirms the democratic message that every vote counts, which in turn empowers Chinese immigrants, nurtures a greater sense of civic duty, and facilitates their incorporation into the American polity. Today, the Asian constituency extends beyond Monterey Park to other cities in the San Gabriel Valley. Joaquin Lim was elected to the Walnut city council in 1995 and became mayor in 1999. In 1997 Wen P. Chang, a Taiwan-born businessman, became the first person of Chinese descent to be elected to the Diamond Bar city council. He served as mayor the following year and was re-elected for two consecutive terms. In 2001 Ben Wong became mayor of West Covina. In 2002 John Wuo was elected to Arcadia city council; he served as mayor in 2005. In 2003 Judy S. Wong, a Taiwan-born community activist, was elected to the city council of Temple City, its first Chinese American member. Mike Ten became mayor of South Pasadena in 2004. In 2005 Matthew Lin became the first Chinese American mayor of San Marino. In 2006 Chi Mui, a China-born businesswoman, was sworn in as San Gabriel City's first Asian and first Chinese American mayor. In the same year, Joaquin Lim was re-elected mayor of Walnut City and Mary W. Su was elected to the Walnut city council. At present, Chinese Americans have been elected to the boards of a series of unified school districts (USD): Alhambra, Arcadia, Garvey, Hacienda–La Puente, Montebello, Rowland, San Marino, and South Pasadena. Most significantly, in 2001 Judy Chu was elected, thanks to multiethnic support, to the state legislature, representing the 49th Assembly District: Monterey Park, Alhambra, Rosemead, San Gabriel, San Marino, El Monte, and South El Monte in the San Gabriel Valley. Mike Eng succeeded her in 2006.[57] The increasing numbers of Chinese elected officials are strong indicators of Chinese participation in local politics.

## Conclusion

Recent studies of the suburbanization of new immigrants and the development of ethnoburbs in the San Gabriel Valley shed light on immigrants' spatial assimilation and ethnic community formation.[58] First, new immigrants are socioeconomically diverse. Newcomers continue to converge in central cities as a first stop in the journey to attain the American dream. But many of them are bypassing that traditional staging ground and moving directly into affluent suburbs, situating themselves comfortably on the middle or upper-middle rungs of the mobility ladder. This phenomenon distorts the correlation between levels of acculturation and spatial assimilation predicted by classical assimilation theories. It points to the possibility that immigrants' initial place of residence is not simply a staging ground for somewhere better, but is in fact their final desired destination. Spatial assimilation is not the end result or "reward" for acculturation well done; it may instead be attained at the very inception of immigrants' settlement in the new land. Thus, ethnicization and assimilation are not incompatible.

Second, the tangible socioeconomic resources that immigrants bring, such as money, skills, and other assets, are often linked to intangible ethnic resources: easy access to established local and/or global social networks and material capital. This linkage enhances the value of individual holdings to create a new mode of immigrant incorporation—transnational entrepreneurship and global investment in local development. This mode of incorporation alters the way ethnic economies operate, since they are more integrated than in the past into an increasingly globalized local economy. While high levels of ethnic concentration and ethnic entrepreneurship are not antithetical to spatial assimilation, however, the development of the Chinese ethnoburb has reproduced spatial disparities as immigrants of modest SES have arrived in relatively large numbers and cluster around it.[59] For example, in Monterey Park the median house price was $216,500 in 2000, down from $238,800 in 1990, and the proportion of owner-occupied housing decreased from 65 percent in 1960 to 55 percent in 1990 and 54 percent in 2000. Median household incomes in the ethnoburban core (e.g., Monterey Park, Alhambra, San Gabriel, and Rosemead) were below the average for Los Angeles County (see Table 4.1).

Socioeconomic diversity has implications for both immigrants and natives. For Chinese immigrants, the influx of low-SES immigrants would mean less desirable living conditions, greater social service burdens, and a higher risk of bearing a dual stigma—that of foreigners and that of the poor. To avoid association with low-SES coethnics, the more affluent Chinese immigrants are actually moving out or not considering moving into this ethnoburb. Several immigrant Chinese business owners in Monterey Park told us that they had left Monterey Park recently to avoid "overcrowdedness" and "gangs in schools." Some newcomers even expressed a reluctance to settle in Monterey Park. A Chinese homebuyer moving from New York told us, "I wouldn't want to buy into Monterey Park . . . because it's so congested, crowded, and so many [poor] Chinese."[60] Interestingly, these feelings mirror those of established residents. For natives, the influx of low-SES immigrants would mean a disruption of middle-class lifestyles and the threat of importing inner-city or Third World social problems. Such intraethnic inequality and class division may not be conveniently neutralized by traditional mechanisms of social support and control—bounded solidarity and enforceable trust—as they were in old Chinatowns under legal exclusion and racial segregation.

Third, the size and the economic power of new immigrants heighten ethnic visibility and conflict with the host society. The influx of affluent immigrants and the growth of ethnic economies stir up the tranquility of complacent bedroom towns. Whereas longstanding immigrant enclaves in the inner city continue to absorb the successive waves of immigrants fairly smoothly, when suburban bedroom communities experience widespread in-migration of middle-class immigrants and rapid economic growth, their responses are often confrontational. In the past, the movement of ethnic minorities of lower SES into urban neighborhoods triggered white flight into the suburbs. The current movement of immigrants of higher SES into the suburbs has ushered in a similar trend because the newcomers have settled without going through the time-honored process of acculturation. They pose a new threat to the established white middle-class residents, who fear being "un-Americanized" by the newcomers. The Chinese ethnoburb shows that affluent immigrants from Asia, no less than blacks and Hispanics, can be perceived as a threat to white middle-class communities when they achieve a substantial presence. Their high socioeconomic standing, contribution to the local economy, and adaptive attitude do not make them immune to criticism. Rather, they can pose a different kind of threat, one that undermines longtime residents' sense of place and identity and their notion of "Americanness."[61] Among established residents in Monterey Park, for example, there is a deep-seated fear that their neighborhoods are turning into Chinatowns or microcosms of Taipei, Shanghai, or Hong Kong, which they imagine as the most crowded, congested, and polluted cities in the world. A Japanese American on his return to Monterey Park complained to his father, "Damn it, Dad, where the hell did all these Chinese come from? Shit, this isn't our town any more."[62]

Resistance from native-born residents, in turn, reinforces immigrant ethnicity, giving rise to a politics of diversity.[63]

Fourth, the very fact that Chinese immigrants are residentially assimilated into suburbia and yet have seemingly "returned" to the ethnic community, as illustrated in the development of Chinese ethnoburbs in the San Gabriel Valley, indicates that a fixed notion of the ethnic community as an isolated entity no longer applies. The Chinese ethnoburbs are multiethnic and unlikely to be dominated by a single national-origin group. Diversity at the local level has made intraethnic and interethnic relations key community issues. Among coethnic members, the mixing of coethnics from different socioeconomic backgrounds gives the community the power and vitality to combat the trends of ghettoization and social isolation encountered in the inner city, but simultaneously turns it into another type of "staging area" for the more affluent immigrants. Living side by side with members of other ethnic groups provides opportunities for intimate social contact, but also for potential tension. Even though intergroup conflicts are much more overt in Monterey Park than in Chinatown, often focusing on growth control movements and support for Official English resolutions, intergroup coalitions also seem more effective because native-born Latinos and Asian Americans tend to align with immigrant Chinese to act on racial issues in a city where minority groups form the numerical majority. We should therefore start to look at ethnic communities of the twenty-first century as integral to rather than separate from mainstream society, and view each ethnic group and its culture, despite distinct internal dynamics, as essentially contributing to rather than competing with the mainstream culture.

In sum, the development of Chinese ethnoburbs in the San Gabriel Valley provides some useful insights into the understanding of the paradox of ethnicization and assimilation. To the extent that the new Chinese immigrants comfortably live their own ethnic lives in America, they may, intentionally or unintentionally, bypass opportunities for primary group interaction. One of the main constraints on the ethnic community is its internal socioeconomic diversity. The immigrant success in ethnoburbs has largely overshadowed the plight of low-SES immigrants, some of whom are undocumented and whose mobility prospects remain problematic. This situation raises a series of questions that require further study. How does the ethnic community cope with intragroup differences in SES, cultures, and languages? To what extent are existing mechanisms that used to hold the ethnic community together effective or outdated for today's diverse ethnic population and ethnic businesses? Would low-SES coethnic immigrants be trapped in permanent disadvantaged status in relatively affluent ethnoburbs, or would they be able to transcend their disadvantages via ethnic resources made available there?

Another constraint is the ethnic community's exclusivity. We have seen signs that Chinese immigrants are not mixing well with native-born non-coethnics in ethnic enclaves and ethnoburbs.[64] This lack of primary-level or intimate interpersonal relationships may render Chinese immigrants and their children vulnerable to negative stereotyping and racial discrimination. For example, non-Chinese residents in Chinese ethnoburbs often feel that they are being pushed out of their own backyards and being un-Americanized by Chinese immigrants with higher-than-average levels of education and household income but relatively low English proficiency and high linguistic isolation.[65] Native-born Asian Americans are also stereotyped as foreigners and are perennially caught in situations in which they feel compelled to prove their loyalty and patriotism.[66] Thus, Chinese Americans living and/or working in Chinese ethnoburbs must continue to find innovative ways to collectively counter stereotypes and foster interethnic understanding and inclusion.

# III

# The Organizational Structure of the Ethnic Enclave

# 5

# Immigrant Entrepreneurship and the Enclave Economy

*The Case of New York City's Chinatown*

E thnic entrepreneurship as a social phenomenon has long fascinated social scientists and stimulated considerable research and debate. Ethnic entrepreneurs are overrepresented among first-generation immigrants. These entrepreneurs are often referred to simultaneously as owners and managers (or operators) of their own businesses. Their chosen occupations are tied to their ethnic group membership, and they are often known to outsiders as having a cultural inclination for business ownership. More importantly, they are embedded in particular social structures that constrain individual behavior, social relations, and economic transactions.[1] To the lay person, the idea of an ethnic entrepreneur often evokes images of petty traders, merchants, dealers, shopkeepers, or even peddlers and hucksters, along with their restaurants, sweatshops, laundries, greengrocers, liquor stores, nail salons, newsstands, swap meets, taxicabs, and so on. Indeed, few would regard Computer Associates International (a large public firm specializing in computer technology based in New York) and Watson Pharmaceuticals (a large public firm based in Los Angeles) as *ethnic* businesses and their founders, Charles B. Wang, an immigrant from mainland China, and Allen Chao, an immigrant from Taiwan, as *ethnic* entrepreneurs. These immigrants appear to have successfully shed their ethnic distinctiveness and incorporated their businesses into the center of the mainstream economy.

It is generally known that certain immigrant or ethnic minority groups are more entrepreneurial and more likely than others to adopt self-employment as a strategy to achieve socioeconomic mobility, and that some immigrant groups are more successful than others in utilizing this strategy both for individual success and for community building.[2] In this chapter I aim to document how ethnic entrepreneurship affects individual and collective outcomes. In so doing, I first present the enclave economy theory and then illustrate it with a case study of New York City's Chinatown.

## Conceptualizing Immigrant Entrepreneurship and the Ethnic Enclave

### Middleman-Minority Entrepreneurs versus Ethnic-Enclave Entrepreneurs

The literature of immigrant entrepreneurship analytically distinguishes two main types: middleman-minority entrepreneurs and ethnic-enclave entrepreneurs. "Middleman minorities" are those entrepreneurs who trade between a society's elite and the masses. Historically, middleman-minority entrepreneurs are like sojourners: interested in making a quick profit from their portable and liquifiable businesses and then reinvesting their money elsewhere, often implying a return home.[3] Therefore, they most commonly establish business niches in poor minority neighborhoods or immigrant ghettos in urban areas deserted by mainstream retail and service industries and business owners from a society's dominant group. Typical examples of middleman-minority businesses would include a Jewish shop in a Puerto Rican neighborhood, a Korean grocery store in a black neighborhood, or a Chinese restaurant in a Latino neighborhood. Middleman-minority entrepreneurs have few intrinsic ties to the social structures and social relations of the local community in which they conduct economic activities.

Ethnic-enclave entrepreneurs, in contrast, are bounded by coethnicity and the coethnic social structures of a particular ethnic community. In the past, they typically operated businesses in their own, often self-sustaining, ethnic enclave. Today, as ethnic enclaves evolve into multiethnic neighborhoods and new ones develop in affluent middle-class suburbs, those who run businesses in a particular location may simultaneously play a double role—as both middleman-minority and ethnic-enclave entrepreneur. For example, a Chinese immigrant who runs a restaurant in Chinatown is an enclave entrepreneur. But to his or her Latino clients who live in Chinatown, he or she would be a middleman-minority entrepreneur.

The analytical distinction is sociologically meaningful because the economic transactions of these two types of entrepreneurs are conditioned by different social structures and relations. For example, the stone face of a Chinese restaurant owner in a Latino neighborhood may be taken as rude or even racist, its effect exacerbated by a lack of Spanish- or English-language proficiency. But the same facial expression is likely to be taken matter-of-factly by the Chinese in Chinatown, where a common language often eases potential anxiety.

## The Ethnic Economy versus the Enclave Economy

The sociologists Edna Bonacich, John Modell, and Ivan Light were among the first to theoretically develop the concept of the ethnic economy, which broadly includes any immigrant or ethnic group's self-employed, employers, and coethnic employees.[4] Light and his colleagues later rearticulated the concept to a higher level of generality.[5] The reconceptualized ethnic economy includes two key components: one is "ethnic ownership economy," which refers to the ethnic group's maintenance of "a controlling ownership stake" in its economic activities and in its coethnic labor force or unpaid family labor; and the other is "ethnic-controlled economy," which refers to the ethnic group's control over the employment networks to allow the channeling of coethnics into non-coethnic firms and even into the public sector of the larger labor market.[6] In this formulation, "ethnic economy"—with its dual aspects of coethnic ownership and employment network—is a neutral designation for every enterprise that is either owned, supervised, or staffed by members of a racial/ethnic minority group, regardless of size, type, and geographic clustering. It is also agnostic about the intensity of ethnicity, neither requiring nor assuming "an ethnic cultural ambience within the firm or among sellers and buyers."[7]

The ethnic economy concept thus encompasses businesses owned by middleman-minority entrepreneurs in non-coethnic neighborhoods, businesses owned by enclave entrepreneurs in their own ethnic communities, and all other ethnic-owned or ethnic-controlled enterprises in the mainstream economy. Under this conception, the groups that are known to have higher-than-average rates of self-employment, such as Jews, Iranians, Cubans, Japanese, Koreans, and Chinese, have their respective ethnic economies; the groups that are known to have low self-employment rates but have control over recruitment networks in certain industries in non-coethnic firms and even in the public sector, such as Mexicans, Salvadorans, and blacks, would also have their own ethnic economies. Such a conception allows for two types of analyses: one to account for variations in mobility outcomes among ethnic group members who create employment opportunities for themselves and their coethnic workers, and the other to account for variations in the level of economic integration of group members who enter the mainstream economy via coethnic employment networks. However, broadening a concept too much risks weakening its explanatory power because substantive internal differences are so large. For example, coethnic businesses concentrated in an ethnic enclave are very different from those dispersed into other, non-coethnic neighborhoods and serving primarily non-coethnics, a situation more appropriately referred to as middleman-minority entrepreneurship. Similarly, businesses that are owned and staffed by coethnics are very different from those that are owned by non-coethnics but staffed by supervisors and co-workers of the same ethnicity, a situation more appropriately referred to as "ethnic niching," or ethnic occupational segregation.[8] Furthermore, extending ethnic economies beyond bounded ethnicity decontextualizes the ethnic economy concept.

The broader concept may be useful when examining individual outcomes, such as earnings or employment opportunities for the disadvantaged, but it is not of much use when examining processes of community building in immigrant or ethnic minority neighborhoods.

The enclave economy is a special case of the ethnic economy, one that is bounded by coethnicity and location. Not every group's ethnic economy can be called an enclave economy. Likewise, not every ethnic economy betokens a middleman minority.[9] Alejandro Portes and his colleagues were among the first to develop the enclave economy concept, drawing on the dual labor market theory.[10] In its original conceptualization, the enclave economy had a structural and a cultural component. As a distinct type of the ethnic economy, it consisted of a wide range of diverse economic activities that exceeded the limits of small businesses, and traditional mom-and-pop stores, as well as ethnic institutions that mediated economic action, such as merchant associations, chambers of commerce, informal credit associations, and family/hometown associations. It resembled, to varying degrees, some of the key characteristics of *both* the primary and secondary labor markets of the mainstream economy.[11]

Unlike the ethnic economy concept, which includes almost every business under an ethnic umbrella, the enclave economy has several unique characteristics. First, the group involved has a sizable entrepreneurial class. Second, economic activities are not exclusively commercial, but include productive activities directed toward the general consumer market. Third, the business clustering entails a high level of diversity, including not just niches shunned by natives, but also a wide variety of economic activities common in the mainstream economy, such as professional services and production. Fourth, coethnicity epitomizes the relationships between owners and workers and, to a lesser extent, between patrons and clients. Last and perhaps most importantly, the enclave economy requires a physical concentration within an ethnically identifiable neighborhood with a minimum level of institutional completeness. Especially in their early stages of development, ethnic businesses need proximity to a coethnic clientele that they initially serve; proximity to ethnic resources, including access to credit, information, and other sources of support; and a supply of ethnic labor.[12]

The enclave economy also has an integrated cultural component. Economic activities are governed by bounded solidarity and enforceable trust—mechanisms of support and control necessary for economic life in the community and for reinforcement of norms and values and sanctioning of socially disapproved behavior.[13] Relationships between coethnic owners and workers, as well as customers, generally transcend a contractual monetary bond and are based on a commonly accepted norm of reciprocity.

In sum, the enclave economy does not include just any type of ethnic economy. "Enclave" refers to a specific phenomenon, one that is bounded by an identifiable ethnic community and embedded in a system of community-based coethnic social relations and observable institutions. The central argument is that the enclave is more than a shelter for the disadvantaged who are forced to take on either self-employment or marginal wage work in small businesses. Rather, the ethnic enclave possesses the potential to develop a distinct structure of economic opportunities as well as opportunities for rebuilding the social networks that are disrupted by international migration. In this view the ethnic enclave is an effective alternative path to individual as well as group-based social mobility.[14] In the next section I use the case of New York City's Chinatown to illustrate how the enclave economy develops to generate tangible and intangible resources for individual immigrants and the community as a whole.[15]

## The Development of an Ethnic Enclave

### Chinatown as a Residential Enclave

New York's Chinatown in Lower East Manhattan has been an immigrant enclave for over a century.[16] Until 1970 most Chinese immigrants entering New York made Chinatown their home. Although decentralization of the Chinese population began as early as the 1930s, substantial out-migration and outer-borough settlement were not common until much later. According to census counts in 1990, about 50,000 Chinese lived in the core (defined by 14 census tracts),[17] up from 26,700 in 1970; 53 percent of the area's residents were Chinese, an increase from 32 percent in 1970; out of the 14 tracts, 5 had a Chinese majority and another 5 contained 25 percent or more Chinese.[18] Census counts are no doubt too low and miss many undocumented immigrants who are afraid to cooperate with census staff. Probably at least twice as many Chinese live in Old Chinatown and the surrounding area as census figures indicate.

The majority of Chinatown residents are Cantonese who came from the traditional sending regions in South China prior to World War II. In recent years, a noticeable group of Sino-Vietnamese has settled in Chinatown; most are fluent in Cantonese and share many cultural characteristics with earlier migrants, since they originally emigrated to Vietnam from Guangdong and Guangxi provinces. Members of another dialect group, the Fuzhounese, have also established a foothold. Because of cultural differences and coethnic stereotyping, Fuzhounese, who generally arrive as undocumented immigrants, do not mingle with the Cantonese; instead they have built their own sub-enclave in a three-block area on East Broadway under the Manhattan Bridge.[19] Although Chinatown's residents are culturally diverse, they share similar socioeconomic status; many are recent arrivals, have low levels of education, speak little or no English, hold low-wage jobs, and live in poverty. The elderly are a significant presence; 21 percent of the household heads in the core area of Chinatown were 65 years old or older, compared with 15 percent citywide. Some of these elderly people have chosen to keep their residence in Chinatown even after their children and grandchildren have moved to the suburbs.

Walk-up tenement and loft buildings line the streets. Overcrowding characterizes Chinatown living. Over 90 percent of residents live in rental housing, and many housing units are in poor and deteriorating conditions. New immigrants are often shocked by the squalid environment, which strikingly contrasts with the glamorous skyscrapers in the background. One middle-aged woman who arrived to join her daughter's family recalled:

> I'd never imagined my daughter's family living in this condition. My daughter, who was about to give birth to her first child, lived with her husband in a one-room apartment. When I arrived in New York, my daughter had to squeeze me into their apartment. They had only one queen-size bunk bed that almost filled the room. I slept, and later with the baby, at the bottom, and my daughter and her husband on top. In China, I had a spacious three-bedroom apartment. It was just like hell living there.[20]

This woman's family eventually bought a house in Brooklyn. Like her, many immigrants came from relatively affluent middle-class backgrounds but were not wealthy enough to afford adequate housing in New York. Those who came from the working class seemed more optimistic. One Chinatown man remarked, "Sharing a two-bedroom apartment with another family in Chinatown wasn't that bad. In China, I lived just like that, and there were many people who lived in worse conditions. Here, you are pretty sure that this would change in a few years. But in China, you were not so sure."[21] Many Chinese immigrants reluctantly tolerate dank and filthy cubicle dwellings in the hope that someday they will move out of Chinatown. Indeed, many have been able to do so. In Chinatown, most of the residents are either recent arrivals, including those who are undocumented, or the elderly; very few second-generation young people are raising their families there. As a residential enclave, Chinatown has provided a culturally familiar refuge and an economically viable place for new immigrants in their pursuit of the American dream. However, the concentration of the disadvantaged and the out-movement of the upwardly mobile have not led to the kind of ghettoization experienced by native racial minority groups.[22] What accounts for Chinatown's resilience and growth as opposed to decline? A close examination of the enclave economy provides insight.

## Changes in the Ethnic Enclave

For many Chinese immigrants, Chinatown's inferior living conditions are offset by the easy access to jobs and services. With the continuous arrival of new immigrants and the tremendous influx of foreign capital, the physical boundaries of Chinatown have expanded so that it now covers a huge area in Lower Manhattan. The century-old enclave has been transformed. During the Exclusion era, Chinatown's economy was highly concentrated in restaurant and laundry businesses.[23] Early twentieth-century Chinese went into the laundry business in such large numbers that by 1920 well over a third of Chinese workers in New York (38 percent) were occupied in laundry work. Over 300 restaurants and tea houses had opened in the 10-block area of Chinatown by the late 1950s, serving meals for Chinese laborers, most of whom had no families with them, as well as exotic food for non-Chinese tourists. Although ethnic businesses within the enclave may be short-lived and last only one generation, they nonetheless opened up a unique structure of opportunities that corresponded to the needs of early Chinese immigrants, who were mostly poor, uneducated peasants, and enabled disadvantaged coethnics to gain a foothold in society.[24]

By the 1970s the laundry business had declined substantially and the garment industry had become one of Chinatown's major employers. In the 1980s it held more than 500 factories, run by Chinese entrepreneurs and employing more than 20,000 immigrant Chinese, mostly women. In the mid-1990s this industry too showed signs of decline, as many factories moved out of the enclave, but it remained strong as an ethnic niche for immigrant women. It is estimated that three out of five immigrant Chinese women in Chinatown worked in the garment industry. The restaurant business, another backbone industry in Chinatown, has continued to grow and prosper. Listed restaurants run by Chinese in New York City grew from 304 in 1958 to nearly 800 in 1988, employing at least 15,000 immigrant Chinese workers.[25] Other businesses have also experienced tremendous growth, ranging from grocery stores, gift shops, jewelry stores, barber shops, beauty salons, and import-export companies to such professional services as banks, law firms, financial, insurance, real estate, tourist, and employment referral agencies, and doctors' and herbalists' clinics.[26]

Chinatown's economic development is described by the sociologist Jan Lin as a two-circuit phenomenon embedded in a post-industrial global city: sweatshops and tenements are the lower circuit, characterized by low-wage jobs, unskilled labor, sidewalk peddlers, and crowding or slum living; finance and redevelopment are the upper circuit, characterized by high-skilled and professional service jobs, capital-intensive redevelopment, transnational businesses, and modern tourism.[27] I would add that Chinatown's enclave economy constitutes an important part of the larger metropolitan economy, containing industries that reflect characteristics of both primary and secondary sectors of the mainstream economy. Moreover, Chinatown's economy reflects a structural duality that operates largely by its own logic. The duality is made up of a protected sector and an export sector, both characterized by ethnic businesses that are extremely competitive and susceptible to business succession even within the enclave.

The protected sector of Chinatown's economy arises within the enclave itself, representing a captive labor market oriented toward ethnic-specific goods and services that are not readily accessible outside the enclave, and also toward solutions for various adjustment and settlement problems relating to immigration. The special consumer demands created by new immigrants provide a direct link between places of origin and the tastes and buying preferences of coethnic members, substantially reducing the level of competition from mainstream firms. These demands also allow ethnic firms to stay competitive in times of crisis in the larger economy because the enclave economy is secured by its own exclusive capital market, labor market, and consumer market. Firms in the protected sector include not only labor-intensive industries such as restaurants and grocery stores but also knowledge-intensive industries such as professional services.

The protected sector may seem constrained within the enclave. When it develops alongside the other sector—the export sector—and reaches out globally, however, the enclave economy can expand its interface with the mainstream economy and the world economy to exploit opportunities and resources that feed its further development. The export sector has a non-coethnic market characteristic and contains mostly leftover niches of the larger secondary economy, such as underserved or abandoned businesses and businesses that serve unstable or fashionable demands, provide exotic goods, or require low economies of scale.[28] Relative to the protected sector, the export sector does not have a combination of the three captive ethnic markets (capital, labor, and consumer) and thus does not have control over production, business operation, and distribution. Furthermore, firms in the export sector are predominantly labor-intensive, small-scale, and highly sensitive to broader economic changes, resembling those in the mainstream secondary economy.

Before 1965 Chinatown's export sector was dominated by the laundry business. There used to be about 2,700 laundries in New York City, serving a non-Chinese clientele.[29] Technological innovations in both machinery and fabrics caused the industry's decline. Historically and in the present day, Chinatown's tourist industry has been an important component of the export sector via ethnic restaurants and gift shops.[30] More recently, the enclave economy has found another niche to capture Chinatown's large pool of unskilled, low-wage labor. The growth of the garment industry points to several main characteristics of the export sector: it has a non-coethnic consumer market; it is largely in the hands of the non-coethnic manufacturers and retailers with whom the work is contracted; and it is highly subject to interethnic competition in the larger secondary economy. Although protected by a coethnic labor market, Chinese garment factory owners depend on the demands of larger consumer markets and must compete with other ethnic groups for a share of the pie. Because of these structural constraints, the enclave economy has often been charged with being highly exploitative of coethnic workers—more so than the larger secondary economy.[31] This charge is simplistic and even misleading in that it reinforces a negative stereotype of the enclave and discounts the many benefits—convenience, employment, and entrepreneurial opportunities—that the enclave creates for immigrants, especially those who are poor and have little English-language ability, low levels of education, and few transferable job skills.

The success of Chinatown's economy depends in large part on three things: the ability to mobilize capital, the ability to control the cost of labor and business operation, and access to consumer markets. For an ethnic enclave to grow, capital for reinvestment is necessary. The interaction of the two sectors of the enclave economy produces a dialectical relationship between internal consumption and reinvestment. On the one hand, the protected sector secures a steady circulation of capital within the enclave, preventing economic resources from being drained away. Although intraethnic competition within the enclave can be fierce, it does not necessarily harm the enclave economy as a whole. Rather, a pattern of business takeover among coethnic members prevails. That is, someone may be outcompeted, but he or she is more likely to be succeeded by a coethnic entrepreneur than by someone from outside the enclave, or by some middleman-minority entrepreneur. When a Chinese restaurant fails, for whatever reason, there is always another, more ambitious Chinese who takes over and tries to do a better job. Many Chinatown restaurants change hands frequently, but the absolute number continues to grow.

On the other hand, profit and income generated from the export sector enrich the reinvestment capital of entrepreneurs or potential entrepreneurs and strengthen the buying power of workers, allowing economic resources to flow from the larger economy into the enclave. High rates of business failure in the enclave's export sector, such as the closing down of factories, may not necessarily mean failure for enclave entrepreneurs. It may well be that the more ambitious entrepreneurs simply use their initial businesses as a long-term strategy to pursue more challenging ventures after accumulating capital and work experience for a number of years.

## The Development of Ethnic Institutions

Economic development in Chinatown is also intertwined with the enclave's sociocultural development. When an ethnic group is legally excluded from participating in the mainstream host society, effective community organizing can mobilize ethnic resources to counter the negative effects of adversarial conditions. During the Exclusion era, various ethnic institutions arose to meet the needs of immigrants. The strength of community organization can be measured by the density and diversity of community-based institutions and establishments. Among the most visible and influential ethnic organizations in Chinatown were family, clan, or kinship associations, district or regional associations, merchants' associations, and the *tongs*.[32] These organizations functioned primarily to meet the basic needs of sojourning workers, helping them obtain employment, offering different levels of social support, and organizing economic activities. Powerful tongs controlled most of the economic resources in the community and shielded Chinatown from outsiders while preserving the status quo within it.[33] The single most important social organization was the Chinese Consolidated Benevolent Association (CCBA), which represented some 60 organizations in Chinatown, including family and district associations, the guilds, the tongs, the Chamber of Commerce, and the Nationalist Party. Controlled by a few powerful tongs, the CCBA cooperated with all voluntary associations and operated as an unofficial government in Chinatown.[34] Traditional organizations secured the standing of Chinatown in the larger society and provided a refuge for sojourning laborers. Some also formed underground societies and portioned out territories to profit from illicit activities: extortion of local businesses, gambling, prostitution, and drugs.[35]

The rapid demographic change in contemporary Chinese immigration since the 1960s has created pressing demands for services associated with resettlement and adjustment problems. These have overwhelmed traditional organizations in Chinatown and forced them to redefine their role. In addition, Chinatown has witnessed the birth and growth of new ethnic, civic, and religious institutions. A glance at one Chinese-language business directory, for example, reveals over 100 voluntary associations, 61 community service organizations, 41 community-based employment agencies, 16 daycare centers, 27 career training schools, 28 Chinese- and English-language schools, and 9 dancing and music schools in New York City in the early 1990s.[36] Most are located in Manhattan's Old Chinatown, but some are in the new satellite Chinatowns in Flushing, Queens, and Sunset Park, Brooklyn.[37]

Traditional ethnic institutions have changed their orientation from sojourning to settlement and assimilation. To appeal to the settlement demands of new immigrants and their families, the CCBA has established a Chinese-language school, an English night school for adults, and a career training center, along with a variety of social service programs, including employment referral and job training services. The CCBA also operates one of the largest Chinese schools and the largest children- and youth-oriented organization in Chinatown.[38] The Chinese American Planning Council (CPC), established in the late 1960s in Chinatown, is a rival to the CCBA, representing an assimilationist and mainstream agenda similar to that of labor organizations such as the International Ladies' Garment Workers' Union (ILGWU) and the Chinese Staff and Workers' Association (CSWA). Led by educated second- or 1.5-generation Chinese Americans who are devoted to the community, the CPC challenges the traditional patriarchal structure and conservative stance of the CCBA through grassroots class mobilization and support from federal and local governments and private foundations. It offers a broader array of services to families and children than the CCBA (though the CCBA's Chinese school has a much larger enrollment than the CPC's), aiming to provide access to services, skills and resources to promote economic self-sufficiency and integration into the American mainstream.[39]

Many smaller civic and voluntary ethnic organizations address the concerns and demands of new immigrants and their children. The Chinatown History Museum, now the Museum of Chinese in the Americas, was established in 1980 primarily to reclaim, preserve, and share Chinese American history and culture with a broad audience. The member-supported museum offers historical walking tours, lectures, readings, symposia, workshops, and family events year-round, not only to Chinese Americans but also to the general public. The museum also provides school programs for elementary and high school students, guided and self-guided tours for college students, and videotapes, slide presentations, and exhibits.

Ethnic religious institutions have also played an important role in helping immigrants adjust to life in the United States. Although Chinese immigrants are mostly nonreligious, many initially affiliate with religious institutions for practical support and later are converted through intense participation. In the larger Chinese community in New York City, the number of churches or temples has doubled since 1965, now including over 80 Christian churches and 18 Buddhist and Taoist temples; about three-quarters are located in Manhattan's Chinatown. Although Buddhist and Taoist temples tend to attract adults, including some college students and the elderly, Christian churches generally have well-established afterschool youth programs in addition to their regular Sunday Bible classes.

Overall, accelerated Chinese immigration has stimulated the growth of the enclave ethnic economy, accompanied by the development of community-based ethnic institutions. These developments have strengthened and expanded Chinatown's existing social structures. The ethnic community, in turn, furnishes a protective social environment, helping immigrants cope with racism, unemployment, family disruption, problems with school, drug abuse, and crime, and providing access to resources that can help immigrants and their children move ahead in mainstream American society.[40] Yet there is a counterargument: some would say that Chinatown's economy reinforces the traditional patriarchal social structure, privileging the elite while exacerbating coethnic exploitation and trapping the working-class immigrants into permanent subordination.[41]

## Enclave Economy and Immigrant Adaptation: Evidence from Quantitative Analysis

A key proposition of the enclave economy theory is that the ethnic enclave opens opportunities for its members that are not easily accessible in the larger society. The enclave housing, labor, and capital markets partially shelter coethnic members from competition from other ethnic minority groups, from discrimination and abuse on account of their ethnic origins, and from government surveillance and regulation. In many respects, as I have discussed previously, the enclave economy, along with ethnic social structures, provides economic and cultural resources to group members and seems to offer a positive alternative path toward social mobility. In what specific ways does the enclave economy facilitate or inhibit social mobility?

### Earnings Returns on Human Capital for Immigrant Men: Workers versus Entrepreneurs

In empirical research, there has been disagreement over the proposition that immigrant workers in the enclave labor market achieve greater returns on human capital than those who participate in the outside economy. That is, if human capital investments yielded greater returns for persons tied to the enclave, such returns should show up as effects of education and labor market experience, and possibly English-language ability, on earnings. Surveying immigrants in Miami's Cuban community, Alejandro Portes and Leif Jensen found that those who worked within the enclave were more likely to become self-employed entrepreneurs.[42] Compared with immigrants employed in the secondary labor market, those in the enclave had occupations that corresponded more closely with their educational attainment, and earnings that corresponded more closely with their occupational status. These findings were questioned by Jimy Sanders and Victor Nee, who analyzed census data for Cuban immigrants in Miami and for Chinese immigrants in San Francisco, finding that earnings return on human capital in enclave economies is mostly limited to entrepreneurs.[43]

If earnings returns on human capital characteristics such as education and labor market experience were limited to ethnic entrepreneurs, the positive function of the enclave would be sharply circumscribed. In their response, Portes and Jensen accepted the general strategy of comparing models of earnings for persons within and outside the enclave and comparing models for workers with models for entrepreneurs, but criticized Sanders and Nee for incorrectly operationalizing the concept of the ethnic enclave.[44] For Portes and his associates, enclave entrepreneurs were owners of firms in an area where similar enterprises concentrate. Enclave workers were employees of these firms.[45] If the enclave was operationalized in terms of the place of residence, as in Sanders and Nee's study, the central element in the concept would be lost. Further, the place-of-residence definition was inherently biased because it excluded better-off enclave participants, who were likely to move out of the residential enclave to more affluent neighborhoods or suburbs, and overrepresented the worse-off segment of the population, who were concentrated in the geographic enclave.[46] However, the definition based on workplace and the one based on residence have one thing in common: they are both geographically bound. Neither is sensitive to ethnic ownership or to the ethnic composition of the workers of a firm. Moreover, any study relying on census data is liable to define the enclave in a way that includes many non-enclave workers, leading to an underestimation of differences between enclave and non-enclave labor markets and an overestimation of the absolute size of the enclave labor market.

In addressing the controversy over the earnings returns on human capital in the ethnic enclave, I replicated the studies by Portes and Jensen and by Sanders and Nee, but examined and compared three possible ways of defining the enclave economy: by place of residence,[47] by place of work,[48] and by industry.[49] I was not specifically interested in where people lived, where they worked, or what industry they were employed in; I simply used these measures as indicators of the likelihood that a person worked in the enclave. Each of these definitions partially captured the concept of the enclave economy. Whether the enclave economy was defined by residence, workplace, or industry, there was a large amount of overlap between the three measures.[50]

## Definition 1: Place of Residence

When the earnings-return model for male immigrant workers is estimated using the place of residence as the definition of enclave, there were significant positive effects on earnings of labor market experience, college education, and English-language ability among those within the enclave. Labor market experience and college education were similarly related to earnings among male immigrant workers outside the enclave. It was curious, however, that English-language ability had no effect in this latter group. One would expect, from the enclave model, that this variable would have greater effects outside the enclave than within.[51]

The model for male immigrant entrepreneurs within the enclave shows no effect for labor market experience or college education. Unlike the results reported for California Chinese by Sanders and Nee, it appeared that these human capital variables were more important for workers than for entrepreneurs in the ethnic enclave in New York. English-language ability was an important predictor for enclave entrepreneurs, as were the hours worked and occupation control variables. The model for immigrant entrepreneurs outside the enclave showed still another pattern: labor market experience and English-language ability have no significant effects. The effect of a college education was positive and significant, but the effect of a high school education was negative, though not significant.

These results differed from those that might be predicted from a reading of the existing literature. Unlike Sanders and Nee, I found positive returns on human capital for workers both inside and outside the enclave. And, unexpectedly, college education had a positive effect for entrepreneurs outside the enclave, but not inside. Finally, challenging the portrait of the enclave as a place where cultural assimilation was unnecessary, I found positive returns on English-language ability and U.S. citizenship for workers within the enclave, but not outside.[52]

## Definition 2: Place of Work

When the enclave is defined by place of work, the model for male immigrant workers employed in the enclave showed positive returns on labor market experience and college education, but not English-language ability. The model for male immigrant workers employed outside the enclave showed a comparable effect for college education, but no effect for labor market experience or English-language ability. Using the place of work definition, entrepreneurs within the enclave had positive returns on labor market experience and college education comparable to (possibly larger than) effects for workers. There was a very strong effect for English-language ability.[53]

## Definition 3: Industrial Sector

Finally, I ran regression models using industrial sector to categorize people as within or outside the ethnic enclave. Once again, I found that college education yielded positive earnings returns for enclave workers. Labor market experience did not, but there was a positive effect for English-language ability. For workers outside the enclave, all three of these predictors had significant positive effects.[54]

In sum, the same human capital variables that predicted earnings for male enclave workers also predicted earnings for male enclave entrepreneurs: college education, English-language ability, and U.S. citizenship. College education was significant for entrepreneurs outside enclave industries, as was labor market experience; English-language ability was not.

## Earnings Returns on Human Capital for Immigrant Women

Up to this point, the analysis has been limited to immigrant men in order to maintain comparability with previous studies. Substantively, however, this limitation is indefensible. Women constitute a major share of the labor force. More importantly, it is well known that women's position in the labor market is not the same as men's, and there is no reason to believe that mobility processes experienced by men are in any way applicable to women. In fact, separate analysis of Chinese immigrant women working in the New York metropolitan area reveals some very different patterns.[55] In New York, the labor force participation of Chinese women was around 60 percent. Women's concentration in the garment industry was extraordinary: more than 55 percent of all Chinese immigrant women were employed there.[56]

The specific question here is whether participation in the enclave economy affects immigrant women's ability to reap earnings returns on human capital, as hypothesized for men.[57] My analyses show a total absence of human capital effects: neither education nor labor market experience nor English-language ability nor U.S. citizenship had any significant effects for women within the enclave, regardless of the definition of "enclave."[58] These findings for women workers require a careful interpretation of the positive functions of the enclave economy. Researchers need to ask to what degree the positive functions of the enclave for men are derived from the subordinate position of women.[59] The explanation may depend on the structure of the enclave economy and its relationship to the larger economy: what kinds of industries can prosper, with what labor requirements, and at what wages? It may also depend upon the values and motives of the immigrants themselves. While I encourage caution in evaluating women's status, I emphasize that paid work in a job incommensurate with one's education and other attainments has both a negative and a positive side. Viewed from an individualistic perspective, the enclave labor market appears clearly exploitative of women. But we must remember that Chinese immigrants have historically placed a priority not on individual achievement but on the welfare of the family as a whole, and that women's labor force participation is part of a family strategy.[60]

## What's in the Residual?

Aside from the situation of women workers, how does the enclave economy function for men, and what differences are there between workers and entrepreneurs? One consistent finding here is that college education has positive returns on earnings for male enclave workers, regardless of how the enclave is defined. Labor market experience and English-language ability had positive effects for these workers in two out of three equations. The findings from New York's Chinatown suggest that Chinese immigrant workers in the enclave are able to take advantage of human capital resources to increase earnings (although not consistently more than workers outside the enclave). But there is no consistent evidence that entrepreneurs in the enclave or outside it have greater returns on human capital than do similarly situated workers.

There are two ways to interpret this main result, and the choice between them depends upon one's reading of the facts about San Francisco and Miami. Suppose that a methodologically correct analysis of census data for San Francisco and Miami does reveal significant earnings returns on human capital for enclave workers, as Portes and Jensen argue. In that case, my findings for New York's Chinese would be one more confirmation of Portes' hypothesis *as a general rule about ethnic enclaves*. This ethnic enclave hypothesis would be weakened, however, by my finding that human capital returns for men are no greater within the enclave than outside it. To make a stronger case would require that persons outside the enclave be further classified into the primary or secondary labor market, which I have not been able to do here. Alternatively, suppose that Sanders and Nee's findings were confirmed. This is theoretically more interesting, because then my results for New York City would indicate that there are *differences among enclaves*, even enclaves of the same ethnic group but in different regions (San Francisco versus New York). If in fact there were also important differences among enclave economies—if male enclave workers got earnings returns on human capital in New York but not in San Francisco and perhaps not in Miami—then there would be an opportunity to develop a comparative theory of ethnic enclaves. The most positive outcome of this controversy would be to stimulate other researchers to extend the investigation to other minorities in other places.

Why might the Chinese experience in New York differ from that in San Francisco? Or why might the Chinese experience in San Francisco differ from the Cuban experience in Miami? Why might the Chinese experience in New York be similar to the Cuban experience in Miami? I am not able to offer a comparative theory here, or to explain these particular cases. However, I must stress that the enclave economy theory is neither uniform nor static; it requires more empirical testing with newer and more representative data. Even with the most elaborate and best-specified statistical model, there would still be a large residual, something left unaccounted for by available statistics. It is this residual that stimulates further research to arrive at a fuller understanding of the enclave phenomenon.

# Chinatown: A Better Alternative
# or the Only Option?

Census or survey data provide only proxies for more direct measures of the ethnic enclave, because these data lack detailed information on the ethnicity of owners and the ethnic composition of a firm's work force. While quantitative analyses have their limitations, fieldwork data can supplement and further explain my empirical findings, particularly in three respects. First, there is a real possibility of moving into self-employment in the enclave. Second, education has an effect on socioeconomic achievement in the enclave, just as it does outside it. Third, work within the ethnic enclave has intangible benefits for immigrants.

## Self-Employment as a Measure of Success

Owning a business is part of the threefold American dream as defined by Chinese immigrants (the other two are owning a house and sending children to prestigious colleges). A "boss" enjoys higher status and prestige, makes more money than a worker, and has the power to control things. Working in Chinatown allows workers to see real opportunities to climb up to the rank of self-employment. Mr. Liang, an immigrant store owner, commented:

> In Chinatown, a growing demand for goods and services, with the resulting development of the local economy, provides ample opportunities for self-employment. Chinatown workers learn to work hard and save money to become a boss, because they know the opportunity is there. If they didn't see this, they might not be so motivated. A couple of my former employees have taken off to start a business similar to mine. They acquired all the necessary tricks to operate the business while working for me and have now turned around to be my competitors. It doesn't matter that much to me, since I always anticipate competition.[61]

Mr. Kuang, a waiter in Chinatown, who had saved money for nearly six years and was about to open a fast food takeout in Long Island, shared Liang's view of self-employment in Chinatown:

> I have been working at least 66 hours per week for all these years, and the hourly pay has not been so good, only about four dollars per hour, but I have been able to accumulate enough to make a significant move. I am not sure whether I could have done it if I had been employed outside of the Chinatown economy; maybe I could, but I just would not have even thought of trying.
>
> In Chinatown, I always have a sense of security around people of my own kind, whereas outside, I would be scared simply because I would feel like I look foreign and sound foreign. . . .

To own a small business in New York City is all I want and all I could possibly achieve. Being a boss, I can enjoy more economic freedom and be more in control. I don't think I could get any farther if I left Chinatown and the city.[62]

Young Li, an immigrant who obtained his master's degree in engineering in New York, worked for an import-export firm in Chinatown, trading between Chinatown and Asia. I asked whether he had chosen to work in the enclave. "Yes," he replied:

I can give you reasons why I do. It is quite simple. There is a lot of potential in doing business with China, Hong Kong, and Taiwan. There are so many immigrants here who need ethnic consumer goods and foodstuff imported from the Orient. Also, Americans have started to compete for a share of the markets in the Orient, particularly China. Doing business here in Chinatown, you can take full advantage of ethnicity. Just being Chinese, with a smart brain of course, will help you a lot. You are familiar with the culture, the mentality, and the ways of doing business in China. That is the advantage of trading with China. I could get a job outside without much difficulty if I wanted. But then I would have lost this advantage.[63]

Li was traveling back and forth between the United States and China frequently and was doing very well. He seemed to enjoy his work. He was confident about his career in the trading business and had plans to start his own firm.

Mr. Lee, an immigrant from Hong Kong who arrived in New York in 1980, was equally optimistic. "Everything is good here [New York]":

If you work hard and focus straight, you can make it no matter what you do or where you are. However, Chinatown to me, and probably to most of the newcomers, is a good place to start. People keep saying that jobs in Chinatown are worse and pay less. But when they go out, they find comparable jobs which do not pay much higher; and most of the time, they find that their weekly paycheck is much less than the amount of take-home cash of a Chinatown worker. So they come back here, by choice. There are many different kinds of jobs available outside of Chinatown, jobs that pay much more. The question is: can you get it?

Lee had worked as a waiter for seven years. At the time of the interview, he was an owner of two restaurants, one in Chinatown and the other in Sunset Park, Brooklyn. For him, "it feels good to be a boss."[64]

Within the enclave, workers are apparently inspired by the success of coethnic entrepreneurs and are motivated to work hard, spend less, and save more in order to realize the goal of self-employment. This is possible in Chinatown, because of the continuous influx of cheap immigrant labor, the growing consumer demands from immigrants, and the connection to the emerging market economies across the Pacific.

## How Education Matters in the Ethnic Enclave

Despite the fact that the enclave is dominated by low-wage and labor-intensive jobs, education pays off in Chinese men's socioeconomic attainment in the enclave economy as much as in the open economy, as quantitative findings indicate. It is misleading to assume that one does not need much education to move ahead within the ethnic enclave. It is probably true that education is not a requirement for most of the low-wage, labor-intensive work. Yet Chinatown has developed a far wider range of economic activities than before. It is difficult for a person with little education to capture new opportunities in the enclave.

One example comes from my direct observation in several employment agencies in Chinatown. Most of the jobs listed in these agencies were restaurant jobs, and thus those who looked for jobs through the agencies were mostly uneducated immigrant men (a few foreign students who were not eligible to work in the United States came to seek temporary off-the-books jobs). Once, after I had been sitting in an agency for just 15 minutes, I heard a staff member lecturing a young man, apparently a newcomer, loudly and impatiently: "You must be crazy! Go look at yourself in that mirror! How much education have you got? How much English do you know? You don't look like you have either, and you are asking for a $1,500 monthly salary? I only have a dishwashing job that pays $800 per month. If you don't like it, you do not have any job here."[65] The man was quite embarrassed, and people around me told me that well-educated people were less interested in restaurant jobs and were not likely to drop by the agencies. Even if they had to take a restaurant job, they were more likely to read ads and walk in to bargain directly with the boss. They were also more likely to get front-of-the-house and supervisory positions that paid better. "When you come here, they [the staff] assume that you only want a job of any kind. They don't expect you to bargain for wages, because you do not know what's going on."[66]

Mr. Chen's experience provided another example. He said in an interview:

> I immigrated three years ago. I first worked as a dishwasher for half a year and then changed to my present job as a mechanic in a fortune cookie factory. Before immigration, I was trained in a vocational school as a mechanic and had a few years of work experience. Education and work experience did not matter much for dishwashing, but they did for my present job. If I hadn't had the skills and experience, I would have been confined to operative work in the factory, and I would have been paid at least one-third less.[67]

Many enclave workers shared similar views on the effect of education. Mr. Chiu, who started a Chinatown garment factory after finishing college, felt very strongly that education played an important role in running a business:

> In Chinatown, everybody talks about opening a garment shop. It seems that the garment industry can bring easy and quick cash for whoever invests in it. This is not true. People are overly optimistic about the industry and do not see the high turnover rate and the cutthroat competition within the industry.

In such a severely competitive business environment, if you do not know the business well enough, if you do not know English, if you do not have enough education, your chance of success will be a lot slimmer.

I have three years of college education. My wife also has an associate degree in dress design. Our education helped us a lot in our business startup and operation. I feel that if you are well educated, you are better able to plan, budget, and control your business both at present and in the long run. Moreover, education can enable you to avoid unnecessary operating costs, allow you to bargain for prices with the manufacturers more effectively and become more flexible. In a word, your business would not survive the competition if you did not have a good brain. I believe experience and education can make a difference in succeeding in business.[68]

Mr. Li's story is also telling. Li immigrated with his family when he was five years old. Three years before the time of the interview, he had earned a bachelor's degree in mechanical engineering. After graduating from college, he chose to take over his father's garment factory on Elizabeth Street in Chinatown. When asked why he did not try to look for a job outside Chinatown, and how important his college education was to the business, he explained:

First of all, I am lucky because I have my father's business. But even if I hadn't, I still think I could have taken a job somewhere temporarily just to save enough money to run my own business. Suppose racial discrimination does not have an effect in the larger economy (I think it does), I would still prefer to take over my father's business, because being somebody's boss is far better than being supervised by somebody else. I believe if you have a good education, if you work hard and manage well, you will have a much better chance to increase your income than a wage earner will. The starting salary for a junior mechanical engineer is from $20,000 to $24,000 a year. I made more than that in the first year in my business.

Indeed, I am doing much better than my father because my education helps. For example, my father used to hire a mechanic for the factory and a middleman to negotiate with the manufactures, both of which I do myself. That saved a lot of the operating cost. My father did not know the benefits of the "laws" and how to deal with the labor unions, the workers, and the government, whereas I can turn these around to work to my benefit. My father did not make long-term plans for business expansion and was content with what he had, whereas I know better how to plan for the future. Instead of saving money in the bank, I reinvest it back into the business.

Now I own not only this garment shop but also a restaurant. I am thinking of opening a noodle factory. I am not saying that my father failed the past 10 years because he did not achieve what I have done in the last 3 years. His poor education only led him that far. In Chinatown, there are two types of businessmen: one is conservative and narrow-minded like my father, and the other is ambitious and adventuresome like myself. The level of education determines, to a large extent, what category one would fall into, and it certainly makes a difference in business.[69]

The positive effect of education, particularly college education, on socioeconomic achievement is important both inside and outside Chinatown. The implication is that those who are better educated have more choices, whether in the enclave or elsewhere.

## Intangible Benefits of Working in the Ethnic Enclave

Chinese immigrants cluster in Chinatown for certain intangible benefits as well. First, Chinese immigrants, especially those with little education and English, feel more comfortable working for coethnic employers in the enclave than for noncoethnic employers in the larger economy. Many garment workers who had once worked for *lofan* ("whites" in Cantonese) eventually returned to the enclave partly because they were frustrated at not being able to understand their bosses or make themselves understood. Some workers complained that their *lofan* bosses showed no concern for the workers' language problem.

Second, new immigrants are constantly confronted with the discriminatory hiring practices of native employers. A recent study by the New York State Inter-Agency Task Force on Immigration Affairs found that the Immigration and Reform Act of 1986, which offered amnesty to eligible illegal aliens, led to three specific forms of discrimination. Employers refused to accept legally valid proof of residency, denied employment to those who experienced minor delays in gathering necessary documentation, and screened out applicants who looked or sounded foreign. Frustrated and harassed by discriminatory employers in the larger labor market, immigrants turn back to the enclave for employment whenever possible.

Third, Chinese immigrants tend to be more willing than natives to work longer hours for more pay in cash. Newcomers often think of their wages in terms of *renminbi* (the Chinese currency). The prevailing wage in China in 1988 was about $30 a month, and this served as a frame of reference for newcomers. New immigrants often viewed minimum-wage jobs in Chinatown as good jobs because they were allowed to work more hours and because they were paid in cash with no tax dollars withheld. These workers were well aware of their options, and they knew that the jobs open to them in the larger labor market were likely to pay the minimum wage, and that taxes would be withheld from their paychecks. Many felt that they were being swindled when they saw that taxes had been deducted from their wages.

Fourth, Chinese immigrants, especially women, usually prefer to work for firms that tolerate flexible work schedules. For example, many working women in Chinatown's garment industry could step out of the factory to see their young children in nearby daycare centers or private homes and take care of household chores. Mothers were often allowed to bring their small babies to work and have their older children come to the workplace after school. As long as the job got done, employers did not object to these interruptions.[70]

Fifth, Chinese immigrants generally worry less about finding jobs in China-town than in the open labor market. Even in a period of economic downturn, when some factories are laying off workers, others have job openings. Because Chinatown's economy has gone global, it is less susceptible to changes in the local economy. One way or another, one can always find something to do, though pay is lower in hard times. "I don't hear about joblessness in Chinatown. I hear about laziness blamed on those who are unwilling to work," said a staff member of a Chinatown employment agency.[71]

In sum, the enclave economy produces a reciprocal relationship between immigrant entrepreneurs and workers, interdependent and mutually beneficial. This unique relationship should not be simply interpreted in Marxist terms as a class relationship, because it is bounded by ethnicity and enforced by trust.[72] The availability of low-wage labor and the willingness to tolerate low wages for the common goal of social mobility are keys to success for immigrant entrepreneurs, especially those in small businesses, because lowering the cost of labor is the only effective way to retain market competitiveness. Few coethnic entrepreneurs in the enclave are capitalists according to a Marxist definition. Most of them are workers in their own business, and many have worked their way up from sewing machine operators and restaurant workers to garment factory subcontractors and restaurant owners. To compensate for low wages they offer their coethnic workers flexible working hours, show cultural understanding, and guarantee jobs even during periods of recession. Coethnic workers, in return, show their loyalty by working hard and not challenging substandard labor practices. This kind of ethnic solidarity, however, is more instrumental than sentimental. As workers acquire better education, English-language ability, and work experience, and become more acculturated into American ways, they may seek better options outside the enclave and move up to self-employment.

## Pitfalls of Working in the Ethnic Enclave

To argue that the enclave economy offers a positive alternative route to social mobility is by no means to overlook the fact that the absolute earnings gap between workers within and outside the enclave has remained substantial. Many jobs in the enclave are characterized by low wages, long hours, and poor working conditions, making them seem highly exploitative from the outside. Yet the avail-ability of a reliable ethnic work force represents an important condition for the survival of immigrant families and the success of ethnic businesses.

In Chinatown, downward mobility for immigrants is not uncommon. In addition to disadvantages associated with immigrant status, newcomers are often intimidated by the unfamiliar environment of the host society and the main-stream economy. They are also blocked from entering into the larger labor mar-ket because of cultural and language barriers as well as perceived discrimination. Thus, some Chinese immigrants, like their earlier counterparts, have no choice but to stay in the enclave. Many of them find themselves taking jobs that actually depreciate the human capital that they accumulated prior to immigration. Mr. Hu, who emigrated from Hong Kong four years before I interviewed him, was working as a clerk in a Chinatown bookstore. He had a college degree in finance and had held a well-paid professional job at the Hong Kong and Shanghai Bank before emigrating. When asked why he did not try to look for jobs in the financial sector in Manhattan, he sighed:

> What can you do? You come here with broken English; you don't know what is going on outside [Chinatown]; nobody seems to care much about your education and credentials; and every single piece of job information you can possibly get is associated with Chinatown.
>
> I got this job through a friend who happened to know the boss. At first, I felt very depressed because this job suggested downward mobility for me. Yet people thought I was lucky to get such a nice, clean, "white-collar" job. I guess I have to be satisfied.
>
> Now, I have decided that I like the job. When you tried to escape the 1997 uncertain future in Hong Kong, you should also be prepared to lose something from emigration. You can't get both, can you?[73]

Mr. Lai told a different story. Before emigration he was a full professor in political science from a prestigious university in Guangzhou. At the time of the interview, he was 58 years old and was working in a food-processing factory in Chinatown. He was bitter, frustrated, and angry about his current work situation:

> I never expected to end up making tofu in Chinatown. I feel as if I am deprived of all the prestige and achievement I had worked so hard for over my lifetime when I was in China.
>
> ... I can't teach here because my English isn't good enough. People around here seem to recommend nothing but menial jobs to you. When I got this job making tofu, they told me that this was the right job for an old person like me. It is a bad job, but I have to take it. I have three children at college, and I have to work until they graduate from school.[74]

Mr. Lai went back to China a year later to resume his teaching post at the university. For him, working in Chinatown was not anywhere close to the American dream that most Chinese immigrants had in mind.

This is the other side of Chinatown. Chinese immigrants participating in the ethnic enclave are often in a disadvantaged position. To a large extent, the survival and success of small enterprises in Chinatown depend on the continuous influx of cheap immigrant labor. Because of the tangible and intangible benefits gained through ethnic solidarity, both entrepreneurs and workers in the ethnic enclave become entangled in a web of coethnic obligations that interferes with their rational pursuit of economic opportunities on the one hand and reinforces ethnic segregation on the other. Nevertheless, the gains in the ethnic enclave cannot be calculated exclusively in economic terms or by mainstream standards. In this respect, Chinatown functions to channel the majority of immigrants, especially those from modest socioeconomic backgrounds, toward achieving their mobility goals.

## Conclusion

The case of Chinatown suggests that the enclave economy is advantageous not only for entrepreneurial immigrants but also for other working immigrants. Enclave entrepreneurs and workers are interdependent, bound by coethnicity. From the point of view of coethnic workers in Chinatown in the late 1980s, ethnic businesses offered material and symbolic compensations that could not be accounted for simply in dollar terms. Although jobs in the ethnic enclave were characterized by low wages, long hours, and poor working conditions, immigrant workers were provided with a familiar work environment in which they were effectively shielded from deficiencies in language, education, and general knowledge of the larger society. They could obtain first-hand information on employment and business opportunities through family members, kin, and coethnics, without spending time and effort looking for "good jobs" in the larger market. They were able to work longer hours and quickly accumulate family savings for future plans. They could gain access to rotating credit and financial support from family or clan associations and other ethnic organizations.[75] Moreover, they could get job training and cultivate an entrepreneurial spirit at work, preparing in some cases for eventual transition to self-employment.[76] Many garment factory and restaurant owners built their businesses on family savings accumulated from wages earned in the garment industry.[77] Such benefits are largely absent in the mainstream labor market or in middleman-minority businesses, where coethnicity is atypical of owner-worker relationships and reciprocity is not an enforceable norm. In fact, middleman-minority entrepreneurs who run businesses in non-coethnic neighborhoods or who employ non-coethnic workers can effectively evade the social control of the ethnic community while causing unintended consequences in the form of interethnic conflicts and other social costs.

The fact that many enclave workers have chosen Chinatown as a better alternative indicates that being confined to the ethnic enclave does not necessarily mean the failure of socioeconomic incorporation. In theory, Chinese immigrants have the option of seeking jobs in the larger labor market, since that market is wide open and discrimination is much more covert and subtle than before, especially in entry-level, low-wage industries. In practice, however, because of their poor English-language ability and other initial disadvantages, immigrants can only find jobs in the larger secondary labor market that pay minimum wages with few fringe benefits. Taking ethnic advantages into account, the ethnic enclave becomes preferable. Therefore, Chinese immigrants choose to work in the ethnic enclave not simply because they are out-competed or discriminated against in the larger labor market but because they see working in the enclave as a better strategy. After all, Chinatown's economy is not as isolated as many think. Although the enclave's protected sector remains relatively stable, thanks to global migration networks, the interface with the mainstream economy has greatly expanded the export sector. Especially for self-employment, an important measure of socio-economic achievement, immigrants see fewer obstacles in Chinatown than in the larger economy.

One should be careful not to jump to the conclusion that immigrants have no other choices but to stay in the enclave in order to do well. Bounded solidarity and enforceable trust do not inhere in the moral conviction of the individual or the culture of origin; rather, they interact with structural factors in the host society to help immigrants organize their social and economic lives in disadvantaged or adverse situations.[78] For many new immigrants, low-paid menial work is a part of a time-honored path toward economic independence and upward mobility for their families over the course of more than one generation in America.

# 6

# Chinese-Language Media in the United States

hinese-language newspapers, television, and radio are influential ethnic institutions, pillars of Chinese diasporic communities around the
world.[1] Recently, the Internet has joined these traditional media. In
the United States, the upsurge of Chinese-language media in the past few
decades mirrors the linguistic, cultural, and socioeconomic diversity of the
Chinese immigrant community, its vibrant enclave economy, and its multifaceted ethnic life. The New York–based *World Journal*, also known as the
*Chinese Daily News* (世界日报), the U.S. edition of the Hong Kong–based
*Sing Tao Daily* (星岛日报), and the New York–based *China Press* (侨报) are
among the largest-circulation and most influential newspapers in the United
States. These three dailies command a disproportionate share of the Chinese-
speaking consumer market in major U.S. cities, with a national circulation
ranging between 120,000 and more than 300,000. On a smaller scale, numerous nationally or locally circulated newspapers and magazines are published
daily, weekly, biweekly, monthly, or quarterly. Especially since the early 1990s,
Chinese-language television, radio, and online publications have also grown
rapidly, with a strong presence in the very cities where ethnic printed publications have established strongholds.

This chapter explores the causes and consequences of the growth of
ethnic-language media and their impact on Chinese immigrants in the
United States. It is based on a content analysis of a selection of major Chinese-
language newspapers, television and radio programs, and online publications, supplemented by telephone or face-to-face interviews with a convenience sample of ethnic newspaper reporters, television and radio producers,

readers, viewers, and listeners.[2] I attempt to answer a fundamental question: do Chinese-language media inhibit or promote the adaptation and integration of immigrants into American society? I look first at the driving forces behind the development of Chinese-language media and then provide a descriptive analysis, exploring what they offer to immigrants. Finally, I examine how Chinese-language media function as a social institution to influence processes of immigrant adjustment and assimilation. I argue that these media not only connect immigrants to their places of origin but also serve as a roadmap for their incorporation into their new homelands by promoting homeownership, entrepreneurship, and education for the second generation.

## The Expanding Market for Chinese-Language Media

Chinese-language media in the United States have existed almost as long as the first Chinatowns but have achieved the status of an influential ethnic institution fairly recently. In isolated Chinatowns during the Chinese Exclusion era, Chinese-language media were relatively insignificant, partly because of low levels of literacy among the old-timers, partly because of the predominance of the face-to-face mode of interpersonal communications, and partly because of the limited scale of the enclave economy. However, community papers and association newsletters were published and circulated. Back issues of newspapers and magazines published in China and focusing almost entirely on the homeland or international events related to it also circulated, within a small, elite circle. Not until the 1940s did Chinese-language media take root in American soil.[3] They have grown rapidly since the 1970s and burst into full bloom in the 1990s. Changes in contemporary Chinese immigration and the development of ethnic economies perpetuate and encourage the development of these media.

### Demographic Change and Consumer Demand for Chinese Media

Before World War II, the Chinese American community was essentially a bachelor society consisting of a small merchant class and a vast working class of sojourners whose lives were oriented toward an eventual return to China.[4] Racism and legal exclusion, crystallized by the Chinese Exclusion Act of 1882, reinforced the sojourning orientation and residential segregation of early immigrants. In 1900 there were about 119,000 Chinese in the United States according to official counts, more than 90 percent of them male. They were mostly concentrated in historic gateway cities on the Pacific west coast, particularly in San Francisco, working in mining and railway construction.[5] Later, they moved east to such urban centers as New York, Chicago, and Boston, to escape both violent and subtle forms of anti-Chinese discrimination and look for better job opportunities. But most ended up in Chinatowns, clinging to one another for comfort and self-protection in a hostile land while they toiled for an eventual return to China.

The 1943 repeal of the Chinese Exclusion Act recognized the legitimacy of the Chinese presence and their basic human rights as immigrants. Yet U.S. immigration policy continued to impose restrictions on Chinese immigration. The Chinese American community remained segregated and male-dominant, though families and native-born children began slowly to appear.[6] In 1950 there were only 150,000 Chinese (63 percent of them male) in the United States.

Passage of the Immigration Act of 1965 (Hart-Celler) brought dramatic changes, favoring family reunification and skilled labor.[7] Contemporary Chinese immigration to America is thus a post-1970 phenomenon. Since then, America's ethnic Chinese population has not only increased many times in absolute numbers, but has also become culturally, linguistically, and socioeconomically diverse.

Contemporary Chinese immigrants differ from the old-timers in several remarkable respects.[8] They come not only from traditional sending regions but from all over China, as well as from the greater Chinese Diaspora: Hong Kong, Taiwan, Vietnam, Cambodia, Malaysia, and the Americas. More than 80 percent of Chinese Americans speak a language other than English at home, and while most share a written language (using traditional or simplified characters), they do not necessarily share a spoken language. Hundreds of local dialects are spoken in China. Most immigrants from the traditional sending regions of mainland China and those from Hong Kong and some parts of Southeast Asia speak Cantonese, which is not easily understood by Mandarin speakers. Immigrants from other regions in mainland China and Taiwan speak Mandarin (the official language of both), as well as Min, Hakka, Chaozhounese, Shanghainese, and so forth. Today, while Cantonese continues to be the dominant dialect in the Chinatowns of San Francisco, Los Angeles, and New York, Mandarin is more and more often heard in Chinese ethnoburbs and even in Chinatowns. Whichever dialect they speak, the great majority of contemporary immigrants are proficient in written Chinese, unlike the illiterate and semi-literate immigrants of older times.

Contemporary immigrants are also extremely diverse in socioeconomic background. Unlike the old-timers, who were mostly uneducated peasants, today's immigrants are disproportionately drawn from the urban, highly educated, and professional segments of the populations in their respective sending regions. As of 2000, for example, 65 percent of foreign-born Chinese between 25 and 34 have four or more years of college education, compared with 30 percent of native-born non-Hispanic whites; immigrants from Taiwan have significantly higher educational attainment than those from the mainland and Hong Kong. The influx of highly educated and highly skilled immigrants from mainland China into the United States was accelerated by the Tiananmen Square protests of 1989 and the U.S. government response to their suppression, the so-called June Fourth green cards.[9] Immigration from the mainland is more diverse in terms of place of origin, and there is a new trend of transnational movement between America and China in which immigrants return to their homeland to seek better economic opportunities. All these developments have profound implications for Chinese-language media, especially printed and online publications.[10]

Differences in origin and socioeconomic background lead to variations in settlement patterns. The traditional pattern of regional concentration in gateway cities continues to hold, as over half of the ethnic Chinese population is concentrated in just three metropolitan regions—New York, Los Angeles and San Francisco.[11] Within each of these regions, however, the settlement pattern tends to be bimodal, with ethnic concentration and dispersion equally significant. Currently, only 14 percent of the Chinese in New York, 8 percent of the Chinese in San Francisco, and less than 3 percent of the Chinese in Los Angeles live in the old Chinatowns. The majority of the Chinese American population is spreading into outer areas or suburbs around traditional gateway cities as well as into new urban centers of Asian settlement. Half of all Chinese Americans live in suburbs. Mandarin-speaking coethnics from mainland China, those from Taiwan, and those of higher socioeconomic status tend to stay away from Cantonese-dominant Chinatowns. Once settled, they tend to establish new ethnic communities, often in more affluent urban neighborhoods and suburbs, such as the "second Chinatown" in Flushing, New York, "Little Taipei" in Monterey Park, California, and emerging Chinese ethnoburbs in the San Gabriel Valley.[12]

The differences in origin and socioeconomic background also have important implications for community organization. Pre-existing ethnic communities are rooted in immigrant gateway cities and have maintained strong cultural infrastructures. Contemporary Chinese immigration has functioned to strengthen and revitalize these pre-existing ethnic communities through family and kin networks while stimulating the development of new ones in suburbs. As of 2000, close to 90 percent of the ethnic Chinese population in the United States was either foreign-born (first generation) or of foreign-born parentage (second generation).

The sharp rise of immigration in the past four decades has not only replenished the Chinese immigrant community but also created an enormous demand for Chinese-language media as immigrants—socioeconomically diverse and with limited English proficiency—look for ways to obtain information, rebuild social networks, and conduct their lives in the new homeland effectively and efficiently. As they strive to get settled, many contemporary immigrants, including the upwardly mobile, find themselves in a paradoxical situation. They have voluntarily left their old homeland but remain emotionally attached to it; they aspire to become a part of their new homeland but often find their paths to success blocked by language and cultural barriers. They thus need ethnic institutional support to ease adjustment difficulties. Chinese-language media are among the numerous new ethnic institutions that have grown up to serve that need.

## Economic Change and the Market for Chinese-Language Media

Economic development in the immigrant community is another driving force behind the rise of Chinese-language media. During the Exclusion era, the immigrant community was spatially and socially isolated. Ethnic economies that developed in the original Chinatowns were oriented to sojourning and confined either to ethnically specific niches, such as restaurants, or to low-skilled, labor-intensive niches unattractive to native workers, such as the hand laundry business or garment manufacturing.[13] For two decades after the repeal of the Chinese Exclusion Act, Chinatown economies remained small in scale and limited in variety, as the immigrant population aged with little replenishment and the second generation gradually moved out of the enclave.[14]

Small-scale traditional ethnic economies could not afford to support ethnic-language media and had little need for them. Advertising was uncommon, since ethnic businesses were closely intertwined with coethnic networks of individuals and organizations. Information about goods and services and about business or employment opportunities was channeled primarily through word of mouth and face-to-face interaction. For example, the owner of a popular restaurant was likely to be the head of a hometown association and was inclined to hire his fellow villagers, who, in turn, would spread the word about his restaurant. A laundry worker was likely to shop at the same place as his neighbors, who could share shopping tips and exchange information about the price and quality of goods and services in the enclave. As a result, coethnic business owners and workers met their respective needs without having to step outside of Chinatown.

Since the 1970s, unprecedented Chinese immigration, accompanied by an enormous influx of human and financial capital, has set off a new stage of economic development in the Chinese immigrant community in the United States.[15] From 1977 to 1987, the U.S. Census reported that the number of Chinese-owned firms grew by 286 percent, compared with 238 percent for Asian-owned firms, 93 percent for black-owned firms, and 93 percent for Hispanic-owned firms. From 1987 to 1997, the number of Chinese-owned businesses grew at a rate of 180 percent (from less than 90,000 to 253,000). As of 1997, there was approximately one ethnic firm for every 9 Chinese and for every 11 Asians, but only one ethnic firm for every 42 blacks and one for every 29 Hispanics. Chinese American–owned business enterprises made up 9 percent of the total minority-owned business enterprises nationwide, but 19 percent of the total gross receipts.[16]

The increase in the scale and variety of the Chinese ethnic economy is visible in major American metropolitan centers. On the one hand, ethnic businesses have grown rapidly, not only in central-city Chinatowns but also in suburban areas, or Chinese ethnoburbs. On the other hand, ethnic businesses have expanded from traditional mom-and-pop retail establishments (e.g., restaurants, grocery stores, and gift shops) and small manufacturing into a wide range of retail, wholesale, and import-export businesses as well as professional services, high-tech manufacturing, banking, and other capital-intensive investments.[17]

Although traditional Chinatowns used to be the center of immigrant Chinese economic life, the Chinese ethnic economy has developed in a multinuclear pattern, dispersing widely into ethnoburbs.[18] The influx of immigrant labor and capital has extended and revitalized Chinatowns, but most of the new development has occurred in the suburbs of major metropolises. Los Angeles' San Gabriel Valley is a prime example.[19] Many new ethnic businesses have expanded beyond the geographic boundaries of the ethnic enclave to tap into the non-coethnic consumer market. Yet they still tend to cluster in metropolitan areas with a visible concentration of coethnic consumers and coethnic businesses, and to maintain close ties to the ethnic community. This phenomenon is captured by the sociological concept of the "enclave economy," which connotes both a spatial dimension (based on the geographic concentration of ethnic businesses and coethnic populations) and a social dimension (embedded in and with profound impacts on the social structures of an ethnic community).[20] Some ethnic businesses have become incorporated into the mainstream economy, such as Computer Associates International in Long Island, or Kingston Technology and Sybase in California's Silicon Valley. These ethnic businesses rely on neither a distinctive ethnic labor market nor a coethnic consumer market and thus have relatively little tangible impact on the immigrant community as a whole, except for being celebrated as models of success. The enclave economy, in contrast, depends almost entirely on the ethnic capital, labor, and consumer markets and serves as an anchor, or identity marker, for the immigrant community.[21] Although the enclave economy contains certain features of the primary sector of the mainstream economy and provides opportunities for upward mobility, such as self-employment, it remains marginal (not necessarily disadvantaged) in relation to the mainstream economy in that it operates largely within a culturally and linguistically distinct environment.

Compared with the traditional Chinatown economy, which was largely restricted to the retail and service sectors, the new enclave economy is more diverse, comprising such fast-growing industries as high-tech and durable goods manufacturing, communications, wholesale trade, FIRE (finance, insurance, and real estate), and professional services. Related ethnic enterprises may be further diversified into various specialties. Take the medical profession as an example. In New York City, the Chinese business directory listed 12 doctors' offices in 1958 and 30 in 1973, compared with 300 in 1988. That number includes a wide range of specialists, ranging from internists, pediatricians, obstetricians, and gynecologists to dentists, optometrists, orthopedists, cosmetic surgeons, acupuncturists, and chiropractors.[22] New ethnic businesses are also much larger in size and scale than traditional ones. In the restaurant business, for example, traditional family-run restaurants are supplemented by trendy corporate-managed restaurants equipped with banquet halls, private dinning rooms, karaoke and other entertainment facilities, and seating capacities of 500 or more.

To a great extent, the survival and growth of the enclave economy depend heavily on ethnic resources: foreign capital, pooled family savings, the ethnic labor force, ethnic consumers, and transnational markets. To compete for a greater share of the ethnic consumer market, ethnic businesses can no longer depend on word of mouth or face-to-face interaction to facilitate information flow. They must find new ways to communicate with potential consumers who are diverse in dialects, origins, socioeconomic status, and settlement patterns, but share similar tastes and needs for goods and services that the larger economy cannot adequately provide. Consequently, Chinese-language media have emerged in the immigrant community, not simply to serve ethnic businesses through marketing and advertising, but also as a new type of ethnic business in and of themselves.

## The Development of Chinese-Language Media: A Descriptive Analysis

At present at least 200 Chinese-language media outlets exist across the United States: print publications, television, radio, and mostly recently online media.[23] Affected by contemporary immigration trends and the booming ethnic Chinese economy, Chinese-language media function as both an economic enterprise and a social institution. They are most developed and thriving in the old and new immigrant-receiving centers where the Chinese and their ethnic economies are concentrated, even though they have transcended geographic boundaries through modern technologies. More than half of all Chinese adults (nearly 2.5 million) read an ethnic newspaper on a regular basis.[24]

### Printed Publications: Dailies, Weeklies, and Community Papers

The press dominates the ethnic-language media. A 1998 survey by Kang & Lee Advertising found that four major dailies have a U.S. circulation surpassing the 100,000 mark (Table 6.1). The *World Journal,* by far the largest and most influential Chinese-language daily circulating in the United States is affiliated with the Taiwan-based United Daily Group. Since its debut in New York in 1976, the *World Journal* has been published by independent operations in New York, Los Angeles, San Francisco, Chicago, Houston, Vancouver, and Toronto, and has distribution offices in major cities in the United States, Canada, Europe, and Latin America. Its mission is to serve all overseas Chinese by helping immigrants bridge the gap to mainstream society, keep in touch with their homeland and local Chinese community news, and improve their quality of life.[25] The newspaper currently contains five or six sections, 64 to 128 full pages, a Sunday magazine, and an online version at worldjournal.com (世界新闻网). In the United States it has eight metropolitan editions (San Francisco, Los Angeles, New York, New Jersey/Pennsylvania, Washington, D.C., Boston, Chicago, and Atlanta/Florida)

**TABLE 6.1  MAJOR CHINESE-LANGUAGE DAILIES AND WEEKLIES WITH NATIONAL OR REGIONAL CIRCULATION IN THE UNITED STATES**

| Name | Date Established | Original Base | Metropolitan Editions |
|---|---|---|---|
| *World Journal* (*Chinese Daily News*) | 1976 | New York | New York, San Francisco, Los Angeles, Seattle, Boston, Chicago, Philadelphia/Washington, DC, Atlanta, Texas, Florida, Hawaii, Vancouver, Toronto |
| *Sing Tao Daily* | 1960 | San Francisco | San Francisco, New York, Los Angeles, Boston, Chicago, Philadelphia, Vancouver, Toronto |
| *China Press* | 1990 | New York | Los Angeles, New York, San Francisco |
| *Ming Pao Daily News* | 1997 | New York | New York, Vancouver, Toronto |
| Chinese Today (*International Daily News*) | 1981 | Los Angeles | San Francisco/Seattle, New York/Atlanta/Texas |
| *Chinese Free Daily News* | 1990 | Taiwan | Los Angeles, New York |
| *Epoch Times* | 1995 | New York | West coast, east coast, New Jersey, Atlanta, Washington, DC/Philadelphia, Texas, Florida, New England, Midwest, Canada |
| *People's Daily* overseas edition | 1985 | Beijing | New York, San Francisco, Toronto |
| *Southern Chinese Daily* | 1979 | Houston | Bay Area, Seattle, Boston, Chicago, Washington, DC, St. Louis, Atlanta, Dallas |
| *Chinese American Daily News* | 1990 | Los Angeles | Southern California |
| *United Journal* | 1952 | New York | New York |
| *New Asian American Magazine* (bimonthly) | — | Chicago | New York, San Francisco, Los Angeles, Chicago, Phoenix |
| *China Times Magazine* (weekly) | — | Taiwan | New Jersey |
| *Travel and Recreation Magazine* (weekly) | 1994 | Los Angeles | Southern California |
| *Sino Times* (biweekly) | 1998 | Rowland Heights, CA | Los Angeles, New York, San Francisco, Miami |
| *Sino-U.S. Weekly* | 1994 | San Gabriel, CA | Los Angeles, Seattle, New York, Chicago, Boston, Atlanta, Washington, DC, Denver, Dallas |
| *China Journal* (weekly) | 1992 | Los Angeles | Chicago, Atlanta, Houston, Florida, Canada |

and a daily circulation of 300,000 or more.[26] The newspaper initially reflected and represented the political views and cultural interests of Mandarin-speaking immigrants from Taiwan but has become increasingly neutral and thus more receptive to immigrants from mainland China and Hong Kong in recent years. A 2006 survey revealed that 93 percent of the Chinese-speaking community in New York, Los Angeles, and San Francisco reads Chinese-language newspapers. Of those, 83 percent had read the *World Journal* in the past six months, with most (74 percent) reading it on a regular basis—at least once a week.[27]

The second-largest Chinese-language daily circulating in the United States is the *Sing Tao (USA) Daily*, a subsidiary of the Hong Kong–based Sing Tao Newspaper Group. It has arguably the second-largest international coverage in the world (following the *International Herald Tribune*), with 22 branch offices globally.[28] *Sing Tao (USA) Daily* established its San Francisco office in the early 1960s, its Los Angeles and New York offices in the 1980s, and its Boston, Chicago, and Philadelphia offices in the 1990s. The newspaper contains six sections and 32 to 74 full pages with six editions (including the Bay Area, Los Angeles, and New York), a weekend magazine, and an online version at singtaousa.com (星岛日报网). In the United States, its daily circulation is more than 181,000.[29] *Sing Tao Daily* presents readers with comprehensive local, national, and international news and the most important news from China, Hong Kong, and Taiwan. Its stronghold is in the Bay Area, perhaps due to the dominance of Cantonese influence in the immigrant community. A survey shows that 57 percent of Chinese newspaper readers name *Sing Tao Daily* as their preferred newspaper.[30]

The third-largest Chinese-language daily circulating in the United States is the *China Press*, or *Qiao Bao* (Overseas Chinese Press). It was established in 1990 in New York as an independent paper but has maintained close ties to the official media machine in mainland China. *China Press* contains four or five sections and 40 to 60 full pages with three metropolitan editions (Los Angeles, New York, and San Francisco). It is read mainly in the United States, with a daily circulation of 120,000.[31]

Another large Chinese-language newspaper with increasing visibility in the United States is the Hong Kong-based *Ming Pao Daily News* (明报). The New York edition entered the U.S. market in 1997; the San Francisco edition was added in 2004. Circulating in New York City, New Jersey, Philadelphia, Boston, and Seattle, it has a current U.S. readership of 100,000.[32]

In cities where major Chinese-language dailies are headquartered or have branch offices, they coexist with numerous Chinese-language dailies and weeklies with a national or regional circulation ranging from 15,500 to 90,000 (Table 6.2). Local and community papers as well as weekly, monthly, or quarterly magazines have appeared in the same cities, especially since the 1990s. Community papers, mostly owned and run by new immigrant entrepreneurs, frequently from the mainland, are published weekly or biweekly and typically have a circulation of 5,000 to 12,000 copies. Most of these community papers are distributed at no cost through Chinese-owned businesses (e.g., supermarkets, travel agencies,

TABLE 6.2    CHINESE-LANGUAGE LOCAL OR COMMUNITY WEEKLIES IN SELECTED
U.S. CITIES

| Name | Date Established | Original Base | Place of Circulation |
|---|---|---|---|
| United Times | 1981 | Santa Ana, CA | Southern California |
| China Post | 1990 | Alhambra, CA | Los Angeles |
| Tomorrow Times | 1993 | Los Angeles | Los Angeles |
| Merit Times | 1997 | Monterey Park, CA | Los Angeles |
| Zhong Guo Daily News | 1998 | El Monte, CA | Los Angeles |
| New Immigrant Times | 2000 | S. El Monte, CA | Los Angeles |
| Chinese Weekend | 2001 | City of Industry, CA | Los Angeles |
| Washington China Post | 1982 | Rockville, MD | Washington, DC |
| A & C Business News | 1996 | Rockville, MD | Washington, DC |
| New World Times | 1998 | Rockville, MD | Washington, DC |
| Washington Chinese Times | 2000 | Rockville, MD | Washington, DC |
| Washington Chinese News | 2000 | Rockville, MD | Washington, DC |
| Atlanta Chinese News | 2000 | Rockville, MD | Atlanta |
| San Francisco Chinese Times | 2000 | Rockville, MD | San Francisco Bay area |
| Boston Chinese News | 2000 | Rockville, MD | Boston |
| Chicago Chinese News | 2000 | Rockville, MD | Chicago |
| Dallas Chinese Times | 2000 | Rockville, MD | Dallas |
| Miami Chinese Sun | 2000 | Rockville, MD | Miami |
| Portland Chinese Times | 2000 | Rockville, MD | Portland |
| Seattle Chinese News | 2000 | Rockville, MD | Seattle |
| St. Louis Chinese Journal | 2000 | Rockville, MD | St. Louis |

bookstores, and restaurants); some have a nominal charge. They tend to be established in suburbs rather than in inner cities. For example, almost all of the locally circulated dailies and weeklies in Los Angeles and Washington, D.C., where my fieldwork was conducted, are headquartered in Los Angeles' San Gabriel Valley and in Rockville, Maryland, a suburb of Washington with an increasingly visible Chinese immigrant population.

## Television and Radio

Chinese-language television has developed rapidly since the mid-1980s (Table 6.3). Prior the launching of digital and satellite television, there were three major Chinese-language television networks in the United States: Asian American Television (AATV), Chinese Television Network (CTN), and North American Television (NATV).[33] AATV was based in Los Angeles and received most of its programming from mainland China, including satellite local and international news about China, variety shows, popular or classic Chinese movies, Cantonese operas, and children's shows. It also produced some local programming, including news,

**TABLE 6.3 CHINESE-LANGUAGE TELEVISION BROADCASTING IN THE UNITED STATES**

| Name | Date Established | Headquarters | Coverage Area | Language |
|------|------------------|--------------|---------------|----------|
| **Major Television Networks or Channels** | | | | |
| Asian American Television | — | Los Angeles | Los Angeles via satellite | Cantonese, Mandarin |
| Chinese Television Network | 1994 | Hong Kong | Los Angeles via satellite | Cantonese, Mandarin |
| North American Television | 1994 | Los Angeles | Los Angeles, San Francisco, Seattle, New York via satellite | Cantonese, Mandarin |
| Sino Television Broadcasting | 1998 | New York | New York, New Jersey, Connecticut | Mandarin |
| New Tang Dynasty Television | 2002 | New York | New York via satellite | Cantonese, Mandarin |
| China Central Television-9 (CCTV-9) | 2000 | Beijing | Via cable and satellite | Mandarin |
| Phoenix Chinese Television | 1996 | Hong Kong | Via cable and satellite | Mandarin |
| Jade TV Broadcasts (TVB) | 1967 | Hong Kong | Via cable and satellite | Cantonese |
| Asian Television (ATV) | 1957 | Hong Kong | Via cable and satellite | Cantonese |
| **Selected Television Stations** | | | | |
| Chinese Television Company | 1976 | San Francisco | San Francisco Bay area | Cantonese, Mandarin |
| Texas Chinese Television | 1983 | Houston | Houston | Mandarin |
| TVB (USA) | 1984 | San Francisco | Los Angeles, San Francisco | Cantonese, Mandarin, Vietnamese |
| World Television | 1985 | New York | New York | Cantonese, Mandarin |
| Pacific Television | 1986 | San Francisco | San Francisco Bay area | Cantonese, Mandarin |
| Chinese American Television | 1988 | Los Angeles | Southern California | Mandarin, English |
| Chicago News Television | 1989 | Chicago | Chicago | Mandarin |
| Panda Television | 1989 | Los Angeles | Nationwide | Mandarin with English subtitles |
| Sinovision | 1990 | New York | New York | Cantonese, Mandarin |

commentaries, and special forums on topics related to both mainstream U.S. society and the Chinese American community: current affairs, local politics, education, real estate, and finance. AATV once reached about 87,000 households in Los Angeles via two local cable channels, usually for three to six hours a day, Monday through Saturday, and as many as 100,000 more viewers via satellite dishes. CTN was established in 1994 in Hong Kong to serve the global Chinese community. In the 1990s CTN's major U.S. market was in Los Angeles, where it had a viewership of about 280,000 households via local cable channels and another 285,000 via satellite dishes for its 24-hour programming. At present, CTN claims to be one of the largest television networks reaching out to the global Chinese Diaspora. NATV, established in 1994 in Los Angeles, claims to be the largest Chinese-language television network. It receives most of its Cantonese programs from Hong Kong and its Mandarin programs from Taiwan. Through satellite and local cable services, NATV reaches an estimated viewership of about 860,000 on the west coast and in New York.[34]

Capitalizing on the growing Chinese-speaking consumer market, mainstream American corporations such as DirecTV and EchoStar Communications Corporation's Dish Network have aggressively expanded their Chinese-language programming via satellite television services. DirecTV offers three Chinese-language packages: Jadeworld, Mandarin Direct II, and Mandarin Direct III.[35] Dish Network offers six: Chinese Variety Pack, Chinese Plus Pack, Chinese Super Pack, Chinese Select Pack, Taiwanese Mega Pack, and the Great Wall TV Package.[36] The Great Wall package, launched in the United States in the fall of 2004, is directly broadcast from Hong Kong, China, Taiwan, and other countries in the Asian Pacific region. It bundles 17 popular Chinese-language television channels, including 7 of the very best news and entertainment channels from China Central Television (CCTV), 6 provincial channels from mainland China, and 4 channels provided by partners beyond China.[37] Both DirecTV and Dish Network offer 24 hours of Chinese programming a day, delivering the latest movies, television series, sports, news, entertainment, children's programs, music videos, documentaries, and travelogues to Chinese communities in the United States directly from mainland China, Hong Kong, Taiwan, and other parts of the Chinese Diaspora.

Local stations also broadcast Chinese-language programs, especially in cities with growing numbers of Chinese immigrants (see Table 6.3). These programs are supplied by national and regional networks in China, Hong Kong, and Taiwan and fed to local cable systems with broadcast times varying from 30 minutes to eight hours daily. Except for the San Francisco–based Chinese Television Company, which was established in 1976, most of the Chinese-language networks started broadcasting in the mid- to late 1980s and the 1990s. Sino Television Broadcasting, for example, launched in 1998 in the New York, New Jersey, and Connecticut region, offers a comprehensive 24-hour schedule of Chinese-language programming, including news, sports, entertainment, financial reports, drama, cooking shows, community programs, and movies; it is also available via cable and satellite.[38] In Los Angeles, New York, San Francisco, Houston, and Chicago, local Chinese-language stations claimed viewerships of 100,000 or more.[39] As satellite and digital technologies have revolutionized television broadcasting since the turn of the twenty-first century, Chinese-language viewership has grown exponentially.

Chinese-language radio is also a fairly recent phenomenon in the United States. It first aired in the 1960s and has grown rapidly since the 1990s. The handful of Chinese radio stations in the United States are mostly based in Los Angeles, San Francisco, and New York (Table 6.4).[40] Los Angeles' KAZN AM1300 began broadcasting in Mandarin in 1993, the first and only free-access full-day Chinese-language radio station in the United States. KAHZ AM1600 is simulcast from KAZN in Los Angeles, serving the Chinese-speaking audience in Orange County, California. It combines experienced broadcasters from mainland China, Taiwan, Hong Kong, and the United States and high-quality, varied programming with wide appeal. In addition, KMRB AM1430, Sino Radio Broadcasting, launched in 1998, broadcasts 24 hours a day in Cantonese, the only such station in southern California. WZRC AM1480 is the leading Cantonese 24-hour radio program in New York, New Jersey, and Connecticut. WKDM AM1380, launched in early 2007, is a 24 hour Monday–Friday Mandarin station serving the New York–New Jersey–Connecticut market. The five radio stations mentioned above were acquired by Multicultural Radio Broadcasting Inc. (MRBI) and incorporated into MRBI's Chinese Media Group operations.[41] Many Chinese-language programs are aired through local radio stations at different times in Chinese-concentrated cities, such as KVTO AM1400 in the San Francisco Bay Area, Chinese American Broadcast Network in Boston, and Chinese Radio Houston (see Table 6.4).[42] Overall, radio programs attract larger audiences than television among Chinese Americans. According to a radio survey of the New York and Los Angeles markets in the winter of 2005, 56 percent of radio listening by Chinese-speaking Asian Americans involves Chinese-language radio, and 83 percent of Chinese-speaking Asian Americans aged 12 and older in New York and Los Angeles listen to the radio over the course of a week, spending an average of 16 hours each week on the medium.[43]

Compared with television, radio stations produce a substantially higher proportion of their programming locally, focusing not only on news, rush-hour traffic updates, business and finance, lifestyle, shopping, entertainment, and tabloid gossip, but also on community service. As stated on KAZN's website, for example, "Apart from being the voice of the community, KAZN has actively organized and participated in countless charity events, raising relief funds for people in need all over the world. KAZN is also a proud sponsor and organizer of various events such as seminars, concerts, holiday parties, cultural festivals, tours, competitions and dinner shows, that establish bonds between audiences and their favorite radio station and program hosts."[44]

**TABLE 6.4   CHINESE-LANGUAGE RADIO BROADCASTING IN THE UNITED STATES**

| Name | Date Established | Headquarters | Coverage Area | Language |
|---|---|---|---|---|
| Sino Radio Broadcasting via KAZN AM1300/ KAHZ AM1600 | 1993 | Los Angeles | Los Angeles, Orange County | Mandarin |
| Sino Radio Broadcasting via KMRB AM1430 | 1998 | Los Angeles | Los Angeles | Cantonese |
| Sinocast Radio | 1987 | Los Angeles | US, Canada | Cantonese, Mandarin |
| Sinocast Radio | 1987 | Los Angeles | US, Canada | Cantonese, Mandarin |
| Sinocast Radio via WZRC AM1480 | | New York | New York, New Jersey, Connecticut | Cantonese |
| Sinocast Radio via WKDM AM1380 | 2007 | New York | New York, New Jersey, Connecticut | Mandarin |
| Chinese American Voice via WACD-FM | 1986 | New York | New York, New Jersey, Connecticut | Mandarin, Taiwanese |
| Chinese Radio New York via WNWR | | New York | New York, Philadelphia | Mandarin |
| Chinese Radio Network via WGBB AM1240 | 1998 | New York | New York, Philadelphia | Mandarin |
| San Francisco Chinese Radio | 1990 | San Francisco | San Francisco Bay area | Cantonese, Mandarin |
| Chinese Radio Shows via KVTO AM1400 | 1994 | San Francisco | San Francisco Bay area | Cantonese |
| Chinese American Broadcast Network | 1995 | Boston | Boston | Cantonese, Mandarin |
| Chinese Radio Houston via WCHN | | Houston | Houston | Mandarin |
| Hong Kong Vintage Pop Radio | 2002 | Web-based | New York, global | Cantonese |
| Chinese Radio International via MUST AM1120 | | Beijing | Washington, DC | Mandarin |
| Chinese Radio International via WNWR AM1540 | | Beijing | Philadelphia | Mandarin |
| Radio Taiwan International via WYFR | | Taipei | Okeechobee, FL, via shortwave | Mandarin |

## Online Publishing

At the peak of the information age, Chinese-language media have expanded onto the Internet (Table 6.5). Chinese-language websites run by and for Chinese immigrants have been booming in the United States.[45] Most of the major Chinese-language newspapers circulated in the United States publish online as well. For example, *World Journal, Sing Tao Daily,* and *China Press* launched their online editions in the late 1990s (worldjournal.com, singtaousa.com, and usqiaobao.com). The Los Angeles-based *Zhong Guo Daily News* and *Taiwan Daily News* jointly maintain the website chinesedaily.com. Many other Chinese American media outlets, including print media, television channels, and radio stations, have an online presence.[46] Chinese-language websites hosted in China, Hong Kong, Taiwan, or elsewhere are just a click away.

Some of the most visited multimedia websites are Chinese Yahoo (中国雅虎), Sina North America (北美新浪网), Duowei (多维新闻网), BackChina (倍可亲网), China News Digest (华夏文摘), and China Gate (文学城). Chinese Yahoo (cn.yahoo.com) is not a direct translation from the English site, but contains distinctly Chinese channels and categories; it can be viewed in both simplified and traditional Chinese writing systems. Sina North America (home.sina.com) was developed by Chinese immigrant entrepreneurs in Silicon Valley in the mid-1990s and later merged with a Shanghai-based company; it has since become a leading online Chinese-language resource for global Chinese communities, offering news, entertainment, community affairs, and e-commerce in four localized websites that are produced and updated daily by teams in China, Hong Kong, Taiwan, and the United States. In September 2000, Sina North America enjoyed an average of 46 million daily page views and had 11 million registered users. Because of their strong business interests in China, Chinese Yahoo and Sina

**TABLE 6.5   POPULAR CHINESE-LANGUAGE MEDIA WEBSITES**

| Name | Website | Date Established | Headquarters |
|------|---------|------------------|--------------|
| *World Journal* | http://worldjournal.com/ | 2002 | New York City |
| *Sing Tao Daily (USA)* | http://singtaousa.com/ | 1995 | Hong Kong |
| *China Press* | http://usqiaobao.com/ | 2002 | New York City |
| *Ming Pao Daily News* | http://mingpaousa.com/ | 1998 | Long Island, NY |
| *Chinese Daily* | http://www.chinesedaily.com | 2001 | Los Angeles |
| Chinese Yahoo | http://cn.about.yahoo.com | 1999 | Silicon Valley, Beijing |
| Sina North America | http://home.sina.com/ | 1999 | Silicon Valley, Shanghai |
| Duowei | http://www2.chinesenewsnet.com/ | 1999 | New York City |
| BackChina | http://www.backchina.com/ | 2003 | Houston |
| China News Digest | http://www.cnd.org/ | 1989 | Gaithersburg, MD |
| China Gate | http://www.wenxuecity.com/ | 1997 | Silicon Valley |

North America are suspected by some overseas Chinese readers of being too compliant toward the government of the People's Republic of China (PRC).[47] Duowei (chinesenewsnet.com), whose name can be translated as "multidimensional," was founded in 1999 by Chinese Media Net, Inc. (CMN). This ethnic media group operates in the United States, Canada, and Hong Kong.[48] Following CMN's motto, "multidimensional media in the multidimensional world," Duowei offers high-quality media content, via both traditional and online publication, to global Chinese communities: uncensored real-time coverage of global news and analyses and commentaries from many perspectives, 24 hours a day. Duowei has 500,000 unique users per month and has been the number-one Chinese-language news website outside China and number 51 (in terms of content and audience size) in the United States.[49] The U.S.-based website Back-China (backchina.com) is increasing popular, surpassing North American Sina as one of the sites most favored by educated Chinese immigrants in the United States.[50] BackChina presents a comprehensive mixture of news, information, and entertainment, tailored to their specific needs. China Gate (wenxuecity.com), established in 1997 in the heart of Silicon Valley, boasts the largest overseas Chinese community portal in the world.[51]

Internet users can also easily browse online editions of newspapers and magazines published in China, Hong Kong, and Taiwan, and numerous other websites based in diasporic communities around the world. What distinguishes the homeland-based and U.S.-based websites are their perspectives and approaches. A Chinese American perspective and a transnational approach are clearly articulated in many U.S.-based Chinese-language websites. Moreover, most of the influential online media originating in the United States after 1990 were established by well-educated professionals from mainland China. Once established, they have a global presence and play an important role in reconnecting users not only with mainland China but also with other diasporic Chinese communities globally.[52]

## Content and Coverage

Most of the Chinese media outlets in the United States are owned by ethnic or transnational entrepreneurs; some are owned by overseas Chinese media corporations; and some have been acquired by mainstream media corporations. Almost all are managed and staffed by Chinese immigrants. These various outlets cover events in the local Chinese community as well as economic, political, social, and cultural news in the homeland and around the world, with varying degrees of emphasis on China, Hong Kong, and Taiwan. They also provide information that is especially important to new immigrants on jobs, housing, schooling, childcare, healthcare, welfare, taxation, traffic rules, and immigration services, along with classified advertisements for rental housing and second-hand goods, carpooling notices, listings for tourist attractions, and online and print Chinese yellow pages and business directories. Online media seamlessly integrate news with treaded discussion groups, forums, bulletin boards, chat rooms, and blogs to encourage and facilitate interaction among users, thus creating an international virtual community. The contents are not just rich in homeland news absent from mainstream media; they are also directly relevant to immigrants' multifaceted life in America.

Coverage, however, reflects not only the diverse material needs and cultural tastes of coethnic consumers, including both immigrants and business owners, but also the ideological positions of editors-in-chief, producers, and, to a lesser extent, reporters. Moreover, media outlets' editorial focus, content selection, and programming are heavily influenced by place of origin and homeland political affiliation. For example, the *World Journal* used to be politically pro-Taiwan, and "anti-communism" is one of its founding principles. In contrast, the *China Press* is pro-PRC; "promoting unification" is one of its founding principles.

Although ideological and political differences persist, many outlets strive for professionalism, adopting the principle of honest, fair, and impartial reporting in order to gain credibility in the Chinese immigrant community. Most of the media outlets have in their mission statements such phrases as "connecting immigrants to mainstream America," "assisting immigrants to assimilate into American society," "promoting better relations and dialogues between China and Taiwan," and "promoting integration to the global Chinese community." The *World Journal*, the biggest Chinese-language daily circulating in the United States, leads the ethnic media in this direction. Although its editorial focus is on political, economic, and social developments in Taiwan, and it maintains its anti-communist stand, it has become increasingly sensitive to the needs and tastes of its diverse constituents, most of whom are immigrants from the mainland. Since the mid 1980s, the *World Journal* has hired reporters of mainland origin and increased the proportion of mainland coverage in each of its main sections. For instance, it has invited both Taiwanese and mainlanders to participate in special forums to discuss the hotly contested issue of unification versus independence. It has published readers' letters that voice different views and added two full pages to the entertainment section to cover mainland movie stars and celebrities. Moreover, it has changed from the traditional vertical typesetting format to the modern horizontal left-to-right one, which has been widely used in mainland China since the 1950s.[53] As a result, the *World Journal* has significantly increased its circulation among immigrants from mainland China and has won substantial consumer loyalty. One mainland Chinese immigrant, who was a strong supporter of the PRC, admitted to me that he shifted his subscription from the *China Press* to the *World Journal* because the latter was not only "richer and more comprehensive in its content coverage" but also "the best Chinese-language paper" available. Many other Chinese media outlets encourage uncensored, objective, and independent reporting.

News is the key component of all Chinese-language media outlets, whether in print, on air, or online. Coverage includes: (a) local and national news highlights directly transmitted from major media outlets in China, Hong Kong, and

Taiwan; (b) U.S. and local news, current affairs, special reports, and weather reports, based on mainstream media sources such as the *New York Times, Los Angeles Times,* Associated Press, *Wall Street Journal, USA Today, Time,* CNN, ABC, and NBC, and translated into Chinese; and (c) news about the local, national, and global Chinese community produced by ethnic media outlets. Most print and online publications also feature thematic sections on politics, community life, business and finance, entertainment, leisure, and sports, editorial columns, and readers' responses. The thematic sections often, and to varying degrees, reflect editorial biases.

Smaller Chinese-language media players lack the financial, human, and institutional resources to compete with the big dailies in providing comprehensive news coverage. Instead, they devote a significant part of their coverage to issues related to the immediate settlement needs of new immigrants, such as education, job training, employment, and entrepreneurship.

In the United States, Chinese-language television programming features headline news from China, Hong Kong, and Taiwan and breaking news from the United States and the rest of the world, along with a wide variety of special reports on current affairs or historical events, sports, and arts and entertainment programs. There is a heavy focus on entertainment: homeland-produced classics or popular movies, Chinese operas, soap operas, concerts, sitcoms, and animated shows for young children. In recent years, Chinese television networks have increased the proportion of locally produced programming, which includes news reporting and forums on health, family, education, finance, real estate, and entrepreneurship in which local experts are invited to participate, as well as locally recorded, taped, and edited concerts and performances by popular singers and dancers from mainland China, Hong Kong, and Taiwan.

Radio, too, focuses heavily on news and entertainment (e.g., popular and folk music, traditional Chinese operas, and contemporary soap operas) and sports (major U.S. sports and sports in China or Taiwan). The proportion of locally produced programs is higher for radio than for television: local programming includes community news, ethnic politics, education, home or business ownership, rush-hour traffic reports, and commercial advertisements.

Clearly, Chinese-language media in the United States do not simply import content from the homeland media, nor do they merely offer a translation of mainstream American content. Rather, they respond to the diverse needs of their co-ethnic Chinese-speaking clientele. Newspaper readers, television viewers, and radio listeners tend to be diverse in educational and occupational statuses, ranging from cooks, waiters, and seamstresses to engineers, scientists, and teachers. Online media users tend to be predominantly middle-class professionals who are not only well educated, but also English-proficient and assimilated. Through an increasing proportion of local reporting and locally produced programming, the ethnic media fulfill an important function as an information agent by keeping immigrants of diverse backgrounds well-informed about their multiple social worlds.

## Effects on Immigrant Adaptation and Integration

Chinese-language media are thriving and show no sign of slowing down. Many of these media outlets are themselves independent business enterprises, but they collectively serve as an important ethnic social institution in the Chinese immigrant community. How does this ethnic institution affect immigrant life and immigrants' integration into their new homeland? There are two approaches to this question, each guided by a different assumption. The assimilationist approach assumes that the ethnic community and the host society are inherently in conflict and mutually exclusive; that there is a natural process by which diverse ethnic groups shed their cultural baggage and come to share a common culture and identity; and that, once set in motion, this process moves inevitably and irreversibly toward assimilation.[54] The multicultural approach, in contrast, assumes that the ethnic community is an integral part of the host society and that each ethnic culture, despite its distinct internal dynamics, contributes to the host society as a whole. New immigrants, with limited English-language proficiency, few marketable or transferable skills, and limited information about their new homeland, have to cluster in ethnic enclaves upon arrival and rely on coethnic networks and institutions to find housing, jobs, and their way around. The assimilationists would predict that immigrants will eventually withdraw from their ethnic institutions as they become assimilated. In contrast, the multiculturalists would predict that immigrants will find an identifiable place in their host societies through these ethnic institutions.[55]

In my view, Chinese-language media can be understood as a social institution that is complementary rather than oppositional in relation to the host society. There is ample evidence to support this view. First and foremost, they effectively connect immigrants to the host society through media that are familiar to them and keep them informed. News coverage about the host society and the immigrant community is substantial. Without speaking a single word of English, immigrants know what is going on in the world around them, from big headline news about a U.S. military surveillance plane's crash-landing on Hainan Island in 2001, Judy Chu's election to the California State Assembly in 2002 and to the California State Board of Equalization in 2006, California's energy crisis, a high court's decision on marijuana use in 2008, or the Beijing Olympics, to tabloid gossip about Hollywood movie stars. In one of my interviews, a 60-something acupuncturist in Los Angeles' Chinatown, who did not speak English well, surprised me with an incredibly vivid description of a recent NBA playoff game. When I asked how he came by such detailed knowledge, he smiled, pointed to the *International Daily News* on his desk, and said, "I watched the game on CBS, and then read the newspaper and listened to the radio on my way to work the next day. The radio had better coverage." He even invited me to quiz him on other current events. In this case, Chinese-language media are not only a source of information in themselves but also a supplement to the mainstream media. This example also suggests that non-English-speaking immigrants are acculturated to the host society via the Chinese-language media—a point developed below.

Second, the ethnic media provide immigrants with a detailed roadmap, pointing out the best ways to advance through unknown territory. Newcomers, even those with some proficiency in English, want to know how to go about finding suitable housing, jobs, business and investment opportunities, schools for their children, and various services. But they are not well connected to the service and employment networks in the mainstream society, and their own family or friendship networks are no longer sufficient to meet these diverse needs. As an information agent, the ethnic media fill needs that are not met in the larger society. A non-English-speaking newcomer can pick up a phone and possibly find a rental apartment and a job in the same day because housing and job advertisers also speak Chinese. Locally produced newspaper forums and television and radio programs routinely discuss topics that are of special interest to immigrants: how changes in immigration laws affect them, how to invest in their children's education, how to purchase and finance a home, how to apply for a business loan, how to bridge the generation gap between themselves and their teenage children, and so forth.

Third, Chinese-language media promote and reinforce the mobility goals of the immigrant community. As we have seen, the Chinese immigrant community has shifted its orientation from sojourning to settling: the plan is to move up in American society rather than to make money and go back. The community's biggest concerns are making a living, homeownership, and the education of children. Many immigrants regard themselves as successful if they run their own business or become a *laoban* (boss), if they own their own home (even if they have to rent out part of the house), or if their child goes to an Ivy League college. As an ethnic social institution, the media consistently support and reinforce these mobility goals. In the local business and community sections of newspapers, for example, news reports and editorial columns, as well as numerous advertisements, inform readers about business opportunities, the best time and place to purchase a home, and children's problems and educational achievements. The *World Journal* annually publishes a chart listing the top 25 colleges according to the ranking in *U.S. News & World Report.* On a visit to a Chinatown worker's home, I saw such a chart clipped from the paper and posted on the refrigerator door. I also heard people talking about these rankings during the period when high school students file their college applications. Winners of regional and national academic awards who are of Chinese ancestry get front-page coverage in major dailies, with photographs and extensive writeups about the winners' families. Ka-ming Lui, editorial director of *Ming Pao Daily News,* stated in an interview: "That's what draws people. Every immigrant worries about getting his kid into a good school. We run lots of education stories to meet that need."[56]

Ethnic-language media have a subtle but profound role in reinforcing the values of educational achievement and financial success for immigrants and their children. A high school senior who volunteered in a nonprofit organization in Los Angeles' Chinatown told me: "My father always read aloud news reports on winners of something, anything. When he did that, my whole body got stiffened. I felt he was talking to me and expecting me to do the same." A Chinese immigrant who is fluent in English, has a master's degree in accounting, and is a certified public accountant moved to Washington, D.C., from the Deep South to take up a job in a mainstream firm for a six-digit salary, while maintaining his own business as a tax consultant. He told me that he constantly advertised his business in the local Chinese newspaper even though he did not intend to expand it: "The purpose is not to get new business but to make a statement about yourself. It is important to show that you *exist* and that people know about you." Indeed, in his circle of new Chinese friends in Washington, he is known as a boss, not an employee.

Fourth, Chinese-language media work, often subtly and gradually, to acculturate the immigrants. This may sound counterintuitive—how can ethnic-language media contribute to acculturation when the key measure is the adoption of the host language? I have found that the media subtly influence certain habits and behaviors that are not typically Chinese. One example is buying takeout food, which is not a traditional Chinese practice. Because so many restaurants provide convenient takeout and delivery services, and so many immigrant women work, takeout food has become quite common within the ethnic enclave. Restaurants are the primary advertisers in many newspapers, and immigrants can easily select a place from which to order takeout just by glancing over the front or back page of a paper. Politics offers another example. The ethnic media encourage immigrants to practice democracy by providing them with an outlet for voicing their opinions—something that they did not normally or comfortably do in their homeland (particularly in the PRC). This practice causes behavioral change. I have both systematically and casually observed that customers will threaten to write to the press to report a problem with business people. When I interviewed a Taiwanese housewife who is a regular listener to Radio Chinese (Los Angeles), her husband teasingly warned: "Don't cite her wrong. She will call in to the station to 'sue' you."

While the ethnic-language media serve as a bridge between the Chinese-speaking immigrant community and mainstream society, they also keep immigrants in close contact with the homeland, thus easing the psychological and emotional problems of being a foreigner. New immigrants are concerned about what goes on in their original homeland as well as in the host country, wondering how politics and the economy are affecting families and friends who were left behind, and how events or policies developed in the homeland, the host society, or elsewhere will affect U.S.-China relations and their own lives. Mainstream media outlets usually lack detailed coverage on issues of this type, and the ethnic media fill the gap.

Moreover, ethnic-language media create a cultural space enabling immigrants to enrich their lives. New immigrants are interested in things that they have been personally connected to or have grown up with: art and literature, entertainment, favorite movie, music, and sports stars, the familiar faces and voices of television anchors, the writings of sports commentators, comedians, and novelists. The cultural scene in the host society may be unfamiliar and irrelevant—and sometimes even unsettling in the case of racial stereotyping, insensitive ethnic jokes, and biased depiction of the group. The language barrier exacerbates the sense of cultural emptiness. An immigrant writer described this painful feeling as "being in a cultural desert." He remarked: "You try to look ahead but see no destination; you try to turn back but can't retrace your footsteps; and you end up drifting aimlessly without direction." While Chinese-language media fill the emptiness by offering the familiar and thus easing the pain, they also open up a cultural space where immigrants can express their experience and share it with others. The family section of the *World Journal,* for example, publishes short stories, poems, and essays that reflect immigrant life in the United States.

Clearly, Chinese-language media have a profound effect on immigrant life in America, directly and indirectly shaping the familiarization process and reclaiming a sense of home among Chinese immigrants in the United States. However, I have also observed those media, interacting with a concentration of ethnic economies and institutions, set barriers to improving intergroup relations at the individual level. As a social institution, the ethnic media reinforce immigrants' sense of "we-ness" to the exclusion of "other-ness" and lower the incentive to expand social and personal networks to include members of other racial and ethnic groups. Thus, immigrants may be well informed about what is going on in their community, but they may not feel compelled to make friends with their non-Chinese neighbors because of their own lack of English proficiency and the perceived low instrumental value of such personal relationships. Indeed, in Chinese ethnoburbs in Los Angeles, as well as many sub-enclaves in cities, some Chinese immigrants feel as if they are living in Hong Kong, Taipei, Shanghai, or Guangzhou, and are not particularly motivated to learn English or seek out informal contacts with their non-Chinese neighbors.

## Survival and Growth: Some Constraints

Like all mass media, Chinese-language media are economic enterprises with a dual objective: delivering professional services to the business community and the ethnic population and generating revenues to sustain and expand themselves. If we assume that more than half of all Chinese immigrants who do not speak English well and even a large number of those who do prefer to use Chinese-language media either entirely or selectively, the ethnic consumer market in the United States would amount to at least 1.5 million. Taking into account the strong purchasing power of this population and the thriving ethnic economies, this market is potentially lucrative. Intraethnic competition for advertising and readers, viewers, and listeners is inevitable. The biggest challenge facing the Chinese-language media is to balance their professional and profit-oriented goals.

Yet the Chinese-language media face several constraints. First, subscription rates are low in the ethnic media market, and the media themselves are often free or inexpensive. This means that advertising sales to ethnic businesses generate most of the revenue. Since there are so many Chinese-language outlets available in the immigrant community, ethnic business owners can exercise pressure through the allocation of advertising, causing media outlets to pay more attention to advertisers than to readers. This business orientation and overdependence on ethnic businesses can reduce the outlets' incentive to enrich content coverage.

Second, most staff reporters are not professionally trained in the United States, and some of those who were professional journalists in their homelands are not proficient in English. In the former case, the quality of reporting may suffer; in the latter case, there may be problems with English-Chinese translation and production or selection of U.S. national and local news.

Third, regardless of professional training and experience, work in the ethnic media is a low-paid job. For example, my interviews with Chinese-language news reporters and producers indicated that full-time starting salaries were similar to those for low-end clerical jobs in the mainstream service sector, and much lower than those for mainstream media jobs. As a result, many ethnic reporters work several jobs to make a living. For example, it is not unusual to report for a Chinese-language media outlet while also working as an insurance or real estate agent in the ethnic enclave. Someone with a journalism degree who is proficient in both Chinese and English would naturally be attracted to mainstream media outlets, though he or she might use ethnic media as a stepping stone. Uncommitted or overloaded journalists may produce lower-quality work.

Fourth, reporters may face ethical challenges when potential advertisers request special treatment. Many Chinese media outlets run paid advertisements in the form of short articles (150–300 words) written by reporters; radio stations may broadcast short product-related interviews. This kind of paid advertisement is an important source of revenue for the outlet, but it suggests bias or favoritism on the part of individual reporters, threatening the outlet's credibility. Similarly, donations from homeland governments or political organizations may compromise the principles of impartiality and media independence.

These constraints undoubtedly impede the development of Chinese-language media and interfere with their effort to meet high professional standards while sustaining themselves. Such problems are inherent in the structure of the enclave economy and the dynamics of Chinese immigration. As the editor-in-chief of a Los Angeles–based weekly put it: "Ours is a small ethnic press. I never intend to make my paper comparable [to the] New York Times or Los Angeles Times, and I don't think anybody else in my business does. . . . For us, no Chinese businesses, no Chinese immigrants, no Chinese-language papers. Fierce internal competition has been what drives the quality of my paper. I guess it's a good thing."[57]

## Conclusion

In this overview of Chinese-language media and their impact on immigrant life in the United States, I have shown that these media have risen in sync with contemporary Chinese immigration and that their development has not only responded directly to broader changes in the Chinese American community but has also helped shape individual orientation and achievement goals in the new homeland. My descriptive analyses also suggest that Chinese-language media, while constituting a type of ethnic business, connect immigrants to the host society, providing them with a detailed map of their environment, promoting and reinforcing their mobility goals, and creating a cultural space in which they can enrich their lives. The ultimate question, however, is whether Chinese immigrants who are involved in this ethnic institution are being integrated into American life. The answer is both yes and no—yes, because they feel comfortable in their new home thanks to the rich cultural life enhanced by the Chinese-language media; and no, because some may never learn to speak English if they are comfortable depending exclusively on the ethnic media. What can we make of this paradox? If we took the assimilationist approach, we would expect the immigrant community and ethnic institutions to diminish in instrumental importance and eventually become obstacles to assimilation. Judged from a strictly assimilationist standpoint, the ethnic media are potentially harmful. Intentionally or unintentionally, they discourage immigrants from learning English and Western ways, stifle their incentive to make contact with members of the host society's dominant group and mainstream institutions, and trap them in permanent isolation. Indeed, there is evidence that Chinese immigrants are not mixing well with native-born American neighbors or co-workers, especially at the individual level.

From a multicultural approach, however, the picture is different. We have not seen strong evidence for permanent isolation. Non-English-speaking immigrants seem to be well informed about the mainstream host society. English-proficient and assimilated immigrants who have moved out of the enclaves and melted into the mainstream seem to return to the ethnic community in larger numbers and with greater frequency. Some of them are forming new ethnic organizations and are actively involved in them, and many subscribe to or turn to the ethnic media for information and entertainment, even when they have access to mainstream media.[58] The children of immigrants, young people who were born or raised in the United States and who have now attained college educations and well-paid jobs in the mainstream economy, are seen returning to ethnic enclaves or ethnoburbs to open up professional offices, and they turn to Chinese-language media to advertise their services. Some mainstream marketers, such as AT&T, Motorola, and Prudential, have started to seek out ethnic-language media to advertise their products, just as they use Spanish-language media.[59] In fact, a great deal of crossover is occurring between generations and between ethnic and mainstream businesses.

I thus reiterate my argument that ethnic-language media cannot simply be viewed as an ethnic institution isolated from the mainstream host society; rather, they are important facilitators of immigrant adaptation and integration. Even though Chinese-language media in the United States are largely a first-generation phenomenon and may gradually die out with decreasing immigration, their current growth continues to be strong and follows an upward trajectory. At present, more than two-thirds of Chinese immigrants in the United States speak Chinese at home, even among those who are proficient in English. And immigration to the United States has remained high in volume, sustaining a critical mass of ethnic clientele for Chinese-language media in the near future.

# 7

# Chinese Schools and the Ethnic System of Supplementary Education

C hinese schools have long been an integral part of the organizational structure of Chinatowns in the United States as well as in the Chinese Diaspora worldwide. In this chapter I examine how a particular type of ethnic organization generates resources conducive to educational success. By looking specifically into Chinese schools in Los Angeles' Chinese immigrant community, I also unfold an ethnic system of supplementary education that not only offers tangible academic support but also reinforces cultural norms pushing immigrant children to succeed in school.[1]

## Behind the Ethnic Success Story: Community Forces and Ethnic Social Environment

The 2000 U.S. Census shows that nearly three-quarters (73 percent) of U.S.-born Chinese Americans between ages 25 and 34 (and half of U.S.-born Asian Americans) have attained at least a bachelor's degree, compared with 15 percent of African Americans and 30 percent of non-Hispanic whites.[2] What is more striking is that children of low-income Chinese immigrants or refugees who live in inner-city Chinatowns and attend urban public schools in poor neighborhoods also show up, in disproportionately large numbers, as high school valedictorians or freshmen at prestigious colleges and universities.[3] In fact, the high educational achievement of Chinese Americans and other Asian Americans perpetuates the stereotype of the model minority.

## Behind the Success: Culture versus Structure

What is behind the ethnic success story is more complicated than the statistical data suggest. For a long time, educators and researchers have sought to explain the unequal educational outcomes of different ethnic minorities by focusing on either cultural factors, such as a group's traits, qualities, and behavioral patterns, or structural factors, such as its special historical experience of domination and subjugation, members' socioeconomic backgrounds, immigrant selectivity, labor market conditions, and residential patterns. For example, some studies have found that the residential segregation and social exclusion of the poor give rise to distinct values and norms that are at odds with those of mainstream society in regard to work, money, education, home, and family life. Sometimes exclusion provokes an oppositional collective social identity that entails a willful refusal of mainstream norms and values relating to school success.[4] This in turn leads to a set of self-defeating behavioral problems, such as labor force nonparticipation, out-of-wedlock births, welfare dependency, school failure, drug addiction, and chronic lawlessness.[5] Other studies, in contrast, have found that low-income families of racial/ethnic minorities tend to concentrate in poverty-stricken and unsafe inner-city neighborhoods. Parents who lack human capital (e.g., education, professional job skills, and English proficiency in the case of immigrants) have few options other than to send their children to dilapidated urban schools that have inadequate facilities and resources, poorly trained and inexperienced teachers, and large proportions of low-achieving students, thus putting their children at a much higher risk of school failure.[6] These explanations, however, largely overlook certain ethnic social settings that create resources conducive to education for coethnic group members to the exclusion of non-coethnic members who may share the same neighborhood and the same access to public education.

In my view, ethnicity cannot be simply viewed as a measure for either culture or structure. Rather, it encompasses values, norms, and behavioral patterns that are constantly interacting with both internal and external structural exigencies, such as group-specific contexts of exit and reception.[7] In American society, the concept of ethnicity is inherently interacted with social class status. That is, the educational experience of Chinese Americans in Los Angeles may not be the same as that of Mexican Americans in the same metropolis, because the children of these two ethnic groups grow up in different informal social settings. One particular type of setting is what I term the ethnic social environment.

What is in the ethnic social environment that affects education? We know that social class shapes both formal and informal social settings and has a powerful impact on children's educational experience and their future life chances.[8] Children of middle-class and upper-middle-class backgrounds have access to high-quality public schools in their neighborhoods or well-equipped private schools. These children are also exposed to informal social settings that support academic achievement. Highly educated and well-informed parents practice "concerted cultivation" in communities where positive and caring adult role models are next door and preschool education, afterschool tutoring, and extra-curricular activities are around the corner.[9] Children of low-income families, in contrast, live in homes and communities with fewer resources in terms of human, cultural, and social capital. They have to attend poor urban schools that are often understaffed and insufficiently funded. Their lived experiences in socioeconomi-cally disadvantaged cultural communities are usually not reflected in school cur-ricula, readers, textbooks, and other learning materials.[10] Furthermore, they are disproportionately tracked into low-ability and low-performing classes.[11] The disadvantages of their formal educational settings are exacerbated by disruptive informal social settings characterized by extreme poverty, high crime rates, social disorganization, and economic disinvestment.[12]

However, informal social settings are also mediated by race and ethnicity to reinforce or undercut class disadvantages.[13] Native-born African American par-ents, Latino immigrant parents, and Asian immigrant parents in low-income neighborhoods all stress the value of education for their children, and the chil-dren of these racial groups all agree that education is imperative in securing a good job.[14] Yet only the children of Asian immigrants as a group seem to have managed to actualize that value, showing higher rates of academic success than other minority groups.[15] It seems that what determines a child's learning and development is not merely social class, but also what John Ogbu and his associ-ates call "community forces," both of which affect informal social settings in ethnic-specific ways.[16]

According to Ogbu and his associates, community forces are the products of sociocultural adaptation embedded within a cultural community. They entail specific beliefs, interpretations, and coping strategies that a racial/ethnic group adopts in response to hostile societal treatment or social exclusion.[17] Ethnic minorities can turn their distinctive heritages into a kind of ethnic armor and establish a sense of collective dignity. This strategy enables them to cope psycho-logically, even in the face of discrimination and exclusion, or to accept and inter-nalize the socially imposed inferiority as part of their collective self-definition, and develop an "oppositional outlook" toward the dominant group and main-stream institutions, including education.[18]

## Cultural Values and Structural Supports for Educational Achievement

While education is generally considered a primary means to upward social mobility in all American families, its value is emphasized in some unique ways in the immigrant Chinese family. First and foremost, the children's educational success is very much tied to the honor of the traditional Chinese family as trans-planted to the new homeland. Education of the younger generation is high on the family agenda. Parents in China and Chinese immigrant parents in the United States often explicitly or implicitly remind their children that achievement is a duty and an obligation to the family rather than an individual goal, and that failure will bring shame to the family. This time-honored value, carried over to America, creates a community force that drives both children and parents in the area of education. Children are under pressure to excel at every step along the path to a good college education. Their success is not only bragged about by parents among relatives, friends, and coethnic co-workers; it is also featured in Chinese-language newspapers, club or organization newsletters, and even radio and television programs. Parents, for their part, are under pressure to facilitate their children's education, not just to honor the family and vindicate their own immigration-related sacrifices, but also to show the community that they are good parents.

Chinese immigrant parents take a pragmatic stance on education. They see it not as the most effective road to success in society, but as the *only* road.[19] They are keenly aware of their own limitations and the larger structural constraints: limited family wealth, even among middle-income immigrants; lack of access to social networks connected to the mainstream economy and social and political institutions; and entry barriers to certain occupations because of racial stereotyping and discrimination. Their own experience tells them that a good education in the right fields will guarantee their children good jobs in the future. These fields include science, math, engineering, and medicine, as well as business and, to a lesser extent, law. In practice, then, the parents are concerned more about their children's academic coursework, grades, majors, and college rankings than about a well-rounded learning experience. They would discourage their children's interest in history, literature, music, dance, sports, or anything that they consider unlikely to lead to well-paid, stable jobs, but they pressure their children to get involved in these academic fields and extracurricular activities to the extent that involvement might enhance the chance of getting into Ivy League colleges and other prestigious universities. Even though the children are often frustrated by their parents' insistence on choosing their educational path and making decisions for their future, many end up internalizing their parents' educational values.

Cultural values and norms are one thing; everyday practices and outcomes are quite another. How does the immigrant family ensure that norms are effective and values get actualized? In American society, the immigrant family alone cannot ensure that the children excel in school, even if that family has sufficient socioeconomic resources. U.S.-born or U.S.-raised children can fight back if they feel that their immigrant parents are imposing on them old-world norms and values that are at odds with those of the American mainstream. Yet the Chinese immigrant community possesses specific structural supports, in the form of nonprofit and for-profit institutions, to assist immigrants in actualizing educational values.

The social environments with which the children of Chinese immigrants are in daily contact may be understood through ethnic institutions in the immigrant community, including various economic, social, and cultural organizations, as well as the social networks arising from coethnic members' participation in them.

Therefore, an examination of specific ethnic institutions serving young children and youth can provide insight into how ethnicity interacts with social class to create an ethnic social environment fostering academic development for the second generation. In the next section I describe a growing ethnic system of supplementary education composed of Chinese schools and a range of for-profit ethnic institutions serving young children and youth in the Chinese immigrant community in Los Angeles.[20] My aim is not to explain the differences in educational outcomes between Chinese Americans and members of other ethnic groups, but rather to describe a particular type of ethnic social environment to which a successful group of immigrant children is routinely exposed. I try to find out why the children of Chinese immigrants, regardless of socioeconomic background, excel and succeed in the educational arena in disproportionately large numbers.

## Chinese Schools

Chinese schools (*zhongwen xuexiao*)—pillars of ethnic Chinese communities throughout the worldwide Chinese Diaspora—date back to the late 1880s in the United States, if not before.[21] Like other ethnic-language schools in immigrant German, Scandinavian, Jewish, and Japanese communities, Chinese schools initially aimed to preserve language and cultural heritage in the second and succeeding generations.[22] They were cultural institutions independent of the public school system and were often regarded as competing with it.[23] From the passage of the Chinese Exclusion Act to the outbreak of World War II, most Chinese immigrants were confined in Chinatowns, and so were Chinese schools. As I was repeatedly told when I was conducting my fieldwork in Chinatowns around the United States or during research visits to Chinatowns in Vancouver, Toronto, Kuala Lumpur, Singapore and elsewhere: "Wherever there is a visible Chinese enclave, there is at least one Chinese-language school."

### Early Development: The Era of Legal Exclusion

Chinese immigrants initially came to the United States from the southern region of China's Guangdong Province.[24] Many were young men leaving behind their parents, wives, and children in rural villages in search of a sojourner's dream—to make money and then return home. They helped develop the American West and built the most difficult part of the transcontinental railroad west of the Rockies, but ended up being targets of nativism and racism when their work was no longer needed. Poor economic conditions in the late 1870s exacerbated anti-Chinese agitation, leading to the passage in 1882 of the Chinese Exclusion Act, which was enforced until 1943.[25] Immigrant Chinese built Chinatowns and reorganized their sojourning lives within these socially isolated enclaves, not only on the west coast, but also in other major urban centers, such as New York and Chicago. Within Chinatown, levels of coethnic interaction and solidarity were high. Most worked in Chinese-owned businesses and socialized through family or kinship associations, hometown or district associations, and *tongs* or merchants' associations.[26]

During the Exclusion era, few women, families, or children were found in these bachelor societies. The sex ratio was nearly 27 males to 1 female in 1890, and 9 to 1 in 1910. Males still outnumbered females by more than 2 to 1 in the 1940s. The shortage of women combined with the continued illegal entry of young men stifled the formation of "normal" families and the natural reproduction of the ethnic population.[27] The size of the second generation was small, but the children of immigrants have been increasingly visible among the aging bachelors since the early 1930s.

This is the historical backdrop against which Chinese schools came into existence and gradually developed. The first Chinese school appeared in San Francisco's Chinatown in 1884 to provide a basic education for immigrant young men and the children of immigrants, keep their culture, customs, heritage, and language alive in the United State, and prepare young people eventually to return to China with their families.[28] These early schools were mostly private, financed primarily by tuition (four or five dollars a month) and donations from churches, temples, family associations, and Chinese businesses. Each school was governed by a board consisting mostly of elite members of ethnic organizations and businesses in Chinatown.[29] Typically there were one or two part-time teachers, instruction was in Cantonese, and classes were held daily for three to four hours in the evenings and on Saturday mornings, usually in the basement of a teacher's home or in a room inside a family association building. Teachers were not certified in any formal way, and their pedagogical approaches tended to emphasize cramming and rote memorization, which were popular teaching methods of the time in China. Prior to World War II, about a dozen Chinese schools in San Francisco's Chinatown served nearly 2,000 children and adolescents; there were four in Los Angeles' Chinatown, and at least one each in New York, San Diego, Chicago, Minneapolis, Washington, D.C., and New Orleans.[30]

There were also quasi-public Chinese schools financed directly by the Chinese government. The first, called *Da Qing Shu Yuan* ("College of the Qing Empire"), was established at the turn of the twentieth century in San Francisco's Chinatown. Starting with two classes held daily from 3 p.m. to 9 p.m. during the week and 9 a.m. to 9 p.m. on Saturdays, *Da Qing Shu Yuan* had an initial enrollment of about 60 students under the supervision of two teachers. Tuition was 50 cents a month, and the curriculum was formal and centered on the essential texts used to prepare students for the primary civil service exams in China: *The Great Learning, The Doctrine of the Mean, The Analects of Confucius,* and the writings of Mencius. Similar schools were later established in other major Chinatowns under the management of the Chinese Consolidated Benevolent Association (CCBA), the unofficial government of Chinatown.[31] In recent years these quasi-public Chinese schools have evolved into multifunctional cultural centers in Chinatowns with significant financial support from governments in mainland China and Taiwan.

Aimed primarily at making children proficient in the Chinese language and culture, these early Chinese schools were perceived by mainstream America as competing with public education and inhibiting assimilation. There was some truth to such perceptions. Under legal and social exclusion, Chinatown's children attended segregated public schools during regular school hours and spent many more hours after school, on weekends, and during summer vacations learning Chinese in ethnic schools. Immigrant parents believed that proficiency in the Chinese language was more practical than educational success in American schools, since their children's future options were limited to either returning to China or finding jobs in the ethnic enclave.[32] Parents also believed that a strong Chinese identity and ethnic pride, instilled through Chinese cultural and moral teachings, were necessary to help the children cope with racism and discrimination. Children attended Chinese schools in their neighborhoods after regular school as a matter of course. Even though most children lacked enthusiasm and interest, many, like their parents, recognized the practical value of Chinese schooling.[33] Few expected to find jobs in the mainstream economy commensurate with their levels of education. Like other ethnic organizations in Chinatown, these early Chinese schools had very little contact with mainstream institutions, and their curriculum was *not* complementary to public schooling. Past research (discussed below) noting the lack of effect or the significantly negative effect of Chinese schooling on the academic performance and physical and mental health of immigrant Chinese children seems to have missed the point: at that time public education and assimilation were irrelevant to the excluded Chinese.

## Post–World War II Developments

The repeal of the Chinese Exclusion Act in 1943 marked a new era for Chinese Americans. For the first time in history, immigrant Chinese and their offspring were legally allowed and encouraged to participate in American society. The founding in 1949 of the People's Republic of China (PRC) and subsequent political and economic sanctions against China further eroded the sojourners' dreams of returning to the homeland. These broader social and political changes in the United States and abroad had a powerful impact on the immigrant Chinese community, shifting its orientation from sojourning to putting down roots and reinforcing its commitment to socioeconomic integration. Meanwhile, the coming of age of a large second generation quietly altered the demographic makeup of the bachelor society, turning it more and more into a family-centered community. By 1960 the sex ratio had become more balanced (133 males to 100 females), and the U.S.-born outnumbered the foreign-born (61 versus 39 percent).

Between World War II and 1960, residential out-movements of the more affluent families and U.S.-born young adults grew into an irreversible trend. Chinatown-based Chinese schools suffered from stagnant growth and even decline as mainstream American society became more open to immigrant

Chinese families and their children and put greater pressure on them to assimilate. The children, especially adolescents, started to question the necessity of Chinese schooling and the practical value of Chinese-language proficiency. Public schools indirectly encouraged them to break away from the ethnic-language schools, on the rationale that such ethnic education placed too great a burden on their young minds and served to confuse and ultimately impede their social and intellectual development. Indeed, some studies designed according to this rationale found that students who attended ethnic-language school were more likely than non-attendees to show unfavorable outcomes such as sleepiness, eye strain, a lack of outdoor and leisure activities, low academic performance on standardized tests, a lack of leadership quality, and a double identity dilemma (feeling partly Chinese, partly American, but belonging to neither group).[34]

Other factors that caused Chinese schools to decline included the aging of the teachers, who were mostly non-English-speaking and slow to adjust to changes in the community, the rigidity of the curriculum and teaching methods, residential dispersion, and the opening of educational and vocational opportunities outside Chinatown. Thus, going to Chinese school became a burden on the child and a source of parent-child conflict. Children continued to attend Chinese schools because their parents made them, but most dropped out by the sixth grade. Parents were ambivalent: they wanted their children to learn English and excel in school, but many feared that they would lose them if they became too Americanized.

## The Post-1965 Revival

Contrary to the assimilationist prediction, the past 40 years have witnessed the revival and rapid growth of ethnic institutions in Chinatowns and new Chinese ethnoburbs. A significant turning point in the development of Chinese schools occurred in the late 1960s. Growth continued in the 1980s and peaked in the mid-1990s as a direct result of phenomenal levels of Chinese immigration. Post-1965 Chinese immigrants from China, Hong Kong, Taiwan, and other parts of the world are no longer uniformly poor, uneducated peasants from traditional sending villages. Many are cosmopolitan urbanites, college-educated professionals, skilled workers, and independent entrepreneurs. Upon arrival in the United States, a majority bypass Chinatown and settle in more affluent outer areas or suburbs in traditional gateway cities, or in the new multiethnic, immigrant-dominant suburban municipalities known as ethnoburbs.[35] Today, more than half of Chinese immigrants live in suburbs; Chinatowns have shrunk in relative numbers. For example, less than 3 percent of Los Angeles County's ethnic Chinese population lived in Chinatown as of 2000.

Openness in mainstream American society does not guarantee desirable outcomes of economic mobility and social integration. Decades of legal exclusion, social isolation, discrimination, and persistent racial stereotyping have left the Chinese with one feasible channel for upward social mobility: public education. Whereas children's education was never a survival issue in a society full of bachelors and sojourners, it has now become an urgent and central issue for the immigrant family and the entire ethnic group. As immigrant families and the ethnic community redefine their goals, the ethnic community and its social and cultural institutions are simultaneously transformed to meet new demands. Consequently, the past 30 years have witnessed the revival and rapid growth of child-centered ethnic institutions in Chinatowns and new Chinese ethnoburbs.

Contemporary Chinese schools have evolved to fill a much broader range of functions than instruction in language and culture, and they facilitate, rather than compete with, children's formal education.[36] The 1995 survey conducted by the National Council of Associations of Chinese Language Schools (NCACLS) counted a total of 634 registered Chinese schools in the United States (223 in California) with 5,542 teachers serving 82,675 K–12 students.[37] Even though the number of Chinese schools has not changed much in Los Angeles' Chinatown, the number in Chinese ethnoburbs in the San Gabriel Valley and other suburbs in the Los Angeles metropolitan area has increased exponentially.[38] In the summer of 2006, the Southern California Council of Chinese Schools listed 106 member schools, 7 in Los Angeles itself (3 in Chinatown) and 88 in Los Angeles suburbs.[39]

These "afterschools" offer ethnic-language instruction and elective classes such as Chinese geography and history, Chinese painting and calligraphy, Chinese and Western-style chess, crafts, cartooning, music and performing arts, computers, basketball and badminton, kung fu, lion and dragon dance, and Chinese cooking and cuisine. Some schools, particularly those in Chinatown and Chinese ethnoburbs, run classes seven days a week, from 3:00 to 6:30 p.m. on weekdays, with a half-day on weekends. The majority of the suburban schools operate on weekends, using space in local public schools or churches. Students usually spend two hours learning Chinese and one hour or more on regular schoolwork or electives. Many schools also offer academic tutoring, standardized test preparation (SAT, SAT-II, AP, etc.), math and science drill, and special training in speech, classical poetry reading, debate, and leadership. For example, Thousand Oaks Chinese School, founded in an affluent white suburb northwest of Los Angeles, started with just 8 students and one teacher in 1975; by 2005 it had 560 students and 50 teachers and offered 30 language classes and 20 enrichment or cultural classes, ranging from SAT preparation for the Chinese-language test and calculation with an abacus to calligraphy, dancing, and ping-pong.[40] Some Chinese schools are accredited institutions where students can gain extra credits in Chinese to fulfill the foreign-language requirement in their regular high schools. As nonprofit institutions, Chinese schools charge a nominal fee to offset operating expenses ($150–$450 per child per semester) and depend largely on parental volunteerism in fundraising and administration. Teachers are college-educated Chinese immigrants who may or may not have prior teaching experience or certification. They are recruited mainly through informal referrals within the ethnic network.

Each school has a parent volunteer association (PVA), which is similar to parent-teacher associations (PTA) in public schools, and parental involvement is highly expected. Suburban Chinese schools also organize activities for parents and other adults, giving parents the option to stay at the school instead of dropping off their children and returning later to pick them up. These parent-run activities include seminars on parenting, doing business, real estate and other financial investments, and family financial management; information sessions on helping children select Advanced Placement courses, prepare for standardized tests, and apply for colleges and college financial aid; and leisure classes, such as t'ai chi chuan, chorus singing, and folk dancing. Chinese schools in the United States at any given time enroll only about 10 to 25 percent of the school-age children (5–14 years old) of Chinese ancestry.[41] However, most of the children of Chinese immigrants have been to a Chinese school or a Chinese-language class at some point. "Going to Chinese school" is a common Chinese American experience.

## Changing Functions

Contemporary Chinese schools, both in and out of Chinatown, differ in several ways from those founded prior to World War II. First, their chief goal is to assist immigrant families in their efforts to push their children to excel in American public schools, get into prestigious colleges and universities, and eventually attain well-paid, high-status professions that secure a decent living in the United States. This effort reflects in part the traditional pragmatism of Chinese immigrant families, only this time it is U.S.-centered rather than China-centered. Parents are enthusiastic about sending their children to Chinese schools, but not because they think that Chinese is the only thing that is important. Rather, many parents are dissatisfied with American public schools and believe that Chinese schools and other ethnic supplementary education institutions will ensure that their children meet parental expectations.

Second, where traditional Chinese schools were relatively homogeneous and rigid in institutional form and governance, today's schools have become more diverse and flexible. Nonprofit schools may be sponsored by a church or temple or by a community or family association; some are independent. For-profits are independent enterprises functioning in the same way as other ethnic businesses. Most schools in Chinatowns or Chinese ethnoburbs offer regular afterschool, weekend, and summer programs (including overseas camps), as well as day-camp programs during spring and Christmas breaks. This scheduling accommodates the needs of dual-worker families living in the ethnic community. Other suburban Chinese schools are mostly half-day Saturday or Sunday schools, since families in non-coethnic neighborhoods tend to be more dispersed.

Schools are financed mainly by student tuition, but nonprofits are supported by donations and community fundraising as well. Nonprofits charge nominal fees. For-profit tuition varies greatly depending on the ownership of the school, the type of program, the number of students enrolled, and the students' family incomes. The fee for a typical afterschool or weekend program serving low-income families ranges from $70 to $250 per 10- to 17-week semester, but fees for some private tutoring programs can be as high as $400 weekly. Special programs charge extra fees. Private lessons cost $10–$50 per hour. Each school has a principal, a part-time staff, and teachers. It is governed by a board consisting of parents, teachers, ethnic business owners, and community leaders. Nonprofits rely heavily on parent volunteers who act as teacher aides, chauffeurs for the schools' pickup and dropoff services, fundraisers, and even janitors. Many Chinese schools have PVAs modeled after the PTAs in public schools. Such parental voluntarism is evident even in for-profits, but for-profits do not have PVAs. Parental involvement is direct and intense in Chinese school, but minimal in public schools because of language and cultural barriers.

Third, unlike traditional schools, where Chinese language and culture were at the core of the curriculum, today's Chinese schools have shifted to a more comprehensive, well-rounded curriculum geared to the requirements of public education and college admission. In fact, the Chinese classics have almost disappeared, and language teaching no longer takes priority. (I have observed that teachers, staff members, and even parents habitually use a mixture of English and Chinese to communicate with the children.) Instead, schools now offer a variety of academic and tutoring programs and *buxiban* (afterschool tutoring class) in such subjects as English (including English as a Second Language), social studies, math and science, and SAT prep, as well as the varied extracurricular programs listed above. Some Chinese schools have excellent Chinese-language programs (mostly in Mandarin) that aim to give students high school foreign-language credits from the formal education system and good scores on the SAT-II Chinese-language test.

Fourth, the focus on moral teaching and passing on cultural heritage is more subtle in today's Chinese schools. These institutions provide a cultural environment where the children are surrounded by other Chinese people, as well as by Chinese-language books and Chinese cultural artifacts, and are thus under external pressure to feel and act Chinese. Teachers reinforce the values of filial piety, respect for authority, hard work, and discipline. During traditional Chinese holiday seasons, such as the Chinese New Year, the spring Dragon Festival, and the Mid-Autumn Moon Festival, Chinese schools participate in celebratory parades, evening shows, and other community events, such as sports and choral or dance festivals. Participation in these cultural activities not only exposes children to their cultural heritage, reaffirming their ethnic identity, but also provides opportunities for the children to work closely with their parents and other adults in the community on common projects.

## For-Profit Institutions: Afterschool Tutoring, Academic Drill, College Preparation, and Enrichment

A relatively recent development has been the rapid growth since the late 1980s of for-profit ethnic afterschool institutions. Geared solely to promote educational achievement and college admissions, these institutions include *buxiban* and *kumon*,[42] academic cram schools, college prep centers, and enrichment programs, as well as early childhood intellectual development programs. The *2005 Southern California Chinese Consumer Yellow Pages* listed 135 academic afterschool tutoring establishments, including *buxiban* and *kumon*, 50 art schools/ centers, 90 music/dance studios, and 14 daycare centers and preschools. Hundreds of afterschools held in private homes are not listed in phone directories. Many are run by stay-at-home mothers who take care of three to five children of the same ages as their own children; they can be found through the advertisement sections of nationally circulated or local Chinese-language newspapers.

Private afterschools have been incorporated into the region's burgeoning Chinese enclave economy.[43] Like other Chinese ethnic businesses, they concentrate in Chinatown and Chinese ethnoburbs in Los Angeles' San Gabriel Valley. They vary in scale, specialty, quality, and formality. Some are transnational enterprises with headquarters or branches in Taiwan and mainland China, offering highly specialized curricula and formal structures. At the other end of the scale are less formal one-person or mom-and-pop operations. Some of these private institutions offer comprehensive academic programs, as Chinese schools do; others tend to be highly specialized and have concrete objectives that are often more academically than linguistically oriented, even though some of the instruction or tutoring may be bilingual. For example, many private institutions offer English, math, chemistry, and physics tutoring and intensive drilling courses that aim solely to help children perform better in formal schools. Thus, their core curricula are supplementary to, rather than competing with, those of the public schools. These for-profit programs are sometimes embedded in nonprofit Chinese schools as well as in other ethnic organizations serving immigrants, such as family, kin, and district associations and churches. As in nonprofit Chinese schools, teachers may or may not have prior teaching experience and are recruited through informal coethnic networks. For some specialized programs, such as SAT tutoring and coaching in English skills, these institutions prefer to recruit non-Chinese certified teachers from mainstream schools. Programs with such teachers tend to be the most expensive. Unlike the nonprofits, for-profit institutions often do not require parental involvement and do not have programs for parents. However, parents do have an opportunity to become acquainted with one another during brief dropoff or pickup times.

Students enrolled in ethnic afterschools are almost exclusively from Chinese immigrant families of varied socioeconomic backgrounds. Daily programs tend to draw students who live nearby, while weekend programs draw students from both the local community and elsewhere in greater Los Angeles. Driving through the commercial corridor of Monterey Park, Alhambra, and San Gabriel, the growing Chinese ethnoburbs east of Los Angeles, one can easily see the flashy bilingual signs of these establishments: "Little Harvard," "Ivy League School," "Stanford-to-Be Prep School," "IQ180," "Hope Buxiban," "Little Ph.D. Early Learning Center" (a preschool), and "Brain Child" (a daycare center).

Major Chinese-language newspapers, such as the *Chinese Daily News, Sing Tao Daily,* and *China Press,* publish weekly education editions with success stories, educational news and commentaries, and relevant information, such as standardized test schedules, high school and college rankings, and application deadlines for major schools, programs, and tests. For-profit institutions advertise in these newspapers.[44] Chinese-language advertisements are targeted more to the parent than to the child, promising to "bring out the best in *your* child," "turn *your* child into a well-rounded superstar," and "escort your child into *your* dream school" (emphasis added); other ads offer to "improve your test scores by 100 points" and "open the door to UC admission." Many youths whom I interviewed agreed that going to a Chinese school or a Chinese-run *buxiban* or *kumon* program had been a shared experience as Chinese Americans, even though they generally disliked being made to attend them.[45] As the ethnic system of supplementary education takes root in the Chinese immigrant community, the children of Chinese immigrants are drawn by community forces into an ethnic social environment with ample resources devoted to the mission of ensuring that "every student is a success."

## Intangible Benefits, Costs, and Tradeoffs

So far, the findings about the ethnic system of supplementary education support my argument that community forces must arise from and be supported by the institutions of an ethnic community. "Community forces" consist of a common cultural heritage along with a set of shared values, beliefs, behavioral standards, and coping strategies with which members of a cultural community are generally identified. Thus, the ethnic community should not be understood simply as a neighborhood where a particular ethnic group's members and/or businesses concentrate, or as a geographically unbounded racial or ethnic identity in the abstract. Rather, it contains various ethnic institutions, such as ethnic businesses, sociocultural organizations, and interpersonal networks established, operated, and maintained by group members. Because community forces dictate the orientation, coping strategies, and corresponding behaviors of different ethnic groups in regard to mobility goals and means of achieving them, the different social environments created and regulated by these forces are likely to facilitate or hinder educational achievement and other long-term mobility goals independent of social class.[46]

The supplementary education system has intangible benefits, too. Nonprofit and for-profit ethnic institutions do not merely provide educationally relevant services supplementing public education; they also serve as a locus of social support and control, network building, and social capital formation.

First, the ethnic system of supplementary education provides an important physical site where formerly unrelated immigrants (and parents) come to socialize and rebuild social ties. Reconnecting with coethnics often helps ease the psychological and social isolation associated with uprooting. Even though parental interaction occurs mostly at dropoff and pickup times or in parent-run activities, these moments are important for the formation of coethnic ties. Moreover, coethnic ties help connect immigrants to the mainstream society, rather than isolating them from it, by making their social life richer and more comfortable.

Second, the ethnic system of supplementary education serves as an intermediate ground between the immigrant home and the American school, helping immigrant parents—especially those who do not speak English well—learn how to navigate the American education system and make it serve their children, even when they are unable to get involved personally in public schools and their PTAs. Through these ethnic institutions, immigrant parents are indirectly but effectively connected to formal schools and become informed about specific factors crucial to their children's educational success. They can exchange valuable information about child rearing and share success stories or lessons learned from failure. Such coethnic interaction reaffirms the educational goals of the immigrant family while putting pressure on, and even creating competition among, parents. In other words, these ethnic institutions carve out a place for parental involvement, which nurtures social capital conducive to educational achievement.

Third, the ethnic system of supplementary education fosters a sense of civic duty in immigrants who are often criticized for their lack of civic participation in mainstream U.S. society. In nonprofit institutions, many parents volunteer their time and energy while also taking the initiative in organizing community events such as ethnic and American holiday celebrations. Immigrants gain valuable experience from their involvement in ethnic institutions, which often motivates them to participate in community affairs beyond ethnic boundaries.

The intangible benefits for children are also multifold. First, Chinese schools and other relevant child-centered or youth-oriented ethnic institutions offer an alternative space where children can express and share their feelings about growing up in immigrant Chinese families. A Chinese schoolteacher I interviewed said:

> It is very important to allow youths to express themselves in their own terms without any parental pressures. Chinese parents usually have very high expectations of their children. When children find it difficult to meet these expectations and do not have an outlet for their frustration and anxiety, they tend to become alienated and lost on the streets. But when they are around others who have similar experiences, they are more likely to let out their feelings and come to terms with their current situation.[47]

Second, these ethnic institutions provide unique opportunities for immigrant children to form different peer networks, giving them greater leverage in negotiating parent-child relations at home. In immigrant families, parents are usually more comfortable and less strict with their children when they hang out with coethnic friends—they either know the friends' parents or feel that they can communicate with coethnic parents if things should go wrong. Children can use their coethnic friendship network as a bargaining chip or screen to avoid conflict with parents. A Chinese girl may simply tell her mother that she will be studying with so-and-so from Chinese school (whose parents are family friends), while actually spending time with her non-Chinese boyfriend.

Third, these ethnic institutions nurture an ethnic identity and pride that might otherwise be rejected because of the pressure to assimilate. In ethnic-language schools and other ethnic school settings, children are exposed to something quite different from what they learn in their formal schools. For example, they read classical folk stories and Confucian sayings about family values, behavioral and moral guidelines, and the importance of schooling. Ethnic folk songs reveal different aspects of their cultural heritage. Such cultural exposure reinforces family values and heightens a sense of ethnic identity, helping children to relate to their parents' or their ancestor's "stuff" without feeling embarrassed. More importantly, being part of this particular ethnic environment helps alleviate the bicultural conflicts that are rampant in many immigrant families. Many children we interviewed, especially the older ones, reported that they did not like being made to go to these ethnic institutions and do extra work but that they reluctantly did so without rebelling because other coethnic children were doing the same. As the sociologist Betty Lee Sung observed in her study of immigrant children in New York City's Chinatown, bicultural conflicts are

> moderated to a large degree because there are other Chinese children around to mitigate the dilemmas that they encounter. When they are among their own, the Chinese ways are better known and better accepted. The Chinese customs and traditions are not denigrated to the degree that they would be if the immigrant child was the only one to face the conflict on his or her own.[48]

However, the ethnic effect is by no means uniformly positive. Overemphasis on educational achievement has costs. Tremendous pressure on both children and parents for school achievement can lead to intense intergenerational conflict, rebellious behavior, alienation from the networks that are supposed to assist them, and even withdrawal from formal education. Alienated children easily fall prey to street gangs and are also vulnerable to suicide. Ironically, in a resourceful ethnic environment, pressures and conflicts can also advance parental expectations. Children are motivated to do well in school because they believe that education is the only way to escape their parents' control. This motivation, arising from parental pressure and reinforced through participation in ethnic institutions, often leads to desirable outcomes.

What are the tradeoffs? Chinese immigrants perceive education as the only feasible means of social mobility that will yield observable returns. They tend to be extremely pragmatic and realistic about what to do and what not to do. Not only parents but also children are expected to make sacrifices. The organizer of a nonprofit program summed up the tradeoff in these words:

> Well, tremendous pressures create problems for sure. However, you've got to realize that we are not living in an ideal environment. Without these pressures, you would probably see as much adolescent rebellion in the family, but a much *larger* [emphasis in tone] proportion of kids failing. Our goal is to get these kids out into college, and for that, we have been very successful.[49]

For the majority, the expected outcomes seem well worth the sacrifice. But for a small minority, outcomes such as depression, running away, and even suicide can be devastating to families. It should also be noted that the ethnic system of supplementary education is less accessible to working-class families than to middle-class ones. Although nonprofit and for-profit afterschool programs have varied price tags and are thus affordable for most families, high-quality academic and specialized enrichment programs tend to be more expensive. Many high-quality private *buxiban,* college prep schools, music and dance lessons, and other rivals to mainstream institutions such as the Princeton Review and Kaplan are extremely expensive. A high demand for afterschool services from immigrant parents with above-average socioeconomic status (SES) and high rates of self-employment in the immigrant community stimulates new business opportunities. Prospective coethnic entrepreneurs aim at serving not only middle-class but also working-class immigrant families. When working-class families are exposed to an informal setting where education is seen as a basic need, they are under pressure to provide for their children's education in the same way they provide food and clothing.

## Conclusion: Lessons from the Immigrant Chinese Experience

The chapter addresses the question of whether it is culture or structure that promotes the educational achievement of immigrant children. Existing quantitative data and anecdotal evidence show that the children of Chinese immigrants, even those coming from poor families and attending inadequate inner-city schools, are doing exceptionally well in school, and that they fare better than other native-born racial groups, including whites. One explanation for their success leans on the cultural influence of Confucianism, while the other focuses on immigrant selectivity. This case study of the ethnic system of supplementary education in the Chinese immigrant community shows that culture and structure intersect to create an ethnic social environment promoting school success.

The Chinese case is unique in several significant ways, each pointing to culture-structure interaction.[50] First, the high value Confucianism places on education has been adapted to contemporary mobility aspirations and expectations to affect educational practices in China and among immigrant Chinese families in the United States. In present-day China, a good college education is viewed as the single most important means to upward social mobility. Many families, urban families in particular, are doing everything possible and necessary to ensure that their children eventually get into prestigious universities. Since the best educational opportunities are relatively scarce, aspiring college-bound students must compete with one another through the annual national college entrance examination. Often students have only one chance to take this exam; as a popular saying warns, "*One* exam determines a child's future." Consequently, a family's educational drive is geared almost entirely toward academic outcomes, neglecting the subtleties and intricacies of a child's learning process, often at the expense of his or her well-rounded development. Meanwhile, a wide range of private *buxiban,* exam cram schools, enrichment programs, and English-language programs emerge to fill the growing demand, serving preschoolers and elementary and high school students. Some preschools for two- to five-year-olds are staffed with foreign experts and have rigorous academic curricula, including math, Chinese, English, music, and dance. These homeland practices and after-school institutions are believed to be effective and thus are transferred to America as Chinese immigrants strive to push their children to success in school.

Second, two factors combine to boost the growth of the ethnic system of supplementary education in the Chinese immigrant community: immigrant selectivity and structural barriers. Immigrant selectivity means that some immigrant parents can call on a tremendous amount of human capital and financial resources. At the same time, structural barriers deter many highly educated and economically resourceful immigrants from finding jobs commensurate with their education and skills in the mainstream American economy. As the demand for educational services grows among Chinese immigrant families, nonprofit and for-profit institutions owned and run by immigrants emerge to form an ethnic system of supplementary education. Once that system takes root, it stimulates new demands for more and better services, leading to the rise of an ethnic social environment in which educational values are reaffirmed and tangible resources conducive to school success are easily accessible.

Third, the visibility of a coethnic middle class in the Chinese immigrant community provides role models as well as opportunities for coethnic interaction across class lines. Unlike traditional immigrant enclaves that concentrate new arrivals of low-SES backgrounds and native racial/ethnic minorities, contemporary Chinese immigrant communities tend to grow in suburbs (or ethnoburbs) and comprise immigrants of varied SES backgrounds. Even in inner-city Chinatowns where poor and low-SES immigrant families are clustered, there is a significant presence of coethnic middle-class members who go there on a regular basis to work, do business, shop or entertain, and participate in various activities sponsored by ethnic institutions. The coethnic middle class serves two main functions. On the one hand, the sheer presence of a disproportionately large number of highly educated professionals, particularly those who have been incorporated into the mainstream American economy, provides role models who show that education pays off. On the other hand, the return to the ethnic enclave of middle-class coethnics who are residentially assimilated to the mainstream provides opportunities for cross-class interaction. Social ties formed from coethnic interaction tend to transcend class boundaries and become instrumental bridges, heightening the significance of Bourdieu's conception of social capital.[51] That is, social capital consists not only of the products of embedded social networks or relationships, but also of the processes that reproduce access (or lack of access) to power and resources.

Several lessons may be drawn from the Chinese American experience. First, it suggests that informal social settings are as important as, if not more important than, formal social settings such as schools in affecting children's educational achievement. Within the Chinese immigrant community, a well-established Chinese system of supplementary education makes available and accessible resources that promote and actualize the ethnic community's educational values. However, this system lacks institutional mechanisms to deal with intergenerational conflicts, mental stress, depression, and excessive peer pressure resulting from unhealthy competition. There is also a lack of interconnectedness between these ethnic educational institutions and other nonprofit social service organizations in the community. Moreover, ethnic resources and social capital may be effective only up to a point. That is, they may ensure that immigrant children graduate from high school and get into prestigious colleges, but beyond high school these ethnic resources may become constraining. For example, many children of Chinese immigrants tend to concentrate in science and engineering, not only because their families want them to do so but also because their coethnic friends are doing so. After graduating from college, they often lack the social networks that facilitate job placement and occupational mobility. In these respects, there is much room for improvement in the existing ethnic system of supplementary education.

Second, the ethnic Chinese system of supplementary education is not easily transferable to other ethnic or immigrant minority groups because of variations in immigration histories, group-level socioeconomic characteristics, patterns of incorporation and community organization, and host society reception. Although it is unrealistic to expect other racial minority groups to copy this system, it may be possible to open up ethnic resources through greater interethnic cooperation and public assistance. For example, nonprofit interethnic organizations can help make educationally relevant afterschool services provided by ethnic Chinese (particularly for-profit services) available to other Asian and Latino immigrants who share the same locales. The state could also provide financial assistance to enable families to access private afterschool services.

Third, ethnic entrepreneurship in the area of education may offer an alternative to publicly funded afterschool programs. As the Chinese case shows, nonprofit and for-profit organizations can work together to foster social settings conducive to education. The state should continue to improve existing public afterschool programs while also providing incentives to potential entrepreneurs to develop private afterschools and other education-related programs (such as tutoring, music, sports, etc.), especially in disadvantaged neighborhoods.

In summary, the Chinese ethnic system of supplementary education may not be a direct cause of the extraordinary educational achievement of the children of Chinese immigrants, but it creates a unique social setting in which education-ally relevant resources are both available and accessible. This kind of community-based social setting is not necessarily intrinsic to a specific culture of origin. Rather, it results from the interaction of culture and structure, which is unique to a national-origin group's pre-migration SES, the strength of a pre-existing ethnic community, and the host society's reception. Most immigrant families, Chinese and non-Chinese alike, place a high value on education and consider it the most important path to upward social mobility, but value cannot be actual-ized without the support of the family *and* the ethnic community. The ability of the family and the ethnic community to influence children varies by national origin and generation. National-origin groups that include a significant middle-class component with valuable resources (i.e., education, job skills, and financial assets) upon arrival in the United States have a leg up in the race for success in their new homeland, while those lacking group resources trail behind. Educators and policymakers should be careful not to attribute school success or failure merely to culture or structure alone; the culture-structure interaction is the key.

# IV

# The Family
# and the New
# Second Generation

# 8

# The Other Half of the Sky

*Immigrant Women in Chinatown's Enclave Economy*

"Women hold up half of the sky." This saying accurately describes the role of women in the enclave economy in New York City's Chinatown. Most often than not, when people think of Chinese laborers in the United States, they imagine railroad workers, miners, hand laundrymen, or restaurant waiters and cooks. Women were seldom seen in the old Chinatowns, and past studies of Chinese immigration and adaptation to life in the United States often overlooked women, even as they began to arrive in large numbers after the passage of the Hart-Celler Act of 1965. There was scant recognition that the experience of immigrant women may be different from that of men and that male patterns of socioeconomic adaptation are not necessarily applicable to women.

In New York City's Chinatown in the 1980s, three out of five women worked in the garment industry, the backbone of the growing enclave economy. Most of these working women were new immigrants, married, with school-age and younger children. Day in and day out, row after row, they bent over sewing machines, surrounded by piles of fabric scraps, and sometimes with toddlers and infants at their feet.[1] On the home front, they were expected to attend to the needs of their children and husbands (and parents or in-laws, or both), as well as the household chores: cooking, cleaning, laundry, grocery shopping, paying bills, and so on.

In this chapter I examine how Chinese immigrant women in New York City's Chinatown juggle multiple roles as wives, mothers, and wage workers and how their labor in both home and workplace contributes to the survival of their immigrant families.

## An Alternative Framework for Analysis

To examine work and its place in the lives of Chinese immigrant women in the ethnic enclave, I develop an analytical framework to argue that immigrant women's work is an intrinsic part of a family strategy to survive and eventually adapt to the host society. However, the adoption of such a strategy depends on specific sociocultural contexts—those from which immigrant women came and those into which they resettled in the United States. My task is to demonstrate that the meaning of women's work varies under unique sociocultural circumstances. I aim to reconcile seemingly contradictory elements in the lived experience of immigrant women and to shed light on how cultural components interact with economic factors to affect immigrant adaptation to American society.

First, I analytically distinguish two dimensions of work involved in women's labor force participation: survival and career attainment. Each contains a different set of goals and strategies. Survival entails getting settled and securing from an unfamiliar and often hostile environment the essential means of livelihood. Career attainment involves the socialization of women into the normative structure of an economy traditionally dominated by men, occupational mobility equal to that of men, and economic independence from men.[2] Oftentimes, newly arrived immigrants are busy working in order to put food on the table and make ends meet. Some segments of the immigrant population may quickly bypass the mere survival stage because they bring with them strong human capital and economic resources.[3] However, a disproportionate number have first to secure food, clothing, and shelter in order to proceed to their American dream. The survival strategies of many immigrant families entail not only male employment but also the economic participation of women in paid work. Therefore, the work of immigrant women may not be secondary; rather, it may be a necessary part of the struggle for survival.

Second, I analytically distinguish immigrant workers from native workers. The reason is straightforward. Immigrant workers are often treated differently in the labor market, viewed as aliens threatening the job security and labor rights of native workers, especially in times of economic distress.[4] Historically and routinely, immigrants have been excluded as "the indispensable enemy" from the working class of the host society.[5] A 1992 Business Week poll revealed that more than 60 percent of U.S. residents interviewed believed that new immigrants took jobs away from native workers and drove wages down.[6] Even descendants of immigrants who were born in the United States and have been fully assimilated may be disadvantaged merely because they look like the foreigners "flooding the country" at a given time.[7]

Some disadvantages are associated with immigration itself. Many newcomers lack the English-language ability, economic resources, transferable skills, and legal protection that would allow them to compete on equal terms with native workers. Because of their foreign status, they lack political clout to fight for labor rights and social equality. They tend to distance themselves from the politics of

American labor and to focus on their own struggle for survival. Thus, they appear willing to take "bad" or "abandoned" jobs or accept substandard wages. "Willing," however, is misleading. Immigrants are not cheap labor by nature. Rather, they see low-wage jobs as the best option to meet their survival needs and facilitate social mobility.

Third, I analytically distinguish between the capital-labor relationship in the context of the larger political economy of capitalism and the worker-employer relationship in an enclave economy. From the neo-Marxist approach, the relationship between labor and capital is inherently one of conflict. The employer represents capital, which exploits labor—the worker. Capital extracts surplus value from labor, establishes its dominance over labor, and consolidates its privileges by politically suppressing the entire working class. But this line of argument does not hold up well within the context of an enclave economy. In the ethnic enclave, entrepreneurs enter self-employment as an alternative to low-wage menial work or unemployment. Many ethnic business owners are subcontractors with little power in the larger political economy of capitalism. Some routinely work in their own factories or shops—often putting in longer hours than their employees. Moreover, they depend on the availability of reliable family labor and an ethnic labor force whose levels of human capital and English language proficiency are lower than the minimum requirements for entry into the larger labor market.[8]

From the point of view of coethnic workers, the ethnic enclave offers job opportunities as well as other material and symbolic compensations—such as a familiar cultural environment in which workers can interact in their own language, flexible work hours, and training—that escape a gross accounting of benefits based exclusively on wages. More importantly, a common cultural heritage creates an unusual bond between employers and workers, making for a more personalized work environment than the highly alienating conditions prevalent in comparable employment in the larger secondary economy.[9] Therefore, the close association between class status and ethnicity within a unique cultural context opens an alternative path to social mobility, one that effectively gives immigrant workers a detour around immigrant disadvantages and racial discrimination. In the pages that follow, I apply this analytical framework to a case study of garment workers in New York City's Chinatown.

## Chinatown's Garment Workers: An Illustrative Case

### The Impact of Female Immigration on Chinatown's Garment Industry

New York City's garment industry has been an immigrant trade since the early 1800s. The earliest garment workers were German and Irish immigrants, followed by Polish, Russian, and other eastern European Jews, and Italians.[10] The garment industry grew because of the availability of a large pool of low-wage and mostly female immigrant labor. After World War II, however, New York City lost its predominant place in garment manufacturing because of standardization for economies of scale and the internationalization of capital and labor. A small portion of the industry remains there, thanks to fluctuating demand for non-standardized and quickly changing fashion, which has created a niche for small garment shops. Where growth exists in New York City's garment industry, it continues to be predicated on low-cost immigrant labor. Between 1975 and 1980, the number of Chinese-owned garment factories grew by an average of 36 a year, reaching a peak of 430 in 1980. In 1980, Chinatown contained one-third of all the jobs in Manhattan's women's outerwear industry.[11]

One of the most important factors in the growth of Chinatown's garment industry in the 1980s was the surge of female Chinese immigrants. During the period of Chinese exclusion in the late nineteenth century and the first half of the twentieth, few Chinese women were allowed to enter the United States, even to join their families.[12] Reflecting earlier migration patterns, New York's Chinatown was a bachelor society for the greater part of the twentieth century. In the 1940s, there were six times as many Chinese men as women in New York. Even after the passage of the War Brides Act in 1945, which allowed Chinese women to join their husbands in the United States, Chinese men still outnumbered women by nearly 300 percent in New York City.[13] It was not until after 1965, when the Hart-Celler Act went into effect and U.S. immigration policies were revised to favor family reunification, that Chinese women entered New York in large numbers. By 1970 the sex ratio for its Chinese population had decreased to 117 men per 100 women; a decade later the ratio was 106 men per 100 women; and as of 2000 women outnumbered men by one percent.[14]

Contemporary Chinese America is shaped by a predominant pattern of family migration. Prior to 1978, China was closed off to the outside world and emigration was restricted by the Chinese government even after the relaxation of U.S. immigration policies. Immigrants from mainland China did not fully utilize their annual quotas until the mid-1980s, after which the total number of immigrants admitted as permanent residents from China and Taiwan has exceeded the annual quota, indicating that many have arrived as nonquota immigrants (i.e., immediate family members of U.S. citizens).[15] In 1980, family unification was responsible for 85 percent of all Chinese immigration.[16] According to official immigration statistics, Chinese women have outnumbered men entering the United States every year since the mid-1970s. The majority (around 65 percent) of the women are of working age (20–59).[17]

The arrival of Chinese women has dramatically altered the social fabric of New York City's Chinatown, transforming a bachelor society into a community bustling with young families. As of 1980, more than 80 percent of the Chinese households in New York City were family households, and 87 percent of the Chinese families were married-couple families (10 percent higher than the average for New York).

Further, the large-scale immigration of women has stimulated economic development in two ways. The sheer numbers of immigrants and the shift to a family-centered community have expanded the market for Chinese goods and services inaccessible in the larger society, creating opportunities for ethnic entrepreneurship in the food industry, restaurant business, beauty salons, and elsewhere. At the same time, the availability of a large pool of low-skilled female labor at a critical time in the city's overall economic restructuring has promoted the rapid growth of informal or subcontracted operations in New York City's garment industry.[18]

The concentration of Chinese immigrant women in that industry is extraordinary: while over half of all Chinese working women aged 16 to 64 in New York City were garment workers, 85 percent of the work force in the garment industry in Chinatown were immigrant women.[19] In 1983, 70 percent of garments produced in New York City were sewn by Chinese immigrant women.[20]

## Chinese Immigrant Women in New York City

The 1980 census revealed similarities and differences between foreign- and U.S.-born Chinese women and non-Hispanic white women (Table 8.1). In terms of family situation, foreign-born Chinese women showed some demographic characteristics similar to those of their U.S.-born counterparts and white women in general, except that they had a lower rate of divorce or separation and were more likely to live with school-age children. However, they also showed a severe lack of human capital: the lowest-level of educational attainment and the poorest English-language ability. Less than half of them had finished high school, and only 42 percent of them reported speaking English well.

These women came from a patriarchal tradition that treated females as temporary members of their birth families and regarded women with little education as virtuous. A 58-year-old immigrant from Taiwan explained to me in an interview that she had no schooling at all because it wasn't considered appropriate for girls. Her brothers, however, went to school and received additional tutoring at home.[21] Despite their lack of human capital, Chinese immigrant women displayed a particularly low rate of labor force nonparticipation. To put it another way, their labor force participation (LFP) rate was 73 percent, 24 percentage points higher than that of foreign-born white women and 15 points higher than that of U.S.-born white women. Over 40 percent of Chinese immigrant women in New York City were employed in the garment industry, suggesting that Chinatown indeed provided job opportunities for immigrant women who would have had a hard time finding work in the larger economy because of their deficiencies in education, work experience, and English-language proficiency.

Table 8.2 presents demographic characteristics of working women by industrial sectors as of 1980. Chinese garment workers were generally younger than white garment workers but older than workers in other industries. Compared

TABLE 8.1    MAJOR CHARACTERISTICS OF WOMEN AGED 16–64 FROM FAMILY
HOUSEHOLDS IN NEW YORK CITY BY RACE AND PLACE OF BIRTH, 1980

| Characteristics | Chinese | | Non-Hispanic White | |
|---|---|---|---|---|
| | Foreign-Born | U.S.-Born | Foreign-Born | U.S.-Born |
| Median age | 39.0 | 30.0 | 40.0 | 41.0 |
| Marital status | | | | |
| % Currently married | 85.0 | 69.2 | 87.2 | 73.3 |
| % Divorced or separated | 1.5 | 2.5 | 4.2 | 7.5 |
| % Single or widowed | 15.5 | 28.3 | 8.6 | 19.2 |
| Household types | | | | |
| % Married-couple families | 90.5 | 88.0 | 90.0 | 82.5 |
| % Female-headed families | 9.1 | 11.1 | 9.5 | 16.7 |
| Relationship to household head | | | | |
| % As household heads | 10.6 | 11.1 | 17.8 | 11.2 |
| % As spouses | 80.0 | 61.5 | 82.7 | 67.7 |
| % As children | 9.5 | 27.4 | 5.5 | 15.1 |
| Presence of children | | | | |
| % With own children aged under 6 | 21.8 | 20.6 | 20.1 | 15.1 |
| % With own children aged 6–17 | 35.5 | 25.6 | 29.0 | 25.9 |
| % Without children | 42.8 | 53.8 | 50.9 | 59.0 |
| Number of children ever born | 3.3 | 1.1 | 2.0 | 1.6 |
| Human capital | | | | |
| Mean years of school completed | 9.2 | 23.0 | 10.6 | 12.6 |
| % High school graduates | 45.2 | 78.6 | 56.1 | 79.3 |
| % Speaking English well | 41.8 | 92.3 | 79.9 | 99.6 |
| Labor market status | | | | |
| % In the labor force | 72.6 | 71.8 | 49.1 | 57.2 |
| % In the garment industry | 40.2 | 6.8 | 7.9 | 1.9 |
| % In other industries | 32.7 | 65.0 | 41.2 | 55.3 |
| Total number of cases | 1,307 | 117 | 8,194 | 32,253 |

Source: U.S. Bureau of the Census, 1983.

with Chinese workers in other industries and all white workers, Chinese garment
workers were more likely to be married, to live in married-couple families as
wives, and to live with school-age children, and they had a higher fertility rate.
These intra- and interracial group differences highlighted a unique context: most
Chinese garment workers were married and had young children.

When we look at socioeconomic characteristics of working women by industrial sectors, Chinese garment workers showed several marked differences from
other Chinese workers and white workers (Table 8.3). First, they were extremely
poor in human capital, with an average of 6.5 years of schooling. Only 22 percent
of them had finished high school, and they spoke little English. Second, they were
mostly recent immigrants, a third of whom had been in the United States for less
than five years. Third, as machine operators they disproportionately occupied

TABLE 8.2 DEMOGRAPHIC CHARACTERISTICS OF FEMALE WORKERS AGED 16–64
FROM FAMILY HOUSEHOLDS IN NEW YORK CITY BY RACE AND INDUSTRY, 1980

| | Chinese | | Non-Hispanic White | |
| Characteristics | Garment Industry | All Other Industries | Garment Industry | All Other Industries |
|---|---|---|---|---|
| As % of group total | 51.4 | 48.6 | 5.6 | 94.4 |
| Median age | 44.0 | 34.0 | 49.0 | 40.0 |
| Marital status | | | | |
| % Currently married | 87.4 | 74.0 | 77.7 | 67.7 |
| % Divorced or separated | 1.0 | 3.1 | 5.0 | 8.5 |
| % Single or widowed | 11.6 | 22.9 | 17.3 | 23.8 |
| Household types | | | | |
| % Married-couple families | 91.7 | 85.9 | 83.3 | 80.3 |
| % Female-headed families | 8.3 | 13.3 | 15.6 | 18.7 |
| Relationship to household head | | | | |
| % As household heads | 9.8 | 14.3 | 15.3 | 19.4 |
| % As spouses | 82.9 | 67.0 | 73.2 | 61.3 |
| % As children | 7.2 | 10.7 | 11.3 | 19.3 |
| Presence of children | | | | |
| % With own children aged under 6 | 14.4 | 17.7 | 5.3 | 8.1 |
| % With own children aged 6–17 | 43.5 | 31.6 | 26.7 | 27.4 |
| % Without children | 42.1 | 50.7 | 68.0 | 64.5 |
| Number of children ever born | 2.7 | 1.5 | 1.7 | 1.4 |
| Total number of cases | 533 | 503 | 1,264 | 21,211 |

Source: U.S. Bureau of the Census, 1983.

the garment industry's lowest occupational rank. Compared with other workers, they generally worked longer hours per week, and their unemployment rate was much lower. Fourth, Chinese garment workers worked in low-wage jobs. Over half of them earned minimum or lower wages, but their contribution to the family was substantial. Their median household incomes were the lowest, and their poverty rate the highest. Finally, Chinese garment workers came from households where household heads, mostly males, also had poor education and worked for low wages.

In sum, Chinese immigrant women at work: (1) lacked human capital and English-language ability; (2) were disproportionately recent arrivals; (3) were low-wage workers at the bottom of the occupational hierarchy; (4) were mostly wives of low-wage workers; and (5) were mostly mothers of school-age children. Given these socioeconomic disadvantages, they had few options. Most were limited to working in Chinatown, especially in low-wage menial jobs in the garment industry. If they rejected work in Chinatown's garment factories, they would be unlikely to find work anywhere at all. Because their husbands barely made living wages, withdrawing from the labor market did not appear to be a feasible option

TABLE 8.3   SOCIOECONOMIC CHARACTERISTICS OF FEMALE WORKERS AGED 16–64
FROM FAMILY HOUSEHOLDS IN NEW YORK CITY BY RACE AND INDUSTRY, 1980

| | Chinese | | Non-Hispanic White | |
|---|---|---|---|---|
| Characteristics | Garment Industry | All Other Industries | Garment Industry | All Other Industries |
| Human capital | | | | |
| Mean years of school completed | 6.5 | 12.5 | 9.6 | 13.0 |
| % High school graduates | 22.0 | 74.8 | 43.0 | 84.1 |
| % Speaking English well | 15.4 | 74.4 | 79.1 | 97.6 |
| Immigration status | | | | |
| % Foreign-born | 98.5 | 74.8 | 51.1 | 15.9 |
| % Immigrated 5 years ago* | 32.2 | 18.5 | 9.3 | 13.4 |
| Occupational status | | | | |
| % Executive/professional occupations | 0.4 | 26.2 | 6.5 | 25.9 |
| Operator/laborer occupations | 94.0 | 10.7 | 64.8 | 3.6 |
| Other occupations | 5.6 | 63.1 | 28.7 | 70.5 |
| Work status | | | | |
| Mean usual hours worked per week | 37.5 | 36.6 | 34.2 | 32.6 |
| Full-time, year-round employment† | 45.2 | 59.8 | 40.7 | 55.2 |
| Unemployment | 1.7 | 3.87 | 13.8 | 5.5 |
| Economic status | | | | |
| % Working at minimum wage or lower | 52.3 | 15.9 | 18.0 | 9.8 |
| Earnings as % of household income‡ | 44.8 | 47.3 | 40.0 | 40.3 |
| Median household income in 1979 | $14,000 | $23,000 | $22,000 | $28,000 |
| % Living below 1.00 poverty level | 12.0 | 6.0 | 3.7 | 2.9 |
| Characteristics of household heads | | | | |
| % Male | 88.9 | 81.9 | 80.1 | 75.2 |
| Mean years of school completed | 7.8 | 11.8 | 9.6 | 12.6 |
| % At work | 75.2 | 74.4 | 61.8 | 63.8 |
| Mean earnings in 1979 | $7,200 | $13,000 | $14,000 | $19,000 |
| Total number of cases | 533 | 503 | 1,264 | 21,211 |

*Of all foreign-born persons.

†Employed 35 hours a week and 48 weeks a year.

‡Own earnings divided by the sum of household head's and own earnings; limited to married-couple families only.

Source: U.S. Bureau of the Census, 1983.

for these women. How do Chinese immigrant women cope with these disadvantages? How does their paid work relate to their family's well-being? How do they juggle paid work and home work? How do they perceive low-wage work in the garment industry? What have they achieved through this line of work?

## Immigrant Women's Paid Work and the Family

Traditionally, a Chinese woman's tangible value lies in her ability to provide support to both her birth family and her husband's family through unpaid or paid labor, and her ability to produce sons for her husband's family. She is expected to be responsible for all domestic work and to work outside the home.

Her life is tied to the family to which she belongs, and her own identity is buried in her family. Women's subordinate status is reflected in a popular Chinese folk song:

> Marry a rooster, follow a rooster.
> Marry a dog, follow a dog.
> Married to a cudgel, married to a pestle.
> Be faithful to it. Follow it.[22]

Even though this extreme version has been discarded in modern times, it is still expected of a married Chinese woman that the family comes first, before herself. This cultural value is not just symbolic but is activated after immigration to the United States. Many Chinese women have come to the United States to join their families in search of the American dream. Once settled, they are expected (and expect themselves) to help their families adjust to the new environment, to sponsor other family members to immigrate, or to make regular remittances to their families in their countries of origin. For most immigrant women, the only way to meet these goals and expectations is to work to make money. Some of my interviews are illustrative.

Ah Mei was a trans-Pacific bride, pregnant with her first child. Her husband expected her to rest at home in order to take care of their unborn baby, but she wandered around Chinatown and walked up to a garment shop. She applied at different shops for a couple of days and got a job, making $200 the first week. That was a half-year's pay in China! Besides, she had her own money. She said:

> Nobody I know comes here just to sit around at home. Everybody works. My husband is not rich. If I don't work, I don't see how we can save money. Besides, I need money to send home to my parents. I can't just ask my husband for money.[23]

Mrs. Liu had never touched a sewing machine, nor had she planned to be a "super sewer" before she came to the United States. Her dreams were fancier. After seven years in the apparel trade, she became one of the most skilled sewing women in Chinatown, so good that she could even "fire" her boss if she chose to. With substantial savings from her garment work, Liu's family had just moved from a tiny apartment in Chinatown to their new home in Flushing, Queens. She continued to work in Chinatown full time: her family had a big monthly mortgage note to pay.[24]

Miss Chen was 16 and had been in New York for 11 months. She worked in a garment factory after school because she felt obliged to help her family. Chen worked from 3 until 7 p.m. every day and all day Saturday and Sunday in the same factory as her mother. She didn't really know how much she made because the boss gave the money to her mother.[25]

These cases suggest that Chinese immigrant women's economic contribution to the family is crucial for survival, especially immediately after immigration. These women seem to be more concerned about their families (defined more broadly than the nuclear family) than about their own individual needs. Through my observations of and interviews with garment workers, I noticed that their paid work not only contributed to their families' economic well-being, but also created a sense of confidence and self-fulfillment that they might never have experienced in traditional Chinese society. Some garment workers remarked without hesitation: "My husband dares not look down on me; he knows he can't provide for the family by himself." "I do not have to ask my husband for money, I make my own." "I help pay for the house."[26]

## Juggling Paid Work and Home Work

These women are still bound by their roles as wives and/or mothers, whether they work outside the home or not, and they seldom prioritize their own career development. Rather, they often expect themselves, and are expected, to earn wages in ways that do not conflict with their traditional family roles.

In Chinatown in the 1980s, women were disproportionately concentrated in garment factory work while men worked in the restaurant business. This gender division was associated with traditional roles that expect a man to hold a stable full-time job as principal breadwinner. Chinatown's restaurant business is in the protected sector of the enclave economy. It is relatively independent and stable because it is supported year-round by a large ethnic consumer market. Chinatown's garment industry, in contrast, falls into the export sector of the enclave economy. It depends largely on the fluctuating demand from the larger non-coethnic consumer market and on production decisions by garment manufacturers in the mainstream economy. Lack of control over production and consumption render Chinatown's garment industry vulnerable to market changes and to competition from producers of low-priced standardized lines that are outsourced offshore. In fact, New York City's garment industry retains only the portion of the production that is transient, unstandardized, and susceptible to the quickly changing vagaries of fashion. Domestic consumer demand is highly unpredictable. Most of Chinatown's apparel orders are for low-priced women's sportswear and stylish products that are made to fill in mass-consumption lines that stores leave open in order to take advantage of late changes in demand. The unpredictability and uncertainty of the industry makes Chinatown's garment factory work highly seasonal. When demand declines, fewer orders are contracted into Chinatown, and workers have to be laid off. This makes garment work less attractive to men. A restaurant waiter responded to my question whether he had ever worked in a garment factory:

> No. I would not consider working in a garment factory. You know, in Chinatown a garment factory job is a woman's job. How could one support his family with a woman's job? I have a couple of kids to feed. What would happen to my family if the factory did not get enough orders and I got laid off?[27]

This waiter was implying that men prefer restaurant work because they need a stable income.

Another reason for women to concentrate in Chinatown's garment industry is that it offers both full-time and part-time jobs, regardless of prior labor market experience. Although most of the women have not worked in the job before arriving in the United States, they can learn at work. Within a short period of time, many become experienced sewing machine operators.

Moreover, the garment industry is easily accessible and does not require a strong commitment to work. Chinese immigrant women are expected to act in the best interests of the family. Even though they work outside the home, they are still expected to carry major household responsibilities. Working wives or mothers prefer jobs that leave them flexibility and time for taking care of their children and housework. Garment work does not need to be done on a fixed 8 a.m. to 5 p.m. schedule, and many subcontractors offer flexible work hours and favorable locations.

The majority of Chinatown's garment workers are mothers of small children. They juggle everything: working, arranging babysitters, grocery shopping, cooking, cleaning, and other household chores. They have to rely on family friends and coethnic members for support. Workers bargain with their coethnic employers to take time off during the day to bring their children to school and pick them up afterward, or to nurse their babies. Coethnic employers often allow children to come to the garment shop after school and wait for their mothers to finish work. Some children help their mothers in the shop by hanging up finished garments, turning belts, or preparing garments for sewing.[28] But if the children are not in Chinatown schools, mothers have to arrange pickups and extended daycare for them. Mrs. Chow's story reflects the busy life of these garment workers.

When I interviewed her, Mrs. Chow was a recent immigrant with a 4-year-old daughter and an 18-month-old son. She lived in Woodside, Queens, and worked in a garment factory in Manhattan's Chinatown. She and her husband, who works in a restaurant in the Bronx, were on different work schedules, and they rarely had time together.

Every day, Mrs. Chow got up at 5:00 in the morning to prepare breakfast for the children. She left the house with her two children at 6:30 a.m., while her husband was still sleeping. She fed the children on the subway train. Getting off the subway, she dropped the older child off at the Chinatown Daycare Center and left the smaller one at her babysitter's home, not far from her factory. She started work at 8:00 a.m. and got off at 5:00 p.m. She went to see her baby during the mid-day break. After work, she hurried to pick up some ready-made food and groceries nearby. Then she picked up her kids. The three arrived home around 7:00 p.m. She prepared dinner for the children and herself, bathed them, and put them to bed at 8:30. She went to bed around 9:30, while her husband was still at work.

Mrs. Chow worked about 35 to 40 hours a week, though she was laid off about three months a year when there was not enough work at the factory. She was able to take time off during the day to go to the babysitter's house. When the children were sick, she could take a day or two off, or take the garment work home. She wanted to work as much as she could so that her family could save money to open up a small family business. With two young children and her husband's long working hours, she could only manage a job with a flexible schedule. When asked how she felt about working, she said:

> I lead a very busy life here, but I feel happy working with other women in the factory and making money for my family. Although I have to spend half of my wages on child care, I still can save about one-third. During the time I was laid off, I had too much housework to do and I felt even busier than when I was working. I feel lonely when I am confined at home and do not get to see my co-workers.[29]

Working mothers who live in Chinatown can manage both work and household responsibilities more efficiently because they avoid Mrs. Chow's long daily commute. They thus can work more hours for more pay. In Chinatown, many older retired women take care of their grandchildren, as older women are traditionally expected to. Private daycare in individual homes is another alternative. In my fieldwork, I found that some mothers chose not to work in order to stay home with their children. They usually took care of two or three children in addition to their own, making some extra money and acquiring playmates for their own children. The costs ranged from $14 to $20 (in 1988 dollars) per day, and the service was reliable and flexible. It was an effective solution to the childcare problem. Working mothers like Mrs. Chow usually spent half of their wages on child care, which was usually provided by other Chinese immigrant women.

## The Perception of Low-Wage Work

We have seen that although Chinese immigrant women have particularly high LFP rates, they are disproportionately concentrated in the low-wage garment industry in Chinatown. As U.S. census data show, the average annual wage for immigrant Chinese women working in New York's garment industry in 1979 was $5,300, and the median hourly wage was only $2.90, lower than the minimum wage of $3.10 at the time.[30]

Are Chinese immigrant women willing to accept substandard wages? The answer is that they are not. Then why are they overrepresented in the low-wage work force in the garment industry? Part of the reason is that the women use a different frame of reference in their perception and evaluation of work. As recent arrivals, they tend to translate American wages into Chinese terms, just as their male counterparts do (and as immigrants of other national origins do in relation to the wage scale in their own homeland). Thus, these women consider even low U.S. wages to be higher than the wages they earned in China.

Moreover, many Chinese women are accustomed to working outside the home. Working, even working for long hours, does not seem to create new pressures on them. Most are from rural areas and are used to backbreaking farm work and menial factory work. Long before immigration they knew that the material standard of living in America was better than that in China and that, if they were willing to work just as hard as they did in China, they could make more money. So they are ready and eager to work, either to bring in additional income for their own families or to save money to remit to families in China.

Further, most garment workers are uneducated, unskilled, and speak little English. Few are able to take even garment industry jobs outside Chinatown. Their options are limited to working in garment shops in Chinatown or staying home. Moreover, they can quickly learn the skills required to operate a sewing machine. They perceive the availability of garment work in Chinatown as an opportunity. Holding a job helps them to withstand the social and psychological pressures associated with immigrant status rather than creating pressures related to their self-perceptions. The following examples illustrate how women perceive their work and their wages.

Back in China, Mrs. Cheng quit school in the fourth grade to work with other women in the fields to help support her family, making less than $125 a year. Regarding garment work, she said: "I was paid by the piece. On average, I probably made about $4.50 an hour because I work fast. My weekly wages were a lot more than my annual wages in China."[31]

Mrs. Wu, who had recently immigrated from a village in Taishan to join her husband, had a similar story. She had only three years of schooling, did not know a single word of English, and had few occupational skills; yet she was more than willing to work. A week after she arrived, she got a job in a garment factory through a relative who was also a sewing machine operator. When asked whether the low wages and long hours had been a problem, she said:

> I never thought of it as a problem. I am a semi-illiterate country girl. I know nothing but work. As long as I have a job, I am happy. I have a chance to make money. Here I am paid by the piece, and I can make an average of $3.00 per hour. A lot of my co-workers can make more than this; some make $5.00 per hour. By the end of the week I can bring home about $180 to $200 [for a 60-hour work week]. If I worked for a *lofan* [referring to Americans], my take-home money would be less because of tax deductions and shorter working hours. I like to be able to work extra hours and over the weekend. That's what I was used to when I was in China.[32]

Mrs. Liang, another garment worker, said:

> If you are a new hand, you do not demand higher wages. All you want is some sort of job, and wages would not seem too bad to you even at $2.50 an hour. You always compare this rate to the rate in China, which equaled to a week's pay at the time I left. Thus, having a job is considered lucky. If you complain, you are simply out of work. The boss can easily get a replacement by firing

you. But if you are really good and quick-handed, the boss tends to keep you by offering higher wages, or you can "fire" him too.[33]

Mrs. Zhao added:

Some girls can make as much as $400 a week. That's hard-earned money from backbreaking jobs, of course, but it's more than two years' pay in China. At whatever wages, most of us just want to work. Also, we are used to hard work and long hours. In China, working six days a week is routine, and working overtime without pay is encouraged as some sort of moral obligation to socialism. Here, if you work harder, you make more. You can't compare with *lofan*. If you don't accept the wage, you will have no job at all.[34]

Chinatown's immigrant women are extremely underpaid. Judging from my interviews with garment factory owners and workers, most employers set the hourly rate according to experience. For new hands, it was below or at the minimum wage rate. For more skilled workers, the rate varied from $4.25 to $5.50 an hour, which was then higher than minimum wage. However, older women who did miscellaneous work in the factory (e.g., cleaning, cutting thread, and wrappings) were only paid $2.50 to $3.00 an hour, whether they were fast hands or not.

These workers were keenly aware that factory owners could and did take advantage of coethnic workers. Despite open acknowledgment of "exploitation" in Chinatown, however, they did not seem to feel bitter. Rather, they were extremely pragmatic about their employment conditions, but purposeful and determined to do their best in a difficult transitional situation.[35] From the point of view of the women, who had low levels of education, job skills, and English-language ability, the garment industry is their only opportunity. As Mrs. Chen put it: "I would have to go back to China if there wasn't a garment industry in Chinatown."[36]

This seeming willingness to accept substandard working conditions and wages is certainly a problem because it can create pressures on other enclave workers to reduce what they are willing to work for. However, getting a job and being paid fairly remain two separate issues for many working women. In Chinatown, most immigrant families cannot survive on only one income. Women's paid work is thus an economic necessity. It was estimated that Chinatown's garment workers made a total of $105 million in wages in 1981.[37] Most of those earnings were spent on food, housing, and clothing. Women were well aware of this reality because they were the ones who handled the rent, bills, and everyday expenses, and they were the ones who knew exactly how much is required to meet the basic household needs. Thus, they were more concerned about having a job of some sort to help their families get settled and move ahead than they were about their own rights, particularly during the earliest stages of immigrant adaptation.

## The Prospect of Social Mobility

The strong desire of Chinese immigrant women to work and their acceptance of low wages and labor practices that might be considered abusive or even illegal by U.S. standards cannot be understood simply in terms of an individualistic drive for social mobility. In the eyes of immigrant women, emigration itself is a form of upward social mobility, and they often base their judgments on comparisons with their past work experience. Moreover, their work is part of a collective effort to fulfill family obligations, helping the family to move ahead in the U.S. society. Thus, women's low-wage work in Chinatown's garment industry constitutes a crucial part of the family struggle for upward social mobility.

But beyond survival, Chinese immigrants have their notion of the American dream: to own a home, to own a business, and to send their children to the Ivy League. To realize this dream, women's contribution is indispensable. With women's wages to help pay the household expenses and women's household management, many immigrant families are indeed able to save money. Mrs. Zhao, a garment worker who had just moved into her own home in Brooklyn, stressed the importance of work in a followup interview:

> The worst thing of not working is that you can't even survive. Even if you can afford to stay home, you won't be able to save much money. Every immigrant family here dreams to buy a home eventually. If you don't start working now and saving, you can never make things happen.[38]

Mrs. Cheng, the garment worker whom I interviewed three years earlier in Chinatown, had just opened up a fast food takeout restaurant in Brooklyn with her husband, a former restaurant worker. With savings from her garment work, she not only helped build her family business but also paid all traveling and settlement expenses so that her mother and brother could immigrate. Mrs. Cheng was satisfied and felt that her hard work had paid off:

> Now my husband and I are working for our own business. I work more hours than I did in the garment shop. Neither of us gets paid regularly. If business goes well, we both make money; otherwise, we both lose money. The difference is that the restaurant is ours.[39]

When families open up small businesses, women usually quit their garment factory jobs and become unpaid family labor. When the primary goal is to own a house, women's cash contribution is as important as that of men. Mrs. Chang was an experienced seamstress and had been in the Chinatown garment industry for quite some time. When she was first interviewed in 1988, she and her husband were making plans to buy a small business and to move out of their one-bedroom apartment in Chinatown. Mrs. Chang's income contributed substantially to her family's savings. In the spring of 1992, she was interviewed again in her new home in Brooklyn. Homeownership moved her family a step closer to their

American dream. But Mrs. Chang continued to commute to Chinatown to work. She explained why:

> You can never afford not to work. We used to pay only $75 monthly for the rent-controlled apartment in Chinatown. Now we have a big mortgage note to pay each month. My husband does not have a stable job. So my family depends on me, especially when he gets laid off. You just have to keep on working.[40]

In Chinatown, the availability of jobs enables immigrant women to become major players in the struggle for survival and adaptation to American society. Their wage labor is an indispensable part of the collective family strategy for social mobility. And the payoff is seen in entrepreneurship, home ownership, and, for many, the educational and occupational attainments of their children.

## Conclusion

In Chinatown, working women, wives and mothers alike, are traditionally considered secondary wage earners in the family, and their paid employment is not automatically accompanied by individual occupational attainment. The double burden of work and family responsibilities is compounded by the lack of assets such as English, transferable education and skills, and an employment network in the mainstream labor market. In this chapter, I illustrate the work experience of Chinatown's immigrant women and the special meanings of work to which these women subscribe in the context of the enclave economy. My study shows that their particularly high rate of labor market participation is largely accounted for by the availability of jobs in the enclave economy; that they are overrepresented in low-wage menial jobs, mostly concentrated in Chinatown; and that they tend to perceive their work as meaningful, despite low wages, long working hours, and poor working conditions. Although their labor practices may be incompatible with American middle-class norms and they are poor by American standards, Chinese garment workers do not seem to feel bitter or hopeless.

The experience of Chinese immigrant women yields some significant insights. First, working outside the home is an economic necessity. Participation in paid work is nothing new for these women, since it was a large part of their everyday life before immigration. After they arrived in the United States, socioeconomic adaptation became a family affair for both men and women. Because of disadvantages associated with immigrant status, one's own hard work is not sufficient to move up the socioeconomic ladder. All adult family members must work together to overcome difficulties and contribute to family savings if they want to achieve their common goals. Although women's contributions may be considered secondary, they are in fact indispensable.

Second, Chinese culture gives priority not to individual achievement but to the welfare of the family as a whole. It is a cultural expectation that women's lives are tied to their families. When migration from one country to another puts a family in a difficult economic situation, women are obliged to work outside the home. However, employment does not mean that they neglect their primary responsibilities in the home, such as housework and child rearing. Sewing at piecework rates fits in well with these expectations: working hours are flexible, and a higher income can be gained by working faster and longer, even if the pay per piece is low. Moreover, many women accept a short-term orientation toward work; their goal is not to develop long-term careers of their own (this applies to many who had professional occupations in China), but to contribute to household's immediate needs for the benefit of the family, especially its younger members. Given their disadvantaged circumstances, they usually consider Chinatown employment a viable option.

Third, immigration and employment in Chinatown create a specific socio-cultural situation in which low-wage work may not impoverish workers. Rather, such work is considered an alternative path to social mobility. In Chinatown, there is a consensus that low wages are compensated for by saving the time and effort that would be involved in finding "good" jobs in the larger labor market; by the option of working longer hours and more days; by a familiar work environment where English is not required; and by the prospect of learning skills and accumulating capital for eventual transition to business or home ownership.[41]

The acceptance of substandard wages and labor practices in Chinatown by no means suggests that Chinese immigrant women are docile. Rather, they use their past work experience as a point of reference in evaluating their current position and perceive their labor at home and in the workplace as part of the struggle to achieve the family's American dream. For these women, immigration is a process; and in the earlier stages of immigrant adaptation at least, survival is more important to them than their own rights in the workplace. Thus, low-wage work in Chinatown's garment factories cannot be viewed solely from a frame of analysis that treats men as women's reference group; nor can it be understood from a frame of analysis that compares immigrant working women with native-born American middle-class women. For immigrant women, the choice of reference group is a result of the specific sociocultural conditions that brought them to the United States. Many compare their current situation with their own past, perceiving immigration to the United States as a long-term process of social mobility for their families.

Last but not least, my study raises questions about the role of Chinatown's economy in facilitating, or impeding, socioeconomic mobility. Does the ethnic enclave benefit from exploiting coethnic members and purposely keeping them from integrating into American society, or does it provide coethnic members with an alternative to compensate for lingering labor market disadvantages? To put it differently: is low-wage employment in Chinatown a dead end, or is it an effective strategy enabling coethnic members to fight their way out of poverty? Should public policy be directed toward discouraging or promoting ethnic economies? In my view, the key issue is not what kind of jobs ethnic economies offer. We need to ask instead whether ethnic economies open up employment or self-employment opportunities otherwise unavailable to coethnic members, and, perhaps more importantly, whether ethnic economies strengthen the social structures of an existing ethnic community. The work experience of Chinatown's immigrant women suggests that socioeconomically disadvantaged groups find it difficult to achieve long-term social mobility merely through individual efforts. Families, ethnic networks, and the normative structures of the ethnic community interact to support, or constrain, individual behavior to facilitate socioeconomic success. Therefore, policies dealing with groups mired in poverty and confined to survival on the margins of society should put more emphasis on community development in connection with promoting individual education and job training.

## Postscript

In April 2007, I was attending a conference in New York City. I took the subway from midtown Manhattan to Brooklyn to see my uncle and aunt, who had introduced me to some of my informants in Chinatown's garment industry back in the 1980s, when I was doing my doctoral dissertation research. On the train, I ran into Mrs. Chang and had a conversation with her. In her late 50s, Mrs. Chang was using a walking stick. She told me that her back and knees ached from working long hours at the sewing machine. She was still working but was thinking about retirement because her two daughters have both graduated from college and gotten professional jobs and because she had paid off her home mortgage. With Mrs. Chang's help, I paid a visit to Mrs. Zhao in Brooklyn. She too had no more mortgage payments. Mrs. Zhao also talked about her various tours to other parts of the United States, Canada, or China every fall. Going on vacation was not a topic of conversation when they were young women working in the garment shop. I felt humbled as I listened to these hard-working, goal-oriented, and proud women.

# 9

# Negotiating Culture and Ethnicity

*Intergenerational Relations in Chinese*
*Immigrant Families*

Intergenerational relations in Chinese immigrant families are characterized by conflict, coping, and reconciliation. In the United States, most
children of Chinese immigrants live in two-parent nuclear families, with
a smaller number in extended or transnational families. In these various
immigrant households, a modified version of Confucian values emphasizing
filial piety, education, hard work, and discipline serves as a normative behavioral standard for socializing the younger generation. Many immigrant parents feel that they have made sacrifices so that their children can have a better
future in America. They have clearly articulated expectations that their children will attain the highest possible levels of educational and occupational
achievement, help the family move up to middle-class status, and, most
importantly, take care of the parents when they are old and frail. Deviation
from these expectations is considered a family shame or failure, and is thus
negatively sanctioned by the family and the ethnic community.

It is not easy, however, for immigrant parents to enforce these behavioral
standards, and guarantee that familial expectations are met, because of vulnerabilities associated with parents' foreign birth, bicultural and intergenerational conflicts, and differences between parents and children in the pace
of acculturation. Like all other immigrant children, the children growing up
in Chinese immigrant families simultaneously and constantly encounter
two different sociocultural worlds: the old world from which they attempt
to distance themselves, and mainstream American society, to which they
aspire, and are also pushed, to assimilate. Often children regard their immigrant parents as *lao-wan-gu* ("old stick in the mud" or "stubborn head")

and parental ways as feudal or old-fashioned. A rebellion against tradition almost inevitably results. Parents are convinced that their own ways are the best recipe for success and constantly worry that their children are becoming too Americanized too soon.

Yet these strains rarely break families apart even when they are manifested in young people's rebellious behavior. Other studies have pointed to factors that lead to conciliation, including children's bonds of affection, loyalty, and obligation to parents.[1] These studies have tended to stress dynamics within immigrant families. My emphasis here is on the important role of the social environment in the ethnic community in reducing strains and tensions in Chinese immigrant families. Although diverse sociocultural contexts—ethnic enclaves, ethnoburbs, and white middle-class suburbs—further constrain parent-child relationships, ethnic institutions not only reinforce parental standards but also provide socially acceptable places where young people can meet and interact—and commiserate and let off steam.[2] This chapter examines how immigration and cultural change affect family life in the Chinese immigrant community in the United States.[3] In particular, it explores the paradoxical family process through which children and parents cope with intricate relationships and negotiate priorities in life that benefit both individual family members and the family as a whole.

## The "Old" versus the "New" Second Generation

Chinese Americans are the oldest and largest Asian-origin group in the United States. Their long history of migration and settlement dates back to the late 1840s, including more than 60 years of legal exclusion. However, unlike Japanese Americans, whose fourth generation is coming of age, Chinese Americans are still predominantly members of the first generation. As of 2006, the foreign-born accounted for 63 percent of the ethnic Chinese population in the United States, compared with less than 30 percent foreign-born in the Japanese American population. The majority of the U.S.-born are still very young, living in immigrant families and just beginning to come of age in large numbers.

### The "Old" Second Generation

As is well-documented in the history of Chinese immigration to the United States, Chinese immigrants initially came to this country from the southern region of China's Guangdong Province.[4] Many were young men leaving behind their parents, wives, and children in rural villages in search of a sojourner's dream—to make money and then return home with "gold and glory."[5] They helped develop the American West and built the most difficult part of the transcontinental railroad west of the Rockies, but ended up being targets of nativism and racism when their work was no longer needed.[6] Poor economic conditions in the late 1870s exacerbated anti-Chinese agitation, leading to the passage in 1882 of the Chinese Exclusion Act, which remained in effect until 1943. Consequently, immigrant Chinese built Chinatowns and reorganized their sojourning lives within these socially isolated enclaves on the west coast, in cities such as San Francisco and Los Angeles, and in other major urban centers to which many had fled, such as New York and Chicago. Within Chinatown, levels of coethnic interaction and solidarity were high, almost entirely reinforced through working in Chinese-owned businesses and socializing in various family or kinship associations, hometown or district associations, and *tongs* or merchants' associations.[7]

During the Exclusion era, America's Chinatowns were bachelor societies with relatively few women and children. (Many "bachelor" workers had actually left wives and children behind in their villages in China.) Of the few "normal" families in the enclave, many were the either the wives and children of merchants or workers who, for immigration purposes, claimed to be related to merchants. The shortage of women combined with the "paper son" phenomenon and the illegal entry of young men by other means stifled the formation of families and the natural reproduction of the ethnic population.[8] Yet a small second generation became increasingly visible among the aging bachelors after the early 1930s. In 1900, less than 9 percent of the ethnic Chinese population was U.S.-born, but because of low immigration, the U.S.-born share increased steadily. As of 1930, the proportion of U.S.-born stood at 41 percent.

During and after World War II, more Chinese women than men were admitted to the United States, most of them as war brides, but the annual quota of immigrant visas for the Chinese was only 105, even after the lifting of the Chinese Exclusion Act. In the 1950s, hundreds of refugees and their families fled Communist China to come to the United States. Despite low immigration rates, the arrival of Chinese refugee families contributed to the increased proportion of U.S.-born children. Between 1940 and 1970, the U.S.-born outnumbered the foreign-born in the Chinese American community. This "old" second generation was disproportionately young. The majority had immigrant parents, grew up in Chinatown, and straddled Chinese and American ways while striving to balance the demands of the two cultures.[9]

## The "New" Second Generation

After World War II, the ethnic Chinese community in the United States grew steadily as the old second generation, with its U.S.-born majority, reached adulthood. However, contemporary Chinese immigration has brought about an unprecedented transformation. Under the Immigration Act of 1965, which abolished the national-origins quota system and gave priority to family unification and the importation of skilled labor, the Chinese American community was rapidly transformed from a bachelor society to an immigrant-dominant family community. The more than 10-fold growth of the Chinese American population from 1960 to 2006 (from 237,000 to 3.6 million) represented a turning point for community development and identity formation. What characterizes this social transformation is the tremendous within-group diversity in terms of place of origin, socioeconomic background, patterns of geographic settlement, and modes of social mobility.[10]

At present, the ethnic Chinese population is primarily first generation (foreign-born); approximately a quarter belongs to the second generation (U.S.-born of foreign-born parentage), and only a small fraction (about 10 percent) belongs to the third-plus generation (U.S.-born of U.S.-born parentage). Today's second generation is still very young and has not yet come of age in significant numbers.[11] The 2000 Current Population Survey indicates that 44 percent of U.S.-born Chinese are under the age of 18 and another 10 percent are between 18 and 24.[12]

Drastic demographic and social changes in the Chinese American community have created multiple contexts in which the new second generation (the U.S.-born or -raised children of contemporary immigrants) is coming of age. Three main neighborhood contexts—traditional ethnic enclaves such as inner-city Chinatowns, ethnoburbs, and white middle-class suburbs—are particularly important analytically in understanding the challenges confronting new Chinese immigrant families.

## Community Transformations and Contexts

In the old Chinatowns of the Exclusion era, individuals and families were enmeshed in, and highly dependent upon, the ethnic community for social, economic, and emotional support, and were also subject to its control. Chinatown children grew up in an extended family environment surrounded by and under the watchful eyes of many "grandpas" and "uncles" who were not actually related by blood but were part of an intricate system of family, kin, or parental friendship associations.

The behavior of children and parents in these old Chinatowns was carefully monitored by a closely knit ethnic community. Children were "good"—loyal, *guai* (obedient), and *you-chu-xi* (promising); or they were "bad"—disrespectful, *bai-jia-zi* (family failure), and *mei-chu-xi* (good-for-nothing). They grew up speaking fluent Chinese (mostly local dialects), going to Chinese schools, working in Chinese-owned businesses in Chinatown, and interacting intimately with other Chinese in the ethnic enclave. Many wished to become like other American children but faced resistance from the larger society as well as from their own families. The larger society looked down on the Chinese and set up barriers to keep them apart, such as segregation in schools and workplaces. Like other racial minority children, the children of Chinese immigrants were not permitted to attend public schools with white children. They encountered discrimination in many workplaces and were denied many of the opportunities available to the children of European immigrants.[13] The Chinese family tied their children to Chinatown and its ethnic institutions, Chinese school being the most important, to shield them from overt discrimination. Despite considerable adolescent rebellion and generational conflict within the family, the children often found themselves dependent on ethnic networks without much scope to break free. As they grew up, few were able to find jobs in the mainstream economy commensurate with their levels of education. Some Chinese Americans even felt that their only career option was to "go west to China," where they could find jobs better matched to their abilities.[14]

Whereas members of the old second generation grew up in ethnic enclaves isolated from middle-class America, the new second generation has more diverse socioeconomic backgrounds and has settled in a wider range of neighborhoods. Those who reside in inner-city Chinatowns are generally from low-income families who are recent arrivals. Like the old second generation, they speak Chinese fluently, interact primarily with people in a Chinese-speaking environment, and participate in various cultural and social institutions of the ethnic community. However, they no longer live in a hostile environment that socially and legally excludes the Chinese. Even though they may go to neighborhood schools with mostly immigrant Chinese and other minority children, they have more opportunities to interact with non-coethnic children and adults and a wider range of occupational choices. But because of the structural constraints associated with disadvantaged class status, Chinatown children also face greater risks of being trapped in permanent poverty and downward assimilation than do their middle-class peers.[15]

Members of the new second generation in multiethnic ethnoburbs are mainly from upper-middle and middle-class families. They generally go to higher-quality suburban public schools. They also have access to ethnic institutions unavailable, or less available, in the old Chinatowns, such as afterschool tutoring (buxiban) and academic enrichment, sports, and music programs offered by Chinese-owned private businesses. Although they speak Chinese fluently, interact with other Chinese, and are involved with "Chinese" food, music, and customs, they also interact regularly with people of diverse racial/ethnic backgrounds.

The children of Chinese immigrants in suburban white middle-class neighborhoods tend to have parents who have achieved high levels of education, occupation, income, and English proficiency and who are bicultural, transnational, cosmopolitan, and highly assimilated. These children attend schools with predominantly white students and have few primary contacts with coethnic peers. Many grow up speaking only English at home and have friends who are mostly white.

Overall, compared with the old (pre-1965) second generation, members of the new second generation are growing up in a more open society. They do not face the legal barriers to educational and occupational attainment that blocked the mobility of the old second generation. They tend to live in family neighborhoods and have more sources of social support beyond the ethnic community. They also have much more freedom to "become American" and more leverage to rebel against their parents if they choose. They can even report their parents to government authorities if they feel they have been "abused" at home, because social institutions and the legal system in the larger society provide support.

And, to take another extreme situation, should they decide to run away from home, they would have more options to get by. In today's more open society, conflicts between the parents' social world and the mainstream society are more intense, and immigrant parents often find it harder to raise children "the Chinese way" than parents in the isolated enclave did.

## Challenges Confronting the Chinese Immigrant Family

Post-1965 Chinese immigrants confront profound challenges when they move to America. One has to do with structural changes in the immigrant family. In Taiwan, Hong Kong, and the mainland, Chinese families are often extended in form, with grandparents or other relatives living in the home or in close contact. Migrating to the United States disrupts extended kin and friendship networks, and the associated support and control mechanisms. When immigrant families arrive first in ethnic enclaves or ethnoburbs, they may be able to reconnect to or rebuild ethnic networks, but these new ethnic networks tend to be composed of coethnic "strangers" rather than close kin and friends and tend to be more instrumental than emotionally intimate. Those who reside in white middle-class suburbs are more detached from the existing ethnic community and have a harder time rebuilding social networks based on common origins and a common cultural heritage. Even though affluent Chinese immigrant families may have less need of ethnic networks and ethnic resources than their working-class counterparts, many find them comforting and, at times, helpful in enforcing traditional Chinese values to which they are still closely attached.

A second challenge is the change in roles in the immigrant family. In most Chinese immigrant families, both parents work full time, and some hold several jobs on different shifts. Because of the disadvantages associated with immigrant status, many Chinese immigrant men experience downward mobility and have difficulty obtaining jobs that enable them to be the main breadwinners. Women have to work outside the home, and many contribute half if not more of the family income while also assuming the principal responsibility for child rearing. That women work outside the home often creates difficulties for children in the family. Without the help of grandparents, relatives, and other close friends, many young "latch-key children" are home alone after school hours. Immigration also affects parent-child roles in other ways, particularly in families where the parents have low levels of education and job skills and speak little or no English. Often these parents depend on their children to act as translators and brokers between home and the outside world, which typically diminishes parental authority.

A third challenge is the generation gap between parents and children, which is exacerbated by the cultural divide between the immigrant family and the larger society. There is a pronounced discrepancy in goal orientation—and views of the means of achieving goals—between immigrant parents and their U.S.-born or -raised children. Most immigrants structure their lives primarily around three goals, summed up by one Chinese immigrant as: "To live in your own house, to be your own boss, and to send your children to the Ivy League." They try to acculturate or assimilate into American society but only in ways that facilitate the attainment of these goals. The children, in contrast, want more. They aspire to be fully American. In the words of a U.S.-born high school student in Los Angeles' Chinatown, they seek for "American qualities" such as "looking cool, going to the ball games, eating hamburgers and French fries, taking family vacations, having fun . . . feeling free to do whatever you like rather than what your parents tell you to."

This cultural gap strains a relationship that is often already tense. Children frequently view their immigrant parents as "*lao-wan-gu*" and consciously rebel against parental traditions. The parents, juggling work and household responsibilities that devour most of their waking hours, are worried that their children have too much freedom, too little respect for authority, and too many unfavorable stimuli in school, on the street, and on the television screen at home. They are horrified when their children are openly disrespectful and disobedient. Intergenerational strains are intensified because parents have difficulty communicating with their Americanized children. Further eroding parental power, the parents' customary ways of exercising authority or disciplining children—physical punishment by beating, for example—which were considered normative and acceptable in the old world, have suddenly become obsolete and even illegal.

It should be noted that the cultural gap also affects relations between foreign-born adolescents and their U.S.-born or -raised coethnic peers. Immigrant youths who arrive in the United States as teenagers have spent their formative years in a different society, were schooled in a different language, and were immersed in a different youth culture. In their homeland, they played a leading role in defining what was *in,* what was cool, and what was trendy, and many were average students in their schools. Once in the United States, they find themselves standing out in the wrong way, becoming objects of ridicule and being teased as "FOBs" (fresh off the boat) by coethnic peers.[16] They also experience academic problems in school. Because of language difficulties, many are unable to express themselves and are misunderstood by teachers and fellow students; they are frequently teased, mocked, or harassed by other students because of their different looks, accents, and clothing; and they worry that if they bring up these problems at home, their parents will get upset or blame them. When their problems are unaddressed by the school or by parents, the youths become discouraged. The discouragement is sometimes followed by loss of interest in school and plunging grades, and they may eventually drop out and join gangs. These problems are summed up by a community organizer:

It is sometimes easier to be a gangster. These kids were generally considered "losers" by their teachers, parents, and peers in school. In school or at home, they feel uncomfortable, isolated, and rejected, which fosters a sense of hopelessness and powerlessness and a yearning for recognition. In the streets, they feel free from all the normative pressures. It is out there that they feel free to be themselves and to do things wherever and whenever they want, giving them a sort of identity and a sense of power.

These challenges are real and serious, with a far-reaching impact on the well-being of immigrant parents and children as they both strive to get ahead and gain acceptance in American society. In the next section I explore some of the most intense points of intergenerational conflict and the ways in which parents and children come to understand and reconcile their differences.

## Pressure Points

Children of immigrant parentage lack meaningful connections to the sociocultural world from which their parents came. They are unlikely to consider a foreign country as a point of reference, and are much more likely to evaluate themselves or be evaluated by others according to the standards of their country of birth or the one in which they are being raised.[17] However, these children constantly find themselves straddling two sociocultural worlds—Chinese versus American. This division is at the core of the head-on intergenerational conflicts within the Chinese immigrant family.

In the Chinese cultural context, filial piety dictates parent-child relationships.[18] But this norm makes more demands on the children than on parents and children reciprocally. In its traditional form, the child's filial responsibility is the debt owed to parents for a lifetime; a child is expected to suppress his or her own self-interest to satisfy parental needs, whether these needs are appropriate and rational or not.[19] Related to filial piety is the notion of unconditional obedience or submission to authority—to the parent, the elder, and the superior. The parent is the authority in the home, as is the teacher in the school. The parent, especially the father, is not supposed to show too much affection to children, play with them, or treat them as equals. This image of stone-faced authority often inhibits children from questioning, much less challenging, their parents. Furthermore, the traditional Chinese family has little room for individualism. Every member is tied to the others, and every act of individual members is considered to bring honor or shame to the whole family. Thus, Chinese parents are expected to bring up their children in ways that honor the family, and children are expected to behave accordingly.

Asymmetric filial piety, unconditional submission to authority, and face-saving override other familial values in the traditional Chinese family. Even though modernization has brought changes in China, these traditional influences still loom large among Chinese immigrants. The problem is that in the American context, these familial practices and values are frowned upon, and children and parents are expected to be independent individuals on equal terms.

The immigrant Chinese family is often described by the children as a "pressure cooker" where intense intergenerational conflicts accumulate, sometimes to the point of explosion. Issues related to education, work ethic, consumption behavior, and dating, among others, are sensitive points that can create potentially intense conflicts.[20] For example, a young Chinese American who had returned to college to complete her associate degree recalled:

> I never felt I was good enough to live up to my parents' expectations. So I fought them non-stop through high school. A war broke out when I got accepted into a few UC schools but decided not to enroll in any one of them. I got kicked out of our home. I moved in with my white boyfriend and started to work to support myself. I felt that the only way to get back to my parents was to make them feel ashamed. With a rebellious daughter, they had nothing to brag about and they lost the war. It may seem silly now, but at that time I really liked what I did.

Chinese parents who were raised in the Confucian tradition tend to be particularly demanding and unyielding about their children's educational achievement. While just about all American families consider education a primary means of upward social mobility, it is emphasized in some unique ways in the immigrant Chinese family. First and foremost, the children's success in school is tied to face-saving for the family.[21] Parents consistently remind their children that achievement is a duty and an obligation to the family goal, and that their failure will bring shame to the family. Not surprisingly, children are under tremendous pressure to succeed. Parents are also pressured to ensure children's success because bragging is common among relatives, friends, and coethnic co-workers.

Immigrant parents also have a pragmatic view of education. They see education not only as the most effective means to achieve success in society, but as the *only* means. The parents are keenly aware of their own limitations as immigrants and the structural constraints blocking their own mobility, and their own experience tells them that a good education in certain fields, such as science and engineering, will allow their children to get good jobs in the future.[22] The children are often frustrated—sometimes deeply resentful—that their parents choose the type of education they are to pursue and make decisions for their future. At college, many Chinese American students pursue double majors, one in science or engineering for their parents and the other in history, literature, or Asian American studies for themselves.

Another sensitive issue is the work ethic. Immigrant Chinese parents believe that hard work, rather than natural ability or innate intelligence, is the key to educational success. Regardless of socioeconomic background, they tend to think that their children can get As on all their exams if they just work hard; they put tremendous pressure on their children to get good grades and are not satisfied with any grade below an A. If the children's grades are lower than expected, they will be scolded for not working hard enough. The parents also believe that by working twice as hard, it is possible to overcome structural disadvantages associated with immigrant or racial minority status. And they tend to ignore the fact that not everybody learns English, catches up with schoolwork, and establishes productive relationships with teachers and fellow students at the same rate. As a result, the children often find themselves working at least twice as hard as their American peers and simultaneously feeling that their parents never think that they are working hard enough.

A third sensitive issue is related to the value of thrift. Immigrant Chinese parents emphasize savings as a means of effectively deploying available family resources. They often bluntly reject their children's desire for material possessions and view spending money on name-brand clothes, stylish accessories, and fashionable hairstyles as a sign of corruption, which they see as "bad" or becoming "too American." At the same time, these parents seldom hesitate to spend money on whatever they consider good for their children, such as books and computer software, afterschool programs, Chinese lessons, private tutors, violin and piano lessons, and other educational activities. They are not just acting in the best interest of their children; they are also driven by the goal of "turning sons into dragons [and daughters into phoenixes]," as a Chinese proverb advises.

The fourth sensitive issue is dating, especially dating at an early age. Chinese parents, especially newer arrivals, consider dating in high school not only a distraction from academic work but also a sign of unhealthy, promiscuous behavior, especially for girls. They are concerned about the risk of premarital sex and unwanted pregnancy—and fear that these will interfere with their daughters' educational progress. Over time, immigrant parents' attitudes toward dating in high school have grown more ambivalent. It is interracial dating, rather than early dating in general, that "freaks them out." The parents' extra concern about girls is related more to practical considerations about the risk of pregnancy than to moral objections to having sex.

All these pressure points have become the focus of parent-child conflict as the children rapidly acculturate into American ways and as parents, in a position of authority, insist on their own values and practices. These conflicts seem to be especially severe in the case of working-class immigrant parents, who are unusually demanding and unbending when it comes to their children's education and behavioral standards because they lack the time, patience, cultural sensitivity, and financial and human capital resources to be more flexible. Middle-class immigrant parents are also demanding and have high expectations for their children. But because of their higher socioeconomic status and higher level of acculturation, they consciously try to be more like American parents in some ways. Some middle-class parents develop a sense of guilt for not being like American parents and become more easy-going and less strict with their children. For example, when a child refuses to do schoolwork on Saturday and tells his father that "nobody works on weekends," a middle-class suburban father might simply shrug and let the child run off with his friends, because he himself doesn't work on weekends. A working-class father who has to work on weekends to support the family would get angry and make the child feel guilty about the parents' sacrifices on his behalf.

## Ethnic Networks and Ethnic Institutions as Mediating Grounds

Such tremendous parental pressures to achieve and behave in the Chinese way can lead to rebellious behavior, withdrawal from school, and alienation from ethnic networks. Alienated children are easy prey for street gangs. Even those children who do well in school and hope to make their parents proud are at risk. A high school student said, "But that [doing well enough to make parents happy] never happens. My mother is never satisfied no matter what you do and how well you do it." This remark echoes a frustration felt by many other Chinatown youths, who want to please their parents and succeed in school, but feel overwhelmed and constrained by parental pressures, rules, and orders. Tensions often seethe beneath the surface, often to the point where parents and children feel that they have no room to breathe.

These bicultural conflicts can be painful. An American popular culture that glorifies self-indulgence and youth rebellion poses severe challenges to Chinese immigrant parents' values and circumvents the role of the family in socializing children in the expected direction. Yet there is rarely an all-out war between the children and their parents in the Chinese immigrant family. Many Chinese immigrant children, regardless of socioeconomic background, seem to live up to their parents' expectations. Involvement in the ethnic community is critical in explaining why this is so.

The educational success of Chinese immigrant children is one of the most remarkable features of this group. They outperform other Americans, including non-Hispanic whites, by significant margins. They score exceptionally well on standardized tests and are overrepresented in the nation's most prestigious universities, as well as in the lists of award winners for national or regional academic competitions, such as the Westinghouse Science Talent Search (now renamed the Intel Science Talent Search). At the University of California, Los Angeles, where I teach, the proportion of Chinese Americans in the entering class in the past few years has been higher than the proportion of blacks and Latinos combined.

Is the extraordinary educational achievement of Chinese Americans a result of the parental pressure for success and enforcement of Confucian values? There is no simple answer. A more appropriate question is: how is it possible for parents in the Chinese immigrant family, plagued with intergenerational strains, to exercise authority and enforce Confucian values regarding education? Why do children end up doing what their parents expect them to do? My research in the Chinese immigrant community points to the important role of an ethnic institutional environment and multiple ethnic involvements.

In Chinatowns or Chinese ethnoburbs, an ethnic enclave economy and a range of ethnic social and cultural institutions have developed to support the daily needs of Chinese immigrants. As the community has changed from a bachelor society to a family community, traditional ethnic institutions have also shifted their functions to serve families and children. Among the programs they offer are weekend Chinese schools and numerous educational and recreational activities, such as daily afterschool classes that match formal school curricula, academic tutoring and English-enhancement classes, exam cram schools, college prep schools, and music, dance, and sports studios. These children-oriented enterprises, both nonprofit and for-profit, have developed in both inner-city Chinatowns and Chinese ethnoburbs.[23]

Consider the Chinese-language school. New York City's Chinese Language School (*zhongwen xuexiao*), run by the Chinese Consolidated Benevolent Association (CCBA), is perhaps the largest children- and youth-oriented organization in any of the nation's Chinatowns.[24] During the school year it enrolls about 4,000 Chinese children, from preschool to twelfth grade, in its 137 Chinese-language classes and over 10 specialty classes (e.g., band, choir, piano, cello, violin, t'ai chi, ikebana, dancing, and Chinese painting). The language classes run from 3:00 to 6:30 p.m. daily after regular school hours. Students usually spend one hour on regular school homework and two hours on Chinese or other classes. There are English classes for immigrant youths and adult workers.[25]

As Chinese immigrants have become residentially dispersed, Chinese schools have also sprung up in the suburbs.[26] The Chinese school provides an affirming ethnic experience for most Chinese immigrant children. If asked, "What makes you Chinese?" many Chinese students say that it is "going to Chinese school." There they learn that their own problems with their parents are common in all Chinese families and that their parents are simply acting like all other Chinese parents. They come to terms with the fact that growing up in a Chinese family is different. Within an ethnic social setting, bicultural conflicts are often alleviated, partly because there are other Chinese children around who have encountered similar problems, and partly because Chinese traditions and ways are better known and better accepted there.[27]

Ethnic institutions not only provide a site where Chinese children meet other coethnic peers, but also allow the children to develop strategies to cope with parental constraints. For example, a girl can tell her parents that she is going out with someone whom her parents know from the Chinese school, while she actually goes to a movie with her non-Chinese boyfriend. Her Chinese school friends will provide cover for her, confirming her story when her parents check. Chinese parents usually trust their children's friends from Chinese schools because they know the friends' parents.

In sum, ethnic institutions provide a safe, healthy, and stimulating environment for youngsters, especially the ones whose parents work long hours. The Chinese schools and various afterschool programs not only ensure that the children spend time on homework or other constructive activities; they also help to keep them off the streets and reduce the anxieties of working parents. More importantly, these ethnic institutions offer some space where children can express and share their feelings.

Ethnic institutions also serve as a bridge between a seemingly closed immigrant community and the mainstream society.[28] Immigrant parents and the children who live in ethnic enclaves or ethnoburbs are relatively isolated, and their daily exposure to the larger American society is limited. Many busy parents expect their children to do well in school and go on to successful careers, but they are unable to give specific directions to guide the children's educational and career plans, leaving a gap between high expectations and feasible means of meeting them. Ethnic institutions fill this gap by helping young people to become better aware of their choices and find realistic means of moving up socioeconomically in mainstream society. Afterschool programs, tutoring services, and test preparation programs are readily available in the ethnic community, making afterschool attendance possible and an accepted norm. As one educator said, "When you think of how much time these Chinese kids put in their studies after regular school, you won't be surprised why they succeed at such a high rate."

At the same time, ethnic institutions function as cultural centers where Chinese traditional values and a sense of ethnic identity are nurtured. Students participating in the afterschool programs, especially the U.S.-born and -reared ones, often speak English to one another in their Chinese classes, but they learn some Chinese words each day. In the afterschool programs, they are able to relate to Chinese "stuff" without being teased, as they might be in school. They listen to stories and sing songs that reveal different aspects of Chinese history and culture, and learn to write in Chinese such phrases as "I am Chinese," "My home country is in China." They also recite classical Chinese poems and Confucian sayings about family values, behavioral and moral guidelines, and the importance of schooling. A Chinese school principal made the goal clear:

> These kids are here because their parents sent them. They are usually not very motivated to learn Chinese per se, and we do not push them too hard. Language teaching is only part of our mission. An essential part of our mission is to enlighten these kids about their own cultural heritage, so that they show respect for their parents and feel proud of being Chinese.

Like other ethnic businesses, these schools also attract suburban middle-class Chinese immigrants, encouraging them to return to Chinatown or a Chinese ethnoburb on a more or less regular basis, thus nurturing ethnic identity and creating opportunities for cross-class coethnic contact.

Despite differences in origin, socioeconomic background, and geographic dispersion, Chinese immigrants have many opportunities to interact with one another as they participate in the ethnic community. Working, shopping, and socializing in the ethnic community tie immigrants to a closely knit system of ethnic social relations. Social networks embedded in the broader Chinese immigrant community reinforce norms and standards and operate as a means of control. Especially pertinent here is the fact that involvement in different types of ethnic institutions helps children to cope with—and indeed has the effect of alleviating—parental pressure.

In many respects the ethnic community and the tangible and intangible resources it provides have proven effective. In a well-integrated ethnic community, even pressures and conflicts can serve to fulfill familial and community expectations. Children are motivated to learn and do well in school because they believe that education is their only way to move up in society and escape their parents' control. This motivation, arising from parental pressure and reinforced through participation in the ethnic community, often leads to desirable outcomes.

## Conclusion

In America, many Chinese immigrant families expect their children to attain the highest levels of educational achievement and rely on them to move families up to middle-class status as a way to repay parental sacrifices and honor the family name. Deviation from these normative expectations is considered shameful, a "loss of face" for the family. In this chapter I show that it is not easy for immigrant families to enforce these cultural values and behavioral standards and to guarantee that familial expectations are met. Challenges include structural vulnerabilities associated with disadvantaged immigrant status and intense bicultural conflicts. Both parents and children have to constantly negotiate culture and ethnicity, make compromises, and resolve conflicts in order to navigate the "right" way into mainstream American society. This undertaking is by no means strictly a family matter, but requires the involvement of broader networks of social support. In the case of contemporary immigrants, a well-organized, resourceful ethnic community geared toward social mobility into mainstream American society plays a crucial role, providing not only tangible resources, in the form of ethnic educational institutions and children-oriented programs, but also intangible ethnic networking, serving as an effective mechanism of social control and sanctioning.

As a sociologist of immigration and race and ethnicity, I believe that cultural values and behavioral patterns seemingly unique to an ethnic group are not intrinsic to that group; rather, they emerge from constant interactions with structural circumstances, including favorable (or unfavorable) contexts of reception of the immigrant group by the host society and the group's own orientation toward the host society, as well as its ability to muster moral and instrumental supports. Thus, examining the immigrant family through the perspective of cultural psychology is helpful insofar as we pay close attention to various structural factors mediating the family's role in affecting educational achievement. I thus reiterate that the processes leading to desirable outcomes are highly contingent upon context, in this case a unique ethnic social environment.

It is evident from quantitative data sources that young Chinese Americans are driven to do well in school and are disproportionately represented at the nation's best universities, and that being Chinese has a significantly positive effect on educational achievement. However, what comes next—after college admission—has often gone unnoticed. As an immigrant mother who has raised a 1.5-generation child in America, and as a professor at a university with a large concentration of Asian American students (40 percent of UCLA's undergraduate student body), I feel that the subject explored here holds personal significance for me. Many Chinese immigrant parents, preoccupied with making sure that their children gain admission to prestigious colleges, have overlooked the costs that come with success. My random observations at home and on campus, coinciding with my qualitative fieldwork, indicate that once these young people get into their family's desired colleges, they are more or less on their own, just like everyone else. Without the clear guidance and the family and community support to which they are accustomed, many feel lost, and some even suffer emotional breakdowns. This underscores the importance of shifting focus to the mental health and intellectual growth of the individual. We have to consider how these students will survive and thrive in an academic environment that is simultaneously ultra-liberal and highly competitive—all on their own.

# 10

## "Parachute Kids" in Southern California

*The Educational Experience of Chinese Children in Transnational Families*

Craig, 18, has been a parachute kid since he was 14; his sister, Zeo, 14, joined him from Taiwan a year ago. They live in a sprawling ranch house in San Marino with an elderly servant who speaks no English. They seem to have adjusted well in school: Craig is a straight-A student, and Zeo also gets As in school and is a student-government leader. Their parents pay all the bills and make up for what the children lack in intimacy with a $3,000 monthly allowance.[1]

Te-Jen arrived in Los Angeles in 1989 when he was 12. His parents ensconced him in a home with a housekeeper who had his favorite meals waiting each evening. At first he called home daily, running up a $500 monthly phone bill. But now he manages to live his own life without calling home so often. Worried about theft, he does not let friends know that he lives alone; he drives his Mercedes-Benz 500 SL for daily jaunts and a beat-up Oldsmobile for late-night hanging out. He takes honors classes and maintains a 4.0 grade point average.[2]

Gina, 16, lived with another parachute kid at a relative's home in Hacienda Heights. Her relative enforced strict rules around the house and applied traditional Chinese home discipline. Gina had trouble obeying her host family and had frequent clashes with the caretaker. Out of rage and disorientation, she once threatened to bomb the house. In December 1995 she actually made a bomb, all by herself, and set it off in the house, even though she knew that the other parachute kid was sleeping in her room. She was arrested for arson and attempted murder. She pleaded guilty.[3]

Hong, 16, was a parachute kid in Los Angeles. On his way home to Taiwan in May 1996, he was arrested at the international airport in Taipei for arms smuggling.[4]

These stories of Chinese adolescents on their own in the United States sound dramatic, but they are not simply the products of media sensationalism. The phenomenon is real and increasingly visible in the immigrant-concentrated ethnoburbs of southern California, where it has drawn special attention from public school administrators, teachers, and the press. The children involved are known as "parachute kids"—a highly select group of young people, aged 8 to 17, who have arrived in the United States to seek a better education in American elementary, middle, or high schools. This education, their parents believe, will give them an advantage in getting into prestigious colleges and obtaining good jobs. As the nickname suggests, they have been "dropped off" in the United States to go to school.

Parachute kids offer a special case of intergenerational relations within the Chinese immigrant community.[5] The phenomenon is particularly prominent in southern California for some obvious reasons—large coethnic concentration in middle-class ethnoburbs, convenient transportation links to Taiwan, Hong Kong, and mainland China, and reasonably good public schools and universities, to name just a few. Most parachute kids live with relatives, friends, or unrelated caretakers in suburban middle-class neighborhoods. Out of sight does not mean out of mind, but absence and separation lessen the potential for conflict with parents. At the same time, parental authority—as well as the sense of obligation to parents—may lose force with distance. This chapter looks into the adjustment experience of parachute kids with a focus on how changes in the conventional family context affect educational achievement.

## Background

Parachute kids are a recent phenomenon coinciding with an unprecedented increase in immigration from Asia and rapid economic growth in the Asian Pacific Rim. These children fly across the Pacific, either with their parents, who make the necessary arrangements for them and then return home, or alone, wearing "Unaccompanied Minor" tags and being met at the airport by relatives or paid caretakers. Southern California parachute kids are disproportionately Chinese, but the phenomenon can be observed among Koreans, Indians, and Filipinos as well. Most of the Chinese parachute kids in the 1980s and 1990s came from Taiwan (my estimate would peg the Taiwanese share at over 80 percent during these two decades). Between 1980 and the mid-1990s, some 40,000 parachute kids arrived in the United States from Taiwan (based on information from visa applications), and smaller numbers have come from Hong Kong, mainland China, and Southeast Asia's Chinese Diaspora, including Singapore and Malaysia.[6] Although it is difficult to gauge the extent of "parachuting," actual numbers of parachute kids are believed to be much larger than the visa information indicates. After 1995 the number from mainland China grew exponentially as the children from one-child families came of age and as the competition for quality education became increasingly fierce there.

Unlike conventional foreign students, who have completed their secondary education and come to the United States to attend college, parachute kids are mostly minors. Although many come on F-1 foreign student visas, approximately one-third come on other non-immigrant visas, such as B-2 visitor visas, later adjusted to student visas. Since the mid-1990s, a growing number of immigrant children have also joined the parachuting world. These children arrive with their families on immigrant visas (holding green cards), but are left on their own because their parents (known as "astronaut parents") are running their own businesses or managing transnational businesses on both sides of the Pacific.

Wealthy families from abroad historically sought to educate their children in American colleges and universities, but Chinese parachute kids of the 1980s and 1990s were a unique group. They were much younger; most of them came to attend elementary, middle, or high schools. Their arrival was influenced by macrostructural factors—the gap between the educational opportunities and skill demands of the homeland and the transnational economic activities of the parents—and they were geographically concentrated in Chinese ethnoburbs in southern California, living in private homes rather than in student quarters. Construed as a social phenomenon, the parachuting world has been growing because of new patterns of transnational familial relations established by both entrepreneurial parents who maintain trans-Pacific careers and middle-class Chinese parents who wish to equip their children with competitive American college degrees.

How has the parachuting phenomenon come about? Its origins lie in a complex set of interrelated factors—not just the usual "pushes" and "pulls," but a new set of conditions giving rise to a "transnational" or "transmigratory" situation in which people try to live concurrently in two societies. On the push side, concern with education is the single most important factor. Chinese culture emphasizes excellence in learning as the key to prestigious social positions, which in turn makes school attendance a crucial step toward upward social mobility. However, opportunity structures in China and many Chinese diasporic societies around the world have historically constrained the realization of this Confucian precept, even among middle-class families. Until after World War II, the Chinese educational system deliberately selected only the most talented, rather than offering an equal opportunity to everyone who desired to learn. Educational opportunities were further restricted by gender and class: only young men were encouraged to obtain an education, and only those from well-to-do families were able to do so.

Since World War II, dramatic social changes and rapid industrial development in Taiwan, Hong Kong, and mainland China have slowly opened up the rigid educational system to girls and children from working-class urban families as well as peasant families, but secondary and postsecondary schooling have remained highly selective. Taiwan made junior secondary education compulsory in 1968. In the late 1980s, the transition rate from elementary to junior secondary schools was almost 100 percent (up from 62 percent in 1967), and the transition rate from junior to senior secondary schools was 80 percent. Less than half (44 percent) of senior secondary school graduates went on to postsecondary schools, and a much smaller proportion were admitted to accredited universities and colleges.[7] Hong Kong extended compulsory education to nine years only after 1978, but was close to universalizing secondary education in the 1980s.[8] Comparatively speaking, mainland China lagged far behind. Although tremendous progress has been made since 1949, the Cultural Revolution (1966–1976) resulted in a major setback whose consequences were still being felt in the 1990s. The expansion of the educational infrastructure simply did not keep pace with the rapid growth of the population. Only 46 percent of youngsters aged 12 to 14 were enrolled in junior secondary schools in 1983, down from 63 percent in 1979; the transition rate from junior to senior secondary schools was only 24 percent, also down from 37 percent in 1979; and only about 10 to 15 percent of senior secondary school graduates went on to college.[9] Throughout the 1990s, China was still striving to universalize elementary education.

Another hurdle is the system of rigorous unified national examinations, at both the high school and college levels. In the 18-year-old cohort, only 8 percent were enrolled in college in Taiwan, compared with 30 percent in Japan, and 50 percent in the United States.[10] The proportion for Hong Kong was much lower, and the proportion for mainland China was less than one percent.[11] Whether in Taiwan, Hong Kong, or mainland China, a college education is a highly desirable but hard-to-attain goal for most high school graduates.

The emphasis on educational attainment and the fierce competition for limited educational opportunities at home have produced class-based outcomes. Average working-class families in urban areas and peasant families generally give up on higher education for their children, except for a few who push extremely hard for their most promising children (usually boys). Many middle-class families seek to "purchase" an alternative means of educating their children. In this sense, parachuting is partly a forced-choice alternative, reflecting disappointment with the educational system at home. If the educational system were more liberal and open, the families would not seek to send their young children so far away from home. Of the students interviewed, all of them list education as their sole or primary motive for parachuting.

Political considerations also play a part. Fear and anxiety over Taiwan's relationship with the mainland, uncertainty about the future of Hong Kong, and unpredictable government policies in China have pushed many wealthy families to choose parachuting as a strategy for protecting their children's future. The effects of these combined factors can best be traced in the Hong Kong case. Less than 10 percent of senior secondary school graduates in Hong Kong were admitted to just a few accredited universities, polytechnics, and colleges in the 1980s.[12] In the late 1980s, about 34,000 went abroad to study, with most heading for the United States, Canada, and Australia. That figure far exceeds the 19,000 full-time students in Hong Kong's five major institutions of higher education.[13] While the number of students studying abroad rose sharply, the average age declined, reflecting a growing eagerness to find an escape route as the 1997 reunification of Hong Kong with mainland China approached. The number of students who left for secondary or even primary schools grew steadily. Many families viewed studying abroad not only as a way to gain credentials but also as a possible way to obtain residence in the host country.[14]

The United States has been the preferred destination for students from mainland China, Hong Kong, and Taiwan, partly because of its liberal educational system and partly because of immigrant and foreign student networks. The multiple layers of the U.S. educational system guarantee relatively open and equal access to anyone who desires to learn. Moreover, the U.S. system is geared toward practical training for the global economy.[15] Since the United States leads the world economy, degrees from U.S. colleges of any rank are highly valued at home and ensure successful placement in the labor market. In the 1980s, students from Taiwan dominated the pool of foreign students on U.S. college campuses, and Taiwanese families have led the trend of sending parachute kids into U.S. elementary and high schools. During the same decade, mainland China sent about 60,000 students, and Hong Kong about 12,000, to study in the United States to study in U.S. colleges.[16] Both joined the practice of parachuting in the early 1990s. This influx of college-bound students, coinciding with more liberal immigration policies and a rapid increase in immigration, has in turn created networks of information and support that perpetuate the parachuting phenomenon.

However, the impetus is broader than that. The dynamism of the East Asian economies and the gains to be realized by maintaining business operations on both sides of the Pacific Rim have induced changes in the familial system and, most importantly, in the location of its parts. Many first-generation immigrants and potential international migrants are deciding that the West no longer offers as many promising economic opportunities as home. This "reverse brain drain" in part reflects the activities of Asian governments and private sector leaders who have sought to recruit the best-educated and most qualified expatriates and emigrants by showering them with promises of high salaries and rapid career advancement, as well as patriotic appeals to help rebuild their home countries.[17] A 1992 study reported that in the 1980s over 40 percent of Taiwanese students went back home each year upon completion of their studies abroad, up from less than 10 percent in the 1950s and 1960s.[18] Another 1992 study showed that roughly one in three Asian immigrants was leaving the United States or maintaining homes in two countries or running a businesses across the ocean. The same study found that only 5 percent of those holding advanced degrees had returned to South Korea, Taiwan, China, the Philippines, Singapore, and Indonesia in the 1960s; whereas in 1980 almost a quarter of them returned.[19] As entrepreneurial immigrants have discovered new opportunities in the homeland, they have decided to capture them by turning themselves into transnationals, or "astronauts."

But for a variety of reasons, these new transnationals seek to have their children educated in the United States. The same factors that encourage college and university students to seek education abroad discourage transnational parents from bringing their school-age children back to the homeland. Even as they pursue economic opportunities at home, moreover, wealthy Chinese entrepreneurs want an "insurance policy" abroad. Many families expect their parachute kids to return home after the completion of their schooling, but eventual settlement in the United States would be an acceptable alternative. If circumstances make return difficult or impossible, the children can stay in the United States to pursue careers, adjust their immigrant status, and eventually get permanent residence. In this sense, dropping parachute kids into the United States not only fulfills the family's educational goals; it is also a practical way of investing in the future.

Another reason for parachuting specifically affects young people from Taiwan, and helps explain why Taiwanese dominate the parachuting phenomenon. In Taiwan, young men aged 18 and over must serve in the military for a minimum of two years before they are allowed into the labor market. To prevent the evasion of military service, boys over 15 are forbidden to leave the country for an extended period. This law applies to every family, rich or poor. Many families choose to send their sons abroad before they reach the age of 15: three of my male interviewees who had arrived before that age mentioned that their parents would not have sent them away when they were so young had it not been for the military service requirement, and that they were aware of this reason at the time.

There are other reasons for sending young children abroad. (At least 40 percent of the parachute kids are girls, for whom military service is not an issue.) Families believe that their children will be more proficient in English and better prepared for college culturally if they spend most of their high school years in America. All the parachute kids are clear about their goals before arrival, and they articulated them in our interviews: being in America means going to school.

## Transnational Living and Its Risks

Unlike immigrant children who live with their parents and whose adaptational experience is influenced by intergenerational clashes and the economic hardships of settlement, most parachute kids live in a world that American teenagers can only dream of: a fully furnished house of their own in an upscale neighborhood, a fancy car, a cell phone, plenty of cash, and no parents. For these children, going to school in America is not only an opportunity for a better future, but an extraordinary adventure—a chance for self-exploration. However, this transnational path is not without risks.

### Intact Families Living Separately

One of the most distinctive features of the parachute phenomenon is the trans-Pacific living arrangement in which parents either remain in the homeland or travel across the ocean on more or less frequent visits. In the United States, "home alone" living for minors is illegal; separation between minor children and parents is extremely rare except in cases of severe family disruption, such as divorce or a sudden change in the parents' socioeconomic, physical, or mental condition.

Studies comparing children in intact families with children living in institutions, one-parent families, or even blended families show socioeconomic, physical, and psychological disadvantages for the latter.[20]

For parachute kids, however, the risks may be associated less with the family's physical separation than with the social environment. Most of these children actually come from intact married-couple families. Although Chinese families today tend to show nuclear living arrangements similar to those found in the United States, separate living arrangements for children and parents are not uncommon. In China, Hong Kong, and Taiwan, a small but visible number of parents will organize their family life in this way because of better schools in certain cities or a change in a parent's workplace, and these arrangements are presumed to be in the children's best interests. One of the parachute kids talked about this experience with a shrug: "It [living apart] has happened for a good part of my life. Nothing's really changed. It's not bad or anything." Because education takes priority, the children involved tend to relate their situation to the fact that their parents care about them and have sought out the best available option. Although the children express their dislike for being away from their parents, they generally accept this family decision. The following remarks reflect interviewees' feelings:

> I didn't like being away from my parents and my family. But think about the kind of money my parents have spent on me just to get a good education. I feel they really care about me and love me.—Taiwanese female

> I don't think the nature of the relationship with my parents changes. I no longer talk to my parents as much as before, but that is just part of growing up. Teenagers don't want to have anything to do with their parents. My parents do not have to send us away, but they do it because they care and because they want us to have a better future.—Taiwanese male

> I am glad I'm here now because there's so much more freedom here compared to Taiwan—more freedom to pursue my goals. And I thank my parents for it.—Taiwanese male

> I feel my parents have always taken care of me.—Taiwanese male

An intact family provides parachuting children with a sense of security, and the practice of separate living arrangements among many Chinese families offers some justification for the parachuting phenomenon. Neither parents nor parachute kids, however, seem to anticipate the drastic difference between separate living quarters in the homeland and transnational living. In the homeland, children living apart from parents are likely to be placed in a familiar sociocultural environment where similar values, norms, and behavioral standards are enforced. They are also likely to confront, as well as be controlled by, an adult society similar to the one of which their parents are a part. In a foreign country, parachute kids are not only away from their families; they are cut off from social networks of support and control and from the customary patterns of social relations between children and adults.

Parents use their financial resources to ensure that their children are in the care of reliable relatives or caretakers, live in safe neighborhoods, and attend good schools. Most of them are well aware that the quality of American schools depends largely on the socioeconomic standing of the neighborhood, so they tend to choose host families or purchase homes for their children in upscale middle-class neighborhoods with reputable schools. However, what these parents can no longer provide is access to social capital resources. These are the resources that help children in a foreign country not only cope with adjustment difficulties but also ease bicultural tensions—between the sending society and the host society, and between the immigrant community and the mainstream community. These parents have little knowledge about the potential risks arising from transnational living—an arrangement that detaches parachute children from an environment in which support and control are exercised effectively through particular social networks connecting children, their parents, and other adults.

Looking back on their experiences, several parachute kids in college said that they had had too much "free" time after school and too little adult supervision. Their parents were not there to supervise homework and arrange the afterschool activities in the local community that are crucial to a child's educational experience. Even if parents managed to set up some extracurricular activities (Chinese school was the most popular), they could not ensure that their children actually attended. Youth-oriented consumerism and anti-intellectualism lured even the most self-disciplined parachute kids. One college student summed up the powerful influence of American popular culture:

> Three to 10 is a long time to be on one's own. I didn't like it at all. I got bored, turned on the TV, played video games, ate junk food, hung out in cafes with other parachute kids and friends. Good thing that none of my friends were in gangs.

## Changing Parent-Child Relationships

Parachute kids do not have intimate, face-to-face interaction with their parents on a daily basis; but this experience is shared with many children of Chinese immigrants. In Chinese families, there is a general lack of demonstrative affection among members. Parent-child interaction tends to be more formal and rigid and less emotionally expressive than that in American families. The parents, especially the father, are the authority in the home. They are expected not only to provide for the children's basic needs but also to exercise *jiajiao* (moral education, discipline, and parental control) and to make sure that their expectations are met. They are discouraged from playing with children, treating them as friends, showing emotion, or expressing love directly or in public.[21]

In the parachuting world, routine interaction between parents and children takes place through weekly phone calls. Many children miss physical closeness among family members, although they feel freer of parental control. When asked what they disliked most, over half of the 33 young people I interviewed said that it was being away from their parents or being unable to talk to them in person. The same group of respondents said that what they valued most as parachute kids was being independent from parental control and being able to do things without parental consent (e.g., filling out parental consent forms themselves in school).

Over time, many parachute children become used to living away from home and feel more emotionally distant from their parents. Trans-Pacific communication becomes a matter of routine, and phone calls become less frequent. One male interviewee recalled:

> I used to call home twice a week in the first few months, telling my parents what I did during the week and letting them know that I did well, and that I missed them. They would also give lectures like they did at home, things like to work hard, to focus, no drugs, no smoking, no dating, and no this, no that. Those kinds of phone calls got boring after a while. Now I call home only because I am expected to. I really don't have much to say on the phone with them.

Another parachute kid said:

> I call home regularly just so my mom doesn't get worried, but I really don't have much to say. My parents don't live here and don't know what problems and what needs we have here. I don't think they understand what I have to say.

Parents are indeed concerned about the gradual change in their relationship with their children. A Taiwanese mother who flew to the United States to visit her parachute children (a 17-year-old son and 14-year-old daughter) recalled:

> I remember in the first few months, my children called frequently. They cried on the phone saying that they missed home. I was sad but kept saying to them that they were not babies anymore, and that they should act like a big boy or a big girl. But after a while, they called less frequently. When they did, there were just those simple responses such as "yes" or "no" or "OK." Then I became very worried.

Both children and parents feel some bitterness about being so far apart. Many parents have developed a sense of guilt and become more easygoing with their children. Children, on the other hand, have gotten used to living by themselves and have become more independent; some even manipulate their parents' sense of guilt. A potential risk is that children who grow alienated from their parents may escape from their parents' social networks in the United States, on which most parents depend for information and control.

## From Direct Control to Remote Control

Parachuting poses a challenge to parental authority in the Chinese transnational family. Traditionally, if children do not show respect for elders and maintain self-discipline or proper behavior, they are considered to be without *jiajiao,* and parents are blamed for not raising children properly. When children live apart from parents, this central mechanism of control is placed under stress.

Two means of remote control allow parents to ensure that their parachute children hold on to the *jiajiao* principles they learned at home: parental networks with caretakers and monthly allowances. Parents usually arrange, at least initially, to settle their children in the homes of relatives, family friends, or unrelated caretakers whom their friends know well. They believe that these connections give them ears and eyes to monitor their children's behavior. Children who live with grandparents, close relatives, or close family friends who make a strong commitment to help are likely to feel pressure to conform to parental expectations. One high school senior explained:

> I am living with my aunt. My parents do not pay her for taking care of me. I guess she is doing my family a favor. She's more than my mother when it comes to rules and discipline. I don't like her much, but I have to obey her because she's my mother's eye. Whatever I do that she knows, my mother knows too.

A college student who lived with her grandmother for the first two years of parachuting recalled:

> My grandma was quite nice. She did not nag as much as my mother, except that she tried to feed me more than I needed. But one thing I used to get annoyed with was that my mother seemed to know a lot of details about my life and behavior here. So I had to watch my behavior in front of my grandma.

Another college student who used to live with a family friend said, "Because they are my parents' friends, I will have to watch my behavior." Many parachute kids agreed that the chief reason for their parents' choice of Los Angeles was the presence of relatives and family friends. Of course, things do not always go smoothly. Some parachute kids rebelled violently against relatives who were considered too "nosy" and too strict. Gina's example, cited at the beginning of this chapter, is just one of those cases.

For children living with paid caretakers (related or unrelated), the remote control button does not always work as intended. Usually parents pay these caretakers to supply room and board and a homelike atmosphere, expecting them to take care of their children and watch out for improper behavior. Many caretakers and host families live up to these expectations. One young man said:

> I had few problems communicating with my caretaker. She gave me general direction and told me what to do. I basically could tell her my problems and

she would give advice in return. But sometimes I had difficulty communicating with her, especially when she overreacted to problems and yelled at me to discipline me.

But some caretakers are reluctant to deal with children's problems. They fear that any active intervention will strain their relationship and may lead to losing income if the parents remove the children from their homes or if the children decide to leave. In my research, I heard of no case of serious, open conflict with paid caretakers, although quite a few parachute kids reported that they disliked or were indifferent to their caretaker.

After a few years parachute kids, especially those in high school, generally move out of the caretaker's home to live—with their parents' support—in a rented house or one owned by their parents. Independent living frees them from parents' networks of control. Without adult supervision or even an adult presence in the home, they are in a high-risk situation.

Wherever they live, monthly allowances are a means of parental control. School performance is of great concern to parents. Parachute kids are expected to report weekly on their schoolwork, and parents double-check these reports with caretakers. They are also expected to fax copies of graded homework and report cards. When these reports do not fit parents' expectations, monthly allowances will be cut as punishment. "They can't ground us, since they are so far away," a parachute kid said in an interview. "But if I don't listen to them, get good grades, they don't send money."

On average, the cost of sending a parachute kid to the United States in the mid-1990s was estimated at $40,000 annually—higher, obviously, when a family sent more than one. In my sample, about a quarter of the parachute kids came with one or two siblings. Apart from caretakers' fees and tuition, parents sent each child an average of $15,000 per year, usually from their home countries, although in some cases the money came from rental properties the parents owned in the United States.

Sally, one of my interviewees, had been a parachute kid for three years. She received approximately $40,000 a year for her expenses. When she went to college, her parents bought her a house and a Mercedes and spent another $12,000 on college tuition. A high school student who had been a parachute kid since he was 14 years old received a $1,200 monthly allowance from his parents; they promised to buy him a new car when he went to college. Parachute kids are aware that the money and material promises are rewards for educational achievement. If they do not do well in school, the ultimate punishment is usually an airplane ticket home and a return with shame.

Although many parachute kids who get good grades are willing to fax their report cards, others are not willing or do so selectively. One young woman said, "When they [parents] are here, I watch what I do. When they're not here, there are no restraints. When they call and I'm not here, I make up an excuse, like I was in the shower or something." There is also a lot of room for what parents consider improper behavior. One parachute kid in my sample got married in order to help a friend get a green card. His parents had not been told at the time of our interviews.

In the parachuting world, children basically control their own lives. Parents may visit them once or twice a year, and the children can make home visits once a year. Many parachute kids do not feel the same about their parents. They still respect them, but they no longer obey them the way they used to when they were younger. Parents gradually, but often reluctantly, accept this change with the hope that their children will turn out to meet their expectations. One parent commented:

> We have always kind of bet on our belief that our children are good kids. If they decide to go the opposite way, you lose them. You really can't do much to make things work for them. They are on their own.

## Determinants of Success

In the absence of parents and in a new social environment, the majority of the parachute kids were doing well in school. According to high school counselors who worked with parachute kids, most graduated from high school with honors and went on to college. Of those who attended college, over 90 percent graduated with a degree, and quite a few expressed interest or enrolled in graduate studies. If the attainment of a college degree is the measure of success, what accounts for this success? Based on my sample of college students and high school seniors with a strong intention of going to college, the subsequent discussion focuses on what really works and highlights some of the main factors influencing success.

Parachute kids are overwhelmingly from upper-middle-class or middle-class families. In my sample, all but two were from upper-middle families, and all were from two-parent families; two-thirds reported that their parents either held professional occupations or operated their own businesses. Mothers' educational level was generally lower than fathers', but over 60 percent of the children reported that their mothers had college degrees. The family's economic standing affects school performance contextually and both directly and indirectly. High-income families can afford desirable neighborhoods, providing access to better schools and more resources,[22] and the family's socioeconomic status arguably works indirectly through the formation of a particular form of social capital. James Coleman and his associates found that success in school depended on the social and family backgrounds of schoolmates, as well as on the social and family backgrounds of individual students.[23] These researchers contended that families provided unequal advantages in schools through tangible supports such as income and social position, as well as intangible supports such as family stability, consistent norms for educational achievement, and expectations for future achievement.

Parachute kids enjoy socioeconomic advantages similar to those of their American peers who attend schools in middle-class communities. However, their exposure to sociocultural advantages in their community is quite limited because of their double isolation—from their own families and from local communities. This lack of access to the social capital available through dense networks of social relationships can jeopardize their chance of success.

This source of vulnerability may be offset by the cultural resources on which parachute kids can draw. The frequently cited cultural value affecting Asian American schooling is Confucianism, which emphasizes education as a means to mobility and stresses the values of consensus, respect, discipline, and hard work, the centrality of the family, and social harmony.

Advocates of the cultural approach to explaining educational outcomes contend that these particular home cultural values have been transplanted to America with few modifications and used by Asian American families to socialize the younger generation in accordance with traditional expectations, helping children to overcome language and other cultural difficulties and withstand adversarial peer pressures.[24] With the family seen as the chief transmitter of cultural characteristics, cultural explanations have dominated attempts to explain the scholastic achievement of the newest group of Asian Americans. The study by Nathan Caplan and his associates of the children of Vietnamese boat people attributes their successful school adaptation to respect for education, hard work, and cooperative family patterns. The researchers conclude that "cultural values are as important to successful adaptation as gravity is to physics."[25] More recent studies of immigrant children from Asia and Central America have shown consistent results.[26] Overall, the cultural approach focuses on how socialization patterns and institutional practices within an ethnic group bring about positive outcomes.

Culture, however, is a convenient but simplistic explanation for the unsettling differences in educational achievement and attainment among ethnic and racial minority groups. Culture is dynamic and is often constrained by structural factors. The case of parachute kids provides a unique opportunity to illustrate how pre-migration cultural values interact with structural opportunities. These children's social class backgrounds and family characteristics are similar. As mentioned previously, most came from families that held a strong belief in Confucianism, adhered to the values of education, hard work, and self-discipline, and exercised strict *jiajiao*. These pre-migration cultural values were indeed crucial prerequisites for success in school. Almost all of the respondents in my sample agreed that Chinese culture accounted for their success there. But why do some Chinese children, in the homeland as well as abroad, who presumably hold the same cultural values, fail to attain their educational goals? Previous studies examining the effect of cultural values have suggested that culture can facilitate or hinder the educational process.[27] When educational opportunities are scarce and the entrance to the system is too competitive, cultural values help the most talented few but discourage the average majority. When the educational system is liberal and open, cultural values may have a positive influence only in particular contexts in which these cultural values are not only highly regarded but also enforced.

In this case, longstanding cultural practices as well as situational response breed a strong commitment to educational success. Individual motivation requires a strong sense of self, appreciation, and self-discipline. Many parachute kids were aware of the fierce competition at home and actually initiated parachuting themselves. As one remarked: "You have to be certain that you are doing it for yourself, not for your parents or anyone else." A parent who was visiting her two parachute children provided a similar remark from her perspective:

> We think parachuting is the best option possible for our children. They were very good students and probably would have gotten into any universities they liked in Taiwan. But they said they wanted to do it, so we simply supported them. The "push" only came later, because we had invested so much and wanted to make sure that they did well and would not be distracted too much.

In my sample, over two-thirds of the respondents said that they had wanted to parachute and had initiated the journey. Some even said that they had persuaded their parents to send them abroad. For parachute kids, success in school is not only their parents' expectation; it is a value internalized through early socialization at home, in kindergarten, and in elementary school. Since education defines the parachuting phenomenon, doing well in school becomes the sole goal and an important measure of self-actualization:

> I want to come to America because I want to learn more about computers, including graphic design. The schools here are better. The knowledge is more advanced. I am not trying to prove to anybody but myself.

My interviews and field observations indicated that those children who took the initiative in making the decision were likely to fare better than those who took orders from their parents. Self-motivation is fed by the belief in educational rewards and a sense of optimism about the future. Parachute kids who make their own decision to go abroad tend to be more appreciative of the educational opportunity and more optimistic about future educational rewards than those who were forced to go by their parents. A high school senior explained:

> You need a college degree to get a good job in Taiwan, but it's very difficult to get into good universities. Going abroad is the best option if your family can afford it. Also, a U.S. college degree is worth more than a degree from an average local school when you compete for jobs. So I am not just trying to please my parents, I'm doing this [parachuting] for myself.

Another high school senior echoed that thought:

> We were raised to respect education. In school in Taiwan, getting good grades is not just for your parents but for yourself. But getting good grades is not enough, you have to be able to compete and stay on top all the time. You may be the best in your class but may still flunk the entrance exams for college. In

Taiwan, people almost have to kill themselves to survive annual comprehensive entrance examinations for high school and college. You feel fortunate that you can be here. In Taiwan, even if you are highly motivated and work hard, you are not sure whether you can succeed. But over here, you know that if you focus and work hard, you can succeed. That's a big difference!

A college student said:

I never take it for granted; it would be lot nicer, of course, if I wasn't a parachute kid. I'm very fortunate that I did the right thing. Otherwise, I couldn't have made college.

Although the liberal educational system in the United States allows these young people to pursue their educational goals, the social environment that they encounter is filled with contradictory and conflicting demands and expectations that may erode their commitment to educational success. In particular, the social environment that parachute kids encounter upon arrival in America is unlikely to be fully supportive. The prevailing youth culture glorifies contempt for authority and overemphasizes peer recognition, materialism, and the freedom of personal choice, especially in dress, dating, and sexual practices. Pressures to acculturate can overwhelm these young newcomers.[28]

Nonetheless, a variety of factors can offset these pressures from the broader social environment. Most of the parachute kids have been carefully screened by their parents. Jane, a college freshman who had been a parachute kid since she was 15, explained: "Not anyone who wants to come here can come. Those allowed to come are the ones whose parents believe them to be capable of self-discipline and self-control." This selectivity interacts with pre-migration cultural values. When asked what determined success, a parachute kid responded:

It's just self-discipline, I guess. I learned this long before I came here. I guess I know what is right and what is wrong. I think it is myself, I know what to do. That keeps me out of trouble.

Second, the parachute kids remain involved in parental social networks even if the parents themselves are not on site. My study showed that parental control is channeled through the children's involvement with people whom the parents know well. The evidence from my study suggests that those who live with or near close relatives and family friends are more likely to watch their behavior and the kind of activities they engage in after school.

A third important factor is the pattern of peer-group association. Ironically, the social world of many parachute kids is limited. When they move to America, their connection to their original friendship circle is broken by physical distance. Entering the U.S. school system at a relatively late stage, they find it hard to make friends with American students, including U.S.-born and -raised Chinese Americans, because they are considered foreign students and are outside the school's already established friendship circles. They are further kept out by language and cultural barriers.[29] What kinds of friends do they make, then, and how do these friendships affect their school experience? The following examples are illustrative.

Kent said that at first his English wasn't fluent enough to communicate with other kids in class:

> So I kept quiet for fear that I might say something weird or stupid. Most of the kids already had their groups, and it was really hard to break in. I didn't even try. I ended up hanging out mostly with other parachute kids like myself or other Asian immigrant children who were also transfers.

Emily said that she got through school because she did not have an outgoing personality. She was quiet and did not "fool around" that much. Her only significant outside activity was going to church every week: "Most of my friends were at church." Jimmy hung out with other Chinese immigrant students like himself:

> It's not because of a particular preference or anything. I gotta study and I gotta have friends who also study. It's just so happened that they are mostly Chinese.

Responding to a general question about success or failure, most of the parachute kids agreed that "if you hung out with people who were having too much fun, you would be in trouble too." In their experience: "Some failed because they hung out with the wrong people and didn't work hard."

## Conclusion

In this chapter, I have discussed the phenomenon of parachute kids, the risks they and their parents are likely to encounter, and the determinants of their educational success. Although the findings are inconclusive because of sampling limitations, the experience of parachute kids has implications for understanding the adaptational process of immigrant children. First, like their immigrant peers, parachute kids' adjustment to school is intrinsically linked to the structural opportunities offered by the American educational system. But they are less likely than other immigrant children to take these opportunities for granted, and they tend to have more clearly defined goals. In many respects, parachute kids do not have a choice between going to school or doing something else, which is what makes them a unique group.

Second, like their immigrant peers, parachute kids have experienced significant changes in parent-child relationships. In transnational as well as immigrant families, parents—middle-class and working-class alike—generally believe that education is the key to success in life and thus expect their children to do well in school. But many parents lack the language proficiency and bicultural literacy to supervise their children's schoolwork, communicate with teachers, and keep their children on the right track. Moreover, the dwindling parental authority that results from living apart (for parachute kids) or from role reversal (for immigrant children) has changed the family dynamics and widened the generation gap. Insufficient family communications, in turn, have detrimental effects on children's self-esteem, psychological well-being, and academic aspirations.[30]

Third, changing parent-child relationships within individual transnational or immigrant families can be a risk factor, but they do not necessarily frustrate children's successful adaptation to the host society, because families are not the only influences on immigrant children. The children whose families hold high expectations for them and stress hard work and education may still perform poorly in school, especially when they have close ties to American youths who hold a strong oppositional stand on education.[31] The immigrant community in which individual families are involved can play an important role in mediating bicultural conflicts between the family and the larger social environment.[32] Just as parachute kids are affected by their parents' social networks, immigrant children also can receive support and control from parents' ethnic networks of social relationships in immigrant communities.

Fourth, peer groups play an important role in promoting or hindering immigrant children's school success. The pressure to fit in and to look cool among peers is overwhelming when adolescents are struggling to develop their own identities. When they associate with other young people who are involved in parental networks of social relations in the immigrant community, their goal orientation is likely to be consistent with the one prescribed by the parental world, even though they may display rebellious behaviors and develop separate identities. In contrast, when young people associate with a peer group that is alienated from the parental world, they are likely to be disoriented and take an oppositional stance. In the case of parachute kids, isolation from American peer networks keeps them tied to the parachuting world and to their parents' social networks in the immigrant community, allowing them to maintain conformity with parental expectations.

In sum, my study suggests that cultural values alone cannot ensure positive educational outcomes and that they must interact with three other important factors—individual motivation, involvement in parental social networks, and peer group association—to exert significant effects on educational achievement. The nature of parachuting is somewhat like sojourning, except that the goal is education rather than jobs. Although quite a lot of parachute kids may decide to stay after the completion of their education, many have come to the United States with the intention of returning to the homeland. This sojourning expectation to a large extent sets them apart from other children of immigrants. As one parachute kid commented: "We never thought, 'Should I stay in school, or go to work?' To go to school was like, hey, just natural. If you don't go to school, you're not a parachute kid."

# V

# The Future of Chinese America

# 11

## Rethinking Assimilation

*The Paradox of "Model Minority" and*
*"Perpetual Foreigner"*

Mr. Leung, 73, worked as a cook in various restaurants in New York's Chinatown for thirty-some years after arriving penniless from Hong Kong in the early 1960s. Now retired, Mr. Leung is reaping the benefits of his lifelong hard work and sacrifices—all five of his children have degrees from Ivy League colleges, hold professional jobs, own their own homes in middle-class suburbs, are happily married with children, and, most importantly, contribute cash support on a monthly basis for his (and his wife's) retirement. Now he and his wife live with one of his children in a New Jersey suburb, and he travels by train daily to Chinatown to play mahjong in his family association building. Mr. Leung still cannot speak English, but he knows his way around and feels comfortable and settled. He says that America is home and his children are his social security.[1]

Drs. Li and Xia arrived in the United States to attend graduate school in the mid-1980s. Now Li is a senior scientist at a federal government research institute, while Xia runs her consulting firm in Washington, D.C. The couple lives in a beautiful suburban home with two school-age children. They speak flawless English, albeit with a slight accent, and do the "American thing" in their leisure time—hanging out with friends at bars or restaurants after work, going to the theater, movies, or ballgames, bicycling and river-rafting in the summer, and skiing in the winter. They vote in local and national elections and volunteer their time for their children's school's PTA and neighborhood events. One way in which they differ from their suburban neighbors is that they helped establish a suburban Chinese-language school and actively participate in it. Xia says [in Chinese], "Saturday [when the Chinese school is in session] is the day I very much look forward to. That's when I can speak Chinese, crack some Chinese jokes, and share some nostalgic feelings about the good old days, or bad old days, rather. It's sort of like going to church."[2]

Congressman David Wu emigrated from Taiwan with his family in 1961, at age six. He has lived the American dream and become the first person of Chinese descent ever elected to Congress. In May 2001 he was invited by Asian American employees of the U.S. Department of Energy (DoE) to give a speech to celebrate Asian American Heritage Month. He and some of his Asian American staff members were not allowed into the DoE building even after presenting their congressional ID. They were repeatedly asked about their citizenship and country of origin. They were told that this was standard DoE procedure and that congressional ID is not a reliable document. A congressman of Italian descent went to the DoE the next day with the same ID. No questions were asked.[3]

T hese vignettes are suggestive of the varied nature of assimilation in American life. Is Leung assimilated? Arguably not. He still cannot speak English after several decades of living in the United States, and his social life has continued to be confined to Chinatown, even after he has retired into a white middle-class suburb. However, he has raised his five children to be quintessential Americans who are also practicing the longstanding Chinese tradition of supporting their elderly parents.

Are Li and Xia assimilated? Arguably yes. But after they have made it by all observable measures—English proficiency, college education, professional occupation, suburban residence, Western lifestyle, and civic participation—they find themselves taking the initiative to return to the ethnic community.

Is Congressman David Wu assimilated? Yes, but ... He has made it via the normative path like other Americans, but also on the strength of his family support, and he gave up a lucrative legal career for public service because he wants to "make a real difference in the real lives of real people."[4] His fellow Oregonians have trusted his words and elected him to five terms as their representative in Congress. Yet he cannot escape the stereotype of his ethnic group as perpetual "foreigners."

Of course, we could easily pick another set of vignettes that tell different stories. For example, an immigrant worker has worked hard all his life, but is unable to move his family out of the inner-city enclave and out of poverty. Or a teenage immigrant drops out of high school, joins a youth gang, and ends up in jail because his parents are too busy working to provide needed supervision. Or an immigrant with a college degree, a high-paid professional job, and a suburban home shows no interest in fitting in with his American colleagues or neighbors, getting involved in community activities, or participating in politics. But the fact is, whether assimilation is defined objectively or subjectively and whether it faces enthusiastic endorsement or vehement resistance, immigrants and their offspring are becoming more like average Americans—one way or another, sooner or later. In practice or discourse, assimilation is an enduring phenomenon. Only in the past few decades has it become controversial and unpopular. As Nathan Glazer keenly notes, the immigrants subjected to the force of assimilation are now allowed more voice and agency.[5]

In this chapter, I am not questioning the political correctness, or incorrectness, of the term "assimilation," nor am I attempting to offer a more concise conceptualization or an alternative model with stronger predictive power. Instead, I aim to focus on the role of ethnicity in shaping the process of immigrant adaptation to American society. I base this discussion on the experience of Chinese Americans because I believe that their contradictory image as both "model minority" and "perpetual foreigner" has significant implications for how we understand the future of Chinese America and assimilation at the turn of the twenty-first century.

## The Challenges for Immigrants and Their Offspring

First-generation immigrants do not usually articulate the process of adaptation to their new homeland in terms of "assimilation." When asked what they expect of life in America, average immigrants would say that they want to be like other Americans. More specifically, they want to hold jobs that pay well, own homes, raise children to be educated and occupationally successful, and have financially secure retirements. In sum, their definition of success is to achieve middle-class status and to freely pursue their dream wherever it takes them. To many Chinese immigrants, the American dream is threefold. In the words of a Chinese immigrant, it is "to live in your own home, to be your own boss, and to send your children to Ivy League colleges."

Yet realizing the American dream is no small project. For average Americans, the normative means is via education. But many other factors determine whether one gets a high-quality education that will eventually pay off. Family socioeconomic status is perhaps the most important factor because it determines where people live and go to school and what human, material, and community resources they can access. The economy is another factor. Economic restructuring since the late 1970s has removed some crucial rungs in the mobility ladder. It is now more difficult than in the past to climb up to the top because of higher educational and skill requirements, and easier to fall into or be trapped at the very bottom because of the lack of jobs that pay living wages. Race is yet another factor. The historical legacies of slavery, civic exclusion, and legal segregation, combined with deep-seated racism, reinforce the system of racial stratification, so that race intertwined with class affects the life chances of group members and reproduces a system of class stratification that disproportionately concentrates racial minorities at the bottom. In reality, nonetheless, most Americans tend to stay in the same stratum in which their parents have established themselves, even though the United States is an open society and mobility across social strata is possible.

For average immigrants, we can expect not only intergenerational mobility, but also convergence to the mean. From my experiences as a researcher and an immigrant, I have noticed that following exactly what other Americans do is not easy for immigrants, whether unskilled or highly skilled. Upon arrival, most immigrants encounter disadvantages associated with immigrant status—lack of proficiency in English, lack of transferable education and skills, unfamiliarity with the host society's economic, social, and political institutions, and disconnection to instrumental social networks tied to the mainstream society.

At one end, poor and unskilled immigrants, a sizable proportion of contemporary Chinese immigration, have few choices but to take low-wage jobs and settle in inner-city Chinatowns, starting their American lives in poverty. For them, trying to approximate the status of average Americans within their lifetime is like joining a marathon race an hour after it starts. For their children, surpassing the parents is not such a big deal, since the parents are already at the lowest social stratum. But skipping several steps to converge to the mean under the precarious conditions most of these children experience—few family resources, a disruptive and unsafe living environment, poorly performing local schools, oppositional youth subcultures, and the hour-glass economy—would be an exceptional achievement.

At the other end, affluent and highly skilled immigrants, a more significant component of Chinese immigration than in the past, manage to secure professional occupations, homeownership, and middle-class livelihoods, achieving higher levels of education, occupation, and income than the average American shortly after arrival. Yet sustaining their middle-class status requires these immigrants to work hard and be constantly on the lookout for corporate downsizing, the glass ceiling, and other hazards. Downward mobility is always a threat because they lack the wealth and membership in corporate old-boy networks, social clubs, or cliques needed to root them securely at the social status they have achieved. For their children, converging to the mean is the default condition, but surpassing their parents is a challenge. To meet that dual expectation, they too would have to work twice as hard.

If we go beyond the first generation to measure success in immigrant adaptation, Chinese Americans seem to have done remarkably well as a group. Their extraordinary educational achievement is a case in point. Research on the new second generation has repeatedly shown that high school students of Chinese ancestry outperform non-Hispanic white students, who in turn outperform black and Hispanic students by a significant margin.[6] This is true even for Chinese American students from relatively modest socioeconomic backgrounds. For example, the 2004 American Community Survey reports that 50 percent of adult Chinese Americans (25 years or older) have attained four or more years of college education, compared with 30 percent of non-Hispanic whites. Immigrants from Taiwan display the highest levels of educational attainment, with nearly two-thirds completing at least four years of college, followed by those from Hong Kong (just shy of 50 percent) and from mainland China (about a third). Professional occupations are also more common among Chinese American workers (16 years or older) than among non-Hispanic white workers (52 versus 38 percent). The annual median household income for Chinese Americans was $57,000 in 2003, compared with $49,000 for whites.[7] More strikingly, the children of Chinese restaurant workers or seamstresses outperform the children of middle-class whites in school.[8] They also score higher than other groups on a series of belief and behavioral measures—conviction that schooling pays off, attributional style, and peer group association—that are considered important determinants of school success.[9] And they attend college at a rate significantly higher than that of whites and other racial minority groups.[10] At the dawn of the twenty-first century, Chinese Americans are dramatically overrepresented at the most prestigious campuses of public universities such as UC Berkeley and UCLA, as well as the most prestigious private colleges such as Harvard, MIT, Caltech, and Stanford.

## The Significance of Ethnicity in Understanding Immigrant Success

Clearly, Chinese immigrants and their children in the United States are making it—and doing so better and faster than members of other immigrant groups. Some of these differences are significantly associated with class differences among the immigrants themselves, who are far more diverse in socioeconomic circum stances than previous waves and than most other contemporary immigrant groups. But if class background explains why foreign-born Chinese physicians, engineers, and computer specialists make it into the ranks of the middle and upper-middle classes, and why their children show up in elite universities, it is more difficult to explain how their coethnic peers reach the same end and at the same speed despite much more modest circumstances.

One can easily fall into the trap of looking for a cultural explanation. Francis Fukuyama argues that old-country values and ways are not entirely inconsistent with the normative systems and social structures of the host country. Just as some immigrant cultural patterns may continue in a state of uneasy coexistence with the requirements of the host country, other aspects may "fit" the requirements of life there. Many cultural traits of Chinese immigrants—strong families, tight webs of moral obligations, delayed gratification, personal sacrifice for the nurturance of children, a high valuation of education, hard work, discipline, respect for others, responsibility, temperance, and good citizenship—are virtues that Americans have traditionally regarded highly but are now arguably losing. These traits, according to Fukuyama, are actually prerequisites for successful assimilation.[11] Thomas Sowell uses "human capital" to describe this "whole constellation of values, attitudes, skills and contacts"; he believes that group differences in IQ tests and scholastic achievement represent real differences in the cultural assets with which groups are endowed.[12] In dissent, John Ogbu argues that group-specific cultures do not emerge from the homeland, or from poverty or ghetto life; they come from unique structural conditions associated with the group's initial mode of entry and societal reception. Ogbu finds that minority groups may accept and internalize a socially imposed inferiority as part of their collective self-definition, thereby fostering an oppositional outlook toward the dominant group and mainstream institutions; or else they create a positive view of their heritage on the basis of cultural and ethnic distinctions, thereby establishing a sense of collective dignity.[13] The latter approach yields survival strategies that enable members to cope psychologically with structural barriers, keeping the host society at arm's length—precisely the ethnic pattern that I will elaborate on shortly. The former approach often produces a different strategy, that of reacting to structural disadvantages by constructing resistance to assimilation.[14] In this case, symbolic expressions of ethnicity and ethnic empowerment may hinder, rather than facilitate, social mobility. That pattern is exemplified by the forced-choice dilemma confronting black, Chicano, and Puerto Rican youth studied by Signithia Fordham, Margaret Gibson, and Philippe Bourgois, all of whom find that black, Chicano, and Puerto Rican students who do well in school are forcefully excluded by their coethnic peers as "turnovers" who act "white."[15] After all, assimilation can also trap immigrant children at the bottom of American society, via integration into the underclass, as elucidated in my work with Alejandro Portes on "segmented assimilation."[16]

Just how cultural patterns interact with social structures to be transmitted from one generation to the next is the crux of the matter. The foreign-born generation is a transitional generation. Immigrants are likely to assess their American condition by a dual frame of reference, to regard their current disadvantaged status as temporary, and to hold an optimistic outlook on the life ahead. By contrast, the second generation, born American or raised to be American, expects to be judged by the same standards to which other Americans aspire. The children have little tolerance for the inferior treatment that their parents' generation may have found objectionable but still bearable; and they may not be deferential to the elders whose roles they are often reluctant to repeat. In order to succeed, immigrants and their children must find a *different* way, because the *normative* path is full of barriers and uncertainties. My past and recent research on Chinese American communities, as shown in previous chapters in this volume, consistently suggests that Chinese Americans and their children are making it, largely through the ethnic community that they have collectively developed since arrival in the United States as well as through the strong coethnic networks that they have built and expanded beyond the ethnic community and beyond national boundaries.

The role of the ethnic community in immigrant adaptation has long been recognized, starting with studies of European-origin groups at the turn of the twentieth century. But much of the emphasis has been on the ethnic community as a temporary refuge for disoriented, helpless newcomers or as a springboard assisting immigrants to jump into mainstream American society. New immigrants cluster in ethnic enclaves upon arrival and rely on coethnic networks and institutions to find housing, jobs, and their way around. In the long run, however, the ethnic community and the social structures that emerge from it will become obstacles to assimilation, as they intentionally or unintentionally discourage immigrants from learning the English language and American ways, stifle their incentive to make contacts with members of the dominant group and mainstream institutions, and trap them in permanent isolation. Immigrants are expected eventually to move out of the enclave as they achieve socioeconomic success. The earlier European immigrants and their offspring have indeed followed this path to successful assimilation, or to becoming white, in just one or two generations.[17]

In twenty-first-century America, however, ethnic enclaves are changing. Some have experienced decline or even dissolution as the more successful coethnic members become assimilated and move out. Others have persisted as new immigrants arrive. Still others are thriving, despite continuous out-migration of the successful, attracting immigrants of diverse socioeconomic backgrounds and new money from overseas. So ethnic enclaves should not be indiscriminately regarded as urban ghettos where poor immigrants cluster. As a sociological concept, the ethnic enclave has a structural and a cultural component. On the one hand, it includes a distinct enclave economy that exceeds the limits of traditional mom-and-pop stores and small businesses and a wide range of ethnic institutions. Through this ethnic structure, immigrants can easily access opportunities for employment and self-employment, housing, goods and services, and information. They can also reestablish ethnic networks and systems of self-help and social support. On the other hand, it is an integrated cultural entity maintained by bounded solidarity and enforceable trust—a form of social capital necessary for ethnic entrepreneurship and the reinforcement of community norms and individual or family mobility goals.[18]

My study of New York City's Chinatown offers a concrete case.[19] This study and my subsequent research on the Chinese immigrant community presented in the preceding chapters focus on how Chinatown and its social institutions create resources that help immigrants fight a general struggle to make it in America without losing their ethnic identity and solidarity. First, Chinatown is no longer an isolated bachelor society. It is an integral part of American society, having redirected its original sojourning goals toward settlement and integration. Immigrant families mostly share this communal goal. In the simple words of a Chinatown worker, "We want to buy a home and move out of here, and we want our children to get a job in those office buildings down the street [Wall Street]." Second, the well-developed enclave economy and a wide range of social institutions provide convenient and easy alternatives to the mainstream economy with respect to employment and self-employment opportunities as well as goods and services. Such opportunities provided by the community tie coethnic members from diverse socioeconomic backgrounds to Chinatown despite their spatial dispersion. These ties, in turn, have directly or indirectly broadened the base of ethnic interaction and thus increased both ethnic cohesion that cuts across class lines and a sense of identity and community. Third, multiple institutional involvement in Chinatown allows coethnic members living in or outside the enclave to reinforce common values and create new mechanisms for mutual support and for sanctioning nonconformity.

The example of working women is most telling.[20] Immigrant Chinese women with little English and few job skills often find working in Chinatown a better option than working elsewhere despite low wages, because the enclave enables them to fulfill their multiple roles as wage earners, wives, and mothers more effectively. In Chinatown, jobs are easier to find, working hours are more flexible, employers are more tolerant of children's presence, and private child care within close walking distance of work is accessible and affordable. Convenient grocery shopping and availability of takeout foods make dinner preparation easier. At work, women are able to socialize with other coethnic women, who may not come from similar socioeconomic backgrounds, but who share similar goals and concerns about family, child rearing, and mobility. At their sewing machines, they can gossip, brag about children, complain about insensitive husbands or nagging relatives back in the homeland, exchange coping strategies and information, and comfort each other. It is not surprising to hear non-English-speaking garment workers in Chinatown talking in a detailed and sophisticated way about SAT scores, admissions to Stuyvesant High School (a highly selective magnet public school), Harvard, and MIT, or winners of the Intel (formerly Westinghouse) science competition. These Chinatown workers get such valuable information not only from personal interactions, in Chinese, with employers and middle-class coethnics in multiple sites in the community, such as Chinese-language schools, cultural centers and events, churches or temples, restaurants, shops, and stores, but also from the extensive Chinese-language media: radio, television, and print.[21] These ties, built on multiple involvements, serve as sources of psychological comfort and instrumental support, as well as pressure to conform to family and community expectations.

The ethnic community and its institutions also have a lasting impact on the adaptation of immigrant children. Obedience, hard work, and success in school are taken for granted in Chinatown. These expectations cannot possibly be instilled in the children without the support of the ethnic community.[22] In other words, the pressure to achieve comes not only from within the family but also from the ethnic community. Illustrative are some common exchanges between adults and children overheard in Chinatown's homes, streets, and restaurants: "How was school?" "How was that test you took today?" "Did you do your homework?" Or, looking at a straight-A report card: "How come you got an A-minus? Shouldn't you have gotten an A-plus?" Relatives and family friends often ask: "Have you been obeying your parents?" "Have you been working hard in school?" "Have you been making good grades?" The children are expected to give positive answers. In the ethnic enclave, children also have access to a wide range of afterschool tutoring (*buxiban*) and academic programs offered at Chinese-language schools and various ethnic institutions.[23] Intense involvement in the community not only gives immigrant children instrumental support necessary for school success; it also helps them alleviate parental pressure and bicultural conflicts.

The way in which many Chinese immigrants and their children have made it in America—via the ethnic community—seems unconventional, but it is nonetheless typically American. The America of the twenty-first century is very different from the one receiving massive immigration from Europe at the start of the twentieth century. In the past, children and grandchildren of European origin were subjected to uniform pressure to assimilate into a white Anglo-Saxon Protestant (WASP) core. It took them two, three, or more generations to make it, but they did so under conditions no longer present for contemporary immigrants: a society dominated by a WASP hegemony, an immigrant stock that was overwhelmingly European, an expanding manufacturing-based economy, a powerful trade union movement, and a long period of restricted immigration. In today's arguably more open, inclusive society, new immigrants from diverse backgrounds have more agency in determining the meaning, pace, and direction of assimilation and in choosing their own destinies. But at the same time, they are still subjected to a racial stratification system that accords differential privilege and power based on ascribed characteristics.

## Becoming American: Identity Formation

### Asian American versus Chinese American Identity

Post-1965 immigration has changed America's face. The U.S. population was 68 percent non-Hispanic white, 12 percent non-Hispanic black, 15 percent Hispanic, and 4 percent Asian at the dawn of the twenty-first century (compared with 80 percent white, 12 percent black, 6 percent Hispanic, and 1.5 percent Asian in 1980). It is projected that by the year 2050, the nation's face will be 51 percent white, 16 percent black, 24 percent Hispanic, and 8 percent Asian. In California, the concept of "white majority" no longer holds. The state's population as of 2006 was 43 percent non-Hispanic white, 6 percent non-Hispanic black, 36 percent Latino, and 12 percent Asian; and this single state concentrates about 30 percent of the nation's Hispanic population and 34 percent of the Asian-origin population (including a third of its Chinese Americans).[24] Not surprisingly, concerns about assimilation once again occupy a central place in public and academic discourse.

Just as the offspring of Irish, Italian, Jewish, and Polish immigrants are dropping their ethnic hyphens to melt into the indistinguishable category "white," we have seen new hyphens emerging in the American ethnic scene in the past few decades. These new hyphens are often based on racialized groupings beyond black and white (i.e., Latino, Chicano, and Asian), or on non-European national origins (Mexican, Chinese, Japanese, Korean, Filipino, Vietnamese, and Indian). Chinese Americans, like other Americans of Asian origin, are often lumped into a broad racial category of "Asian," as opposed to "white," "black," or "Hispanic," in official statistics. Unlike the racialized identity imposed upon Asian-origin Americans, however, "Asian American" is a self-empowering political identity. The term "Asian American" was coined by the late historian and activist Yuji Ichioka during the ethnic consciousness movements of the late 1960s. To adopt this identity is to reject the western-imposed label of "Oriental."[25]

Before 1970, the Asian-origin population in the United States was largely made up of Chinese, Japanese, and Filipinos. Today, Americans of Chinese and Filipino ancestries are the largest subgroups (at 3.6 million and 3 million, respectively), followed by Indians, Koreans, Vietnamese, and Japanese (at more than one million). Some 20 other national-origin groups, such as Cambodians, Pakistanis, Lao, Thai, Indonesians, and Bangladeshis, were officially counted in government statistics only after 1980, and together amounted to more than 2 million residents at the dawn of the twenty-first century. Currently, about 60 percent of the Asian-origin population is foreign-born (the first generation); another 28 percent are U.S.-born of foreign-born parents (the second generation); and just 12 percent are born to U.S.-born parents (the third generation and beyond). The only exception to this pattern are Japanese Americans, who have a fourth generation and many U.S.-born elderly.

"Asian American" is now an umbrella category that includes both U.S. citizens and immigrants whose ancestors came from Asia east of Pakistan. However, differences in national origins, timing of immigration, affluence, and settlement patterns profoundly affect the formation of a stable panethnic identity. For example, recent arrivals are less likely than those born or raised in the United States to identify as Asian American. They are also so busy settling in that they have little time to think about being Asian or Asian American, or, for that matter, white. Their diverse origins evoke drastic differences in languages and dialects, religions, foodways, and customs. Many nationalities also brought to America their histories of conflict (such as the Japanese colonization of Korea and Taiwan, the Japanese invasion of China, and the Chinese armed conflict with Vietnam). Immigrants who are predominantly middle-class professionals (such as the Taiwanese and Indians) or predominantly small business owners (such as the Koreans) share few concerns and priorities with those who are predominantly uneducated, low-skilled refugees (such as Cambodians and Hmong). Finally, Asian-origin people living in San Francisco or Los Angeles among many other Asians and self-conscious Asian Americans develop sharper ethnic sensitivities than those living in, say, Latin-dominant Miami or white-dominant Minneapolis. A politician might get away with calling Asians "Orientals" in Miami but would get into big trouble in San Francisco. All of these differences can create obstacles to fostering a cohesive pan-Asian solidarity. As Yen Le Espiritu shows in her research, pan-Asianism is primarily a political ideology of U.S.-born, American-educated, and middle-class Asians rather than of Asian immigrants, who are conscious of their national origins and overburdened with their daily struggles for survival.[26]

Although it is widely used in public discussions, most Asian-origin Americans are ambivalent about this label. Their reservations reflect the difficulty of being American and still keeping some ethnic identity: is one, for example, Asian American or Chinese American? In their private lives, few Americans of Chinese ancestry would spontaneously identify themselves as Asian or Asian American. They instead link their identities to specific places or ethnic origins, such as

Chinese, Taiwanese, Cantonese, Fujianese, Hakka (Kejia), and so on. Although some Chinese Americans have family histories in the United States longer than those of many Americans of eastern or southern European origin, Chinese Americans as an ethnic group became numerous only after the passage of the Hart-Celler Act of 1965. According to the U.S. Citizenship and Immigration Services (USCIS), the United States admitted approximately 17 million immigrants between 1971 and 1995, matching the scale of the "old" immigration of the first quarter of the twentieth century (17.2 million between 1901 and 1925), and another 8.8 million between 1996 and 2005. About 1.7 million from China, Hong Kong, and Taiwan were admitted as permanent residents between 1970 and 2006.[27] High rates of contemporary immigration will continue to influence the identity formation of Chinese Americans, who are members of the nation's oldest immigrant group.

## What Does It Mean to Be White?

In the United States, "white" is an arbitrary label having more to do with privilege than biology. Historically, some ethnic groups initially considered nonwhite, such as the Irish, Italians, and Jews, have attained membership in the "white" race by acquiring status and wealth. It is hardly surprising, then, that nonwhites would aspire to becoming "white" as a mark of and a tool for material success. However, becoming white can mean distancing oneself from "people of color" or selling out one's ethnicity. Panethnic identities—Asian American, African American, Hispanic American—are one way in which the politically vocal in these respective groups try to stem defections; yet these collective identities may restrain aspirations for individual mobility.

Are Chinese Americans becoming white? For many public officials, the answer to this question must be positive, because they classify Chinese (and other Asian) Americans with European-origin Americans for equal-opportunity programs; neither group is underrepresented, as blacks, Latinos, and American Indians are. But this answer is premature and based on false premises. Although Asian Americans as a group have attained the level of career and financial success equated with being white, and although many have moved near to or even married whites, they remain culturally distinct and suspect in a white society.

The paradox of Asian Americans being celebrated as a "model minority" while simultaneously viewed as "perpetual foreigners" is a case in point. The "model minority" image surfaced during World War II and became crystallized in the popular media in the mid-1960s, at the peak of the civil rights and ethnic consciousness movements but *before* the rising waves of immigration and the refugee influx from Asia.[28] Two articles from 1966—"Success Story, Japanese-American Style," by William Petersen in the *New York Times Magazine,* and "Success of One Minority Group in U.S.," by the *U.S. News & World Report* staff—marked a significant departure from the traditional depiction of Asian immigrants and their descendants in the media.[29] Both articles extolled Japanese and Chinese

Americans for their persistence in overcoming extreme hardships and discrimination to achieve a level of success unmatched even by U.S.-born whites, through "their own almost totally unaided effort" and with "no help from anyone else," winning wealth and respect in American society through hard work, family solidarity, discipline, delayed gratification, nonconfrontation, and eschewing welfare.

The model-minority stereotype buttresses the myth that the United States is devoid of racism and accords equal opportunity to all, so that those who lag behind do so because of their own poor choices and inferior culture. Celebrating this model minority can help thwart other racial minorities' demands for social justice, pitting minority groups against each other. It can also pit Asian Americans against whites. On the surface, Asian Americans seem to be on their way to becoming white, just like the offspring of earlier European immigrants. But the model-minority image implicitly casts Asian Americans as different from whites. By placing Asian Americans above whites, it sets them apart from other Americans, white or nonwhite, in the public mind.

"What's wrong with being a model minority?" asked a black student in a class I taught on race. "I'd rather be in the model minority than in the downtrodden minority that nobody respects." Let me point to two less obvious effects. Whether people are in a model minority or a downtrodden minority, they are judged by a *different* standard. The model-minority stereotype holds Asian Americans to higher standards than average Americans. And it places particular expectations on members of the group so labeled, channeling them into specific avenues of success, such as science and engineering, and unintentionally reinforcing barriers for Asian Americans pursuing careers outside these designated fields. Falling into this trap, a Chinese immigrant father might be upset if his son told him that he had decided to change his major from engineering to English. Disregarding his son's passion and talent for creative writing, the father would rationalize his concern: "You have a 90 percent chance of getting a decent job with an engineering degree, but what chance would you have of earning income as a writer?" This rationale reflects more than the simple parental concern over career choices typical of middle-class families; it constitutes the self-fulfilling prophecy of a stereotype.

In the end, the celebration of Asian Americans as a model minority is based on the judgment that many Asian Americans perform at levels above the American average, which sets them apart not only from other minorities but also from whites. The truth of the matter is that the larger-than-average size of the middle and upper-middle class in some Asian-origin groups, such as the Chinese, Indians, and Koreans, paves the way for the immigrants and their offspring to regain their middle-class status in the new homeland. The financial resources that immigrants bring with them to this country also help build viable ethnic economies and institutions, such as private afterschool programs, that help the less fortunate members of the group to move ahead in society much faster than they would without these ethnic resources.

## "It's Not So Much Being White as Being American"

I never asked to be white. I am not literally white. That is, I do not have white skin or white ancestors. I have yellow skin and yellow ancestors, hundreds of generations of them. But like so many other Asian Americans of the second generation, I find myself now the bearer of a strange new status: white, by acclamation. Thus it is that I have been described as an "honorary white," by other whites, and as a "banana" by other Asians ... to the extent that I have moved away from the periphery and toward the center of American life, I have become white inside.—Eric Liu[30]

Many Chinese immigrants and their U.S.-born or -raised children seem to accept that "white" is mainstream, average, and normal, and they look to whites as their frame of reference for attaining a higher social position. Similarly, researchers often use non-Hispanic whites as the standard of comparison for other groups, even though there is great diversity among whites, too. Like most immigrants to the United States, Chinese immigrants tend to believe in the American dream and measure their achievements in material terms. Those with sufficient education, job skills, and money move into white middle-class suburban neighborhoods immediately upon arrival, while others work intensively to accumulate enough savings to move their families up and out of the old inner-city Chinatowns. Consequently, many children of contemporary Chinese immigrants spend their entire childhood in white communities, make friends with mostly white peers, and grow up speaking only English. In fact, Chinese Americans are one of the most acculturated non-European groups in the United States. By the second generation, most have lost fluency in their parents' native languages.[31] Chinese Americans also intermarry extensively with whites and with members of other minority groups.[32]

Yet U.S.-born or -raised Chinese Americans may be more ambivalent about becoming white than their immigrant parents. Many are cynical about the equation of "white" with "American." Although they recognize whites as a frame of reference, many children of Asian immigrants reject the idea of becoming white themselves: "It's not so much being white as being American," commented a Korean American student in my class on the new second generation. This aversion to becoming white is particularly common among well-educated and privileged second-generation college students who have taken ethnic studies courses, and among Asian American community activists. However, most of the second generation continues to strive for the privileged status associated with whiteness, just like their parents. For example, most U.S.-born or -raised Chinese American youths end up studying engineering, medicine, or law, believing that these areas of study guarantee well-paid jobs and middle-class lives, as well as enhancing social contact with whites.

Chinese Americans are also more conscious of the disadvantages associated with being nonwhite than their parents, who as immigrants tend to be optimistic about overcoming disadvantages. A second-generation Chinese American in her sixties succinctly described the situation in these words: "The truth is, no matter how American you think you are or try to be, you do not look *American*. If you have almond-shaped eyes, straight black hair, and a yellow complexion, you are a foreigner by default. People will ask where you come from but won't be satisfied until they hear you name a foreign country, and they will naturally compliment your perfect English. So you can certainly be as good as or even better than whites, but you will never become accepted as white."[33] These remarks echo a common frustration among second-generation Asian Americans, who detest being treated as immigrants or foreigners. Their experience suggests that whitening has more to do with the beliefs of white America than with the actual situation of Asian Americans. Speaking perfect English, effortlessly adopting mainstream cultural values, and even marrying members of the dominant group may help reduce this "otherness" at the individual level, but it has little effect on the group as a whole. New stereotypes can emerge and un-whiten Asian Americans anytime and anywhere, no matter how "successful" and "assimilated" they have become. Congressman David Wu's story, quoted at the beginning of this chapter, is illustrative.

The stereotype of the "honorary white" or model minority goes hand in hand with that of the perpetual foreigner. At this point in time, Chinese Americans, like their Asian American peers, are in an ambivalent position as nonwhite and nonblack.[34] Globalization and U.S.-China relations, combined with continually high rates of immigration, affect how Chinese Americans are perceived in American society and how they evaluate themselves in relation to members of other racial and ethnic minorities, as well as their coethnics in China and the Chinese Diaspora.[35] Most of the historical stereotypes, such as the "yellow peril" and "Fu Manchu," have found their way into contemporary American life. Consider the murder of Vincent Chin, a Chinese American mistaken for Japanese and beaten to death by a disgruntled white auto worker in the 1980s; the trial of Wen Ho Lee, a nuclear scientist suspected of spying for the Chinese government in the mid-1990s; the 1996 presidential campaign finance scandal, which implicated Asian Americans in funneling foreign contributions to the Clinton campaign; and, in 2001, the Abercrombie & Fitch tee-shirts that depicted Chinese cartoon characters in stereotypically negative ways—with slanted eyes, thick glasses, and the Qing queue (a long pigtail at the back of the head).[36] The ambivalent, conditional nature of white acceptance of Chinese Americans prompts them to organize panethnically to fight back—which consequently heightens their racial distinctiveness. So becoming white or not may be beside the point, since Chinese Americans, like other Asian Americans, still constantly have to prove that they are truly loyal Americans, especially in situations where U.S.-China relations are in the spotlight.[37]

Ironically, it is the very fact that Asian Americans are assimilated but conditionally accepted that prompts them to organize on the basis of ethnicity. In the end, this Asian paradox overlaps the paradox of assimilation. In order to advance to the rank of average Americans, the first generation chooses the ethnic way and succeeds. In order to fight the negative stereotype of perpetual foreigners, the "assimilated" second generation falls back on ethnicity and ethnic self-consciousness for empowerment. Their ethnic strategy, which is qualitatively different from the one adopted by their parents, is effective: that is, becoming assimilated via the ethnic way and becoming American by becoming ethnic.[38]

## Conclusion

The Chinese way, or the ethnic way, may not fit all Asian-origin groups, much less non-Asian groups, because of the different contexts and circumstances under which immigrants leave their various old countries and are received on American soil. In order to reach the goal in the race for social mobility, every group must find its own strategies and its own path. The truth is that ignorant and stupid bigots may still shout hysterically at Chinese Americans to "go back to China," but they cannot stop Chinese Americans, or any other "foreign-looking" groups, from making equal claims on this land they call home. As American society becomes increasingly multiethnic, and as ethnic communities and ethnic Americans become integral components of the society, the time will come, sooner or later, when the ethnic way is accepted as the American way. Whether "assimilation" is a meaningful concept remains arguable. After all, Chinatown and ethnic distinctiveness are quintessentially American.

# Appendix:
# Recommended Films on the
# Chinese American Experience

Adachi, Jeff. *The Slanted Screen: Asian Men in Film and Television* (documentary, 60 min.). 2006.

Chen, Amy. *The Chinatown Files* (documentary, 57 min.). 2001.

Choy, Christine, and Renee Tajima. *Who Killed Vincent Chin* (documentary, 87 min.). 1988.

Cohn, Peter. *Golden Venture* (documentary, 70 min.). 2006.

Ding, Loni. *On New Ground* (documentary, 30 min.). 1982.

———. *From Madera, California, to Kaiping, China* (documentary, 17 min.). 1996.

———. *Ancestors in the Americas: Coolies, Sailors, Settlers* (documentary, 64 min.). 1998.

———. *Canton Army in the High Sierras: America's First Continental Railroad, 1863–1869* (documentary, 28 min.). 1998.

———. *Chinese in the Frontier West: An American Story* (documentary, 60 min.). 1998.

———. *Island of Secret Memories: The Angel Island Immigration Station in San Francisco Bay (1910–1941)* (documentary, 20 min.). 1998.

———. *Mamie Tape and the Fight for Equality in Education, 1885–1954* (documentary, 21 min.). 1998.

Doug, Arthur. *Living Music for Golden Mountains* (documentary, 27 min.). 1981.

———. *Sewing Woman* (documentary, 14 min.). 1982.

———. *Forbidden City, U.S.A.* (documentary, 56 min.). 1989.

———. *Claiming a Voice* (documentary, 59 min.). 1990.

———. *Hollywood Chinese: The Chinese in American Feature Films* (documentary, 89 min.). 2008.

Fung, Richard. *Orientations* (documentary, 52 min.). 1984.

———. *My Mother's Place* (documentary, 50 min.). 1990.

———. *Dirty Laundry* (documentary, 30 min.). 1995.

Gee, Deborah. *Slaying the Dragon* (documentary, 60 min.). 1988.

Gow, William, and Sharon Lee. *More to the Chinese Side* (documentary, 17 min.). 2003.

Hima, B. *Coming Out/Coming Home: Asian and Pacific Islander Family Stories* (documentary, 44 min.). 1996.

Hom, Montgomery. *We Served with Pride: The Chinese American Experience in WWII* (documentary, 60 min.). 1999.

Hosley, David, and Dennis Yep. *Bittersweet Roots: The Chinese in California's Heartland* (documentary, 60 min.). 2002.

Huang, Renata. *Tribute and Remembrance: Asian Americans after 9/11* (documentary, 69 min.). 2003.

Hwang, Jason. *Afterbirth* (documentary, 34 min.). 1982.

Kelly, Nancy. *Thousand Pieces of Gold* (drama, 105 min.). 1991.

Kirk, Michael. *From China with Love* (documentary, 60 min.). 2004.

Koster, Henry. *Flower Drum Song* (comedy). 1961.

Lee, Ang. *Tui Shou* (*Pushing Hands*) (drama, 105 min.). 1992.

———. *The Wedding Banquet* (drama, 106 min.). 1993.

Lee, Joyce. *Foreign Talk* (drama, 11 min.). 1993.

Lew, Jennifer F. *Separate Lives, Broken Dreams: Saga of Chinese Immigration* (documentary, 47 min.). 1994.

Lowe, Felicia. *Carved in Silence* (documentary, 45 min.). 1988.

———. *Claiming a Voice: The Visual Communications Story* (documentary, 60 min.). 1990.

Mock, Freida Lee. *Maya Lin: A Strong Clear Vision* (documentary, 98 min.). 1995.

Moyers, Bill. *Becoming American: The Chinese Experience* (documentary, three parts, 360 min.). 2003.

Nakasako, Spencer. *Talking History* (documentary, 30 min.). 1984.

Nakasako, Spencer, and Vincent DiGirolamo. *Monterey's Boat People* (documentary, 29 min.). 1982.

Ning, Stephen C. *Freckled Rice* (documentary, 48 min.). 1983.

Niwa, Paul. *Overshadowed: Boston's Chinatown* (documentary, 27 min.). 2005.

Sakya, Sapana, Donald Young, and Kyung Yu. *Searching for Asian America* (documentary, 90 min.). 2003.

Soe, Valerie. *All Orientals Look the Same* (experimental, 2 min.). 1986.

———. *Picturing Oriental Girls* (documentary, 12 min.). 1992.

Tajima-Peña, Renee. *My America . . . or Honk if You Love Buddha* (documentary, 85 min.). 1997.

———. *Labor Women* (documentary, 35 min.). 2002.

Tom, Pam. *Two Lies* (documentary, 25 min.). 1990.

Wang, Peter. *A Great Wall* (comedy, 97 min.). 1986.

Wang, Wayne. *Chan Is Missing* (comedy, 80 min.). 1982.

———. *Dim Sum: A Little Bit of Heart* (drama, 88 min.). 1985.

———. *Dim Sum Take Out* (drama, 12 min.). 1988.

———. *Eat a Bowl of Tea* (drama, 102 min.). 1989.

———. *The Joy Luck Club* (drama, 139 min.). 1993.

Winn, Robert. *Grassroots Rising* (documentary, 60 min.). 2005.

Xu, Anhua. *My American Grandson* (drama, 90 min.). 1991.

# Notes

## INTRODUCTION

1. Gans, *The Urban Villagers*; Suttles, *The Social Order of the Slum*.

2. I left China to come to the United States when my son was barely 10 months old. I initially came to study for a master's degree in sociology and promised my family to return in no more than two years. But I was inspired and encouraged to pursue a doctorate after I earned my M.A. in December 1985, and I stayed on to work for my Ph.D. After receiving it in May 1989, I accepted a faculty position in one of the best universities in Guangzhou, shipped my belongings to China, and traveled to Switzerland for a short break. Events in Tiananmen Square on June 4, 1989, changed my career course and pushed me back to the United States.

3. I was trained as a quantitative sociologist and taught myself qualitative methodologies largely through practice; that is, I learned by doing fieldwork and interviews in Chinatown. Since this original research, I have always preferred to employ mixed methods in my work on contemporary Chinese America and other Asian immigrant communities, combining quantitative data (e.g., data from the U.S. Census Bureau and U.S. Citizenship and Immigration Services [formerly Immigration and Naturalization Service] and from surveys) and qualitative data derived from face-to-face interviews, extensive fieldwork and participant observation, and historical documents and media accounts.

4. Portes, "The Social Origins of the Cuban Enclave Economy of Miami"; Portes, "Economic Sociology and the Sociology of Immigration"; Wilson and Martin, "Ethnic Enclaves"; Wilson and Portes, "Immigrant Enclaves"; Portes and Bach, *The Latin Journey*. Also see Portes and Shafer, "Revisiting the Enclave Hypothesis."

5. The mainstream economy is segmented into a primary and a secondary sector with corresponding labor markets. The primary labor market is dominated by industries that are capital- or knowledge-intensive and high paying, with fringe benefits, good working conditions, and opportunities for promotion. In contrast, the secondary labor markets is

dominated by industries that are labor-intensive and low paying, with minimal or no fringe benefits, poor working conditions, and few opportunities for promotion.

6. Portes and Zhou, "Gaining the Upper Hand"; Portes and Zhou, "Self-Employment and the Earnings of Immigrants."

7. See Chapter 5 in this volume.

8. The subject-centered approach is further developed and applied in Zhou et al., "Success Attained, Deterred, and Denied."

9. See Zhou, *Chinatown*; Zhou and Logan, "Returns on Human Capital in Ethnic Enclaves."

10. See Chapters 5 and 8 in this volume.

11. See Chapter 8 in this volume.

12. See Chapter 3 in this volume.

13. My doctoral dissertation, "The Enclave Economy and Immigrant Incorporation in New York City's Chinatown," won the 1989 President's Distinguished Doctoral Dissertation Award from SUNY–Albany. My book *Chinatown,* based on my dissertation, received an honorable mention in 1993 from the Community and Urban Sociology Section of the American Sociological Association.

14. *Chinatown* was well received by book reviewers for academic and popular journals and has been extensively cited in the social science literature on international migration, immigrant adaptation, ethnic economies, Chinese immigration, residential mobility, geography, and urban sociology; it has been adopted as a main text for undergraduate and graduate courses.

15. Zhou, *Tang Ren Jie* (唐人街), has become a classic reference and text for programs in overseas Chinese studies in Chinese universities.

16. Among the scholars whose works are cited in the Bibliography, two were particularly influential in shaping my postdoctoral intellectual development in the area of Chinese American studies. Sucheng Chan took issue with two prevailing perspectives in the field: that of exploited victims and that of agents and sensible decision makers capable of shaping their own lives. Her actor-oriented approach shows how individuals make history and initiate adaptive responses to the social, economic, and political milieu in which they find themselves (see the introductory chapters in her book *This Bitter Sweet Soil* and her co-edited book *Chinese Americans and the Politics of Race and Culture*). Her passionate and extraordinary commitment to Asian American studies (see *In Defense of Asian American Studies*) has made her my role model even though I do not know her well at a personal level. Him Mark Lai is legendary and inspirational, one of the few U.S.-born Chinese American scholars who are fluently bilingual and bicultural. His contributions to Chinese American history are numerous, the most remarkable being his painstaking effort to collect and preserve Chinese-language data generated by Chinese immigrants in the United States, his mixed-method approach and meticulous research employing both Chinese- and English-language sources, and his conceptual framework, which brings Chinese Americans and Chinese immigrants (especially those who do not speak English) to the center of analysis, shaking off stereotypical depictions and giving them voice, agency, and respect as unique human beings.

17. Park, "Human Migration and the Marginal Man"; Stonequist, *The Marginal Man.*

18. Park, "Human Migration and the Marginal Man."

19. Warner and Srole, *The Social Systems of American Ethnic Groups.*

20. Alba, *Italian Americans*; Handlin, *The Uprooted*; Lieberson and Waters, *From Many Strands.*

21. Hsu, "From Chop Suey to Mandarin Cuisine"; Lee, *The Chinese in the United States*

*of America*; Tsai, *The Chinese Experience in America*; Wong, "From Pariah to Paragon"; Yuan, *Chinese-American Population*.

22. Portes and Rumbaut, *Legacies*; Suárez-Orozco and Suárez-Orozco, *Children of Immigration*; Telles and Ortiz, *Generations of Exclusion*.

23. Gans, "Second Generation Decline."

24. Ibid., pp. 173–174.

25. Chinese cultural products such as foods, music, and martial arts play an important role in this process. They are domesticated to appeal to American consumers, yielding significant economic returns. See Hsu, "From Chop Suey to Mandarin Cuisine"; Liu, *The Transnational History of a Chinese Family*; Liu, "The Resilience of Ethnic Culture."

26. See Chapters 5 to 8 in this volume. Whether ethnicity and the ethnic community have positive or negative effects on socioeconomic incorporation depends upon group-specific contexts of exit and reception.

27. Massey and Denton, *American Apartheid*; Wilson, *The Truly Disadvantaged*; Wilson, *When Work Disappears*.

28. Wilson, *The Truly Disadvantaged*.

29. Breton, "Institutional Completeness of Ethnic Communities and the Personal Relations of Immigrants."

30. Breton speculated that respondents from communities with no ethnic publications were most likely to make contacts outside their ethnic group (ibid., p. 198).

31. I use "institution" and "organization" interchangeably to refer to registered (formal) and nonregistered (informal) establishments in a given neighborhood. For example, I view community centers, churches, and nonprofit community-based organizations (CBOs) as local institutions, just as restaurants, doctor's offices, travel agencies, banks, and tutoring centers are. For-profit establishments are not merely economic institutions; they often serve as physical sites where local residents interact, socialize, and establish community. See Zhou, "How Do Neighborhoods Matter for Immigrant Children?"

32. This is the basic argument I am developing in my forthcoming book, *Chinatown, Koreatown, and Beyond*.

33. Coleman, "Social Capital in the Creation of Human Capital."

34. Portes and Sensenbrenner, "Embeddedness and Immigration," p. 1323.

35. Sampson, "Neighborhood and Community."

36. Putnam, *Making Democracy Work*.

37. See Bourdieu, "The Forms of Capital."

38. Loury, "A Dynamic Theory of Racial Income Differences."

39. The idea of ethnic capital was originally proposed by the economist George J. Borjas; see *Friends or Strangers* and "Ethnic Capital and Intergenerational Mobility." In my article co-written with Mingang Lin, "Community Transformation and the Formation of Ethnic Capital," we conceptualize ethnic capital differently, using a community perspective.

40. See Chapters 5 and 8 in this volume for a detailed discussion.

41. Zhou, "The Ethnic System of Supplementary Education"; Zhou and Kim, "Community Forces, Social Capital, and Educational Achievement." Also see Chapter 7 in this volume.

42. Korean immigrants in the United States have also developed an ethnic system of supplementary education that is arguably more sophisticated and better organized than the Chinese one. See Zhou and Kim, "Community Forces, Social Capital, and Educational Achievement." Findings are inconclusive because long-term, or lagged, effects of these supplementary programs are unclear and require future study.

43. At present, national-level survey data on Asian Americans and on Asian American subgroups are scarce.

## CHAPTER 1. THE CHINESE DIASPORA AND INTERNATIONAL MIGRATION

This chapter is based on "The Chinese Diaspora and International Migration," in *Social Transformations in Chinese Societies*, vol. 1 (Boston: Brill, 2006), pp. 161–190. © 2006 Brill Academic Publishers, used by permission. It has been rewritten and updated.

1. Ma and Cartier, *The Chinese Diaspora*; Zhuang, 世纪之交的海外华人 (*Ethnic Chinese at the Turn of the Centuries*); also see China Qiaowang: http://www.chinaqw.com.cn/node2/node116/node119/node158/index.html, accessed April 3, 2008.

2. Hong Kong became a special administrative district of China when it was returned to China in 1997. Under the "one China, two systems" policy, it is treated as a nation-state but only in an analytical sense. I shall treat Taiwan similarly in this chapter and throughout the book despite the controversy over its status.

3. Poston et al., "The Global Distribution of the Overseas Chinese around 1990"; Ma, "Space, Place and Transnationalism in the Chinese Diaspora"; Qiu, "国际人口迁移与华侨华人研究" ("International Migration and Research on Overseas Chinese").

4. Most recently, based on my calculations using *The World Factbook, 2005* (published by the Central Intelligence Agency online: https://www.cia.gov/library/publications/the-world-factbook), the countries with the largest Chinese-ancestry populations are Thailand (9.2 million), Indonesia (8.0 million), Malaysia (5.8 million), Singapore (3.4 million), and the United States (2.9 million). See also Ma, "Space, Place and Transnationalism in the Chinese Diaspora."

5. Qiu, "International Migration and Research on Overseas Chinese."

6. Liao, 福建海外交通史 (*A History of Overseas Communications of Fujian*).

7. Wang, *China and the Chinese Overseas*.

8. Zhuang, *The Feudal Chinese State and Its Policies toward Overseas Chinese*; Zhuang, 华侨华人与中国的关系 (*The Relationships between Chinese Overseas and China*).

9. More precisely, *Nanyang* refers to the region immediately to the south of China, including the Philippines, the Dutch East Indies, Malaya and Borneo, Siam, Burma, Vietnam, Cambodia, and Laos. Pan, *The Encyclopedia of the Chinese Overseas*, p. 16.

10. Reid, *Sojourners and Settlers*.

11. Pan, *The Encyclopedia of the Chinese Overseas*.

12. Liao, *A History of Overseas Communications of Fujian*; Pan, *Son of the Yellow Emperor*; Pan, *The Encyclopedia of the Chinese Overseas*; Zeng, *Marine Migration to Taiwan and the Philippines in the Qing Dynasty*; Zhuang, *The Relationships between Chinese Overseas and China*.

13. Pan, *The Encyclopedia of the Chinese Overseas*.

14. Wang, *Anglo-Chinese Encounters since 1800*; Zhuang, *The Relationships between Chinese Overseas and China*.

15. Wang, *China and the Chinese Overseas*.

16. Zhuang, *The Relationships between Chinese Overseas and China*.

17. Zhuang, *The Feudal Chinese State and Its Policies toward Overseas Chinese*; Zhuang, "China's Policies toward Overseas Chinese."

18. Zeng, 东洋航路移民: 明清海洋移民台湾与菲律宾的比较研究 (*Marine Migration to Taiwan and the Philippines in the Qing Dynasty*).

19. Liao, *A History of Overseas Communications of Fujian*; Zeng, *Marine Migration to Taiwan and the Philippines in the Qing Dynasty*; Zhuang, *The Feudal Chinese State and Its Policies toward Overseas Chinese*; Zhuang, "China's Policies toward Overseas Chinese."

20. Kyo, "Japan"; Zeng, *Marine Migration to Taiwan and the Philippines in the Qing Dynasty*.

21. Pan, *The Encyclopedia of the Chinese Overseas*; Purcell, *The Chinese in Southeast Asia*; Reid, *Sojourners and Settlers*.

22. Reid, "Introduction"; Reid, "Chinese and Southeast Asian Interactions."

23. Reid, "Introduction."

24. Ibid.

25. Reid, *Sojourners and Settlers*; Trocki, "Chinese Pioneering in Eighteenth-Century Southeast Asia."

26. Andaya, "Adapting to Political and Economic Change."

27. Abeyasekere, "Slaves in Batavia," p. 296.

28. Blythe, *The Impact of Chinese Secret Societies in Malaya*.

29. Reid, *Sojourners and Settlers*.

30. Reid, "Chinese and Southeast Asian Interactions."

31. Trocki, "Chinese Pioneering in Eighteenth-Century Southeast Asia"; Wickberg, "Localism and the Organization of Overseas Chinese Migration in the Nineteenth Century."

32. The Portuguese reached China by sea in 1514 and are believed to be the first Europeans to have done so. Pan, *The Encyclopedia of the Chinese Overseas*, p. 365.

33. Brown, "History [of the Philippines]."

34. Cribb, "History [of Indonesia]."

35. Li, 欧洲华侨华人史 (*A History of Chinese Immigrants in Europe*); Wang, *Anglo-Chinese Encounters since 1800*; Zeng, *Marine Migration to Taiwan and the Philippines in the Qing Dynasty*.

36. Smith, "History [of Viet Nam]."

37. Storry, "History [of Japan] Up to 1952."

38. Meagher, *The Coolie Trade*; Stewart, *Chinese Bondage in Peru*; Wang, *China and the Chinese Overseas*; Yun, *The Coolie Speaks*.

39. Pan, *The Encyclopedia of the Chinese Overseas*; World Book, *The World Book Encyclopedia* (1990), 3:502–503.

40. The foreign powers wanted the Qing dynasty to survive so that its unequal treaties would remain in effect. *World Book* (1990), 3:503.

41. Pan, *The Encyclopedia of the Chinese Overseas*.

42. Ibid.

43. Zhuang, *The Relationships between Chinese Overseas and China*.

44. Pan, *The Encyclopedia of the Chinese Overseas*.

45. Irick, *Ch'ing Policy toward the Coolie Trade*; Meagher, *The Coolie Trade*; Stewart, *Chinese Bondage in Peru*; Wang, *China and the Chinese Overseas*; Yun, *The Coolie Speaks*.

46. Ching-Hwang, *Coolies and Mandarins*; McKeown, *Chinese Migrant Networks and Cultural Change*; Zhuang, *The Relationships between Chinese Overseas and China*.

47. Zeng, *Marine Migration to Taiwan and the Philippines in the Qing Dynasty*; Zhuang, *The Relationships between Chinese Overseas and China*.

48. Pan, *The Encyclopedia of the Chinese Overseas*.

49. Zhu, *Overseas Emigration from China*.

50. See, "Chinese Clanship in the Philippines"; Wickberg, "Localism and the Organization of Overseas Chinese Migration in the Nineteenth Century"; Wickberg, "The Philippines."

51. Willmott, "Cambodia."

52. Pan, *The Encyclopedia of the Chinese Overseas*.

53. The Si Yi region, located in southwest Guangdong, includes four counties—Taishan, Kaiping, Enping, and Xinhui. The San Yi region includes three counties—Nanhai,

Panyu, and Shunde. See Chan, *This Bitter Sweet Soil*; Chan, *Chinese American Transnationalism*; Ling, *Chinese St. Louis*; Zhou, *Chinatown*.

54. Burusratanaphand, "Chinese Identity in Thailand"; Chan and Tong, *Alternate Identities*.

55. Meagher, *The Coolie Trade*; Stewart, *Chinese Bondage in Peru*; Yun, *The Coolie Speaks*.

56. Zhu, *Overseas Emigration from China*.

57. Skinner, *Chinese Society in Thailand*.

58. Zhu, *Overseas Emigration from China*.

59. This number probably included the refugees who walked across the border to Vietnam after the Communist takeover in 1949.

60. The credit ticket system and labor contracts were also the main means of labor migration to the South Pacific, Hawaii, and the Americas.

61. Blythe, *The Impact of Chinese Secret Societies in Malaya*.

62. Pan, *The Encyclopedia of the Chinese Overseas*.

63. Meagher, *The Coolie Trade*; Stewart, *Chinese Bondage in Peru*; Wang, *China and the Chinese Overseas*.

64. Meagher, *The Coolie Trade*; Stewart, *Chinese Bondage in Peru*.

65. Zhu, *Overseas Emigration from China*.

66. Melendy, *Asians in America*.

67. Irick, *Ch'ing Policy toward the Coolie Trade*, offers a counterargument, asserting that the Qing government effectively negotiated the treaty system to achieve regulation and eventual prohibition of the coolie trade.

68. Qiu, "International Migration and Research on Overseas Chinese."

69. Azuma, "Brief Historical Overview of Japanese Emigration, 1868–1998"; Cribb, "History [of Indonesia]."

70. Brown, "History [of the Philippines]"; Cribb, "History [of Indonesia]"; Liu, 中国东南亚学 (*Southeast Asian Studies in China*); Smith, "History [of Viet Nam]"; Turnbull, "History [of Singapore]."

71. Fitzgerald, *The Third China*; Fitzgerald, "The History of China Up to 1966."

72. Chang, *The Global Silicon Valley Home*; Chang, *Taiwan's Brain Drain and Its Reversal*; Chee, *Taiwanese American Transnational Families*.

73. Hugo, "The Demographic Underpinnings of Current and Future International Migrations in Asia."

74. Abella, "Contemporary Labor Migration from Asia."

75. Turnbull, "History [of Singapore]."

76. Hugo, "The Demographic Underpinnings of Current and Future International Migrations in Asia"; Martin et al., "Overview"; Tyner, "Global Cities and Circuits of Global Labor."

77. Hugo, "The Demographic Underpinnings of Current and Future International Migrations in Asia"; Martin et al., "Overview."

78. Martin et al., "Overview."

79. Hugo, "The Demographic Underpinnings of Current and Future International Migrations in Asia."

80. Skeldon, "Labor Migration to Hong Kong."

81. Ng and Lee, "Hong Kong Labor Market in the Aftermath of the Crisis."

82. Skeldon, "Labor Migration to Hong Kong"; Wong, "Hong Kong Immigrants in San Francisco."

83. Tsay, "Taiwan."

84. Chan, *Chinese American Transnationalism*; Chang, *Taiwan's Brain Drain and Its Reversal.*

85. Tsay, "Taiwan."

86. Ibid.

87. Lee, "The Impact of the Asian Financial Crisis on Foreign Workers in Japan."

88. Chew and Chew, "Immigration and Foreign Labor in Singapore."

89. Ibid.

90. Liu, *Southeast Asian Studies in China*; Liu, "New Migrants and the Revival of Overseas Chinese Nationalism."

91. Arnold and Shah, "Asia's Labor Pipeline"; Goldstone, "A Tsunami on the Horizon?"

92. Weidenbaum and Hughes, *The Bamboo Network*. "Bamboo network" refers to overseas Chinese business families in Southeast Asia and their enormous family-run conglomerates.

93. Forbes, "Toward the 'Pacific Century.'"

94. Zhou, Chen, and Cai, "Chinese Language Media and Immigrant Life in the United States and Canada."

95. Li, *Chinese in Canada.*

96. Zhou, Chen, and Cai, "Chinese Language Media and Immigrant Life in the United States and Canada."

97. Martin et al., "Overview."

98. Battistella and Paganoni, *Philippine Labour Migration.*

99. Zhuang, *The Relationships between Chinese Overseas and China.*

100. Chan, *Cities with Invisible Walls.*

101. Chin, *Chinese Subculture and Criminality*; Chin, *Smuggled Chinese*; Li, *A History of Chinese Immigrants in Europe*; Kwong, *Forbidden Workers*; Liang, "Demography of Illicit Emigration from China"; Myers, "Of Qinqing, Qinshu, Guanxi, and Shetou"; Smith, "Chinese Migrant Trafficking."

102. Goldstone, "A Tsunami on the Horizon?"

103. Chin, *Smuggled Chinese.*

104. Smith, "Chinese Migrant Trafficking."

105. Goldstone, "A Tsunami on the Horizon?"

106. Smith, "Chinese Migrant Trafficking."

107. Ibid., p. 14.

108. Smith, "Chinese Migrant Trafficking."

109. Chan, *Chinese Business Networks*; Li, "Mass Migration within China and the Implications for Chinese Emigration"; Pillai, "The Impact of the Economic Crisis on Migrant Labor in Malaysia."

110. Lee, "The Impact of the Asian Financial Crisis on Foreign Workers in Japan."

111. Massey et al., "An Evaluation of International Migration Theory."

112. Koehn and Yin, *The Expanding Role of Chinese Americans in U.S.-China Relations*; Reid, *Sojourners and Settlers.*

113. Goldstone, "A Tsunami on the Horizon?"; Qiu, "International Migration and Research on Overseas Chinese."

## CHAPTER 2. DEMOGRAPHIC TRENDS AND CHARACTERISTICS OF CONTEMPORARY CHINESE AMERICA

This chapter is based on "Chinese: Once Excluded, Now Ascendant" in Eric Lai and Dennis Arguelles, eds., *The New Faces of Asian Pacific America* (Los Angeles: Asian Week, UCLA Asian American Studies Center, and the Coalition for Asian Pacific American Community Development, 2003), pp. 37–44. © 2003 Asian American Studies Center Press, used by permission. It has been rewritten and updated.

1. 2006 American Community Survey, at the website of the U.S. Bureau of the Census: http://factfinder.census.gov. See S0201: "Selected Population Profile in the United States Population Group: Chinese alone or in any combination."

2. Forty-three Chinese were admitted to the United States between 1820 and 1849 according to official immigration statistics. The total number of Chinese immigrants legally admitted from 1850 to 1959 was 424,897. In contrast, 716,916 were admitted between 1960 and 1989; 591,599 between 1990 and 1999; and 460,678 between 2000 and 2006. Figures are based on country of last residence. U.S. Department of Homeland Security, *Yearbook of Immigration Statistics: 2007,* table 2: see http://www.dhs.gov/ximgtn/statistics/publications/LPR07.shtm.

3. 2006 American Community Survey.

4. Cassel, *The Chinese in America;* Chan, *This Bitter Sweet Soil;* Chan, *Asian Americans;* Chang, *The Chinese in America;* Daniels, *Asian American;* Glick, *Sojourners and Settlers;* Hom, *Songs of Gold Mountain;* Sung, *Mountain of Gold;* Takaki, *Strangers from a Different Shore;* Valentine, "Chinese Placer Mining in the United States"; Zhou, *Chinatown.*

5. Aarim-Heriot, *Chinese Immigrants, African Americans, and Racial Anxiety in the United States, 1848–1882;* Chan, *Asian Americans;* Chiu, *Chinese Labor in California;* Coolidge, *Chinese Immigration;* Gyory, *Closing the Gate;* Kung, *Chinese in American Life;* Lee, *At America's Gates;* Liu, *The Chinatown Trunk Mystery;* McClain, *In Search of Equality;* Miller, *The Unwelcome Immigrants;* Peffer, *If They Don't Bring Their Women Here;* Salyer, *Laws Harsh as Tigers;* Sandmeyer, *The Anti-Chinese Movement in California;* Saxton, *The Indispensable Enemy;* Shah, *Contagious Divides;* Takaki, *Strangers from a Different Shore.*

6. Chan, *This Bitter Sweet Soil;* Chan, *Asian Americans;* Chow, *Chasing Their Dreams;* Lydon, *Chinese Gold;* Zhu, *A Chinaman's Chance;* Zo, *Chinese Emigration into the United States.*

7. Chan, *This Bitter Sweet Soil;* Chen, *Chinese San Francisco, 1850–1943;* Chow, *Chasing Their Dreams;* Dicker, *The Chinese in San Francisco;* Hsu, *Dreaming of Gold, Dreaming of Home;* Lydon, *Chinese Gold;* McCunn, *An Illustrated History of the Chinese in America;* Nee and Nee, *Longtime Californ'.*

8. Chan, *Asian Americans;* Lee, *The Chinese in the United States of America;* Lee, *The Growth and Decline of Chinese Communities in the Rocky Mountain Region;* Lyman, *Chinese Americans;* Tchen, *New York before Chinatown;* Zhang, "The Origin of the Chinese Americanization Movement"; Zhu, *A Chinaman's Chance.*

9. "Paper sons" claimed to be sons of American citizens and immigrated to the United States using false papers during the Chinese Exclusion era. Chin, *Paper Son;* Fry, "Illegal Entry of Orientals into the United States between 1910 and 1920"; Hsu, "Gold Mountain Dreams and Paper Son Schemes"; Lau, *Paper Families;* Siu, "The Sojourner"; Wong, *American Paper Son.*

10. Sung, *The Adjustment Experience of Chinese Immigrant Children in New York City;* Zhao, *Remaking Chinese America.*

11. Wong, "Chinese Americans."

12. Si Yi (Sze Yap) includes four counties—Taishan, Kaiping, Enping, and Xinhui—whose people share a similar local dialect. San Yi (Sam Yap) includes three counties—Nanhai, Panyu, and Xunde. The Pearl River Delta counties (such as Zhongshan) were among the main sources for migrants from the Canton region.

13. U.S. Bureau of the Census, *The American Community, Asians.*

14. Ibid.

15. Consolidated Metropolitan Statistical Areas (CMSA): New York–Northern New Jersey–Long Island, Los Angeles–Anaheim–Riverside, and San Francisco–Oakland–San Jose. Chapters 3 and 4 in this volume offer a detailed description and analysis of Chinese New York and Chinese Los Angeles.

16. Fan, "Chinese Americans"; Fong, *The First Suburban Chinatown*; Horton, *The Politics of Diversity*; Laguerre, *The Global Ethnopolis*; Li, *From Urban Enclave to Ethnic Suburb*; Ling, *Chinese St. Louis*; Ng, *The Taiwanese Americans*; Tseng, "Suburban Ethnic Economy"; Wong, "Monterey Park"; Yang, *Post-1965 Immigration to the United States*; Zhou, "How Do Places Matter."

17. Chen, *Chinatown No More*; Fong, *The First Suburban Chinatown*; Lin, *Reconstructing Chinatown*; Zhou, "Chinese"; Zhou and Kim, "A Tale of Two Metropolises."

18. The term "ethnoburb" was first proposed by the Chinese American geographer Wei Li in 1997 to refer to a suburban community with a significant concentration of a particular ethnic group in residence and business ownership. Ethnoburbs are hybrids of multiethnic enclaves and middle-class suburbs (see Fig. 4.1 in this volume).

19. Horton, *The Politics of Diversity*; Saito, *Race and Politics*; see also Chapters 3 and 4 in this volume.

20. Zhou, *Chinatown.*

21. Tsai, "Contextualizing Immigrants' Lived Experience."

22. Zhou, "Contemporary Immigration and the Dynamics of Race and Ethnicity"; Zhou and Lin, "A Study on Ethnic Capital and the Transformation of Chinese Migrant Communities in the United States."

23. U.S. Bureau of the Census, *Survey of Minority-Owned Business Enterprises, 1987*; *Survey of Minority-Owned Business Enterprises, 1992.*

24. U.S. Bureau of the Census, *Survey of Minority Owned Business Enterprises, 2002.*

25. Zhou, *Chinatown*; see also Chapters 5 and 8 in this volume.

26. Kwong, *The New Chinatown*; Kwong, *Chinatown, N.Y.*; Lee, "Jing Fong"; Loo, *Chinatown*; Louie, *Sweatshop Warriors*; Shah, *Contagious Divides*; Trauner, "The Chinese as Medical Scapegoats in San Francisco, 1870–1906."

27. Breton, "Institutional Completeness of Ethnic Communities and the Personal Relations of Immigrants." Raymond Breton developed the concept of institutional completeness for his study of immigrant adaptation in Montreal in the early 1960s. He defined it in terms of the ability of complex neighborhood-based formal institutions to satisfy community members' needs. He measured the degree of social organization in an ethnic community on a continuum: at one extreme an informal network of interpersonal relationships, such as kinship, friendship, or companionship groups; at the other, a set of informal and formal organizations ranging from welfare and mutual aid societies to commercial, religious, educational, political, professional, and recreational organizations and ethnic media. Breton found that the presence of a wide range of formal institutions in an ethnic community had a powerful effect, keeping immigrants' social relations within its boundaries and minimizing out-group contacts, thus inhibiting assimilation.

28. Kasinitz et al., *Inheriting the City.*

29. While religion is not a focus of my work, it is an important part of Chinese immigrant life and of the ethnic community. For more on the topic, see Chen, *Getting Saved in America*; Guest, *God in Chinatown*; Jeung, *Faithful Generations*; Yang, *Chinese Christians in America*; Yoo, *New Spiritual Homes*.

30. See Chapter 11 in this volume for a more detailed discussion.

31. See Chapters 3 and 4 in this volume.

32. See Chapter 11 in this volume.

## CHAPTER 3. IN AND OUT OF CHINATOWN

This chapter is based on Chapter 8, "Residential Mobility and Ethnic Segregation," of *Chinatown: The Socioeconomic Potential of an Urban Enclave* (Philadelphia: Temple University Press, 1992). © 1992 Temple University Press, used by permission. It has been rewritten and updated. The analysis was based on 1980 U.S. census data and my fieldwork in New York's Chinatown in 1988–1989. I have selectively updated census information and observational data where necessary.

1. Dillon, *The Hatchet Men*; Kuo, *Social and Political Change in New York's Chinatown*; Kwong, *The New Chinatown*; Leong, *Chinatown Inside Out*; Sung, *The Adjustment Experience of Chinese Immigrant Children in New York City*; Wang, *Surviving the City*; Wong, *Chinatown*.

2. Earlier Chinese had landed and settled in New York City even before Chinatown took shape: see Tchen, *New York before Chinatown*.

3. Kwong, *The New Chinatown*; Kwong, *Forbidden Workers*; Kwong, *Chinatown, New York*.

4. Chen, *Chinatown No More*; Lin, *Reconstructing Chinatown*; Zhou, "Chinese"; Zhou and Kim, "A Tale of Two Metropolises"; Zhou and Lin, "Community Transformation and the Formation of Ethnic Capital"; Zhou and Logan, "In and Out of Chinatown."

5. Personal interview, May 1993.

6. In this chapter "Flushing" refers the core area in downtown Flushing, which was officially defined by Queens Community Board #7 as including 11 contiguous census tracts in both the 1980 and 1990 censuses: 797, 845, 851, 853, 855, 857, 859, 865, 867, 871, and 875. See Zhou and Kim, "A Tale of Two Metropolises."

7. Ng, *The Taiwanese Americans*.

8. Parvin, "Immigrants Migrate to International City," p. 22.

9. Ibid.

10. Winnick, *New People in Old Neighborhoods*.

11. NYCDCP, *The Newest New Yorkers*.

12. Zhou, *Chinatown*, pp. 191–192.

13. Kwong, *Forbidden Workers*.

14. Aloff, "Where China and Brooklyn Overlap"; Mustain, "Chinatown Grows in Brooklyn, Too."

15. Gladwell, "Rebirth in New York."

16. On October 3, 1965, President Johnson signed the Immigration and Nationality Act (the Hart-Celler Act), which rejected the use of national origin as a basis for selecting immigrants and gave preference to family reunification. As a direct result, the population of Chinese ancestry increased from 237,292 in 1960 to 435,062 in 1970, and to 812,178 in 1980.

17. Lieberson, *A Piece of the Pie*.

18. Alba, *Italian Americans*; Gans, *The Urban Villagers*.

19. Massey and Denton, "Trends in Residential Segregation of Blacks, Hispanics, and Asians." Using the census data involved certain limitations. First, the census data they used were aggregated to average group characteristics in metropolitan areas, with no analysis of predictors of residential location at the individual level. Second, their results were mixed. In predicting a group's degree of suburbanization, their main indicator of the group's SES, median family income, was not significant at the .05 level for either Hispanics or Asians. A second indicator, occupational dissimilarity with Anglos, was significant for Hispanics but not for Asians. The proportion of U.S.-born, seen as an indicator of acculturation, was positively related to suburbanization for Asians, but English-language ability was not (language ability is negatively related to suburbanization for Hispanics). For more detail, see Zhou, *Chinatown*, chap. 8.

20. Alba and Logan, "Variations on Two Themes."

21. Wilson and Portes, "Immigrant Enclaves"; Portes and Bach, *The Latin Journey*. For a more detailed discussion of the enclave economy, see Chapter 5 in this volume.

22. Portes and Jensen, "What's an Ethnic Enclave?" See also Zhou and Logan, "Returns on Human Capital in Ethnic Enclaves."

23. Massey and Denton, "Trends in Residential Segregation of Blacks, Hispanics, and Asians." See also Bean and Tienda, "The Hispanic Population of the United States"; Frey and Speare, "Regional and Metropolitan Growth and Decline in the United States."

24. Segregation across census tracts was measured in terms of evenness of distribution, indicated by the Index of Dissimilarity (D). I used the census-tract-level data in summary tape file 3A (STF3A) of the 1980 Census of Population and Housing. My sample included New York City and adjacent counties in New York and New Jersey. For the calculation of D, see Lieberson, *A Piece of the Pie*, p. 254; Cortese, Falk, and Cohen, "Further Consideration of the Methodological Analysis of Segregation Indices." I calculated D for the segregation of the Chinese from three major groups: non-Hispanic whites, non-Hispanic blacks, and Hispanics. I also included D scores between major Asian groups: the Chinese, Japanese, Koreans, and Filipinos. According to prior research, D scores between 0 and .30 generally suggest a low degree of residential segregation, those between .30 and .60 a moderate degree, and those above .60 a high degree. For more detail, see Zhou and Logan, "In and Out of Chinatown."

25. Measuring segregation of blacks from non-Hispanic whites, Massey and Denton, "Trends in Residential Segregation of Blacks, Hispanics, and Asians," reported that in 1980 the average value of D for all central cities in their study was .69. They found that segregation of Asians from non-Hispanic whites averaged only .41 for central cities, with a value of .49 for New York City, both scores considerably lower than my findings for the Chinese in New York City. Langberg and Farley, "Residential Segregation of Asian Americans in 1980," also found that in selected standard metropolitan statistical areas (SMSAs) across the nation, the average segregation scores for the Asian subgroups, except for the Japanese, were higher than what Massey and Denton found for Asians, with the Vietnamese being the most segregated from non-Hispanic whites (.69). Thus, lumping all the Asians into the same category obscured subgroup differences in spatial assimilation. In fact, there were high levels of segregation between these subgroups. The Asian label simply masked real national and ethnic differences.

26. However, I calculated the baseline values for Chinese and Asians both in New York City as a whole and in Manhattan. I found that the order of magnitude of random effects on D in Manhattan was minimal compared with the actual values of D and differences in D for Chinese and Asians. For more detail, see Zhou, "The Enclave Economy and Immigrant Incorporation in New York City's Chinatown."

27. For this purpose, I exploited the Public Use Microdata Sample (PUMS) of the 1980 Census of Population and Housing. To avoid double counting within the same household, the logistic models were based on samples limited to householders who are 25 years old or older. This choice also had a substantive justification because location decisions are made by households, not individuals. For more detail, see Zhou, "The Enclave Economy and Immigrant Incorporation in New York City's Chinatown."

28. For the 1970 NORC occupational prestige scale, a two-digit score was assigned to each respondent's occupational category to create the occupational prestige variable.

29. Sectoral employment is a dummy variable, with the enclave industries coded as 1 and all other industries 0. The definition of enclave industries is based upon overrepresentation of the Chinese in the work force; data on ethnic ownership of businesses are not available. The enclave economy includes the garment industry, restaurant business, and ethnic retail and service firms. Precise definitions used here include the PUMS standard industry codes 132–152, 500–542, 550–571, 580–691, 771–780, and 812–830.

30. The interpretation of the effects of the continuous variables is straightforward; that is, one unit change in education, household income, or occupational prestige increases the log odds of living elsewhere by its logit, controlling for all other independent variables. However, the logit coefficients of the dummy variables are not sufficient to interpret the model, for it is difficult to grasp concretely the magnitudes of effects in a logarithmic scale: see Alba, "Interpreting the Parameters of Log-Linear Models." The actual magnitude of effects in a logit model is not fixed, which has been an obstacle to interpretation. Alba's procedure is to begin from the mean values on all variables and measure the effects of changes in the independent variables from that standard reference point. Thus, I first translated logit parameters into multiplicative parameters (odds ratios relative to the omitted category), and then derived illustrative percentage differences that showed the magnitude of effects of the predictors. The reference percentages for suburban residence (percent living outside New York City) for the Chinese and whites were 20.0 percent and 60.2 percent, respectively. The reference percentages for residence in the outer boroughs for the Chinese and whites were 53.3 percent and 74.5 percent, respectively. For more detail, see Zhou, "The Enclave Economy and Immigrant Incorporation in New York City's Chinatown."

31. For detailed results see Zhou, "The Enclave Economy and Immigrant Incorporation in New York City's Chinatown"; Zhou and Logan, "In and Out of Chinatown."

32. Fieldwork data were collected in 1988 and 1989 through periodic observations in Chinatown and extensive interviews with city government officials; community leaders and organizers; Chinatown's investors, bankers, real estate agents, and business owners; enclave and non-enclave Chinese immigrant workers; longtime residents of Chinese enclaves in Brooklyn, Manhattan, and Queens; and other informants of various occupations. Questions directed to both enclave and non-enclave workers involved the immigration process, education before and after immigration, English proficiency, family and kinship relations, residential choices, ethnic identity, past employment, experience of racial discrimination, inter- or intraethnic labor market experiences, job satisfaction, and experience with labor unions. I personally conducted these face-to-face and telephone interviews with informants as part of my doctoral dissertation research. For the sake of confidentially, pseudonyms are used here. See Zhou, *Chinatown*, for details.

33. Telephone interview, January 1989.

34. Personal interview, January 1989. .

35. Kwong, *The New Chinatown*.

36. Kwong, *The New Chinatown*; Wang, "Behind the Boom"; Zhou, "The Enclave Economy and Immigrant Incorporation in New York City's Chinatown."

37. Kwong, *The New Chinatown*.

38. Personal interview, May 1988.

39. Though illegal, this was a common practice in Chinatown. Because most of Chinatown's rental apartment units were rent-controlled, landlords could not raise the rent substantially unless they drove the old tenants out. See Kwong, *The New Chinatown.*

40. Personal interview, September 1988.

41. Personal interview, May 1988.

42. Personal interview, December 1988.

43. Personal interview, January 1989.

44. Sung, *The Adjustment Experience of Chinese Immigrant Children in New York City*; Zhou, "The Enclave Economy and Immigrant Incorporation in New York City's Chinatown."

45. Yuan, "Voluntary Segregation."

46. Personal interview, December 1988.

47. Personal interview, September 1988.

48. Personal interview, September 1988.

49. Personal interview, September 1988.

50. Loo and Mar, "Desired Residential Mobility in a Low Income Ethnic Community"; Yuan, "Voluntary Segregation."

51. Personal interview, September 1988.

52. NYCDCP, *Asians in New York City.*

53. Zhou and Logan, "Returns on Human Capital in Ethnic Enclaves."

## CHAPTER 4. SUBURBANIZATION AND NEW TRENDS IN COMMUNITY DEVELOPMENT

The chapter is rewritten from Min Zhou, Yen-Fen Tseng, and Rebecca Y. Kim, "Rethinking Residential Assimilation through the Case of a Chinese Ethnoburb in the San Gabriel Valley, California," *Amerasia Journal* 34 (2008): 55–83. © 2008 Asian American Studies Center Press, used by permission. Yen-Fen Tseng is professor of sociology at National Taiwan University in Taipei. Rebecca Kim is assistant professor of sociology at Pepperdine University in Malibu, California.

1. Zhou and Kim, "A Tale of Two Metropolises"; Zhou et al., "Rethinking Residential Assimilation."

2. Li, "Spatial Transformation of an Urban Ethnic Community from Chinatown to Chinese Ethnoburb in Los Angeles." For the definition of an ethnoburb, see note 18 in Chapter 2 in this volume.

3. Portes and Rumbaut, *Immigrant America*; Sassen, *Cities in a World Economy.*

4. Ng, *The Taiwanese Americans*; Yang, *Post-1965 Immigration to the United States*; Zhou and Gatewood, "Mapping the Terrain."

5. Edwards, *Contested Terrain*; Tolbert, Horan, and Beck, "The Structure of Economic Segmentation."

6. Waldinger, "Ethnicity and Opportunity in the Plural City."

7. Ibid.

8. Fong, *The First Suburban Chinatown*; Horton, *The Politics of Diversity*; Li, "Spatial Transformation of an Urban Ethnic Community from Chinatown to Chinese Ethnoburb in Los Angeles"; Lin and Robinson, "Spatial Disparities in the Expansion of the Chinese Ethnoburb of Los Angeles"; Saito, *Race and Politics*; Tseng, "Beyond 'Little Taipei'"; Tseng, "Suburban Ethnic Economy"; Wong, "Monterey Park"; Zhou, "Ethnic Networks as Transactional Networks."

9. Zhou, *Chinatown.*

10. The first generation (the foreign-born) and the second generations (the U.S.-born of foreign-born parentage) combined make up nearly 90 percent. See Zhou and Gatewood, "Mapping the Terrain."

11. Tseng, "Beyond 'Little Taipei'"; Tseng, "Suburban Ethnic Economy."

12. Xie and Goyette, *A Demographic Portrait of Asian Americans.* Nationwide, 48 percent of adult Chinese Americans (aged 25 and over) had a college degree, compared with 24 percent in the general U.S. adult population, as shown in the 2000 U.S. Census.

13. Lin, *Reconstructing Chinatown*; Zhou, *Chinatown.*

14. For details, see Zhou and Kim, "A Tale of Two Metropolises."

15. See Chapter 3 in this volume.

16. Li, "Ethnoburb versus Chinatown."

17. Conway, *San Gabriel Valley Regional Demographic Profile.* Also see Wikipedia, "The San Gabriel Valley," http://en.wikipedia.org/wiki/San_Gabriel_Valley, accessed January 30, 2007.

18. Fong, *The First Suburban Chinatown*; Horton, *The Politics of Diversity*; Li, "Spatial Transformation of an Urban Ethnic Community from Chinatown to Chinese Ethnoburb in Los Angeles"; Lin and Robinson, "Spatial Disparities in the Expansion of the Chinese Ethnoburb of Los Angeles"; Tseng, "Beyond 'Little Taipei'"; Tseng, "Suburban Ethnic Economy"; Zhou, "Ethnic Networks as Transactional Networks."

19. Fong, *The First Suburban Chinatown*; Horton, *The Politics of Diversity.*

20. Fong, *The First Suburban Chinatown*; Horton, *The Politics of Diversity.*

21. Horton, *The Politics of Diversity.*

22. Tseng, "Suburban Ethnic Economy."

23. USINS, *Statistical Yearbook of the Immigration and Naturalization Service.*

24. Tseng, "Suburban Ethnic Economy."

25. Tseng, "Suburban Ethnic Economy"; Yoon, "The Changing Signification of Ethnic and Class Resources in Immigrant Businesses."

26. Tseng, "Suburban Ethnic Economy."

27. Fong, *The First Suburban Chinatown*; Zhou, "'Parachute Kids' in Southern California." See also Chapter 10 in this volume.

28. Diamond Bar is adjacent to the San Gabriel Valley and may be more appropriately considered to be a Pomona Valley city.

29. Table 4.1 displays four Asian-majority cities—Monterey Park, San Gabriel, Rowland Heights, and Walnut. Not listed there are four other Asian-majority cities in the United States: Cerritos (58 percent) in L.A. County, Daly City (51 percent) and Milpitas (52 percent) in the San Francisco Bay Area, and Honolulu City (56 percent) in Hawaii. In 1990, only Monterey Park and Daly City had Asian majorities.

30. Quoted in Arax, "Monterey Park."

31. Ibid.

32. Fong, *The First Suburban Chinatown*, 50.

33. Tseng, "Suburban Ethnic Economy."

34. Eljera, "The Chinese Beverly Hills"; Amy Luu, "The Chinese American Experience in the San Gabriel Valley," http://www.eskimo.com/~camla/history/sangabri.htm, accessed January 15, 2007.

35. Tseng, "Suburban Ethnic Economy," p. 44.

36. Wong, "Monterey Park."

37. Tseng, "Suburban Ethnic Economy."

38. Li, "Building Ethnoburbia"; Li et al., "Chinese-American Banking and Community Development in Los Angeles County"; Zhou, "Beyond Ethnic Enclaves."

39. Light, *Deflecting Immigration*; Tseng, "Suburban Ethnic Economy."

40. Portes and Zhou, "Gaining the Upper Hand."

41. For a more detailed discussion, see Chapter 5 in this volume.

42. Ethnic organizations, Chinese schools, and Chinese-language media have historically been three pillars of Chinese diasporic communities. See Li, "Chinese Diaspora in Occidental Societies."

43. Zhou and Kim, "Formation, Consolidation, and Diversification of the Ethnic Elite."

44. Ibid.

45. Fong, *The First Suburban Chinatown*, p. 153.

46. Zhou and Kim, "Community Forces, Social Capital, and Educational Achievement." Also see Chapter 7 in this volume.

47. Li, "Chinese Diaspora in Occidental Societies."

48. Fong, *Complementary Education and Culture in the Global/Local Chinese Community*. See also Chapter 7 in this volume.

49. Fong, *Complementary Education and Culture in the Global/Local Chinese Community*; Wang, *A View from Within*; Zhou and Li, "Ethnic Language Schools and the Development of Supplementary Education in the Immigrant Chinese Community in the United States." See also Chapter 7 in this volume.

50. See Chapter 7 for details.

51. Horton, *The Politics of Diversity*.

52. Ibid.

53. Ibid.

54. Mayors are not directly elected in Monterey Park; instead, council members become mayors for nine months on a rotating basis. The Chinese American council member was Lily Lee Chen.

55. "The New Ellis Island," *Time*, June 13, 1983, pp. 18–25.

56. Horton, *The Politics of Diversity*, p. 108.

57. Dr. Judy Chu stepped down as California assemblywoman in 2006 because of term limits. She was elected to the California Board of Equalization in 2006, and now chairs the Board of Equalization.

58. Fong, *The First Suburban Chinatown*; Horton, *The Politics of Diversity*; Li, "Spatial Transformation of an Urban Ethnic Community from Chinatown to Chinese Ethnoburb in Los Angeles"; Saito, *Race and Politics*; Tseng, "Suburban Ethnic Economy"; Zhou, "Ethnic Networks as Transactional Networks"; Zhou and Kim, "A Tale of Two Metropolises."

59. Lin and Robinson, "Spatial Disparities in the Expansion of the Chinese Ethnoburb of Los Angeles."

60. Personal interviews, March 1999.

61. Horton, *The Politics of Diversity*.

62. Quoted ibid., p. 10.

63. Horton, *The Politics of Diversity*.

64. Fong, *The First Suburban Chinatown*; Horton, *The Politics of Diversity*; Zhou and Kim, "A Tale of Two Metropolises."

65. Horton, *The Politics of Diversity*; Lin and Robinson, "Spatial Disparities in the Expansion of the Chinese Ethnoburb of Los Angeles."

66. Horton, *The Politics of Diversity*.

## CHAPTER 5. IMMIGRANT ENTREPRENEURSHIP AND THE ENCLAVE ECONOMY

This chapter is based on Chapter 6, "The Ethnic Labor Force and Its Labor Market Experience," of *Chinatown: The Socioeconomic Potential of an Urban Enclave* (Philadelphia: Temple University Press, 1992). © 1992 Temple University Press, used by permission. It has been rewritten and updated. It also draws on material from my "Revisiting Ethnic Entrepreneurship: Convergences, Controversies, and Conceptual Advancements," published in *International Migration Review* 38 (2004): 1040–1074. The analysis uses data from the 1980 U.S. Census and my own fieldwork in New York City. Fieldwork data were collected by systematic participant observations in Chinatown and by extensive interviews with 60 informants through a snowball sample of workers, entrepreneurs, investors, bankers, real estate agents, organizational leaders, union activists, and longtime residents in Chinatown and other immigrant-concentrated neighborhoods in New York City. I conducted all of the face-to-face and followup interviews (including those by phone) during 1988 and 1989. For the sake of confidentiality, I use pseudonyms in this chapter. I have selectively updated the census information and observational data where necessary.

1. Yinger, "Ethnicity"; Aldrich and Waldinger, "Ethnicity and Entrepreneurship."

2. Glazer and Moynihan, *Beyond the Melting Pot*; Zhou, "The Role of the Enclave Economy in Immigrant Adaptation and Community Building"; Zhou, "Revisiting Ethnic Entrepreneurship."

3. Bonacich, "A Theory of Middleman Minorities." See also Zhou, "Revisiting Ethnic Entrepreneurship."

4. Bonacich, "'Making It' in America"; Bonacich and Modell, *The Economic Basis of Ethnic Solidarity*; Light, *Ethnic Enterprise in America*; Light, "Beyond the Ethnic Enclave Economy."

5. Light et al., "Beyond the Ethnic Enclave Economy"; Light and Gold, *Ethnic Economies*; Light and Karageorgis, "The Ethnic Economy." See also Zhou, "Revisiting Ethnic Entrepreneurship."

6. Light, "The Ethnic Economy," p. 650; Light and Karageorgis, "The Ethnic Economy," p. 648.

7. Light and Karageorgis, "The Ethnic Economy," p. 649.

8. Model, "The Ethnic Niche and the Structure of Opportunity"; Waldinger, *Still the Promised City?*

9. Light and Karageorgis, "The Ethnic Economy."

10. Portes, "The Social Origins of the Cuban Enclave Economy of Miami"; Portes, "Economic Sociology and the Sociology of Immigration"; Wilson and Martin, "Ethnic Enclaves"; Wilson and Portes, "Immigrant Enclaves"; Portes and Bach, *The Latin Journey*; Portes and Shafer, "Revisiting the Enclave Hypothesis."

11. The mainstream economy is segmented into a primary sector and a secondary sector, with corresponding labor markets. The primary labor market is dominated by industries that are capital- or knowledge-intensive and high-paying, with fringe benefits, good working conditions, and promotion opportunities. In contrast, the secondary labor market is dominated by industries that are labor-intensive and low-paying, with minimal or no fringe benefits, poor working conditions, and few promotion opportunities.

12. Portes, "The Social Origins of the Cuban Enclave Economy of Miami"; Portes and Jensen, "The Enclave and the Entrants"; Portes and Manning, "The Immigrant Enclave."

13. Portes and Zhou, "Gaining the Upper Hand"; Portes and Zhou, "Self-Employment and the Earnings of Immigrants."

14. Portes and Zhou, "Gaining the Upper Hand"; Portes and Zhou, "Self-Employment and the Earnings of Immigrants"; Portes and Zhou, "Entrepreneurship and Economic Progress in the Nineties"; Zhou, *Chinatown.*

15. The Chinatown case study was based on analysis of 1980 U.S. Census data and my 1988–1989 fieldwork; much of it was published in *Chinatown,* chap. 6. I have selectively updated the census information and observational data where necessary.

16. For a more detailed discussion, see Chapter 3 in this volume.

17. Old Chinatown included 14 tracts in 1980 and 1990. The core area consisted of tracts 6, 8, 16, 18, 27, 29, and 41; the extended area included tracts 2.01, 2.02, 14.02, 22.01, 43, 15.01, and 25. The total population of these tracts in 1990 was 92,873, over half of whom were Chinese. See Zhou, *Chinatown.*

18. Zhou and Kim, "A Tale of Two Metropolises"; Zhou, "Chinese."

19. Kwong, *Forbidden Workers;* Zhou, "Chinese."

20. Personal interview, November 1989; followup interview, May 1993.

21. Personal interview, May 1993.

22. Wilson, *The Truly Disadvantaged.* For a discussion of the differences between a black ghetto and an immigrant enclave, see Massey and Denton, *American Apartheid,* chap. 3.

23. Yu, *To Save China, To Save Ourselves.*

24. Zhou, *Chinatown.*

25. In the 1950s, most of the Chinese-owned restaurants were concentrated in Chinatown. In the late 1980s, Chinese-owned restaurants emerged in significant numbers in satellite Chinatowns in Queens and Brooklyn. See Chin, *Sewing Women;* Kwong, *The New Chinatown;* Zhou, *Chinatown.*

26. Zhou, *Chinatown;* Zhou, "Chinese."

27. Lin, *Reconstructing Chinatown.* Also see Light et al., "Transnationalism and American Exports in an English-Speaking World."

28. Aldrich and Waldinger, "Ethnicity and Entrepreneurship."

29. Wong, *A Chinese American Community;* Yu, *To Save China, To Save Ourselves.*

30. A point made by Jan Lin in his thoughtful review of my *Chinatown.* See also Light and Wong, "Protest or Work."

31. Bonacich, "A Theory of Middleman Minorities"; Sanders and Nee, "Limits of Ethnic Solidarity in the Enclave Economy."

32. Kuo, *Social and Political Change in New York's Chinatown;* Leong, *Chinatown Inside Out;* Wong, *A Chinese American Community;* Zhou and Kim, "Formation, Consolidation, and Diversification of the Ethnic Elite."

33. Ibid.

34. Kuo, *Social and Political Change in New York's Chinatown;* Sung, *The Adjustment Experience of Chinese Immigrant Children in New York City;* Yu, *To Save China, To Save Ourselves.*

35. Dillon, *The Hatchet Men;* Kuo, *Social and Political Change in New York's Chinatown;* Leong, *Chinatown Inside Out;* Sung, *The Adjustment Experience of Chinese Immigrant Children in New York City.*

36. The actual number of community organizations in Chinatown was approximately twice as large as this list indicates because many were not listed in this particular directory. See Chinatown Today Publishing, *Chinese-American Life Guide.*

37. See Chapter 3 in this volume.

38. See Chapter 7 in this volume.

39. Website: http://www.cpc-ny.org/.

40. Zhou, *Chinatown*; Zhou, "The Ethnic System of Supplementary Education"; Zhou and Lin, "Community Transformation and the Formation of Ethnic Capital."

41. Kwong, *The New Chinatown*; Kwong, *Forbidden Workers*; Lin, *Reconstructing Chinatown*.

42. Portes and Jensen, "What's an Ethnic Enclave?"

43. Sanders and Nee, "Limits of Ethnic Solidarity in the Enclave Economy."

44. Portes and Jensen, "The Enclave and the Entrants."

45. Portes and Manning, "The Immigrant Enclave"; Portes and Jensen, "What's an Ethnic Enclave?"; Portes and Jensen, "The Enclave and the Entrants"; Wilson and Martin, "Ethnic Enclaves"; Wilson and Portes, "Immigrant Enclaves."

46. Portes and Jensen, "What's an Ethnic Enclave?" p. 768.

47. The "place of residence" definition assumes that Chinese immigrants who live in New York City are more likely to participate in the ethnic enclave economy than those who live in surrounding areas. This assumption is justified by the concentration of the region's Chinese population in New York City during the 1970s. Census data for 1980 show that 85 percent of New York State's Chinese lived in New York City (for a total of 124,372), and that the majority of New York City's Chinese were concentrated in three counties: New York County (42 percent), Kings County (21 percent), and Queens County (32 percent). A further 73 percent of New York County's Chinese lived in 14 census tracts in Lower East Manhattan. Chinese immigrants, particularly recent immigrants, were likely to seek both housing and jobs in Manhattan's Chinatown, or in the newly developing Chinese enclaves in Flushing, Queens, and Sunset Park, Brooklyn.

Using place of residence for the study of New York's Chinatown seemed more defensible than the residential definition adopted by Sanders and Nee for their study of San Francisco's Chinatown. The City of San Francisco accounted for a little more than a quarter of California's Chinese population, while other large concentrations were found elsewhere in that state: e.g., 18 percent of California's Chinese lived in Oakland and surrounding communities, and 14 percent in the City of Los Angeles. Thus, what Sanders and Nee defined as "outside the enclave" included ethnic enclaves other than San Francisco. Census data show that of those Chinese immigrant employees who lived in New York City in 1980, about 25 percent worked outside the city; they tended to be restaurant workers (61 percent). Chinese immigrants who lived outside New York City were far less likely to work in the city; only 21 percent of the immigrant employees who lived outside the city commuted into it. About 63 percent of those non–New York City residents who worked in the city were in high-ranking managerial, professional, and technical jobs.

48. Under the "place of work" definition, the enclave was delimited as Chinese immigrants working in New York City. Evidence shows that the majority of the Chinese-owned businesses in New York State are located in New York City, where they provide thousands of ethnic jobs for Chinese immigrants. The 1982 Survey of Minority-Owned Business Enterprises by the U.S. Bureau of the Census indicated that 87 percent of all Chinese-owned firms in the state were located in the New York metropolitan area (5,413 of 6,216 businesses). Moreover, of the 5,978 entries in the 1988 *Chinese Business Guide and Directory* for metropolitan New York, the majority (59 percent) of Chinese firms were located either in Manhattan's Chinatown or in Flushing, where they could be supported by the large and concentrated ethnic population. The 1980 Public Use Microdata Sample (PUMS) for New York State also showed that 67 percent of the region's immigrant Chinese labor force, regardless of where they lived, worked in New York City.

49. I also added a definition of the ethnic enclave in terms of industrial sector. Because ownership information was not provided in census data, I relied on information about the

ethnic composition of particular industries. I assumed that sectors in which Chinese immigrants were overrepresented constituted the ethnic enclave economy, while all others were considered non-enclave. Two industries that were easily discernible as dominated by Chinese immigrants were garment factories and restaurants. The PUMS data showed that 23 percent of Chinese immigrant workers in New York State worked in garment and textile-related industries (compared with 3 percent for all workers in the state), and another 23 percent worked in eating and drinking establishments (compared with 4 percent for all workers). Finally, some 14 percent of Chinese immigrants worked in retail shops and services that had an ethnic clientele. The 1988 *Chinese Business Guide and Directory* confirmed this distribution: the garment industry (a total of 437 firms) and the restaurant business (783) by themselves composed 20 percent of the entries. Other Chinese-owned services catering predominantly for a Chinese clientele were also well represented: for example, barbershops and beauty salons (111), offices of herbal doctors (101), herbal stores (53), clinics (23), doctors (300), dentists (98), small department stores (107), entertainment and video-rental stores (61), food stores (303), jewelry stores (97), and travel agencies (115). Thus, the enclave niches are the garment industry, the restaurant business, and ethnic-oriented retail and services (the enclave industries included the 1980 PUMS standard industry codes 132–152, 500–532, 540–542, 550–571, 580–691, 771–780, and 812–830; the non-enclave industries include all other industrial codes except 900–992). This definition was not precise, but there is no doubt that a large proportion of the Chinese immigrant population was engaged in those niches.

50. My procedure was to estimate OLS regression models separately for workers and entrepreneurs, categorized as within or outside the ethnic enclave. I presented three sets of results, one for each alternative definition of the enclave. Significance tests in these tables referred to one-tailed tests of the hypothesis that the population coefficient equaled zero. In addition to these regression models, I also conducted F-tests of the significance of differences in coefficients between different samples. I found significant differences between the models for workers and entrepreneurs within the enclave, regardless of how the enclave was defined. I found two comparisons where the model for workers within the enclave differed significantly from the model for workers outside the enclave (using workplace or industry to define enclave). For more detail, see Zhou and Logan, "Returns on Human Capital in Ethnic Enclaves."

51. The control variables—U.S. citizenship, hours worked, and occupation—had statistically significant and strong effects for those within and outside the enclave.

52. In "Limits of Ethnic Solidarity in the Enclave Economy," Sanders and Nee similarly found that English-language ability is a significant predictor of earnings for both Cuban and Chinese employees who lived within the enclave. See Zhou and Logan, "Returns on Human Capital in Ethnic Enclaves," table 1.

53. See Zhou and Logan, "Returns on Human Capital in Ethnic Enclaves," table 2.

54. Ibid., table 3. Results on the economic effects of the ethnic enclave among other racial/ethnic groups were mixed; see Logan et al., "Ethnic Segmentation in the American Metropolis."

55. For a more complete analysis, see Zhou, *Chinatown*; see also Chapter 8 in this volume.

56. Among those who worked at least 160 hours and earned over $500 based on the 1980 U.S. Census.

57. There were too few cases of female entrepreneurs in my sample to support a separate analysis; my analysis focused on women workers only. The independent variables in these models were the same as those used for men, with the addition of a variable indicating

whether the woman had any children. Note that there were significant differences between the models for men and women (based on F-tests similar to those reported above for workers versus entrepreneurs and enclave versus non-enclave).

58. See Zhou and Logan, "Returns on Human Capital in Ethnic Enclaves," table 4.

59. See Chapter 8 in this volume for more detail.

60. Glenn, "Split Household, Small Producer, and Dual Wage Earner"; Zhou, *Chinatown*; Zhou and Nordquist, "Work and Its Place in the Lives of Immigrant Women." See also Chapter 8.

61. Personal interview, May 1988.

62. Personal interview, May 1988.

63. Personal interview, February 1989.

64. Personal interview, May 1988.

65. Field notes taken by the author, September 1988.

66. Ibid.

67. Personal interview, December 1988. Mr. Chen started work the day after his arrival. A dishwashing job that paid $200 per week was immediately available thanks to his friend's help. Later, by himself, he found a mechanic's job that paid $350 per week. However, as Chen said, many jobs in Chinatown required long working hours. Chen worked 10 to 12 hours a day, six days a week, at both jobs.

68. Personal interview, May 1988.

69. Personal interview, December 1988.

70. For a more detailed discussion of Chinatown's working women, see Chapter 8 in this volume.

71. Personal interview, September 1988.

72. Portes and Zhou, "Gaining the Upper Hand."

73. Personal interview, April 1988.

74. Personal interview, May 1988.

75. Zhou, *Chinatown*.

76. Bailey and Waldinger, "Primary, Secondary, and Enclave Labor Markets."

77. Zhou, *Chinatown*.

78. Portes and Zhou, "Gaining the Upper Hand."

## CHAPTER 6. CHINESE-LANGUAGE MEDIA IN THE UNITED STATES

This chapter draws on Min Zhou and Guoxuan Cai, "The Chinese Language Media in the United States: Immigration and Assimilation in American Life," originally published in *Qualitative Sociology* 25 (2002): 419–440; and Min Zhou, Wenhong Chen, and Guoxuan Cai, "Chinese Language Media and Immigrant Life in the United States and Canada," originally published in Wanning Sun, ed., *Media and Chinese Diaspora: Community, Commerce and Consumption* (London and New York: Routledge, 2006), pp. 42–74.

1. Li, "Chinese Diaspora in Occidental Societies."

2. The study was conducted in New York, Los Angeles, and Washington, D.C., between the fall of 2000 and spring of 2001, and was updated in the fall of 2004 and again in the summer of 2007. I and two research assistants conducted the interviews.

3. Lai, "The Chinese American Press"; Lai, "The Chinese Press in the United States and Canada since World War II"; Zhao, *Remaking Chinese America*.

4. Zhou, *Chinatown*.

5. Aarim-Heriot, *Chinese Immigrants, African Americans, and Racial Anxiety in the United States, 1848–1882*; Barth, *Bitter Strength*; Chan, *This Bitter Sweet Soil*; Chen, *Being*

*Chinese, Becoming Chinese American*; Coolidge, *Chinese Immigration*; Miller, *The Unwelcome Immigrants*; Peffer, *If They Don't Bring Their Women Here*; Salyer, *Laws Harsh as Tigers*; Sandmeyer, *The Anti-Chinese Movement in California*; Saxton, *The Indispensable Enemy*.

6. Zhao, *Remaking Chinese America*.

7. The Immigration Act (Public Law 89-236) was passed in 1965 but did not take effect until 1968. It abolished the national-origins quota system in favor of admittance based on skills and family unification, with seven preference categories: (1) unmarried adults whose parents are U.S. citizens; (2) spouses and unmarried offspring of permanent residents; (3) gifted professionals, scientists, and artists; (4) married offspring of U.S. citizens; (5) siblings of adult U.S. citizens; (6) skilled or unskilled labor needed in U.S. economy; and (7) refugees.

8. See Chapter 2 in this volume.

9. Zhou, "Contemporary Immigration and the Dynamics of Race and Ethnicity." See also Chapter 2 in this volume.

10. Fong, "Transnational Newspapers"; Sun, *Leaving China*; Sun, *Media and the Chinese Diaspora*.

11. Referring to Consolidated Metropolitan Statistics Areas (CMSA) of New York–Northern New Jersey–Long Island, Los Angeles–Anaheim–Riverside, and San Francisco–Oakland–San Jose.

12. Fong, "Transnational Newspapers"; Fong, *The First Suburban Chinatown*; Horton, *The Politics of Diversity*; Zhou and Kim, "A Tale of Two Metropolises." Also see Chapters 3 and 4 in this volume.

13. Siu, *The Chinese Laundryman*; Wong, *Patronage, Brokerage, Entrepreneurship and the Chinese Community of New York*; Zhou, *Chinatown*.

14. Wong, *Patronage, Brokerage, Entrepreneurship and the Chinese Community of New York*.

15. Fong, *The First Suburban Chinatown*; Lin, *Reconstructing Chinatown*; Zhou, *Chinatown*.

16. U.S. Bureau of the Census, *Survey of Minority-Owned Business Enterprises* (1987, 1992, and 1997). Also see Chapter 2 in this volume.

17. Fong, *The First Suburban Chinatown*; Tseng, "Suburban Ethnic Economy"; Zhou, *Chinatown*.

18. Tseng, "Suburban Ethnic Economy"; Zhou, "Beyond Ethnic Enclaves." Also see Chapters 3 and 4 in this volume.

19. For a more detailed discussion, see Chapter 4 in this volume.

20. Portes and Bach, *The Latin Journey*; Zhou and Logan, "Returns on Human Capital in Ethnic Enclaves."

21. Zhou, *Chinatown*.

22. Ibid., p. 95.

23. Zhou et al., "Chinese Language Media and Immigrant Life in the United States and Canada."

24. "Ethnic Media in America: The Giant Hidden in Plain Sight," NCM poll conducted by Bendixen & Associates, June 7, 2005; see http://news.ncmonline.com/news/view_article .html?article_id=0443821787ac0210cbecebe8b1f576a3, accessed October 1, 2007.

25. See http://www.worldjournal.com/About_us-e.php, accessed October 2, 2007.

26. Kang & Lee Advertising, *Asian Media Reference Guide*; Zhou et al., "Chinese Language Media and Immigrant Life in the United States and Canada." In contrast, the *World Journal* is the third-largest Chinese-language daily in Canada, with two metropolitan editions (Toronto and Vancouver) and a daily circulation of 25,000.

27. Chinese American Media Consumption and Purchasing Behavior Survey, 2006, fielded by Interviewing Service of America; see http://www.worldjournal.com/About_us-e .php, accessed October 2, 2007.

28. Sing Tao Daily USA, "*Sing Tao*'s Heritage of Service to the Global Chinese Community": see http://www.singtaousa.com/media/heritage.html, accessed October 1, 2004.

29. In Canada, by contrast, *Sing Tao Daily* is the largest Chinese-language newspaper, with a daily circulation of 40,000. Kang & Lee Advertising, *Asian Media Reference Guide*; Machuca, "The Other War."

30. Corey Canapary McCullough Research report, "You Need to Speak the Right Language—*Sing Tao* Newspaper/Radio Combo Reaches 56%": http://www.singtaousa.com/ media/combo.html, accessed October 2, 2007.

31. Kang & Lee Advertising, *Asian Media Reference Guide.*

32. Ibid.; also see http://www.mingpaony.com/htm/info/intro/, accessed October 3, 2007.

33. Based on the survey by Kang & Lee Advertising, *Asian Media Reference Guide,* and my own pre-2001 survey. Also see AST CTN, http://av.sina.com/ctn/profile.html, accessed October 3, 2007.

34. Zhou and Cai, "The Chinese Language Media in the United States"; Zhou et al., "Chinese Language Media and Immigrant Life in the United States and Canada."

35. See http://www.directv.com/DTVAPP/packProg/channelChart2.jsp?assetId =1200044, accessed October 8, 2007. Chinese-language packages offered by DirecTV include Jadeworld, MandarinDirect II, and MandarinDirect III, etc.

36. See http://www.afreedish.com/dish-network-dish-chinese-great-wall.html, accessed October 8, 2007. The Great Wall Television Package includes 17 channels: 7 from China Central Television (CCT: CCTV-4, CCTV-9, CCTV-E&F, CCTV-Entertainment, CCTV-Opera, PACVIA TV, and China Yellow River TV), 6 from various regions (Beijing TV, Fujian Straight Satellite TV, Guangdong Southern TV, Hunan Satellite TV, Jiangsu International Channel, and Dragon TV), and 4 from Hong Kong or North America (ATV Home Channel, Phoenix North America Chinese channel, Phoenix Infonews, and CMC). Other packages include Chinese Plus (ATV and CCTV-4), Chinese Variety (CTS, CTV, Sky Link TV, Sky Link TV-2, and TTV), and Chinese Select (CTS, CTV, Sky Link TV, Sky Link TV-2, and TTV).

37. See http://www.people.com.cn/GB/14677/14737/22037/2898494.html, accessed October 8, 2007; see also the Great Wall TV Package website: http://www.afreedish.com/ dish-network-dish-chinese-great-wall.html, accessed October 8, 2007.

38. See http://www.mrbi.net/sinotv.htm, accessed October 8, 2007.

39. Zhou and Cai, "The Chinese Language Media in the United States."

40. See http://www.mrbi.net/chinesemediagroup.htm, accessed October 8, 2007; Kang & Lee Advertising, *Asian Media Reference Guide.*

41. See http://www.mrbi.net/chinesemediagroup.htm, accessed October 8, 2007.

42. See http://www.sanfranciscochinatown.com/culture/radio.html, accessed October 8, 2007.

43. Based on a radio study conducted by Arbitron; see http://arbitron.com/ad_agencies/chinese_ratings.htm, accessed October 8, 2007.

44. See http://www.mrbi.net/kazn.htm, accessed October 8, 2007.

45. Yang, "The Internet and the Rise of a Transnational Chinese Cultural Sphere."

46. Jun, "The History and Current Status of Chinese Online Media in North America," http://www.chinanews.com.cn//2003-09-21/136/147.html, October 1, 2004.

47. Based on interviews with Chinese immigrants in Los Angeles in September 2007.

48. See http://www.chinesemedianet.com/index_e.html, accessed October 8, 2007.

49. Ibid. Ranked by Hitwise, a U.S.-based online measurement company.

50. See http://www.backchina.com/, accessed October 8, 2007. A Chinese-language online newspaper, USDragon.com, established in the mid-1990s by a group of Chinese immigrant entrepreneurs in Maryland, was offline in 2007. Like the printed publication, the online version featured four channels (USDragon News, Chinese Community, USDragon Columns, and Leisure and Entertainment, with various categories within each channel) and eight metropolitan editions (Washington, D.C., Los Angeles, New York, San Francisco, Boston, Chicago, Houston, and Detroit). This site was popular among Chinese immigrants in the United States at the turn of the twenty-first century.

51. See http://docs.wenxuecity.com/aboutus/.

52. Sun, *Media and the Chinese Diaspora.*

53. Szonyi, "Paper Tigers"; Zhou and Cai, "The Chinese Language Media in the United States."

54. Gordon, *Assimilation in American Life*; Warner and Srole, *The Social Systems of American Ethnic Groups.*

55. Conzen, "Mainstreams and Side Channels."

56. Quoted in Szonyi, "Paper Tigers"; also cited in Zhou et al., "Chinese Language Media and Immigrant Life in the United States and Canada."

57. Personal interview, April 2001.

58. Zhou et al., "Chinese Language Media and Immigrant Life in the United States and Canada"; also see Chapter 4 in this volume.

59. Veciana-Suarez, *Hispanic Media.*

## CHAPTER 7. CHINESE SCHOOLS AND THE ETHNIC SYSTEM OF SUPPLEMENTARY EDUCATION

This chapter draws material from several previously published works: Min Zhou, "The Ethnic System of Supplementary Education: Non-Profit and For-Profit Institutions in Los Angeles' Chinese Immigrant Community," in Beth Shinn and Hirokazu Yoshikawa, eds., *Toward Positive Youth Development: Transforming Schools and Community Programs* (New York: Oxford University Press, 2008), pp. 229–251; Min Zhou and Xiyuan Li, "Ethnic Language Schools and the Development of Supplementary Education in the Immigrant Chinese Community in the United States," *New Directions for Youth Development: Understanding the Social Worlds of Immigrant Youth* 100 (2003): 57–73; Min Zhou and Susan S. Kim, "Community Forces, Social Capital, and Educational Achievement: The Case of Supplementary Education in the Chinese and Korean Immigrant Communities," *Harvard Educational Review* 76 (2006): 1–29.

1. I draw on the conception of supplementary education developed by E. W. Gordon and his colleagues to frame my study of ethnic organizations serving young children and youth. See Gordon et al., *Supplementary Education,* for details.

2. Xie and Goyette, *A Demographic Portrait of Asian Americans.*

3. Kasinitz et al., *Inheriting the City.*

4. Fordham, *Blacked Out*; Fukuyama, "Immigrants and Family Values"; Kohl, *"I Won't Learn from You" and Other Thoughts on Creative Maladjustment*; Ogbu, *The Next Generation*; Wilson, *When Work Disappears.*

5. Wilson, *When Work Disappears.*

6. Anyon, *Ghetto Schooling*; Kozol, *The Shame of the Nation*; Olsen, *Made in America*; Suárez-Orozco and Suárez-Orozco, "Children of Immigration"; Varenne and McDermott, *Successful Failure.*

7. Contexts of exit and reception are group-level measures. Variables for contexts of exit may include pre-migration socioeconomic characteristics (education, occupation, income, etc.), homeland educational practices, and one's status as a regular or undocumented migrant or refugee. Variables for contexts of reception may include government policy toward a specific national-origin or ethnic group, public attitudes, and the organization of the pre-existing coethnic community. See Portes and Rumbaut, *Immigrant America*, for more detail.

8. Gordon et al., *Supplementary Education*.

9. Lareau, *Unequal Childhoods,* chap. 1; Zhou, "Social Capital in Chinatown"; Zhou, "How Do Neighborhoods Matter for Immigrant Children?" Zhou, "Ethnicity as Social Capital."

10. Scribner and Cole, "Cognitive Consequences of Formal and Informal Education."

11. Kozol, *The Shame of the Nation*; Olsen, *Made in America*; Xiong and Zhou, "Selective Testing and Tracking for Minority Students in California."

12. Ogbu, *The Next Generation*; Portes and Rumbaut, *Immigrant America*; Wilson, *When Work Disappears*.

13. Gordon et al., *Supplementary Education*.

14. Carter, *Keepin' It Real*; Lareau, *Unequal Childhoods*; Tyson et al., "It's Not 'a Black Thing'"; Varenne and McDermott, *Successful Failure*.

15. Portes and MacLeod, "The Educational Progress of Children of Immigrants"; Steinberg, *Beyond the Classroom*.

16. Ogbu and Simon, "Voluntary and Involuntary Minorities," p. 155.

17. Fong, *Complementary Education and Culture in the Global/Local Chinese Community*; Fordham and Ogbu, "Black Students' School Success"; Ogbu, *The Next Generation*; Ogbu and Simon, "Voluntary and Involuntary Minorities."

18. Fordham, *Blacked Out*; Ogbu and Simon, "Voluntary and Involuntary Minorities," p. 155.

19. Louie, *Compelled to Excel*; Sue and Okazaki, "Asian American Educational Achievement."

20. The data on which this chapter is based are drawn from multiple sources. (1) Relevant data from a multisite ethnography of immigrant neighborhoods in Los Angeles, in which Chinatown was selected as one of the main research sites (original study done in 1999–2000, with followup study in 2002–2004). In this study, neighborhood-based ethnic institutions (including nonprofits, for-profit establishments, and other locally based social structures) were closely observed, and face-to-face or phone interviews were conducted to examine how social organization at the neighborhood level affects immigrant children's school adaptation. Relevant data include intensive field observations in ethnic-language schools, private afterschools, and educational institutions as well as interviews with language school principals, parents, and adolescent participants in Chinatown. (2) Two other ethnographic case studies: a weekend Chinese school in a white middle-class suburb west of Los Angeles and a private afterschool in a Chinese ethnoburb east of that city. (3) Content analyses of Chinese-language newspapers and other media accounts, advertisements, and curricular materials. Ethnic newspapers circulating in the Chinese immigrant community heavily advertise academic services such as SAT prep schools and language schools at the beginning of the school year. In addition, sections in these newspapers cover education-related topics on a weekly basis, sometimes through translations of articles from the *Los Angeles Times* and popular mainstream magazines such as *Newsweek* on the best U.S. colleges, college admissions guidelines, admission and graduation rates, etc. This content analysis offers a unique view of the kind of information available to the Chinese immigrant community and the interaction between ethnic institutions and community members.

21. Some suggest that Chinese schools may date as far back as the late 1840s, when Chinese laborers started to arrive in the United States in large numbers. See Wang, *A View from Within.*

22. Acherman, "Strangers to the Tradition"; Beatty, *Preschool Education in America*; Harada, "A Survey of Japanese Language Schools in Hawaii"; Onishi, "A Study of the Attitudes of the Japanese in Hawaii toward Japanese Language Schools"; Shimada, "Wartime Dissolution and Revival of the Japanese Language Schools in Hawai'i"; Svensrud, "Attitudes of the Japanese toward Their Language Schools."

23. Leung, "A Sociological Study of the Chinese Language Schools in the San Francisco Bay Area."

24. Chan, *This Bitter Sweet Soil*; see also Chapter 2 of this volume.

25. Chan, *Entry Denied*; Chiu, *Chinese Labor in California*; Coolidge, *Chinese Immigration*; McClain, *In Search of Equality*; Miller, *The Unwelcome Immigrants*; Peffer, *If They Don't Bring Their Women Here*; Salyer, *Laws Harsh as Tigers*; Sandmeyer, *The Anti-Chinese Movement in California*; Saxton, *The Indispensable Enemy.*

26. Dillon, *The Hatchet Men*; Hoy, *The Chinese Six Companies*; Kuo, *Social and Political Change in New York's Chinatown*; Lai, "Historical Development of the Chinese Consolidated Benevolent Association/Huiguan System"; Wong, *Patronage, Brokerage, Entrepreneurship and the Chinese Community of New York*; Zhou and Kim, "Formation, Consolidation, and Diversification of the Ethnic Elite."

27. Chin, *Paper Son*; Hsu, "Gold Mountain Dreams and Paper Son Schemes"; Lau, *Paper Families*; Wong, *American Paper Son*; Zhao, *Remaking Chinese America.* See also Chapter 2, table 2.1, in this volume.

28. See Lai, "Retention of the Chinese Heritage" (parts 1–2); Wang, *A View from Within.*

29. Fan, "The Chinese Language Schools of San Francisco in Relation to Family Integration and Cultural Identity"; Fong, *Complementary Education and Culture in the Global/Local Chinese Community*; Foreman, "A Study of Chinese Language Schools"; Lai, "Retention of the Chinese Heritage" (parts 1–2); Leung, "A Sociological Study of the Chinese Language Schools in the San Francisco Bay Area"; Lu, "Bicultural Identity Development and Chinese Community Formation"; Tom, "Functions of the Chinese Language Schools."

30. Foreman, "A Study of Chinese Language Schools"; Ma, "Effects of Attendance at Chinese Language Schools upon San Francisco Children"; Tom, "Functions of the Chinese Language Schools."

31. Fan, "The Chinese Language Schools of San Francisco in Relation to Family Integration and Cultural Identity"; Lu, "Bicultural Identity Development and Chinese Community Formation."

32. Kuo, "Excluded, Segregated, and Forgotten"; Leung, "A Sociological Study of the Chinese Language Schools in the San Francisco Bay Area"; Wong, "The Language Situation of Chinese Americans."

33. Chun, "Shifting Ethnic Identity and Consciousness."

34. Chiang, "A Study of the Chinese Language School and the Maintenance of Ethnic Language in the Second-Generation, American-Born Chinese"; Fan, "The Chinese Language Schools of San Francisco in Relation to Family Integration and Cultural Identity"; Leung, "A Sociological Study of the Chinese Language Schools in the San Francisco Bay Area"; Ma, "Effects of Attendance at Chinese Language Schools upon San Francisco Children." But these same studies also found favorable outcomes among Chinese school attendees in terms of general health, posture, nutrition, and grade point averages.

35. Li, "Spatial Transformation of an Urban Ethnic Community from Chinatown to Chinese Ethnoburb in Los Angeles."

36. Fong, *Complementary Education and Culture in the Global/Local Chinese Community*; Lai, "Retention of the Chinese Heritage" (parts 1–2); Lai, *Becoming Chinese American*; Leung, "A Sociological Study of the Chinese Language Schools in the San Francisco Bay Area."

37. Lai, *Becoming Chinese American*; Wang, *A View from Within*.

38. Fong, *Complementary Education and Culture in the Global/Local Chinese Community*.

39. Compiled from the Southern California Council of Chinese Schools website: http://www.scccs.net/, accessed July 31, 2006. The numbers do not include the less-structured, private, and weekend Chinese-language classes.

40. Interview with the principal and a teacher in July 2002. School information can be accessed at http://www.to-cs.org/tocs/.

41. Lai, *Becoming Chinese American*.

42. *Buxiban* afterschool classes tutor students in various subjects included in their regular school curricula. *Kumon* is a supplemental afterschool program aiming to make school-based learning easier, but not to substitute for regular school instruction.

43. Zhou, "The Non-Economic Effects of Ethnic Entrepreneurship"; Zhou, "Revisiting Ethnic Entrepreneurship."

44. Zhou and Cai, "The Chinese Language Media in the United States"; see also Chapter 6 in this volume.

45. Zhou, "Ethnicity as Social Capital"; Zhou, "The Ethnic System of Supplementary Education"; Zhou and Kim, "Community Forces, Social Capital, and Educational Achievement"; Zhou and Li, "Ethnic Language Schools and the Development of Supplementary Education in the Immigrant Chinese Community in the United States"; Zhou and Li, "Ethnic Language Maintenance and Assimilation."

46. Fernandez-Kelly, "Towanda's Triumph"; Fordham, *Blacked Out*.

47. Personal interview, December 1999.

48. Sung, *The Adjustment Experience of Chinese Immigrant Children in New York City*, p. 126. Also see Lu, "Bicultural Identity Development and Chinese Community Formation."

49. Personal interview, July 2002.

50. Bhattacharyya, "Community Support for Supplementary Education"; Zhou and Kim, "Community Forces, Social Capital, and Educational Achievement." In the United States today, only the Korean immigrant community has a comparable ethnic system of supplementary education.

51. Bourdieu, "The Forms of Capital."

## CHAPTER 8. THE OTHER HALF OF THE SKY

This chapter is based on Chapter 7, "The Other Half of the Sky: Socioeconomic Adaptation of Immigrant Women," of *Chinatown: The Socioeconomic Potential of an Urban Enclave* (Philadelphia: Temple University Press, 1992). © 1992 Temple University Press, used by permission. It also draws on material from Min Zhou and Regina Nordquist, "Work and Its Place in the Lives of Immigrant Women: Garment Workers in New York City's Chinatown," *Applied Behavioral Science Review* 2 (1994): 187–211. The analysis was done using 1980 U.S. Census data and my own fieldwork data, collected in New York City by systematic participant observations in Chinatown and extensive interviews with 60 informants through a snowball sample of workers, entrepreneurs, investors, bankers, real estate agents, organizational leaders, union activists, and longtime residents in Chinatown and other neighborhoods with a concentration of Chinese immigrants. I conducted face-to-face interviews and followups (including some phone interviews) during 1988–1989, and additional field observations and six followup interviews between 1991 and 1992. For the sake of confidentiality, I use pseudonyms in this chapter. I have selectively updated the census information and observational data where necessary.

1. As a graduate student, I worked side by side with these women for two summers in the late 1980s. I did this for my doctoral dissertation research, but I was also badly in need of the hard-earned dollars to support myself as a foreign student. I personally experienced what it was like to work in a Chinatown factory, while also learning about the other side of garment workers' lives through my interviews.

2. Mueller and Campbell, "Female Occupational Achievement and Marital Status"; Philliber and Hiller, "The Implication of Wife's Occupational Attainment for Husband's Class Identification"; Van Velsor and Beeghley, "The Process of Class Identification among Employed Married Women."

3. Borjas, *Friends or Strangers.*

4. Saxton, *The Indispensable Enemy.*

5. Ibid.

6. "The Immigrants: How They Are Helping to Revitalize the U.S. Economy," *Business Week,* July 13, 1992.

7. U.S. Commission on Civil Rights, *Civil Rights Issues Facing Asian Americans in the 1990s.*

8. Zhou and Bankston, "Variations in Economic Adaptation."

9. Portes and Zhou, "Gaining the Upper Hand."

10. Bao, *Holding Up More Than Half the Sky;* Chin, *Sewing Women;* Waldinger, *Through the Eye of the Needle.*

11. ILGWU, *The Chinatown Garment Industry Study,* p. 44.

12. Cheng, "Free, Indentured, Enslaved"; Ling, *Surviving on the Gold Mountain;* Ling, "Family and Marriage of Late-Nineteenth- and Early-Twentieth-Century Chinese Immigrant Women"; Peffer, *If They Don't Bring Their Women Here;* Tong, *Unsubmissive Women;* Yung, *Unbound Voices.*

13. The War Brides Act (Public Law 271) was passed on December 28, 1945, to allow wives of members of the U.S. armed forces to enter the United States. The following year fiancées of U.S. servicemen were allowed to immigrate.

14. Sung, *The Adjustment Experience of Chinese Immigrant Children in New York City;* Zhou, *Chinatown;* Zhou, "Low-Wage Employment and Social Mobility."

15. See n. 7 in Chapter 6.

16. Sung, *The Adjustment Experience of Chinese Immigrant Children in New York City,* p. 20.

17. Zhou, *Chinatown;* Zhou, "Low-Wage Employment and Social Mobility."

18. Waldinger, *Through the Eye of the Needle.*

19. Zhou, *Chinatown;* Zhou, "Low-Wage Employment and Social Mobility."

20. Cited from *New York Times,* May 10, 1986.

21. Personal interview, June 1990.

22. Quoted in Kingston, *The Women Warrior,* p. 193.

23. Personal interviews, April 1988, September 1988.

24. Personal interview, April 1991.

25. Lau, "Children at a Sewing Machine."

26. Personal interviews, March 1992.

27. Personal interview, May 1988.

28. Sung, *The Adjustment Experience of Chinese Immigrant Children in New York City*, p. 86.

29. Personal interview, May 1988.

30. Zhou, *Chinatown*, p. 173, table 7-6.

31. Personal interview, May 1988.

32. Personal interview, April 1988.

33. Personal interview, January 1989.

34. Personal interview, January 1989.

35. Sung, *The Adjustment Experience of Chinese Immigrant Children in New York City.*

36. Personal interview, May 1988.

37. ILGWU, *The Chinatown Garment Industry Study.*

38. Followup interview with Mrs. Zhao in her own home, March 1992.

39. Followup interview with Mrs. Cheng in her restaurant, March 1992.

40. Followup interview with Mrs. Chang in her own home, March 1992.

41. Zhou, *Chinatown.*

## CHAPTER 9. NEGOTIATING CULTURE AND ETHNICITY

This chapter is based on one originally published in Ram Mahalingam, ed., *Cultural Psychology of Immigrants* (Mahwah, NJ: Lawrence Erlbaum, 2006), pp. 315–336. © 2006 Taylor & Francis Group LLC, reprinted by permission. It has been rewritten and updated.

1. Foner, "The Immigrant Family"; Mahalingam, *Cultural Psychology of Immigrants.*

2. Zhou and Li, "Ethnic Language Schools and the Development of Supplementary Education in the Immigrant Chinese Community in the United States"; see also Chapter 7 in this volume.

3. This chapter is based on my own qualitative fieldwork data, collected in Chinese immigrant communities in Los Angeles and New York between September and October 1994 and again between 1996 and 2002. All quotations are from my face-to-face interviews with immigrant children, parents, and workers in community-based organizations.

4. Chan, *This Bitter Sweet Soil.*

5. Glenn, "Split Household, Small Producer, and Dual Wage Earner"; Glenn and Yap, "Chinese American Families"; Ling, "Family and Marriage of Late-Nineteenth- and Early-Twentieth-Century Chinese Immigrant Women"; Liu, "The Trans-Pacific Family Pattern in the Chinese American Experience"; McKeown, "Transnational Chinese Families and Chinese Exclusion, 1875–1974"; Zhou, *Chinatown.*

6. Chan, *This Bitter Sweet Soil*; Daniels, "Westerners from the East: Oriental Immigrants Reappraised"; Saxton, *The Indispensable Enemy.*

7. Zhao, *Remaking Chinese America.*

8. Lau, *Paper Families*; Lyman, "Marriage and the Family among Chinese Immigrants to America"; Peffer, *If They Don't Bring Their Women Here*; Yung, *Unbound Voices.*

9. Chung, "Fighting for Their American Rights"; Lu, "Bicultural Identity Development and Chinese Community Formation"; Wong and Chan, *Claiming America.*

10. For a detailed description, see Chapters 2, 3, and 4 in this volume.

11. Estimated from the Current Population Survey (CPS) data 1998–2000. See also Logan et al., "From Many Shores."

12. Compared with 8 percent under 17 and 8 percent between 18 and 24 in the first generation.

13. Chen, *Being Chinese, Becoming Chinese American*; Chun, *Of Orphans and Warriors*; Ngai, "History as Law and Life"; Wong, *Americans First*; Wong and Chan, *Claiming America.*

14. Chan, "Race, Ethnic Culture, and Gender in the Construction of Identities among Second-Generation Chinese Americans, 1880s to 1930s"; Chun, *Of Orphans and Warriors*; Chun, "Shifting Ethnic Identity and Consciousness"; Liu, *The Transnational History of a Chinese Family.*

15. Portes and Zhou, "The New Second Generation."

16. Pyke and Dang, "'FOB' and 'Whitewashed'"; Chiang-Hom, "Transnational Cultural Practices of Chinese Immigrant Youth and Parachute Kids." See also Chapter 10 in this volume.

17. Gans, "Second-Generation Decline"; Portes and Zhou, "The New Second Generation"; Zhou, "Social Capital in Chinatown."

18. Sung, *The Adjustment Experience of Chinese Immigrant Children in New York City.*

19. Yeh and Bedford, "Filial Piety and Parent-Child Conflict."

20. Sung, *The Adjustment Experience of Chinese Immigrant Children in New York City.*

21. Ibid.; Zhou, "Social Capital in Chinatown."

22. See Chapter 7 for a more detailed discussion.

23. See Chapters 4 and 7 in this volume.

24. The CCBA is a quasi government in Chinatown. It used to be an apex group representing some 60 different family and district associations, guilds, tongs, the Chamber of Commerce, and the Nationalist Party, and it has remained the most influential ethnic organization in the Chinese immigrant community. See Zhou and Kim, "Formation, Consolidation, and Diversification of the Ethnic Elite."

25. Zhou, "Social Capital in Chinatown"; Zhou and Li, "Ethnic Language Schools and the Development of Supplementary Education in the Immigrant Chinese Community in the United States"; see also Chapter 7 in this volume.

26. See Chapter 7 in this volume. Also see Chao, "Overview."

27. Sung, *The Adjustment Experience of Chinese Immigrant Children in New York City.* Also see Chapter 7 in this volume.

28. Zhou and Li, "Ethnic Language Schools and the Development of Supplementary Education in the Immigrant Chinese Community in the United States."

## CHAPTER 10. "PARACHUTE KIDS" IN SOUTHERN CALIFORNIA

This is a revised and updated version of my previously published article "'Parachute Kids' in Southern California: The Educational Experience of Chinese Children in Transnational Families," *Educational Policy* (1998): 682–704. © 1998 Sage Publications, used by permission.

1. Quoted from Denise Hamilton, "A House, Cash—and No Parents," *Los Angeles Times,* June 24, 1993.

2. Ibid.

3. Headline news from *World Daily,* April 18, 1996.

4. Headline news from *World Daily,* April 13, 1996.

5. Data on parachute kids are extremely limited. The media have occasionally and selectively reported on them, but only in sensational and exotic terms. Because of the paucity of available data and the lack of substantive understanding of this phenomenon, I rely on field interviews with a snowball sample of 33 parachute kids and a convenience sample of parents, caretakers, school counselors, and community social workers, all from southern California. The sample of parachute kids was made up of 25 college students and 8 high

school students; 55 percent were males; 3 were from Hong Kong, 1 from Singapore, 2 from mainland China, and the rest from Taiwan. I made a handful of prearranged home visits in Monterey Park, Alhambra, and Arcadia and conducted a number of in-home or telephone interviews with parents who were either back in their home country or were visiting their children in southern California at the time. I also talked, either in person or on the phone, to a number of school counselors and community social workers who had worked with parachute kids in Monterey Park, Alhambra, Arcadia, and Hacienda Heights, where many were concentrated. Data were collected during the spring and summer of 1996 by my three research assistants and myself. I believe that this qualitative approach helps the researcher to find out what affects the experience of this group of foreign-born youths and the ways in which their experience may be similar to or different from that of other immigrant youths. There are several obvious limitations associated with such sampling procedures. My sample contains college students and high school students with definite intentions to go to college, so that it leans toward the high achievers; those who have failed are absent from the sample. Though small in number, the dropouts are noticeable. Most of them have been flown back home by their parents, but some have remained in the United States as gang members and troublemakers. Also absent from the sample are those who have graduated from college, since most college graduates have returned to their homeland. The exclusion of these failure and success cases inevitably poses a problem for generalization. However, since my study is an attempt to sort out, rather than measure the effects of, possible factors influencing parent-child relations and educational experiences in a changing family context, the use of interviews with current parachute kids and their parents, and the use of second-hand information from school counselors and social workers, can help us gain insight into the parachute phenomenon. The names of the parachute kids are pseudonyms.

6. Zheng and Yu, *Taiwan's Education Today*.

7. Ibid.

8. Luk, "Opportunities for Women in Tertiary Education in Hong Kong"; Morris, "Preparing Pupils as Citizens of the Special Administrative Region of Hong Kong."

9. Thogersen, *Secondary Education in China after Mao*; World Bank, *China*.

10. Shi, "Returning Home?"

11. U.S.-China Education Clearinghouse, *An Introduction to Education in the People's Republic of China and U.S.-China Educational Exchange*.

12. Morris, "Preparing Pupils as Citizens of the Special Administrative Region of Hong Kong."

13. Bray, "Hong Kong Education in an International Context"; Postiglione, "International Higher Education and the Labor Market in Hong Kong."

14. Mak, "The Schooling of Girls in Hong Kong."

15. Since the late 1990s, the United Kingdom, France, Germany, Australia, New Zealand, and other Western countries have become increasing attractive to Chinese parachute kids, especially those from mainland China. While some children from very wealthy families attend private boarding schools, the majority take advantage of the high-quality education offered by good public schools in host countries.

16. Bray, "Hong Kong Education in an International Context"; Postiglione, "International Higher Education and the Labor Market in Hong Kong."

17. Ong et al., "Migration of Highly Educated Asians and Global Dynamics."

18. Du, *Chinese Higher Education*.

19. Ong et al., "Migration of Highly Educated Asians and Global Dynamics."

20. Hernandez, *America's Children*.

21. Sung, *The Adjustment Experience of Chinese Immigrant Children in New York City*; Zhou, "Social Capital in Chinatown"; see also Chapter 9 in this volume.

22. Ballantine, *The Sociology of Education*; Elliott and Voss, *Delinquency and Dropout*; Fagerlind, *Formal Education and Adult Earnings*; Kiker and Condon, "Transmission of Economic Inequality over Three Generations"; Kiker and Condon, "The Influence of Socioeconomic Background on the Earnings of Young Men"; Wagenaar, "What Do We Know about Dropping Out of High School."

23. Coleman et al., *Equality of Educational Opportunity*.

24. Ogbu and Matute-Bianchi, "Understanding Sociocultural Factors"; Sung, *The Adjustment Experience of Chinese Immigrant Children in New York City*; Zhou, "Social Capital in Chinatown."

25. Caplan et al., *The Boat People and Achievement in America*, p. 149.

26. Gibson, *Accommodation without Assimilation*; Rutledge, *The Vietnamese Experience in America*; Ogbu and Matute-Bianchi, "Understanding Sociocultural Factors"; Suárez-Orozco and Suárez-Orozco, *Transformations*; Suárez-Orozco and Suárez-Orozco, *Children of Immigration*; Sung, *The Adjustment Experience of Chinese Immigrant Children in New York City*; Zhou and Bankston, *Growing Up American*.

27. Sue and Okazaki, "Asian American Educational Achievement."

28. Gans, "Second Generation Decline"; Zhou, "Growing Up American."

29. See also Chiang-Hom, "Transnational Cultural Practices of Chinese Immigrant Youth and Parachute Kids."

30. Ibid.; Rumbaut, "Ties That Bind."

31. Portes and Stepick, *City on the Edge*; Ogbu and Matute-Bianchi, "Understanding Sociocultural Factors."

32. Zhou and Bankston, *Growing Up American*; see also Chapter 9 in this volume.

## CHAPTER 11. RETHINKING ASSIMILATION

This chapter is based on two previously published works: "Are Asian Americans Becoming White?" *Contexts* 3, no. 1 (2004): 29–37, © 2004 University of California Press; and "Assimilation, the Asian Way," in Tamar Jacoby, ed., *Reinventing the Melting Pot: The New Immigrants and What It Means to Be American* (New York: Basic Books, 2003), pp. 139–153, © 2003 Basic Books, used by permission.

1. Personal interview, January 1988. Also see Zhou, "Assimilation, the Asian Way."

2. Personal interview with Dr. Xia in a Washington, D.C., suburb, February 2001 (translation from the Chinese language by the author).

3. Email message from 80-20 Initiative [sbwoo@80-20initiative.net], Sunday, May 27, 2001; Congressman David Wu's website: www.house.gov/wu/.

4. Keynote speech by David Wu at a Chinese American Political Association dinner dance, *CAPA Newsletter*, June 1999.

5. Glazer, "Is Assimilation Dead?"

6. Steinberg, *Beyond the Classroom*.

7. U.S. Bureau of the Census, *The American Community, Asians*.

8. Hirschman and Wong, "Socioeconomic Gains of Asian Americans, Blacks, and Hispanics, 1960–1976"; Hirschman and Wong, "The Extraordinary Educational Attainment of Asian Americans"; Kasinitz et al., *Inheriting the City*; Rumbaut, "The New Californians."

9. Steinberg, *Beyond the Classroom*.

10. Cheng and Yang, "Asians"; Zhou and Kamo, "An Analysis of Earnings Patterns for Chinese, Japanese and Non-Hispanic Whites in the United States."

11. Fukuyama, "Immigrants and Family Values."

12. Sowell, *Ethnic America*, p. 282.

13. Ogbu, *The Next Generation*.

14. Fordham, *Blacked Out*; Kohl, *"I Won't Learn from You" and Other Thoughts on Creative Maladjustment.*

15. Bourgois, "In Search of Respect"; Fordham, *Blacked Out*; Gibson, *Accommodation without Assimilation.*

16. Portes and Zhou, "The New Second Generation"; see also Zhou, "Segmented Assimilation."

17. Alba, "The Twilight of Ethnicity among American Catholics of European Ancestry"; Gordon, *Assimilation in American Life*; Warner and Srole, *The Social Systems of American Ethnic Groups.*

18. Portes and Zhou, "Gaining the Upper Hand"; for a more detailed discussion, see Chapters 5 and 8 in this volume.

19. For a more detailed discussion, see Zhou, *Chinatown.* See also Chapters 5 and 8 in this volume.

20. See Chapter 8 in this volume.

21. Zhou and Cai, "The Chinese Language Media in the United States." Also see Chapters 6 and 8 in this volume.

22. See Chapter 9 for a more detailed discussion.

23. See Chapter 7 for a more detailed discussion.

24. California—ACS Demographic and Housing Estimates from the 2006 American Community Survey, http://factfinder.census.gov/.

25. Louie, "Searching for Roots in Contemporary China and Chinese America"; Wong and Chan, *Claiming America*; Yu, "The 'Oriental Problem' in America, 1920–1960."

26. Espiritu, *Asian American Panethnicity*; Lien, "Homeland Origins and Political Identities among Chinese in Southern California"; Okamoto, "Toward a Theory of Panethnicity"; Zia, *Asian American Dream.*

27. The number was 716,916 between 1960 and 1989; 591,599 between 1990 and 1999; and 460,678 between 2000 and 2006. In comparison, the total number of Chinese immigrants legally admitted into the United States from 1850 to 1959 was 424,897, based on country of last residence. U.S. Department of Homeland Security, *Yearbook of Immigration Statistics: 2007,* table 2; see http://www.dhs.gov/ximgtn/statistics/publications/LPR07.shtm.

28. The model minority image began to take shape during World War II. See Wong, "From Pariah to Paragon." Also see Lee, *Orientals.*

29. See also Petersen, *Japanese Americans.*

30. Liu, *The Accidental Asian,* p. 34.

31. Lopez, "Language Assimilation"; Portes, "English-Only Triumphs, but the Costs are High."

32. Kibria, "The Construction of 'Asian American'"; Lee and Bean, "America's Changing Color Lines"; Liang and Ito, "Intermarriage of Asian Americans in the New York City Region"; Sung, *Chinese American Intermarriage*; Wong, "A Look at Intermarriage among the Chinese in the United States in 1980."

33. Personal communication with a retired Chinatown activist in New York.

34. Wu, *Yellow.*

35. Chan, *Chinese American Transnationalism*; Koehn and Yin, *The Expanding Roles of Chinese Americans in U.S.-China Relations*; Lien, "Transnational Homeland Concerns and Participation in U.S. Politics"; Ma and Cartier, *The Chinese Diaspora.*

36. The Qing queue was a symbol of Han Chinese submission to the Qing dynasty ruled by the Manchus and was cut at the downfall of the Qing empire in 1912, but it became a feature of racist caricatures in the United States long after that date. See also Lee, *My*

*Country Versus Me*; Lee and Zhou, "Conclusion"; Stober and Hoffman, *A Convenient Spy*; Wang, "Class, Race, Citizenship, and Extraterritoriality"; Wu, *Yellow*.

37. Kibria, "The Construction of 'Asian American'"; Koehn and Yin, *The Expanding Roles of Chinese Americans in U.S.-China Relations*; Lien, "Transnational Homeland Concerns and Participation in U.S. Politics"; Lien, "Homeland Origins and Political Identities among Chinese in Southern California"; Wang, "The Structure of Dual Domination"; Wang, *The Dust That Never Settles*.

38. Kibria, *Becoming Asian American*; Louie, "Searching for Roots in Contemporary China and Chinese America"; Tuan, *Forever Foreigner or Honorary White?*; Tung, *Chinese Americans and Their Immigrant Parents*.

# Bibliography

Aarim-Heriot, Najia. *Chinese Immigrants, African Americans, and Racial Anxiety in the United States, 1848–1882*. Champaign: University of Illinois Press, 2006.

Abella, Manolo I. "Contemporary Labor Migration from Asia: Policies and Perspectives of Sending Countries." In Mary M. Kritz, Lin Lean Lim, and Hania Zlotnik, eds., *International Migration Systems: A Global Approach*. New York: Oxford University Press, 1992. Pp. 263–278.

Abeyasekere, Susan. "Slaves in Batavia: Insights from a Slave Register." In Anthony Reid, ed., *Slavery, Bondage, and Dependency in Southeast Asia*. New York: St. Martin's Press, 1983. Pp. 286–314.

Acherman, W. I. "Strangers to the Tradition: Idea and Constraint in American Jewish Education." In Arnold S. Himmelfarb and Sergio Della Pergola, eds., *Jewish Education Worldwide: Cross Cultural Perspectives*. New York: University Press of America, 1989.

Alba, Richard D. "Assimilation's Quiet Tide." *Public Interest* 119 (1995): 1–18.

———. "Interpreting the Parameters of Log-Linear Models." *Sociological Methods and Research* 16 (1986): 45–77.

———. *Italian Americans: Into the Twilight of Ethnicity*. Englewood Cliffs, NJ: Prentice Hall, 1985.

———. "The Twilight of Ethnicity among American Catholics of European Ancestry." *Annals of the American Academy of Political and Social Science* 454, no. 1 (1981): 86–97.

Alba, Richard D., and John R. Logan. "Variations on Two Themes: Racial and Ethnic Patterns in the Attainment of Suburban Residence." *Demography* 28 (1991): 431–453.

Aldrich, Howard E., and Roger Waldinger. "Ethnicity and Entrepreneurship." *Annual Review of Sociology* 16 (1990): 111–135.

Almquist, Elizabeth M., and Juanita L. Wehrle-Einhorn. "The Doubly Disadvantaged: Minority Women in the Labor Force." In Ann H. Stromberg and Shirley Harkess, eds., *Women Working: Theories and Facts in Perspective*. Palo Alto, CA: Mayfield, 1978. Pp. 63–88.

Aloff, Mindy. "Where China and Brooklyn Overlap." *New York Times,* February 7, 1997.

Andaya, Barbara Watson. "Adapting to Political and Economic Change: Palembang in the Late Eighteenth and Early Nineteenth Centuries." In Anthony Reid, ed., *The Last Stand of Asian Autonomies: Responses to Modernity in the Diverse States of Southeast Asia and Korea, 1750–1900.* London: Macmillan, 1997. Pp. 187–215.

Anyon, Jean. *Ghetto Schooling: A Political Economy of Urban Educational Reform.* New York: Teachers College Press, 1997.

Arax, Mark. "Monterey Park: The Nation's First Suburban Chinatown." *Los Angeles Times,* April 6, 1987.

Arnold, Fred, and Nasra M. Shah. "Asia's Labor Pipeline: An Overview." In Fred Arnold and Nasra M. Shah, eds., *Asian Labor Migration, Pipeline to the Middle East.* Boulder: Westview Press, 1986. Pp. 3–16.

Azuma, Eiichiro. "Brief Historical Overview of Japanese Emigration, 1868–1998." In *International Nikkei Research Project, First-Year Report, 1998–99.* Los Angeles: Japanese American Museum, 1999. Pp. 6–8.

Bailey, Thomas, and Roger Waldinger. "Primary, Secondary, and Enclave Labor Markets: A Training System Approach." *American Sociological Review* 56 (1991): 432–445.

Ballantine, Jeanne H. *The Sociology of Education: A Systematic Analysis.* Englewood Cliffs, NJ: Prentice Hall, 1983.

Bao, Xiaolan. *Holding Up More Than Half the Sky: Chinese Women Garment Workers in New York City, 1948–1992.* Urbana: University of Illinois Press, 2001.

Barth, Gunther. *Bitter Strength: A History of the Chinese in the United States, 1850–1870.* Cambridge: Harvard University Press, 1964.

Battistella, Graziano, and Anthony Paganoni, eds. *Philippine Labour Migration: Impact and Policy.* Quezon City: Scalabrini Migration Centre, 1992.

Bean, Frank D., and Marta Tienda. "The Hispanic Population of the United States." *Population and Development Review* 14 (1988): 514–516.

Beatty, Barbara. *Preschool Education in America: The Culture of Young Children from the Colonial Era to the Present.* New Haven: Yale University Press, 1995.

Bhattacharyya, Maitrayee. "Community Support for Supplementary Education." In E. W. Gordon, B. L. Bridglall, and A. S. Meroe, eds., *Supplementary Education: The Hidden Curriculum of High Academic Achievement.* Lanham, MD: Rowman and Littlefield, 2005. Pp. 249–272.

Blau, Peter, and O. D. Duncan. *The American Occupational Structure.* New York: Wiley, 1967.

Blythe, Wilfred. *The Impact of Chinese Secret Societies in Malaya: A Historical Study.* London: Oxford University Press, 1969.

Bonacich, Edna. "Class Approaches to Ethnicity and Race." *Critical Sociology* 10, no. 2 (1980): 9–23.

———. "'Making It' in America: A Social Evaluation of the Ethics of Immigrant Entrepreneurship." *Sociological Perspectives* 30 (1987): 446–466.

———. "Reflections on Asian American Labor." *Amerasia Journal* 18, no. 1 (1992): xxi–xxvii.

———. "A Theory of Middleman Minorities." *American Sociological Review* 38 (1973): 583–594.

Bonacich, Edna, and John Modell. *The Economic Basis of Ethnic Solidarity: Small Business in the Japanese-American Community.* Berkeley: University of California Press, 1980.

Borjas, George J. "Ethnic Capital and Intergenerational Mobility." *Quarterly Journal of Economics* 107 (1992): 123–150.

————. *Friends or Strangers: The Impact of Immigration on the U.S. Economy.* New York: Basic Books, 1990.

Bourdieu, Pierre. "The Forms of Capital." In J. G. Richardson, ed., *Handbook of Theory and Research for the Sociology of Education.* New York: Greenwood, 1985. Pp. 241–258.

Bourgois, Philippe. *In Search of Respect: Selling Crack in El Barrio.* New York: Cambridge University Press, 1995.

Bray, Mark. "Hong Kong Education in an International Context: The Impact of External Forces." In Gerard A. Postiglione, ed., *Education and Society in Hong Kong: Toward One Country and Two Systems.* New York: East Gate, 1991. Pp. 83–94.

Breton, Raymond. "Institutional Completeness of Ethnic Communities and the Personal Relations of Immigrants." *American Journal of Sociology* 70 (1964): 193–205.

Brown, Ian. "History [of the Philippines]." In *The Far East and Australia, 1999.* 13th ed. London: Europe Publications, 1999. Pp. 1011–1015.

Burusratanaphand, Walwipha. "Chinese Identity in Thailand." *Southeast Asian Journal of Social Science* 23 (1995): 43–56.

Caplan, Nathan, Marcella H. Choy, and John K. Whitmore. *The Boat People and Achievement in America: A Study of Family Life, Hard Work, and Cultural Values.* Ann Arbor: University of Michigan Press, 1989.

Carter, P. L. *Keepin' It Real: School Success beyond Black and White.* New York: Oxford University Press, 2005.

Cassel, Susie Lan, ed. *The Chinese in America: A History from Gold Mountain to the New Millennium.* Walnut Creek, CA: AltaMira, 2002.

Castells, Manuel. "Immigrant Workers and Class Struggles in Advanced Capitalism: The Western European Experience." *Politics and Society* 5 (1975): 33–66.

Catell, Stuart H. "Health, Welfare and Social Organization in Chinatown." Manuscript (mimeographed). New York: Community Service Society of New York, 1962.

Chan, Kam Wing. *Cities with Invisible Walls: Reinterpreting Urbanization in Post-1949 China.* Hong Kong: Oxford University Press, 1994.

Chan, Kwok Bun, ed. *Chinese Business Networks: State, Economy, and Culture.* Singapore: Prentice Hall, 2000.

Chan, Kwok Bun, and Chee Kiong Tong, eds. *Alternate Identities: The Chinese of Contemporary Thailand.* Leiden and Singapore: Brill and Times Academic Press, 2001.

Chan, Sucheng. *Asian Americans: An Interpretive History.* New York: Twayne, 1991.

————, ed. *Chinese American Transnationalism: The Flow of People, Resources, and Ideas between China and America during the Exclusion Era.* Philadelphia: Temple University Press, 2005.

————. *Entry Denied: Exclusion and the Chinese Community in America, 1882–1943.* Philadelphia: Temple University Press, 1994.

————. *In Defense of Asian American Studies: The Politics of Teaching and Program Building.* Urbana: University of Illinois Press, 2005.

————. "Race, Ethnic Culture, and Gender in the Construction of Identities among Second-Generation Chinese Americans, 1880s to 1930s." In K. Scott Wong and Sucheng Chan, eds., *Claiming America: Constructing Chinese American Identities during the Exclusion Era.* Philadelphia: Temple University Press, 1998. Pp. 127–164.

————. *This Bitter Sweet Soil: The Chinese in Agriculture, 1860–1910.* Berkeley: University of California Press, 1983.

Chan, Sucheng, and Madeline Y. Hsu, eds. *Chinese Americans and the Politics of Race and Culture.* Philadelphia: Temple University Press, 2008.

Chang, Iris. *The Chinese in America: A Narrative History.* New York: Viking, 2003.

Chang, Shenglin. *The Global Silicon Valley Home: Lives and Landscapes within Taiwanese American Trans-Pacific Culture.* Stanford: Stanford University Press, 2006.

Chang, Shirley L. *Taiwan's Brain Drain and Its Reversal.* Taipei: Lucky Bookstore, 1998.

Chao, Teresa Hsu. "Overview." In Xueying Wang, ed., *A View from Within: A Case Study of Chinese Heritage Community Language Schools in the United States.* Washington, DC: National Foreign Language Center, 1996. Pp. 7–13.

Chee, Maria W. L. *Taiwanese American Transnational Families: Women and Kin Work.* New York: Routledge, 2005.

Chen, Carolyn. *Getting Saved in America: Taiwanese Immigration and Religious Experience.* Princeton: Princeton University Press, 2008.

Chen, Guoxiong. "The Development of Chinese Language TV." http://news.xinhuanet.com/newmedia/2003-09/23/content_1095078.html. Accessed October 1, 2004.

Chen, Hsiang-shui. *Chinatown No More: Taiwan Immigrants in Contemporary New York.* Ithaca: Cornell University Press, 1992.

Chen, Shehong. *Being Chinese, Becoming Chinese American.* Urbana: University of Illinois Press, 2002.

Chen, Yong. *Chinese San Francisco, 1850–1943: A Trans-Pacific Community.* Stanford: Stanford University Press, 2000.

Cheng, Lucie. "Free, Indentured, Enslaved: Chinese Prostitutes in Nineteenth-Century America." In Lucie Cheng and Edna Bonacich, eds., *Labor Immigration under Capitalism: Asian Workers in the United States before World War II.* Berkeley: University of California Press, 1984.

Cheng, Lucie, and Philip Yang. "Asians: The 'Model Minority' Deconstructed." In Roger Waldinger and Mehdi Bozorgmehr, eds., *Ethnic Los Angeles.* New York: Russell Sage Foundation, 1996. Pp. 305–344.

Chew, Soon-Beng, and Rosalind Chew. "Immigration and Foreign Labor in Singapore." *ASEAN Economic Bulletin* 12 (1995): 191–200.

Chiang, M. H. "A Study of the Chinese Language School and the Maintenance of Ethnic Language in the Second-Generation, American-Born Chinese." Ph.D. dissertation, University of Texas at Austin, 2000.

Chiang-Hom, Christy. "Transnational Cultural Practices of Chinese Immigrant Youth and Parachute Kids." In Jennifer Lee and Min Zhou, eds., *Asian American Youth: Culture, Identity, and Ethnicity.* New York: Routledge, 2004. Pp. 143–158.

Chin, Ko-Lin. *Chinatown Gangs: Extortion, Enterprise, and Ethnicity.* New York: Oxford University Press, 1996.

———. *Chinese Subculture and Criminality: Non-traditional Crime Groups in America.* Westport, CT: Greenwood Press, 1990.

———. *Smuggled Chinese: Clandestine Immigration to the United States.* Philadelphia: Temple University Press, 1999.

Chin, Margaret. *Sewing Women: Immigrants and the New York City Garment Industry.* New York: Columbia University Press, 2005.

Chin, Tung Pok, with Winifred C. Chin. *Paper Son: One Man's Story.* Philadelphia: Temple University Press, 2000.

Chinatown Today Publishing. *Chinese-American Life Guide.* Hong Kong: Chinatown Today Publishing, 1993.

Chinese-American Planning Council (CPC). *Chinese-American Planning Council: Program List.* New York: CPC, 1993.

Chinese Business Guide and Directory. *Chinese Business Guide and Directory for Metropolitan New York and Boston, 1988.* New York: Key Publications, 1998.

Ching-Hwang, Yen. *Coolies and Mandarins: China's Protection of Overseas Chinese during the Late Ch'ing Period (1851–1911).* Singapore: Singapore University Press, 1985.

Chiu, Ping. *Chinese Labor in California: An Economic Study.* Madison: University of Wisconsin Press, 1967.

Chow, Lily. *Chasing Their Dreams: Chinese Settlement in the Northwest Region of British Columbia.* Prince George, BC: Caitlin Press, 2000.

Chun, Gloria Heyung. *Of Orphans and Warriors: Inventing Chinese American Culture and Identity.* New Brunswick, NJ: Rutgers University Press, 2000.

———. "Shifting Ethnic Identity and Consciousness: U.S.-Born Chinese American Youth in the 1930s and 1950s." In Jennifer Lee and Min Zhou, eds., *Asian American Youth: Culture, Identity and Ethnicity.* New York: Routledge, 2004. Pp. 113–128.

Chung, Sue Fawn. "Fighting for Their American Rights: A History of the Chinese American Citizens Alliance." In K. Scott Wong and Sucheng Chan, eds., *Claiming America: Constructing Chinese American Identities during the Exclusion Era.* Philadelphia: Temple University Press, 1998. Pp. 95–126.

Citizenship and Immigration Canada. Statistics/Reference, Ottawa. http://www.cic.gc.ca/english/pub/index-2.html#statistics. Accessed October 1, 2004.

Coleman, James S. *Foundations of Social Theory.* Cambridge: Belknap Press of the Harvard University Press, 1990.

———. "Social Capital in the Creation of Human Capital." *American Journal of Sociology* 94 (1988): 95–120.

Coleman, James S., E. Q. Campbell, C. J. Hobson, J. McPartland, A. M. Mood, F. D. Weinfeld, and R. L. York. *Equality of Educational Opportunity.* Washington, DC: U.S. Government Printing Office, 1966.

Conway, Nick. *San Gabriel Valley Regional Demographic Profile: Indicator Report.* Pasadena: San Gabriel Council of Governments, 2003.

Conzen, Kathleen Neils. "Mainstreams and Side Channels: The Localization of Immigrant Cultures." *Journal of American Ethnic History* 11 (Fall 1991): 5–20.

Coolidge, Mary Roberts. *Chinese Immigration.* New York: Henry Holt, 1909.

Cooney, Rosemary, and Vilma Ortiz. "Nativity, National Origin and Hispanic Female Labor Force Participation." *Social Science Quarterly* 64 (1983): 510–523.

Cortese, Charles F., R. Frank Falk, and Jack K. Cohen. "Further Consideration of the Methodological Analysis of Segregation Indices." *American Sociological Review* 41 (1976): 630–637.

Cribb, Robert. "History [of Indonesia]." In *The Far East and Australia, 1999.* 13th ed. London: Europe Publications, 1999. Pp. 415–420.

Daniels, Roger. *Asian American: Chinese and Japanese in the United States since 1850.* Pullman: University of Washington Press, 1988.

———. "Westerners from the East: Oriental Immigrants Reappraised." *Pacific Historical Review* 35 (1966): 373–383.

Dicker, Laverne Mau. *The Chinese in San Francisco: A Political History.* New York: Dover, 1979.

Dillon, Richard H. *The Hatchet Men: The Story of the Tong Wars in San Francisco's Chinatown.* New York: Ballantine Books, 1962.

Dion, Karen K., and Kenneth L. Dion. "Gender and Cultural Adaptation in Immigrant Families." *Journal of Social Issues* 57 (2001): 511–521.

Du, Ruiqing. *Chinese Higher Education: A Decade of Reform and Development (1978–1988).* New York: St. Martin's Press, 1992.

Dugger, Celia W. "Queens Old-Timers Uneasy As Asian Influence Grows." *New York Times,* March 31, 1996.

Edwards, Richard C. *Contested Terrain: The Transformation of the Workplace in the Twentieth Century.* New York: Harper Torchbooks, 1979.

Eljera, Bert. "The Chinese Beverly Hills." *Asianweek,* May 24–30, 1996. http://www.asianweek.com/052496/LittleTaipei.html. Accessed January 15, 2007.

Elliott, Delbert, and Harwin Voss. *Delinquency and Dropout.* Lexington, MA: Lexington Books, 1974.

England, Paula, George Farkas, Barbara Kilbourne, and Thomas Tou. "Sex Segregation and Wages." *American Sociological Review* 53 (1988): 544–558.

Espiritu, Yen Le. *Asian American Panethnicity: Bridging Institutions and Identities.* Philadelphia: Temple University Press, 1993.

Fagerlind, Ingemar. *Formal Education and Adult Earnings.* Stockholm: Almquest & Wiksall, 1975.

Fan, C. Cindy. "Chinese Americans: Immigration, Settlement, and Social Geography." In Laurence J. C. Ma and Carolyn Cartier, eds., *The Chinese Diaspora: Space, Place, Mobility, and Identity.* Lanham, MD: Rowman & Littlefield, 2003. Pp. 261–291.

Fan, C. Y. "The Chinese Language Schools of San Francisco in Relation to Family Integration and Cultural Identity." Ph.D. dissertation, Duke University, 1976.

Fernandez-Kelly, M. Patricia. "Towanda's Triumph: Social and Cultural Capital in the Transition to Adulthood in the Urban Ghetto." *International Journal of Urban and Regional Research* 18, no. 1 (1995): 89–111.

Fitzgerald, C. P. "The History of China up to 1966." In *The Far East and Australia, 1999.* 13th ed. London: Europe Publications, 1999. Pp. 230–234.

———. *The Third China: The Chinese in South-East Asia.* London: Angus & Robertson, 1965.

Foner, Nancy. "The Immigrant Family: Cultural Legacies and Cultural Changes." In Charles Hirschman, Philip Kasinitz, and Josh DeWind, eds., *The Handbook of International Migration: The American Experience.* New York: Russell Sage Foundation, 1999. Pp. 257–274.

Fong, Joe C. *Complementary Education and Culture in the Global/Local Chinese Community.* San Francisco: China Books and Periodicals, 2003.

———. "Transnational Newspapers: The Making of Post-1965 Globalized/Localized San Gabriel Valley Chinese Community." *Amerasia Journal* 22, no. 3 (1996): 65–77.

Fong, Timothy P. *The First Suburban Chinatown: The Remaking of Monterey Park, California.* Philadelphia: Temple University Press, 1994.

Forbes, Dean. "Toward the 'Pacific Century': Integration and Disintegration in the Pacific Basin." In *The Far East and Australia, 1999.* 13th ed. London: Europe Publications, 1999. Pp. 35–43.

Fordham, Signithia. *Blacked Out: Dilemmas of Race, Identity, and Success at Capital High.* Chicago: University of Chicago Press, 1996.

Fordham, Signithia, and Ogbu, John U. "Black Students' School Success: Coping with the 'Burden of "Acting White."'" *Urban Review* 18 (1986): 176–206.

Foreman, H. S. "A Study of Chinese Language Schools." Master's thesis, San Francisco State College, 1958.

Frey, William H., and Alden Speare, Jr. "Regional and Metropolitan Growth and Decline in the United States." *Economic Geography* 65 (1989): 76–79.

Fry, Luther C. "Illegal Entry of Orientals into the United States between 1910 and 1920." *Journal of the American Statistical Association* 23 (1928): 173–178.

Fukuyama, Francis. "Immigrants and Family Values." *Commentary* 95, no. 5 (1993): 26–32.

Gans, Herbert J. "Second-Generation Decline: Scenarios for the Economic and Ethnic Futures of the Post-1965 American Immigrants." *Ethnic and Racial Studies* 15 (1992): 173–192.

———. *The Urban Villagers.* New York: Free Press of Glencoe, 1962.

Gibson, Margaret A. *Accommodation without Assimilation: Sikh Immigrants in an American High School.* Ithaca: Cornell University Press, 1989.

Gladwell, Malcolm. "Rebirth in New York: Neighborhoods Growing Again in the City." *Washington Post,* September 18, 1993.

Glazer, Nathan. "Is Assimilation Dead?" *Annals of the American Academy of Political and Social Science* 530, no. 1 (1993): 122–136.

Glazer, Nathan, and Daniel P. Moynihan. *Beyond the Melting Pot: The Negroes, Puerto Ricans, Jews, Italians, and Irish of New York City.* 2nd ed. Cambridge: MIT Press, 1970.

Glenn, Evelyn Nakano. "Split Household, Small Producer, and Dual Wage Earner: An Analysis of Chinese American Family Strategies." *Journal of Marriage and the Family* 45 (1983): 35–46.

Glenn, Evelyn Nakano, and Stacey G. H. Yap. "Chinese American Families." In Ronald L. Taylor, ed., *Minority Families in the United States: A Multicultural Perspective.* Englewood, NJ: Prentice Hall, 1994. Pp. 115–145.

Glick, Clarence Elmer. *Sojourners and Settlers: Chinese Merchants in Hawaii.* Honolulu: University of Hawaii Press, 1980.

Goldstone, Jack A. "A Tsunami on the Horizon? The Potential for International Migration from the People's Republic of China." In Paul J. Smith, ed., *Human Smuggling: Chinese Migrant Trafficking and the Challenge to America's Immigration Tradition.* Washington, DC: Center for Strategic and International Studies, 1997. Pp. 48–75.

Gong, Eng Ying, and Bruce Grant. *Tong War.* New York: Nicholas L. Brown, 1930.

Gordon, E. W., B. L. Bridglall, and A. S. Meroe, eds. *Supplementary Education: The Hidden Curriculum of High Academic Achievement.* Lanham, MD: Rowman & Littlefield, 2005.

Gordon, Milton M. *Assimilation in American Life: The Role of Race, Religion, and National Origins.* New York: Oxford University Press, 1964.

Guest, Kenneth. *God in Chinatown: Religion and Survival in New York's Evolving Immigrant Community.* New York: New York University Press, 2003.

Gyory, Andrew. *Closing the Gate: Race, Politics, and the Chinese Exclusion Act.* Chapel Hill: University of North Carolina Press, 1998.

Handlin, Oscar. *The Uprooted.* 2nd ed. Boston: Little, Brown, 1973.

Harada, K. G. "A Survey of Japanese Language Schools in Hawaii." M.A. thesis, University of Hawaii, 1934.

Hawkins, J. N. "Politics, Education, and Language Policy: The Case of Japanese Language Schools in Hawaii." *Amerasia Journal* 5, no. 1 (1978): 39–56.

Hernandez, Donald J. *America's Children: Resources from Family, Government, and the Economy.* New York: Russell Sage Foundation, 1993.

Hirschman, Charles, and Morrison G. Wong. "Socioeconomic Gains of Asian Americans, Blacks, and Hispanics, 1960–1976." *American Journal of Sociology* 90 (1984): 584–607.

———. "The Extraordinary Educational Attainment of Asian Americans: A Search for Historical Evidence and Explanations." *Social Forces* 65 (1986): 1–27.

Hom, Marlon K. *Songs of Gold Mountain: Cantonese Rhymes from San Francisco Chinatown.* Berkeley: University of California Press, 1987.

Horton, John. *The Politics of Diversity: Immigration, Resistance, and Change in Monterey Park, California.* Philadelphia: Temple University Press, 1995.

Hoy, William. *The Chinese Six Companies*. San Francisco: California Chinese Historical Society, 1942.

Hsu, Madeline Y. Y. *Dreaming of Gold, Dreaming of Home: Transnationalism and Migration between the United States and South China, 1882–1943*. Stanford: Stanford University Press, 2000.

———. "From Chop Suey to Mandarin Cuisine: Fine Dining and the Refashioning of Chinese Ethnicity during the Cold War Era." In Sucheng Chan and Madeline Y. Hsu, eds., *Chinese Americans and the Politics of Race and Culture*. Philadelphia: Temple University Press, 2008. Pp. 173–193.

———. "Gold Mountain Dreams and Paper Son Schemes: Chinese Immigration under Exclusion." *Chinese America: History and Perspectives* 11 (1997): 46–61.

Hugo, Graeme G. "The Demographic Underpinnings of Current and Future International Migrations in Asia." *Asian and Pacific Migration Journal* 7 (1998): 1–25.

ILGWU (International Ladies' Garment Workers' Union) Local 23–25. *The Chinatown Garment Industry Study*. New York: Abeles, Schwartz, Haeckel & Silverblatt, 1983.

Irick, Robert L. *Ch'ing Policy toward the Coolie Trade, 1847–1878*. Taipei: Chinese Materials Center, 1982.

Jackson, Peter. "Ethnic Turf: Competition on the Canal Street Divide." *New York Affairs* 7, no. 4 (1983): 149–158.

Jeung, Russell. *Faithful Generations: Race and New Asian American Churches*. New Brunswick, NJ: Rutgers University Press, 2005.

Jun, Shao. "The History and Current Status of Chinese Online Media in North America." http://www.chinanews.com.cn//2003-09-21/136/147.html. Accessed October 1, 2004.

Kamo, Yoshinori, and Min Zhou. "Living Arrangements of Elderly Chinese and Japanese Immigrants in the United States." *Journal of Marriage and the Family* 56 (1994): 544–558.

Kang & Lee Advertising. 1998. *Asian Media Reference Guide*. 3rd ed. http://www.kanglee.com. Accessed September 10, 1999.

Kantrowitz, Nathan. "Ethnic and Racial Segregation in the New York Metropolis: Residential Patterns among White Ethnic Groups, Blacks, and Puerto Ricans." *Social Forces* 52 (1974): 429–430.

Kasinitz, Philip, John H. Mollenkopf, Mary C. Waters, and Jennifer Holdaway. *Inheriting the City: The Children of Immigrants Come of Age*. Cambridge: Harvard University Press and Russell Sage Foundation Press, 2008.

Kibria, Nazli. *Becoming Asian American: Second-Generation Chinese and Korean American Identities*. Baltimore: Johns Hopkins University Press, 2002.

———. "The Construction of 'Asian American': Reflections on Intermarriage and Ethnic Identity among Second-Generation Chinese and Korean Americans." *Ethnic and Racial Studies* 20 (1997): 522–544.

———. *Family Tightrope: The Changing Lives of Vietnamese Americans*. Princeton: Princeton University Press, 1993.

Kiker, B. F., and C. M. Condon. "The Influence of Socioeconomic Background on the Earnings of Young Men." *Journal of Human Resources* 16 (1981): 95–105.

———. "Transmission of Economic Inequality over Three Generations." *Social Sciences Journal* 18 (April 1981): 13–24.

Kingston, Maxine Hong. *The Woman Warrior: Memoirs of a Girlhood among Ghosts*. New York: Vintage, 1975.

Koehn, Peter H., and Xiaohuang Yin. *The Expanding Roles of Chinese Americans in U.S.-China Relations*. Armonk, NY: M. E. Sharpe, 2002.

Kohl, Herbert. *"I Won't Learn from You" and Other Thoughts on Creative Maladjustment.* New York: New Press, 1994.

Korstrom, Glen. "Fairchild Expands Media Empire with Web." *Business in Vancouver,* September 2000, pp. 12–18.

Kozol, Jonathan. *The Shame of the Nation: The Restoration of Apartheid Schooling in America.* New York: Crown, 2005.

Kraly, Ellen Percy. "U.S. Immigration Policy and the Immigrant Populations of New York." In Nancy Foner, ed., *New Immigrants in New York.* New York: Columbia University Press, 1987. Pp. 35–78.

Kung, S. W. *Chinese in American Life: Some Aspects of Their History, Status, Problems, and Contributions.* Seattle: University of Washington Press, 1962.

Kuo, Chia-ling. *Social and Political Change in New York's Chinatown: The Role of Voluntary Associations.* New York: Praeger, 1977.

Kuo, Joyce. "Excluded, Segregated, and Forgotten: A Historical View of the Discrimination of Chinese Americans in Public Schools." *Asian Law Journal* 5 (1998): 181–212.

Kwong, Peter. *Chinatown, N.Y.: Labor and Politics, 1930–1950.* Rev. ed. New York: New Press, 2001.

———. *Forbidden Workers: Illegal Chinese Immigrants and American Labor.* New York: New Press, 1997.

———. *The New Chinatown.* New York: Hill & Wang, 1987.

Kyo, Syukushin. "Japan." In Lynn Pan, ed., *The Encyclopedia of the Chinese Overseas.* Cambridge: Harvard University Press, 1999. Pp. 332–339.

Lai, Him Mark. *Becoming Chinese American: A History of Communities and Institutions.* Walnut Creek, CA: AltaMira Press, 2004.

———. "The Chinese American Press." In Sally M. Miller, ed., *The Ethnic Press in the United States: A Historical Analysis and Handbook.* New York: Greenwood Press, 1987. Pp. 27–43.

———. "The Chinese Press in the United States and Canada since World War II: A Diversity of Voices." *Chinese America: History and Perspectives* 4 (1990): 107–156.

———. "Historical Development of the Chinese Consolidated Benevolent Association/ Huiguan System." *Chinese America: History and Perspectives* 1 (1987): 13–51.

———. "Retention of the Chinese Heritage: Chinese Schools in America before World War II." *Chinese America: History and Perspectives* 14 (2000): 10–27.

———. "Retention of the Chinese Heritage: Chinese Schools in America from World War II to the Present." *Chinese America: History and Perspectives* 15 (2001): 1–24.

Laguerre, Michel S. *The Global Ethnopolis: Chinatown, Japantown, and Manilatown in American Society.* London: Macmillan, 2000.

Langberg, Mark, and Reynolds Farley. "Residential Segregation of Asian Americans in 1980." *Sociology and Social Research* 70 (1985): 71–75.

Lareau, Annette. *Unequal Childhoods: Class, Race, and Family Life.* Berkeley: University of California Press, 2003.

Lau, Estelle T. *Paper Families: Identity, Immigration Administration, and Chinese Exclusion.* Durham, NC: Duke University Press, 2006.

Lau, Wendy. "Children at a Sewing Machine: Grim Choice for Immigrants." *Chinese Staff and Worker Association News: The Voice of Chinese American Workers* 2, no. 1 (1990): 8–9.

Lee, Erika. *At America's Gates: Chinese Immigration during the Exclusion Era, 1882–1943.* Chapel Hill: University of North Carolina Press, 2005.

Lee, Jennifer. "Jing Fong: Unfair Labor Practices in Chinatown." *Asian American Policy Review* 7 (Spring 1997): 145–162.

Lee, Jennifer, and Frank D. Bean. "America's Changing Color Lines." *Annual Review of Sociology* 30 (2004): 221–242.

Lee, Jennifer, and Min Zhou. "Conclusion: Reflection, Thoughts, and Directions for Future Research." In Jennifer Lee and Min Zhou, eds., *Asian American Youth: Culture, Identity, and Ethnicity*. New York: Routledge, 2004. Pp. 313–324.

Lee, Joseph S. "The Impact of the Asian Financial Crisis on Foreign Workers in Japan." *Asian and Pacific Migration Journal* 7 (1998): 145–169.

Lee, Robert G. *Orientals: Asian Americans in Popular Culture*. Philadelphia: Temple University Press, 1999.

Lee, Rose Hum. *The Chinese in the United States of America*. Hong Kong: Hong Kong University Press, 1960.

———. *The Growth and Decline of Chinese Communities in the Rocky Mountain Region*. New York: Arno Press, 1978.

Lee, Wen Ho (with Helen Zia). *My Country Versus Me*. New York: Hyperion, 2001.

Leong, Gor Yun. *Chinatown Inside Out*. New York: Barrows Mussey, 1936.

Leung, E. K. "A Sociological Study of the Chinese Language Schools in the San Francisco Bay Area." Ph.D. dissertation, University of Missouri-Columbia, 1975.

Lewis, Oscar. "The Culture of Poverty." *Scientific American* 215 (1966): 19–25.

Li, Ling. "Mass Migration within China and the Implications for Chinese Emigration." In Paul J. Smith, ed., *Human Smuggling: Chinese Migrant Trafficking and the Challenge to America's Immigration Tradition*. Washington, DC: Center for Strategic and International Studies, 1997. Pp. 23–47.

Li, Minghuan. *A History of Chinese Immigrants in Europe* (欧洲华侨华人史). Beijing: Zhongguo Huaqiao Chubanshe, 2002.

Li, Peter S. "Chinese Diaspora in Occidental Societies." In Dirk Hoerder, Christiane Harzig, and Adrian Shubert, eds., *The Historical Practice of Diversity: Transcultural Interactions from the Early Mediterranean to the Postcolonial World*. Oxford and New York: Berghahn Books, 2003. Pp. 134–151.

———. *Chinese in Canada*. Toronto: Oxford University Press, 1998.

Li, Wei. "Building Ethnoburbia: The Emergence and Manifestation of the Chinese Ethnoburb in Los Angeles' San Gabriel Valley." *Journal of Asian American Studies* 2 (1998): 1–28.

———. "Ethnoburb versus Chinatown: Two Types of Urban Ethnic Communities in Los Angeles." *Cybergeo* 70 (October 1998). http://www.cybergeo.presse.fr/culture/weili/weili.htm. Accessed January 30, 2007.

———, ed. *From Urban Enclave to Ethnic Suburb: New Asian Communities in Pacific Rim Countries*. Honolulu: University of Hawaii Press, 2006.

———. "Spatial Transformation of an Urban Ethnic Community from Chinatown to Chinese Ethnoburb in Los Angeles." Ph.D. dissertation, Department of Geography, University of Southern California, 1997.

Li, Wei, Gary Dymski, Yu Zhou, Maria Chee, and Carolyn Akdana. "Chinese-American Banking and Community Development in Los Angeles County." *Annals of the Association of American Geographers* 92 (2002): 777–796.

Liang, Zai. "Demography of Illicit Emigration from China: A Sending Country Perspective." *Sociological Forum* 16 (2001): 677–701.

Liang, Zai, and Naomi Ito. "Intermarriage of Asian Americans in the New York City Region: Contemporary Patterns and Future Prospects." *International Migration Review* 33 (1999): 876–900.

Liao, Da-ke. *A History of Overseas Communications of Fujian* (福建海外交通史). Fuzhou: Fujian Renmin Chubanshe, 2002.

Lieberson, Stanley. *A Piece of the Pie: Blacks and White Immigrants since 1880*. Berkeley: University of California Press, 1981.

Lieberson, Stanley, and Mary Waters. *From Many Strands: Ethnic and Racial Groups in Contemporary America*. New York: Russell Sage Foundation, 1988.

Lien, Pei-te. "Homeland Origins and Political Identities among Chinese in Southern California." *Ethnic and Racial Studies* 31 (2008): 1381–1403.

———. "Transnational Homeland Concerns and Participation in U.S. Politics: A Comparison among Immigrants from China, Taiwan, and Hong Kong." *Journal of Chinese Overseas* 2 (2006): 56–78.

Light, Ivan. "Beyond the Ethnic Enclave Economy." *Social Problems* 41 (1994): 601–616.

———. *Deflecting Immigration: Networks, Markets, and Regulations in Los Angeles*. New York: Russell Sage Foundation, 2006.

———. "The Ethnic Economy." In Neil J. Smelser and Richard Swedberg, eds., *The Handbook of Economic Sociology*. 2nd ed. Princeton: Princeton University Press, 2005. Pp. 650–677.

———. *Ethnic Enterprise in America: Business and Welfare among Chinese, Japanese, and Blacks*. Berkeley: University of California Press, 1972.

Light, Ivan, and Steve J. Gold. *Ethnic Economies*. San Diego, CA: Academic Press, 2000.

Light, Ivan, and Stavros Karageorgis. "The Ethnic Economy." In Neil J. Smelser and Richard Swedberg, eds., *The Handbook of Economic Sociology*. Princeton: Princeton University Press, 1994. Pp. 647–669.

Light, Ivan, George Sabagh, Mehdi Bozorgnehr, and Claudia Der-Martirosian. "Beyond the Ethnic Enclave Economy." *Social Problems* 41 (1994): 65–80.

Light, Ivan, and Charles Choy Wong. "Protest or Work: Dilemmas of the Tourist Industry in American Chinatowns." *American Journal of Sociology* 80 (1975): 1342–1368.

Light, Ivan, Min Zhou, and Rebecca Kim. "Transnationalism and American Exports in an English-Speaking World." *International Migration Review* 36 (2002): 702–725.

Lii, Jane H. "Neighborhood Report: Northern Queens: Common Heritage, but No Common Ground." *New York Times*, April 21, 1996.

Lin, Jan. *Reconstructing Chinatown: Ethnic Enclave, Global Change*. Minneapolis: University of Minnesota Press, 1998.

———. Review of Zhou, *Chinatown*. *Racial and Ethnic Studies* 18 (1995): 671–673.

Lin, Jan, and Paul Robinson. "Spatial Disparities in the Expansion of the Chinese Ethnoburb of Los Angeles." *GeoJournal* 64 (2005): 51–61.

Ling, Huping. *Chinese St. Louis: From Enclave to Cultural Community*. Philadelphia: Temple University Press, 2004.

———. "Family and Marriage of Late-Nineteenth- and Early-Twentieth-Century Chinese Immigrant Women." *Journal of American Ethnic History* 19, no. 2 (2000): 43–63.

———. *Surviving on the Gold Mountain: A History of Chinese American Women and Their Lives*. Albany: State University of New York Press, 1998.

Liu, Eric. *The Accidental Asian: Notes of a Native Speaker*. New York: Vintage Books, 1998.

Liu, Haiming. "The Resilience of Ethnic Culture: Chinese Herbalists in the American Medical Profession." *Journal of Asian American Studies* 1 (1998): 173–191.

———. "The Social Origin of the Early Chinese Immigrants: A Revisionist Perspective." In Susie Lan Cassel, ed., *The Chinese in America: A History from Gold Mountain to the New Millennium*. Walnut Creek, CA: AltaMira, 2002. Pp. 21–36.

———. *The Transnational History of a Chinese Family: Immigrant Letters, Family Business and Reverse Migration*. New Brunswick, NJ: Rutgers University Press, 2005.

———. "The Trans-Pacific Family Pattern in the Chinese American Experience." *Amerasia Journal* 18, no. 2 (1992): 1–32.

Liu, Hong. "New Migrants and the Revival of Overseas Chinese Nationalism." *Journal of Contemporary China* 14, no. 43 (2005): 291–316.

———. *Southeast Asian Studies in China* (中国东南亚学). Beijing: Chinese Social Science Press, 2000.

Liu, Mary Ting Yi. *The Chinatown Trunk Mystery: Murder, Miscegenation, and Other Dangerous Encounters in Turn-of-the-Century New York City.* Princeton: Princeton University Press, 2005.

Logan, John R., Richard D. Alba, Michael Dill, and Min Zhou. "Ethnic Segmentation in the American Metropolis: Increasing Divergence in Economic Incorporation, 1980–1990." *International Migration Review* 34 (2000): 98–132.

Logan, John R., Jacob Stowell, and Elena Vesselinov. "From Many Shores: Asians in Census 2000." Report by the Lewis Mumford Center for Comparative Urban and Regional Research. Albany: State University of New York, 2001. http://mumford1.dyndns.org/cen2000/report.html. Accessed October 6, 2001.

Loo, Chalsa. *Chinatown: Most Time, Hard Time.* Westport, CT: Praeger, 1991.

Loo, Chalsa, and Don Mar. "Desired Residential Mobility in a Low Income Ethnic Community: A Case Study of Chinatown." *Journal of Social Issues* 38, no. 3 (1982): 95–106.

Lopez, David. "Language Assimilation." In Roger Waldinger and Mehdi Bozorgmehr, eds., *Ethnic Los Angeles.* New York: Russell Sage Foundation, 1996. Pp. 139–163.

Louie, Andrea. "Searching for Roots in Contemporary China and Chinese America." In Sucheng Chan and Madeline Y. Hsu, eds., *Chinese Americans and the Politics of Race and Culture.* Philadelphia: Temple University Press, 2008. Pp. 195–217.

Louie, Miriam Ching Yoon. *Sweatshop Warriors: Immigrant Women Workers Take on the Global Factory.* Cambridge: South End Press, 2001.

Louie, Vivian S. *Compelled to Excel: Immigration, Education, and Opportunity among Chinese Americans.* Stanford: Stanford University Press, 2004.

Loury, Glenn. "A Dynamic Theory of Racial Income Differences." In P. A. Wallace and A. Le Mund, eds., *Women, Minorities, and Employment Discrimination.* Lexington, MA: Lexington Books, 1977. Pp. 153–186.

Lu, Xing. "Bicultural Identity Development and Chinese Community Formation: An Ethnographic Study of Chinese Schools in Chicago." *Howard Journal of Communications* 12 (2001): 203–220.

Luk, Bernard Hung-kay. "Opportunities for Women in Tertiary Education in Hong Kong." In Chinese Education Translation Project, *Woman and Education in China, Hong Kong and Taiwan.* Buffalo, NY: Comparative Education Center, SUNY-Buffalo Graduate School of Education, 1990. Pp. 55–62.

Lydon, Sandy. *Chinese Gold: The Chinese in the Monterey Bay Region.* Capitola, CA: Capitola Books, 1985.

Lyman, Stanford M. *Chinese Americans.* New York: Random House, 1974.

———. "Marriage and the Family among Chinese Immigrants to America, 1850–1960." *Phylon* 29 (1968): 321–330.

Ma, Laurence J. C. "Space, Place and Transnationalism in the Chinese Diaspora." In Laurence J. C. Ma and Carolyn Cartier, eds., *The Chinese Diaspora: Space, Place, Mobility, and Identity.* Lanham, MD: Rowman & Littlefield Publishers, 2003. Pp. 1–49.

Ma, Laurence J. C., and Carolyn Cartier, eds. *The Chinese Diaspora: Space, Place, Mobility, and Identity.* Lanham, MD: Rowman & Littlefield, 2003.

Ma, Y. Y. "Effects of Attendance at Chinese Language Schools upon San Francisco Children." Ph.D. dissertation, University of California, Los Angeles, 1945.

Machuca, Paulina. "The Other War." *Convergence Online* 3 (2003). http://magazines.humberc.on.ca/Convergence2003/paulina.html. Accessed October 1, 2004.

Mahalingam, Ram, ed. *Cultural Psychology of Immigrants*. Mahwah, NJ: Lawrence Erlbaum, 2006.

Mainstream Broadcasting Corporation CHMB AM1320. "The Voice of the Community." http://am1320.com/VOC.pdf. Accessed October 1, 2004.

Mak, Grace C. L. "The Schooling of Girls in Hong Kong: Progress and Contradictions in the Transition." In Gerard A. Postiglione, ed., *Education and Society in Hong Kong: Toward One Country and Two Systems*. New York: East Gate, 1991. Pp. 167–180.

Martin, Philip L., Andrew Mason, and Ching-Lung Tsay. "Overview." *ASCEAN Economic Bulletin* 12 (1995): 117–135.

Massey, Douglas S., Joaquin Arango, Graeme Hugo, Ali Kouaouci, Adela Pellegrino, and J. Edward Taylor. "An Evaluation of International Migration Theory: The North American Case." *Population and Development Review* 20 (1994): 699–751.

Massey, Douglas S., and Nancy A. Denton. *American Apartheid: Segregation and the Making of the Underclass*. Cambridge: Harvard University Press, 1995.

———. "Suburbanization and Segregation in U.S. Metropolitan Areas." *American Journal of Sociology* 94 (1988): 592–626.

———. "Trends in Residential Segregation of Blacks, Hispanics, and Asians: 1970–1980." *American Sociological Review* 52 (1987): 802–825.

McClain, Charles J. *In Search of Equality: The Chinese Struggle against Discrimination in Nineteenth Century America*. Berkeley: University of California Press, 1994.

McCunn, Ruthanne Lum. *An Illustrated History of the Chinese in America*. San Francisco: Design Enterprises of San Francisco, 1979.

McKeown, Adam. *Chinese Migrant Networks and Cultural Change: Peru, Chicago, and Hawaii, 1900–1936*. Chicago: University of Chicago Press, 2001.

———. "Transnational Chinese Families and Chinese Exclusion, 1875–1974." *Journal of American Ethnic History* 18, no. 2 (1999): 73–110.

Meagher, Arnold J. *The Coolie Trade: The Traffic in Chinese Laborers to Latin America 1847–1874*. Philadelphia: Xlibris, 2008.

Melendy, H. Brett. *Asians in America: Filipinos, Koreans, and East Indians*. Boston: Twayne, 1977.

Menjívar, Cecilia. *Fragmented Ties: Salvadoran Immigrant Networks in America*. Berkeley: University of California Press, 2000.

Miller, Stuart Creighton. *The Unwelcome Immigrants: The American Image of the Chinese, 1785–1882*. Berkeley: University of California Press, 1969.

Mincer, Jacob, and Solomon Polacheck. "Family Investment in Human Capital: Earnings of Women." *Journal of Political Economy* 82, no. 2 (1974): S76–S108.

Model, Suzanne. "The Ethnic Niche and the Structure of Opportunity: Immigrants and Minorities in New York City." In Michael Katz, ed., *The "Underclass" Debate: Views from History*. Princeton: Princeton University Press, 1993.

Morris, Paul. "Preparing Pupils as Citizens of the Special Administrative Region of Hong Kong: An Analysis of Curriculum Change and Control during the Transition Period." In Gerard A. Postiglione, ed., *Education and Society in Hong Kong: Toward One Country and Two Systems*. New York: East Gate, 1991. Pp. 117–145.

Mueller, Charles W., and Blair G. Campbell. "Female Occupational Achievement and Marital Status: A Research Note." *Journal of Marriage and the Family* 39 (1977): 587–593.

Mustain, Gene. "Chinatown Grows in Brooklyn, Too." *Daily News*, October 27, 1997.

Myers, Willard H., III. "Of Qinqing, Qinshu, Guanxi, and Shetou: The Dynamic Element of Chinese Irregular Population Movement." In Paul J. Smith, ed., *Human Smuggling: Chinese Migrant Trafficking and the Challenge to America's Immigration Tradition*. Washington, DC: Center for Strategic and International Studies, 1997. Pp. 93–126.

Nee, Victor G., and Brett De Bary Nee. *Longtime Californ': A Documentary Study of an American Chinatown.* New York: Pantheon, 1973.

New York City Department of City Planning (NYCDCP). *Asians in New York City.* New York: NYCDCP, 1986.

———. *The Newest New Yorkers: A Statistical Portrait.* New York: NYCDCP, 1992.

Ng, Franklin. *The Taiwanese Americans.* Westport, CT: Greenwood Press, 1998.

Ng, Sek-hong, and Grace O. M. Lee. "Hong Kong Labor Market in the Aftermath of the Crisis: Implications for Foreign Workers." *Asian and Pacific Migration Journal* 7 (1998): 171–186.

Ngai, Mae M. "History as Law and Life: Tape v. Hurley and the Origins of the Chinese American Middle Class." In Sucheng Chan and Madeline Y. Hsu, eds., *Chinese Americans and the Politics of Race and Culture.* Philadelphia: Temple University Press, 2008. Pp. 62–90.

Ogbu, John U. *The Next Generation: An Ethnography of Education in an Urban Neighborhood.* New York: Academic Press, 1974.

Ogbu, John U., and Maria E. Matute-Bianchi. "Understanding Sociocultural Factors: Knowledge, Identity and School Adjustment." In Bilingual Education Service, *Beyond Language: Social and Cultural Factors in Schooling Language Minority Students.* Sacramento: California State Department of Education, 1986. Pp. 73–141.

Ogbu, John U., and H. D. Simon. "Voluntary and Involuntary Minorities: A Cultural-Ecological Theory of School Performance with Some Implications for Education." *Anthropology and Educational Quarterly* 29 (1998): 155–188.

Okamoto, Dina G. "Toward a Theory of Panethnicity: Explaining Asian American Collective Action." *American Sociological Review* 68 (2003): 811–842.

Olsen, L. *Made in America: Immigrant Students in Our Public Schools.* New York: New Press, 1997.

Ong, Paul M., Lucie Cheng, and Leslie Evans. "Migration of Highly Educated Asians and Global Dynamics." *Asian and Pacific Migration Journal* 1 (1992): 543–567.

Onishi, Katsumi. "A Study of the Attitudes of the Japanese in Hawaii toward Japanese Language Schools." M.A. thesis, University of Hawaii, 1948.

Pan, Lynn. *The Encyclopedia of the Chinese Overseas.* Cambridge: Harvard University Press, 1999.

———. *Son of the Yellow Emperor: A History of the Chinese Diaspora.* New York: Kodansha International, 1994.

Park, Robert E. "Human Migration and the Marginal Man." *American Journal of Sociology* 33 (1928): 881–893.

Parvin, Jean. "Immigrants Migrate to International City." *Crain's New York Business,* July 8, 1991.

Peffer, George Anthony. *If They Don't Bring Their Women Here: Chinese Female Immigration before Exclusion.* Urbana: University of Illinois Press, 1999.

Perez, Lisandro. "Immigrant Economic Adjustment and Family Organization: The Cuban Success Story Reexamined." *International Migration Review* 20 (1986): 4–20.

Petersen, Williams. *Japanese Americans: Oppression and Success.* New York: Random House, 1971.

———. "Success Story, Japanese-American Style." *New York Times Magazine,* January 9, 1966, p. 21.

Philliber, William W., and Dana V. Hiller. "The Implication of Wife's Occupational Attainment for Husband's Class Identification." *Sociological Quarterly* 19 (1978): 450–458.

Pillai, Patrick. "The Impact of the Economic Crisis on Migrant Labor in Malaysia: Policy Implications." *Asian and Pacific Migration Journal* 7 (1998): 255–280.

Portes, Alejandro. "Economic Sociology and the Sociology of Immigration: A Conceptual Overview." In Alejandro Portes, ed., *The Economic Sociology of Immigration: Essays on Networks, Ethnicity, and Entrepreneurship*. New York: Russell Sage Foundation, 1995. Pp. 1–41.

———. "English-Only Triumphs, but the Costs Are High." *Contexts* 1 (2002): 10–15.

———. "Foreword." In Min Zhou, *Chinatown: The Socioeconomic Potential of an Urban Enclave*. Philadelphia: Temple University Press, 1992. Pp. xiii–xvi.

———. *The New Second Generation*. New York: Russell Sage Foundation, 1996.

———. "The Social Origins of the Cuban Enclave Economy of Miami." *Sociological Perspective* 30 (1987): 340–472.

Portes, Alejandro, and Robert L. Bach. *The Latin Journey: Cuban and Mexican Immigrants in the United States*. Berkeley: University of California Press, 1985.

Portes, Alejandro, Patricia Fernandez-Kelly, and William J. Haller. "Segmented Assimilation on the Ground: The New Second Generation in Early Adulthood." *Ethnic and Racial Studies* 28 (2005): 1000–1037.

Portes, Alejandro, and Leif Jensen. "The Enclave and the Entrants: Patterns of Ethnic Enterprise in Miami before and after Mariel." *American Sociological Review* 54 (1989): 929–949.

———. "What's an Ethnic Enclave? The Case for Conceptual Clarity." *American Sociological Review* 52 (1987): 768–771.

Portes, Alejandro, and Dag MacLeod. "The Educational Progress of Children of Immigrants: The Roles of Class, Ethnicity, and School Context." *Sociology of Education* 69 (1996): 255–275.

Portes, Alejandro, and Robert D. Manning. "The Immigrant Enclave: Theory and Empirical Examples." In Susan Olzak and Joane Nagel, eds., *Comparative Ethnic Relations*. Orlando: Academic Press, 1986. Pp. 47–68.

Portes, Alejandro, and Rubén G. Rumbaut. *Immigrant America: A Portrait*. 3rd ed. Berkeley: University of California Press, 2006.

———. *Legacies: The Story of the Immigrant Second Generation*. Berkeley: University of California Press, 2001.

Portes, Alejandro, and Steven Shafer. "Revisiting the Enclave Hypothesis: Miami Twenty-Five Years Later." *Research in the Sociology of Organizations* 25 (2007): 175–190.

Portes, Alejandro, and Julia Sensenbrenner. "Embeddedness and Immigration: Notes on the Social Determinants of Economic Action." *American Journal of Sociology* 98 (1993): 1320–1350.

Portes, Alejandro, and Alex Stepick. *City on the Edge: The Transformation of Miami*. Berkeley: University of California Press, 1993.

Portes, Alejandro, and Min Zhou. "Entrepreneurship and Economic Progress in the Nineties: A Comparative Analysis of Immigrants and African Americans." In Frank D. Bean and Stephanie Bell-Rose, eds., *Immigration and Opportunity: Race, Ethnicity, and Employment in the United States*. New York: Russell Sage Foundation, 1999. Pp. 143–171.

———. "Gaining the Upper Hand: Economic Mobility among Immigrant and Domestic Minorities." *Ethnic and Racial Studies* 15 (1992): 491–522.

———. "The New Second Generation: Segmented Assimilation and Its Variants among Post-1965 Immigrant Youth." *Annals of the American Academy of Political and Social Science* 530 (November 1993): 74–98.

———. "Self-Employment and the Earnings of Immigrants." *American Sociological Review* 61 (1996): 219–230.

Postiglione, Gerard A. "International Higher Education and the Labor Market in Hong Kong: Functions of Overseas and Local Higher Education." *International Education* 17 (1987): 48–54.

Poston, Dudley, Jr., Michael Xinxiang Mao, and Mei-yu Yu. "The Global Distribution of the Overseas Chinese around 1990." *Population and Development Review* 20 (1994): 631–645.

Purcell, Victor. *The Chinese in Southeast Asia*. London: Oxford University Press, 1965.

Putnam, Robert D. *Making Democracy Work: Civic Traditions in Modern Italy*. Princeton: Princeton University Press, 1993.

Pyke, Karen, and Tran Dang. "'FOB' and 'Whitewashed': Identity and Internalized Racism Among Second Generation Asian Americans." *Qualitative Sociology* 26 (2003): 147–172.

Qiu, Li-Ben. "International Migration and Research on Overseas Chinese" (国际人口迁移与华侨华人研究). In Zhiyuan Hao, ed., *A Collection of Papers on Overseas Chinese Studies*. Beijing: Social Science Press, 2002. Pp. 40–56.

Reid, Anthony. "Chinese and Southeast Asian Interactions." In Lynn Pan, ed., *The Encyclopedia of the Chinese Overseas*. Cambridge: Harvard University Press, 1999. Pp. 50–52.

———. "Introduction." In Anthony Reid, ed., *The Last Stand of Asian Autonomies: Responses to Modernity in the Diverse States of Southeast Asia and Korea, 1750–1900*. London: Macmillan, 1997. Pp. 1–26.

———. *Sojourners and Settlers: Histories of Southeast Asia and the Chinese*. St. Leonard, NSW: Allen & Unwin for Asian Studies Association of Australia, 1996.

Reynolds, C. N. "The Chinese Tongs." *American Journal of Sociology* 40 (1935): 612–623.

Rumbaut, Rubén G. "The New Californians: Comparative Research Findings on the Educational Progress of Immigrant Children." In Rubén G. Rumbaut and Wayne A. Cornelius, eds., *California's Immigrant Children: Theory, Research, and Implications for Educational Policy*. La Jolla, CA: Center for U.S.-Mexican Studies, University of California, San Diego, 1995. Pp. 17–69.

———. "Ties That Bind: Immigration and Immigrant Families in the United States." In Alan Booth, Ann C. Crouter, and Nancy Landale, eds., *Immigration and the Family: Research and Policy on U.S. Immigrants*. Mahwah, NJ: Lawrence Erlbaum, 1996. Pp. 3–45.

Rumbaut, Rubén G., and Wayne A. Cornelius, eds. *California's Immigrant Children: Theory, Research, and Implications for Educational Policy*. San Diego: Center for U.S.-Mexican Studies, University of California, 1995.

Rutledge, Paul J. *The Vietnamese Experience in America*. Bloomington: Indiana University Press, 1992.

Saito, Leland T. *Race and Politics: Asian Americans, Latinos and White in a Los Angeles Suburb*. Urbana: University of Illinois Press, 1998.

Salyer, Lucy E. *Laws Harsh as Tigers: Chinese Immigrants and the Shaping of Modern Immigration Law*. Chapel Hill: University of North Carolina Press, 1995.

Sampson, Robert J. "Neighborhood and Community: Collective Efficacy and Community Safety." *New Economy* 11 (2004): 106–113.

Sanders, Jimy M., and Victor Nee. "Limits of Ethnic Solidarity in the Enclave Economy." *American Sociological Review* 52 (1987): 745–767.

Sandmeyer, Elmer C. *The Anti-Chinese Movement in California*. Urbana: University of Illinois Press, 1991.

Sassen, Saskia. *Cities in a World Economy*. Thousand Oaks, CA: Pine Forge Press, 1994.

———. *The Mobility of Labor and Capital*. New York: Cambridge University Press, 1988.

Saxton, Alexander. *The Indispensable Enemy: Labor and the Anti-Chinese Movement in California*. Berkeley: University of California Press, 1971.

Scribner, Sylvia, and Michael Cole. "Cognitive Consequences of Formal and Informal Education." *Science* 182 (1973): 553–559.

See, Chinben. "Chinese Clanship in the Philippines." *Journal of Asian Studies* 12, no. 1 (1960): 224–246.

Shah, Nayan. *Contagious Divides: Epidemics and Race in San Francisco's Chinatown*. Berkeley: University of California Press, 2001.

Shapiro, Michael. "Leaving America: A Startling Fact." *World Monitor*, April 1992, p. 44.

Shi, Ying. "Returning Home?" In Lin Zhiping, *I Want to Go Home: Voiced from the Heart of a Parachute Kid*. Taipei: Yuezhifang Press, 1995. Pp. 3–6.

Shimada, Noriko. "Wartime Dissolution and Revival of the Japanese Language Schools in Hawai'i: Persistence of Ethnic Culture." *Journal of Asian American Studies* 1 (1998): 121–151.

Sing Tao Daily USA. *Sing Tao's Heritage of Service to the Global Chinese Community*. http://www.singtaousa.com/media/heritage.html. Accessed October 1, 2004.

Siu, Paul C. P. *The Chinese Laundryman: A Study of Social Isolation*. New York: New York University Press, 1988.

———. "The Sojourner." *American Journal of Sociology* 50 (1952): 34–44.

Skeldon, Ronald. "Labor Migration to Hong Kong." *ASCEAN Economic Bulletin* 12 (1995): 201–218.

Skinner, G. William. *Chinese Society in Thailand*. Ithaca: Cornell University Press, 1957.

Smith, Paul J. "Chinese Migrant Trafficking: A Global Challenge." In Paul J. Smith, ed., *Human Smuggling: Chinese Migrant Trafficking and the Challenge to America's Immigration Tradition*. Washington, DC: Center for Strategic and International Studies, 1997. Pp. 1–22.

Smith, Ralph. "History [of Viet Nam]." In *The Far East and Australia, 1999*. 13th ed. London: Europe Publications, 1999. Pp. 1167–1170.

Sowell, Thomas. *Ethnic America: A History*. New York: Basic Books, 1981.

Steinberg, Laurence. *Beyond the Classroom: Why School Reform Has Failed and What Parents Need to Do*. New York: Touchstone, 1996.

Stewart, Watt. *Chinese Bondage in Peru: A History of the Chinese Coolie in Peru, 1849–1874*. Durham, NC: Duke University Press, 1951.

Stier, Haya. "Immigrant Women Go to Work: Analysis of Immigrant Wives' Labor Supply for Six Asian Groups." *Social Science Quarterly* 97 (1991): 67–82.

Stober, Dan, and Ian Hoffman. *A Convenient Spy: Wen Ho Lee and the Politics of Nuclear Espionage*. New York: Simon and Schuster, 2001.

Stonequist, Everett V. *The Marginal Man*. New York: Charles Scribner's Sons, 1937.

Storry, Richard. "History [of Japan] Up to 1952." In *The Far East and Australia, 1999*. 13th ed. London: Europe Publications, 1999. Pp. 462–465.

Stowe, John E. "The Chinese Language." In Susan Gall and Irene Natividad, eds., *The Asian American Almanac: A Reference Work on Asians in the United States*. Detroit, MI: Gale Research, 1995. Pp. 426–431.

Suárez-Orozco, Carola, and Marcelo M. Suárez-Orozco. *Children of Immigration*. Cambridge: Harvard University Press, 2002.

———. "Children of Immigration." *Harvard Educational Review* 71 (2001): 599–602.

———. *Transformations: Immigration, Family Life, and Achievement Motivation among Latino Adolescents*. Stanford: Stanford University Press, 1995.

Sue, Stanley, and Sumie Okazaki. "Asian American Educational Achievement: A Phenomenon in Search of an Explanation." *American Psychologist* 45 (1990): 913–920.

Sun, Wanning. *Leaving China: Media, Migration, and Transnational Imagination.* Lanham, MD: Rowman & Littlefield, 2002.

———. *Media and the Chinese Diaspora: Community, Communications and Commerce.* New York: Routledge, 2006.

Sung, Betty Lee. *The Adjustment Experience of Chinese Immigrant Children in New York City.* New York: Center for Migration Studies, 1987.

———. *Chinese American Intermarriage.* Staten Island, NY: Center for Migration Studies, 1989.

———. *Mountain of Gold: The Story of the Chinese in America.* New York: Macmillan, 1967.

Suttles, Gerald D. *The Social Order of the Slum: Ethnicity and Territory in the Inner City.* Chicago: University of Chicago Press, 1968.

Svensrud, Marian. "Attitudes of the Japanese toward Their Language Schools." *Sociology and Social Research* 17 (1933): 259–264.

Szonyi, Michael. "Paper Tigers: For the Past Decade, Three Chinese-Language Newspapers Have Battled It out for Market Dominance." *National Post Business,* July 2002, pp. 34–44.

Takaki, Ronald. *Strangers from a Different Shore: A History of Asian Americans.* New York: Penguin Books, 1989.

Tchen, John Kuo Wei. *New York before Chinatown: Orientalism and the Shaping of American Culture, 1776–1882.* Baltimore: Johns Hopkins University Press, 1999.

Telles, Edward E., and Vilma Ortiz. *Generations of Exclusion: Mexican Americans, Race, and Assimilation.* New York: Russell Sage Foundation, 2008.

Thogersen, Stig. *Secondary Education in China after Mao: Reform and Social Conflict.* Aarhus, Denmark: Aarhus University Press, 1990.

Tolbert, Charles, Patrick M. Horan, and E. M. Beck. "The Structure of Economic Segmentation: A Dual Economy Approach." *American Journal of Sociology* 85 (1980): 1095–1116.

Tom, K. F. "Functions of the Chinese Language Schools." *Sociology and Social Research* 25 (1941): 557–561.

Tong, Benson. *Unsubmissive Women: Chinese Prostitutes in Nineteenth-Century San Francisco.* Norman: Oklahoma University Press, 1994.

Trauner, Joan B. "The Chinese as Medical Scapegoats in San Francisco, 1870–1906." *Journal of California History* 57 (1978): 70–87.

Trocki, Carl A. "Chinese Pioneering in Eighteenth-Century Southeast Asia." In Anthony Reid, ed., *The Last Stand of Asian Autonomies: Responses to Modernity in the Diverse States of Southeast Asia and Korea, 1750–1900.* London: Macmillan, 1997. Pp. 27–84.

Tsai, Henry Shih-shan. *The Chinese Experience in America.* Bloomingdale: Indiana University Press, 1986.

Tsai, Jenny Hsin-Chun. "Contextualizing Immigrants' Lived Experience: Story of Taiwanese Immigrants in the United States." *Journal of Cultural Diversity* 10, no. 3 (2003): 76–83.

Tsay, Ching-lung. "Taiwan." *ASCEAN Economic Bulletin* 12, no. 12 (1995): 175–190.

Tseng, Yen-Fen. "Suburban Ethnic Economy: Chinese Business Communities in Los Angeles." Ph.D. dissertation, Department of Sociology, University of California–Los Angeles, 1994.

———. "Beyond 'Little Taipei': The Development of Taiwanese Immigrant Businesses in Los Angeles." *International Migration Review* 29, no. 1 (1995): 33–58.

Tuan, Mia. *Forever Foreigners or Honorary White? The Asian Ethnic Experience Today.* New Brunswick, NJ: Rutgers University Press, 1999.

Tung, May Paomay. *Chinese Americans and Their Immigrant Parents.* New York: Haworth Press, 2000.

Turnbull, C. Mary. "History [of Singapore]." In *The Far East and Australia, 1999.* 13th ed. London: Europe Publications, 1999. Pp. 1053–1058.

Tyner, James A. "Global Cities and Circuits of Global Labor: The Case of Manila, Philippines." *Professional Geographer* 52, no. 1 (2000): 61–74.

Tyson, Karolyn, William Darity, Jr., and Domini R. Castellino. "It's Not 'a Black Thing': Understanding the Burden of Acting White and Other Dilemmas of High Achievement." *American Sociological Review* 70 (2005): 582–605.

U.S. Bureau of the Census. *The American Community, Asians: 2004.* American Community Survey Reports (acs-05). http://www.census.gov/prod/2007pubs/acs-05.pdf. Accessed September 6, 2007.

———. *Census of Population and Housing 1980: Public-Use Microdata Sample A* [MRDF]. Washington, DC: U.S. Bureau of the Census [producer and distributor], 1983. http://www.census.gov/prod/2007pubs/acs-05.pdf. Accessed November 15, 2007.

———. *Survey of Minority-Owned Business Enterprises, 1982.* Washington, DC: U.S. Bureau of the Census, 1982.

———. *Survey of Minority-Owned Business Enterprises, 1987, MB87-1 to 4.* Washington, DC: U.S. Department of Commerce, 1991.

———. *Survey of Minority-Owned Business Enterprises, 1992, MB92-1 to 4.* Washington, DC: U.S. Department of Commerce, 1996.

———. *Survey of Minority-Owned Business Enterprises, 1997, MB97-1 to 4.* Washington, DC: U.S. Department of Commerce, 2001.

———. *Survey of Minority-Owned Business Enterprises, 2002,* SB02-00CS-Asian (RV). Washington, DC: U.S. Department of Commerce, 2006.

U.S.-China Education Clearinghouse. *An Introduction to Education in the People's Republic of China and U.S.-China Educational Exchange.* Washington, DC: Committee on Scholarly Communication with the People's Republic of China, 1980.

U.S. Citizenship and Immigration Service (USCIS). *Statistical Yearbook of the Immigration and Naturalization Service, 2001.* Washington, DC: U.S. Government Printing Office, 2002.

U.S. Commission on Civil Rights. *Civil Rights Issues Facing Asian Americans in the 1990s: A Report.* Washington, DC: U.S. Government Printing Office, 1992.

U.S. Department of Homeland Security. *2003 Yearbook of Immigration Statistics.* Washington, DC: U.S. Government Printing Office, 2004. http://uscis.gov/graphics/shared/statistics/yearbook/2003/2003Yearbook.pdf. Accessed November 8, 2005.

U.S. Immigration and Naturalization Service (USINS). *Statistical Yearbook of the Immigration and Naturalization Service, [1986–1993].* Washington, DC: U.S. Government Printing Office, 1986–1993.

———. *Statistical Yearbook of the Immigration and Naturalization Service, 2002.* Washington, DC: U.S. Government Printing Office, 2002.

*U.S. News & World Report* staff. "Success of One Minority Group in U.S." December 26, 1966. Pp. 73–76.

Valentine, David. "Chinese Placer Mining in the United States: An Example from American Canyon, Nevada." In Susie Lan Cassel, ed., *The Chinese in America: A History from Gold Mountain to the New Millennium.* Walnut Creek, CA: AltaMira, 2002. Pp. 37–53.

Van Velsor, Ellen, and Leonard Beeghley. "The Process of Class Identification among Employed Married Women: A Replication and Reanalysis." *Journal of Marriage and the Family* 41 (1979): 771–778.

Varenne, Herne, and Ray McDermott. *Successful Failure: The School America Builds.* Boulder: Westview Press, 1998.

Veciana-Suarez, Ana. *Hispanic Media: Impact and Influence.* Washington, DC: Media Institute, 1990.

Wagenaar, Theodore. "What Do We Know about Dropping Out of High School." In Ronald G. Corwin, ed., *Research in Sociology of Education and Socialization: A Research Annual.* Greenwich, CT: JAI Press, 1987. Pp. 161–190.

Waldinger, Roger. "Ethnicity and Opportunity in the Plural City." In Roger Waldinger and Mehdi Bozorgmehr, eds., *Ethnic Los Angeles.* New York: Russell Sage Foundation, 1996.

———. *Still the Promised City? African-American and New Immigrants in Postindustrial New York.* Cambridge: Harvard University Press, 1996.

———. *Through the Eye of the Needle: Immigrants and Enterprise in New York's Garment Trades.* New York: New York University Press, 1986.

Wang, Gungwu. *Anglo-Chinese Encounters since 1800: War, Trade, Science and Governance.* New York: Cambridge University Press, 2003.

———. *China and the Chinese Overseas.* Singapore: Times Academic Press, 1991.

Wang, John. "Behind the Boom: Power and Economics in Chinatown." *New York Affairs* 5 (1979): 77–81.

Wang, Ling-chi. "Class, Race, Citizenship, and Extraterritoriality: Asian Americans and the 1996 Campaign Finance Scandal." *Amerasia Journal* 24, no. 1 (1996): 1–21.

———. "Roots and the Changing Identity of the Chinese in the United States." In Tu Wei-ming ed., *The Living Tree: The Changing Meaning of Being Chinese Today.* Stanford: Stanford University Press, 1994. Pp. 185–212.

———. "The Structure of Dual Domination: Toward a Paradigm for the Study of the Chinese Diaspora in the United States." *Amerasia Journal* 21, nos. 1–2 (1995): 149–170.

Wang, Mei-ling T. *The Dust That Never Settles: The Taiwan Independence Campaign and U.S.-China Relations.* Lanham, MD: University Press of America, 1999.

Wang, Xinyang. *Surviving the City: The Chinese Immigrant Experience in New York City, 1890–1970.* Lanham, MD: Rowman & Littlefield, 2001.

Wang, Xueying. *A View from Within: A Case Study of Chinese Heritage Community Language Schools in the United States.* Baltimore: National Foreign Language Center, Johns Hopkins University, 1996.

Warner, William Lloyd, and Leo Srole. *The Social Systems of American Ethnic Groups.* New Haven: Yale University Press, 1945.

Weidenbaum, Murray, and Samuel Hughes. *The Bamboo Network: How Expatriate Chinese Entrepreneurs Are Creating a New Economic Superpower in Asia.* New York: Martin Kessler Books, 1996.

Wickberg, Edgar. "Localism and the Organization of Overseas Chinese Migration in the Nineteenth Century." In Gary G. Hamilton, ed., *Cosmopolitan Capitalists: Hong Kong and the Chinese Diaspora at the End of the 20th Century.* Seattle: University of Washington Press, 1999. Pp. 35–55.

———. "The Philippines." In Lynn Pan, ed., *The Encyclopedia of the Chinese Overseas.* Cambridge: Harvard University Press, 1999. Pp. 187–199.

Willmott, W. E. "Cambodia." In Lynn Pan, ed., *The Encyclopedia of the Chinese Overseas.* Cambridge: Harvard University Press, 1999. Pp. 144–150.

Wilson, Kenneth L., and W. Allen Martin. "Ethnic Enclaves: A Comparison of the Cuban and Black Economies in Miami." *American Journal of Sociology* 88 (1982): 135–160.

Wilson, Kenneth L., and Alejandro Portes. "Immigrant Enclaves: An Analysis of the Labor Market Experience of Cubans in Miami." *American Journal of Sociology* 86 (1980): 295–319.

Wilson, William Julius. *The Truly Disadvantaged: The Inner City, the Underclass, and Public Policy.* Chicago: University of Chicago Press, 1978.

————. *When Work Disappears: The World of the New Urban Poor.* New York: Vintage Books, 1996.

Winnick, Louis. *New People in Old Neighborhoods: The Role of New Immigrants in Rejuvenating New York's Communities.* New York: Russell Sage Foundation, 1990.

Wong, Bernard P. *Chinatown: Economic Adaptation and Ethnic Identity of the Chinese.* New York: Holt, Rinehart, and Winston, 1982.

————. "The Chinese: New Immigrants in New York's Chinatown." In Nancy Foner, ed., *New Immigrants in New York.* New York: Columbia University Press, 1987. Pp. 243–271.

————. *A Chinese American Community: Ethnicity and Survival Strategies.* Singapore: Chopmen Enterprises, 1979.

————. "Elites and Ethnic Boundary Maintenance: A Study of the Roles of Elites in Chinatown, New York City." *Urban Anthropology* 6 (1977): 1–22.

————. *Ethnicity and Entrepreneurship: The New Chinese Immigrants in the San Francisco Bay Area.* Boston: Allyn and Bacon, 1998.

————. "Hong Kong Immigrants in San Francisco." In Ronald Skeldon, ed., *Reluctant Exiles? Migration from Hong Kong and the New Overseas Chinese.* Armonk, NY: M. E. Sharpe, 1998. Pp. 235–255.

————. *Patronage, Brokerage, Entrepreneurship and the Chinese Community of New York.* New York: AMS Press, 1988.

Wong, Charles C. "Monterey Park: A Community in Transition." In Gail Nomura, Russell Endo, Stephen H. Sumida, and Russell Leong, eds., *Frontiers of Asian American Studies.* Pullman: Washington University Press, 1989. Pp. 113–126.

Wong, K. Scott. *Americans First: Chinese Americans and the Second World War.* Philadelphia: Temple University Press, 2008.

————. "From Pariah to Paragon: Shifting Images of Chinese Americans during World War II." In Sucheng Chan and Madeline Y. Hsu, eds., *Chinese Americans and the Politics of Race and Culture.* Philadelphia: Temple University Press, 2008. Pp. 153–172.

Wong, K. Scott, and Sucheng Chan. *Claiming America: Constructing Chinese American Identities during the Exclusion Era.* Philadelphia: Temple University Press, 1998.

Wong, Morrison G. "Chinese Americans." In Pyong Gap Min, ed., *Asian Americans: Contemporary Trends and Issues.* Thousand Oaks, CA: Sage Publications, 1995. Pp. 58–94.

————. "A Look at Intermarriage among the Chinese in the United States in 1980." *Sociological Perspectives* 32, no. 1 (1989): 87–107.

Wong, S. C. "The Language Situation of Chinese Americans." In S. L. McKay and S. C. Wong, eds., *Language Diversity: Problem or Resource?* New York: Newbury House, 1988. Pp. 193–228.

Wong, Wayne Hung. *American Paper Son: A Chinese Immigrant in the Midwest.* Champaign: University of Illinois Press, 2006.

World Bank. *China: Issues and Prospects in Education.* A World Bank Country Study. Washington, DC: World Bank, 1985.

World Book. *The World Book Encyclopedia.* Chicago: World Book, 1990.

Wu, Frank. *Yellow: Race in America Beyond Black and White.* New York: Basic Books, 2002.

Xie, Yu, and Kimberly A. Goyette. *A Demographic Portrait of Asian Americans.* New York: Russell Sage Foundation; Washington, DC: Population Reference Bureau, 2004.

Xiong, Yang Sao, and Min Zhou. "Selective Testing and Tracking for Minority Students in California." In Daniel J. B. Mitchell, ed., *California Policy Options.* Los Angeles: UCLA Lewis Center, 2005.

Yang, Fenggang. *Chinese Christians in America: Conversion, Assimilation, and Adhesive Identities.* University Park: Pennsylvania University Press, 1999.

Yang, Guobin. "The Internet and the Rise of a Transnational Chinese Cultural Sphere." *Media Culture & Society* 25 (2003): 469–490.

Yang, Philip Q. *Post-1965 Immigration to the United States: Structural Determinants.* New York: Praeger, 1995.

Yeh, Kuang-Hui, and Olwen Bedford. "Filial Piety and Parent-Child Conflict." Paper presented at the International Conference on "Intergenerational Relations in Families' Life Course," co-sponsored by the Institute of Sociology, Academie Sinica, Taiwan, and the Committee on Family Research, International Sociological Association, March 12–14, 2003, Taipei.

Yinger, J. M. "Ethnicity." *Annual Review of Sociology* 11 (1985): 151–180.

Yoo, David K., ed. *New Spiritual Homes: Religion and Asian Americans.* Honolulu: University of Hawai'i Press, 1999.

Yoon, In-Jin. "The Changing Signification of Ethnic and Class Resources in Immigrant Businesses: The Case of Korean Immigrant Businesses in Chicago." *International Migration Review* 35 (1991): 303–331.

Yu, Henry. "The 'Oriental Problem' in America, 1920–1960: Linking the Identities of Chinese Americans and Japanese Americans Intellectuals." In K. Scott Wong and Sucheng Chan, eds., *Claiming America: Constructing Chinese American Identities during the Exclusion Era.* Philadelphia: Temple University Press, 1998. Pp. 191–214.

Yu, Renqiu. *To Save China, To Save Ourselves: The Chinese Hand Laundry Alliance of New York.* Philadelphia: Temple University Press, 1992.

Yuan, D. Y. "Voluntary Segregation: A Study of New Chinatown." *Phylon* 24 (1963): 255–265.

Yuan, S. Y. *Chinese-American Population.* Hong Kong: UEA Press, 1988.

Yun, Lisa. *The Coolie Speaks: Chinese Indentured Laborers and African Slaves in Cuba.* Philadelphia: Temple University Press, 2008.

Yung, Judy. *Unbound Voices: A Documentary History of Chinese Women in San Francisco.* Berkeley: University of California Press, 1999.

Zeng, Shaocong. *Marine Migration to Taiwan and the Philippines in the Qing Dynasty* (东洋航路移民: 明清海洋移民台湾与菲律宾的比较研究). Nanchang: Jiangxi Gaoxiao Chubanshe, 1998.

Zhang, Qingsong. "The Origin of the Chinese Americanization Movement: Wong Chin Foo and the Chinese Equal Rights League." In K. Scott Wong and Sucheng Chan, eds., *Claiming America: Constructing Chinese American Identities during the Exclusion Era.* Philadelphia: Temple University Press, 1998. Pp. 41–63.

Zhao, Xiaojian. *Remaking Chinese America: Immigration, Family, and Community, 1940–1965.* New Brunswick, NJ: Rutgers University Press, 2002.

Zheng, Danhua, and Chaomei Yu. *Taiwan's Education Today.* Guangzhou: Guangdong Education Press, 1996.

Zhou, Min. "Are Asian Americans Becoming White?" *Contexts* 3, no. 1 (2004): 29–37.

———. "Assimilation, the Asian Way." In Tamar Jacoby, ed., *Reinventing the Melting Pot: The New Immigrants and What It Means to Be American.* New York: Basic Books, 2003. Pp. 139–153.

———. *Chinatown: The Socioeconomic Potential of an Urban Enclave.* Philadelphia: Temple University Press, 1992.

———. *Chinatown, Koreatown, and Beyond: How Ethnicity Matters for Immigrant Education.* Oxford: Blackwell, forthcoming.

———. "Chinese: Divergent Destinies in Immigrant New York." In Nancy Foner, ed., *New Immigrants in New York.* 2nd ed. New York: Columbia University Press, 2001. Pp. 141–172.

———. "Chinese Americans: Demographic Trends and Intraethnic Diversity." In Eric Lai and Dennis Arguelles, eds., *The New Faces of Asian Pacific America: Numbers, Diversity and Change in the 21st Century.* Los Angeles: Asian Week, UCLA Asian American Studies Center, and the Coalition for Asian Pacific American Community Development, 2003.

———. "Contemporary Immigration and the Dynamics of Race and Ethnicity." In Neil Smelser, William Julius Wilson, and Faith Mitchell, eds., *America Becoming: Racial Trends and Their Consequences,* vol. 1. Commission on Behavioral and Social Sciences and Education, National Research Council. Washington, DC: National Academy Press, 2001. Pp. 200–242.

———. "The Enclave Economy and Immigrant Incorporation in New York City's Chinatown." Ph.D. dissertation, Department of Sociology, State University of New York at Albany, 1989.

———. "Ethnicity as Social Capital: Community-Based Institutions and Embedded Networks of Social Relations." In Glenn Loury, Tariq Modood, and Steven Teles, eds., *Ethnicity, Social Mobility, and Public Policy in the United States and United Kingdom.* London: Cambridge University Press, 2005. Pp. 131–159.

———. "The Ethnic System of Supplementary Education: Non-profit and For-profit Institutions in Los Angeles' Chinese Immigrant Community." In Beth Shinn and Hirokazu Yoshikawa, eds., *Toward Positive Youth Development: Transforming Schools and Community Programs.* New York: Oxford University Press, 2008. Pp. 229–251.

———. "Growing Up American: The Challenge Confronting Immigrant Children and Children of Immigrants." *Annual Review of Sociology* 23 (1997): 63–95.

———. "How Do Neighborhoods Matter for Immigrant Children? The Formation of Educational Resources in Chinatown, Koreatown, and Pico Union, Los Angeles." *Journal of Ethnic and Migration Studies* (forthcoming 2009).

———. "Low-Wage Employment and Social Mobility: The Experience of Immigrant Chinese Women in New York City." *National Journal of Sociology* 9 (Summer 1995): 1–30.

———. "Negotiating Culture and Ethnicity: Intergenerational Relations in Chinese Immigrant Families in the United States." In Ram Mahalingam, ed., *Cultural Psychology of Immigrants.* Mahwah, NJ: Lawrence Erlbaum, 2006. Pp. 315–336.

———. "The Non-Economic Effects of Ethnic Entrepreneurship." In Léo-Paul Dana, ed., *Handbook of Research on Ethnic Minority Entrepreneurship: A Co-Evolutionary View on Resource Management.* Cheltenham and Northampton: Edward Elgar Publishing, 2007. Pp. 279–288.

———. "'Parachute Kids' in Southern California: The Educational Experience of Chinese Children in Transnational Families." *Educational Policy* 12 (1998): 682–704.

———. "Revisiting Ethnic Entrepreneurship: Convergences, Controversies, and Conceptual Advancements." *International Migration Review* 38 (2004): 1040–1074.

———. "The Role of the Enclave Economy in Immigrant Adaptation and Community Building: The Case of New York's Chinatown." In John Sibley Butler and George Kozmetsky, eds., *Immigrant and Minority Entrepreneurship: Building American Communities.* Westport, CT: Praeger, 2004. Pp. 37–60.

———. "Segmented Assimilation: Issues, Controversies, and Recent Research on the New Second Generation." *International Migration Review* 31 (1997): 825–858.

———. "Social Capital in Chinatown: The Role of Community-Based Organizations and Families in the Adaptation of the Younger Generation." In Lois Weis and Maxine S. Seller, eds., *Beyond Black and White: New Faces and Voices in U.S. Schools.* Albany: State University of New York Press, 1997. Pp. 181–206.

————. *Tang Ren Jie* (唐人街). Beijing: Commercial Press, 1995.

————. *The Transformation of Chinese America* (美国华人社会的变迁). Shanghai: Sanlian Publishers, 2006.

Zhou, Min, Jo-Ann Adefuin, Angie Chung, and Elizabeth Roach. "How Community Matters for Immigrant Children: Structural Constraints and Resources in Chinatown, Koreatown, and Pico-Union, Los Angeles." Final report submitted to the California Policy Research Center, 2000.

Zhou, Min, and Carl L. Bankston III. *Growing Up American: How Vietnamese Children Adapt to Life in the United States.* New York: Russell Sage Foundation, 1998.

————. "Variations in Economic Adaptation: The Case of Post-1965 Chinese, Korean, and Vietnamese Immigrants." *National Journal of Sociology* 6, no. 2 (1993): 106–140.

Zhou, Min, and Guoxuan Cai. "The Chinese Language Media in the United States: Immigration and Assimilation in American Life." *Qualitative Sociology* 25 (2002): 419–440.

Zhou, Min, Wenhong Chen, and Guoxuan Cai. "Chinese Language Media and Immigrant Life in the United States and Canada." In Wanning Sun, ed., *Media and Chinese Diaspora: Community, Commerce and Consumption.* London and New York: Routledge, 2006. Pp. 42–74.

Zhou, Min, and James V. Gatewood. "Mapping the Terrain: Asian American Diversity and the Challenges of the Twenty-First Century." *Asian American Policy Review* 9 (2000): 5–29.

Zhou, Min, and Yoshinori Kamo. "An Analysis of Earnings Patterns for Chinese, Japanese and Non-Hispanic Whites in the United States." *Sociological Quarterly* 35 (1994): 581–602.

Zhou, Min, and Rebecca Y. Kim. "Formation, Consolidation, and Diversification of the Ethnic Elite: The Case of the Chinese Immigrant Community in the United States." *Journal of International Migration and Integration* 2 (2001): 227–247.

————. "A Tale of Two Metropolises: Immigrant Chinese Communities in New York and Los Angeles." In David Halle, ed., *Los Angeles and New York in the New Millennium.* Chicago: University of Chicago Press, 2003. Pp. 124–149.

Zhou, Min, and Susan S. Kim. "Community Forces, Social Capital, and Educational Achievement: The Case of Supplementary Education in the Chinese and Korean Immigrant Communities." *Harvard Educational Review* 76 (2006): 1–29.

Zhou, Min, Jennifer Lee, Jody Agius Vallejo, Rosaura Tafoya-Estrada, and Yang Sao Xiong. "Success Attained, Deterred, and Denied: Divergent Pathways to Social Mobility among the New Second Generation in Los Angeles." *Annals of the American Academy of Political and Social Science* 620 (2008): 37–61.

Zhou, Min, and Xiyuan Li. "Ethnic Language Maintenance and Assimilation: A Historical Look at the Development of Chinese Schools in the United States." In Elliott R. Barkan, Hasia Diner, and Alan Kraut, eds., *From Arrival to Incorporation: Migrants to the U.S. in a Global Era.* New York: New York University Press, 2008. Pp. 163–184.

————. "Ethnic Language Schools and the Development of Supplementary Education in the Immigrant Chinese Community in the United States." *New Directions for Youth Development: Understanding the Social Worlds of Immigrant Youth* 100 (2003): 57–73.

Zhou, Min, and Mingang Lin. "Community Transformation and the Formation of Ethnic Capital: The Case of Immigrant Chinese Communities in the United States." *Journal of Chinese Overseas* 1 (2005): 260–284.

————. "A Study of Ethnic Capital and the Transformation of Chinese Migrant Communities in the United States." *Sociological Research* (社会学研究) 111, no. 3 (2004): 36–46.

Zhou, Min, and John Logan. "In and Out of Chinatown: Residential Mobility and Segregation of New York City's Chinese." *Social Forces* 70 (1991): 387–407.

————. "Returns on Human Capital in Ethnic Enclaves: New York City's Chinatown." *American Sociological Review* 54 (1989): 809–820.

Zhou, Min, and Regina Nordquist. "Work and Its Place in the Lives of Immigrant Women: Garment Workers in New York City's Chinatown." *Applied Behavioral Science Review* 2 (1994): 187–211.

Zhou, Min, Yen-Fen Tseng, and Rebecca Y. Kim. "Rethinking Residential Assimilation through the Case of a Chinese Ethnoburb in the San Gabriel Valley, California." *Amerasia Journal* 34 (2008): 55–83.

Zhou, Yu. "Beyond Ethnic Enclaves: Location Strategies of Chinese Producer Service Firms in Los Angeles County." *Economic Geography* 74 (1998): 228–252.

————. "Ethnic Networks as Transactional Networks: Chinese Networks in the Producer Service Sectors of Los Angeles." Ph.D. dissertation, Department of Geography, University of Minnesota, 1996.

————. "How Do Places Matter: A Comparative Study of Chinese Communities in Los Angeles and New York City." *Urban Geography* 19 (1998): 531–553.

Zhou, Yu, and Yen-Fen Tseng. "Regrounding the 'Underground Empires': Localization as the Geographical Catalyst for Transnationalism." *Global Networks* 1 (2001): 131–153.

Zhu, Guohong. *Overseas Emigration from China: A Historical Study of International Migration.* Shanghai: Fudan University Press, 1994.

Zhu, Liping. *A Chinaman's Chance: The Chinese on the Rocky Mountain Mining Frontier.* Boulder: University Press of Colorado, 1997.

Zhuang, Guo-tu. "China's Policies toward Overseas Chinese." In Lynn Pan, ed., *The Encyclopedia of the Chinese Overseas.* Cambridge: Harvard University Press, 1999. Pp. 98–103.

————. *Ethnic Chinese at the Turn of the Centuries* (世纪之交的海外华人). Fuzhou: Fujian Renmin Chubanshe, 1998.

————. *The Feudal Chinese State and Its Policies toward Overseas Chinese* (中国封建政府的华侨政策). Xiamen: Xiamen University Press, 1989.

————. *The Relationships between Chinese Overseas and China* (华侨华人与中国的关系). Guangzhou: Guangdong Gaodeng Xiaoyu Chubanshe, 2001.

Zia, Helen. *Asian American Dream: The Emergence of an American People.* New York: Farrar, Straus and Giroux, 2000.

Zo, Kil Young. *Chinese Emigration into the United States, 1850–1880.* New York: Arno Press, 1978.

# Index

**Min Zhou** is Professor of Sociology and Asian American Studies at the University of California, Los Angeles. She is the author of *Chinatown* (Temple) and *The Transformation of Chinese America*, co-author of *Growing Up American*, and co-editor of *Asian American Youth and Contemporary Asian America*.